STREET
FOOD

STREET FOOD

**Everything You Need to Know
About Open-Air Stands, Carts
& Food Trucks Across the Globe**

Bruce Kraig and Colleen Taylor Sen, EDITORS

AN AGATE IMPRINT

CHICAGO

Printed in the United States.

Street Food
ISBN 13: 978-1-57284-223-6
ISBN 10: 1-57284-223-7
ebook ISBN 13: 978-1-57284-796-5
ebook ISBN 10: 1-57284-796-4

10 9 8 7 6 5 4 3 2 1   17 18 19 20 21

Surrey Books is an imprint of Agate Publishing.
Agate books are available in bulk at discount prices.
Learn more at agatepublishing.com.

CONTENTS

PREFACE

I n August 2016 a historic event took place in the culinary world: A street food vendor in Singapore received a Michelin star for his $2.00 chicken rice and noodle dish. Still, this recognition and honor came as no surprise to the estimated 2.5 billion people who eat street food in some form every day. Street food is not only the main source of nutrition for many people in the world; it also represents some of the most delicious food on the planet.

Once associated mainly with developing countries, street food is also making inroads into the developed world, especially in North America, with the advent of food trucks in major cities. Not to be outdone, top chefs have opened restaurants specializing in street food, and such items as hot dogs, *bhelpuri*, and tacos have been reincarnated as gourmet items on the menus of upscale restaurants. Television programs, even entire series, are devoted to exploring the culinary delights of the street. Street food is one of the centerpieces of culinary tourism for people in pursuit of unique and memorable eating and drinking experiences.

This is the first book of its scope devoted to this important, endlessly fascinating culinary realm. Its purpose is to provide an overview of the world's street food by country or region. It covers not only such street-food superstars as India, China, Thailand, and Mexico (which admittedly deserve volumes of their own) but also countries where street food plays a less important role, such as those in Northern Europe. Our reasoning is that travelers to these countries might also be in search of a street-food experience, which may be somewhat harder to find.

Our contributors include some of the world's leading food historians, academics, and journalists. While we are most grateful for their contributions, any responsibility for errors is our own.

In addition to the contributors listed as authors, we would like to thank the following people: Dr. Carolyn Kirschner (Nigeria), Sharif Islam (Bangladesh), Sharda Thapar (Nepal), Ursula Heinzelman (Germany), Peggy Mohan (Trinidad and Tobago), Michael Kaganiuk and Malgorzata Szkaradek (Poland), Vivek Batra (India), George Macht (China), Geraldine Rounds (China), Kantha Shelke (Food Safety), Michael and Kathleen Frith (Indonesia), Clarisse Zimra (France), Michael Nguyen (Vietnam and Taiwan), and Charles Perry (Yemen).

We also thank our spouses Ashish Sen and Jan Thompson (for bearing up under the burden of having to sample so many interesting foods) and our friends and constant canine companions Gopi and Matilda, who would eat *anything* in this book.

INTRODUCTION

WHAT IS STREET FOOD?

ALL HUMAN BEINGS DINE, meaning that their food is prepared or processed in various ways, and there are rules of conduct in the ways that it is eaten. As social animals, humans usually dine with others—within families, among friends, or in public settings. Public dining comes in many forms, from various kinds of indoor restaurants to such organizational meals as church suppers and fish fries to summer picnics. Worldwide, the most common form of public dining is known as street food. This phrase covers many kinds of venues and lots of varieties of food.

An ordinary definition of the term "street food" is a food prepared by a vendor and sold from an open-air stand, cart, truck, or perhaps a market stall. The food served is usually in the fast and snack food categories; that is, it's prepared quickly from premade ingredients and served in timely fashion. Street food is also usually eaten out of hand, meant to be consumed on the spot or while walking.

Street food has broader definitions and meanings than simply snacks eaten by people on the move. Street food is commercial because it is made by individual entrepreneurs and sold to customers. It is food that belongs to cities and towns, anywhere where people gather for business or recreation. Therefore, the places where these foods are served can include not only streets but also open air and enclosed markets where individuals vend wares. The small stands in Mexico's food markets, called *fondas*, are examples. Other venues include amusement areas such as carnivals, fairs, and boardwalks, and athletic events, bus and train stations, and schools.

The actual food served as street food may be categorized as snacks; junk food; basic foodstuffs—some more nutritionally complete than others; and examples of national or regional cultures. Any of the foods can be made in several ways. Many are premade by commercial manufacturers. Others are made by the individual sellers or their families. For instance, hot dogs are almost always bought from sausage-making companies. Tacos, sold on the streets and in the markets of Mexico, are almost all made by the purveyors themselves. It is these that most people consider to be the best examples of a local culture and the most delicious.

Snack foods, meant to be taken between meals or while doing some activity besides formal dining, are common in the street-food world. Some are more nutritious than others. When going to the movies, Egyptians often stop at street vendor stands to get bags of *foul*, or cooked broad beans mixed with seasonings. Spicy Indian *chaat* is eaten on the run and now found around the world. Americans eat their contribution to world cuisine, popcorn, in large quantities. And in both the Middle East and South Asia, sweets of bewildering variety are made by local sellers and dispensed to ready audiences.

Street food can also be junk in that the individual items sold have little nutritional value and can even be harmful if eaten regularly. Cotton candy, deep-fried candy bars, and fried batters—just about deep-fried anything—are some of the many forms of junk food sold at public events and eagerly consumed by happy fairgoers.

Around the world, in many areas of poverty, street food is a means of feeding large numbers of poor people. Today, billions of people depend on street food as their main source of daily calories. Largely this is because the raw ingredients are bought in local markets, or brought in from the countryside, and made by the seller on the spot or at home. Food of this kind is cheap and usually high in carbohydrates as well. *Gari*, roasted cassava mush served on the streets of Ghana's cities, is one example. Fresh fruit and fruit juices, which are widely sold, provide other essential nutrients.

While street food can be important in providing nutrition to people with little money, many are thought of as integral to a people's culinary culture. Whether cornmeal-based arepas in Venezuela, kebabs in Turkey, dumplings in Russia,

Central Asia, China, and Korea, or even fried or toasted insects in Southeast Asia, all are models of local food culture. Visitors from other countries almost invariably sample street food as important parts of their tourism experiences. Visitors and local people alike have kept street-food industries alive almost everywhere.

The sale of street food is also a widespread form of self-employment for the poor and otherwise unemployed in cities in developing countries. It requires relatively basic skills and small amounts of capital, and provides the vendor's families with a reasonable income. It also provides food security to the urban poor, who may not have the assets to prepare their own meal. It has been estimated that in India alone, there are more than 10 million street vendors, and some studies say they constitute around 2 percent of the population of the major metropolises. In developed countries, food carts and trucks can be a gateway for trained chefs who do not have the resources to launch a brick-and-mortar restaurant.

WHERE IS STREET FOOD FOUND?

Mobile Venues

The first street-food vendors sold their products from trays, baskets, and portable stands. As far back as ancient Mesopotamian civilizations, vendors set up portable stands in primitive bazaars from which people could buy dried dates and fish. So common were serving trays through the history that they are commemorated in the early English nursery rhyme, "Simple Simon." Simple trays or baskets hung by a strap from vendors' necks are still universal, such as Turkish *simit* sellers who can be found in every city and town. Baskets evolved into heated or cooled boxes in the United States, and today, ballpark hawkers sell everything from hot dogs, to peanuts and popcorn to ice cream and beer from such neck-hung containers.

Trays and baskets can hold only so much food, so vehicles of various kinds became widely used early in historical times. The most basic is a wheelbarrow with a flat, open platform. That device is celebrated in a 19th-century song about a fictional shellfish seller, Molly Malone, who "pushed her wheel barrow through streets broad and narrow crying 'cockles and mussels alive, alive oh.'" Humble one or two wheel wooden barrows became pushcarts, either two or four

WORLD'S BEST CITIES FOR STREET FOOD

1. Bangkok, Thailand
2. Singapore
3. Penang, Malaysia
4. Marrakech, Morocco
5. Palermo, Sicily
6. Ho Chi Minh City, Vietnam
7. Istanbul, Turkey
8. Mexico City, Mexico
9. Brussels, Belgium
10. Ambergris Caye, Belize

"Travel Picks: Top 10 cities for street food." *Reuters*, http://www.reuters.com/article/us-travel-picks-food-idUSBRE86J0G220120720.

wheeled, and usually enclosed food cases. By the 19th century, many had heating units where food was kept warm or even cooked on the spot. One variation is the pushcart attached to bicycles. Called *tricyclo* around the world, the most famous in the United States were ice-cream tricycles that are found in neighborhoods across the country. Pushcarts are the most common form of street-food vending, examples ranging from *thattukadas* in South India to *frietcot* in Belgium and Netherlands and ice-cream carts almost everywhere.

More sophisticated mobile venues appeared when horses were attached to wagons in the last third of the 19th century. Often called lunch wagons, these were small versions of railway dining cars. Usually food was served from a service window on the side of the wagon. Others were set up as walk-in fast food restaurants with a serving counter at one end of the wagon. Most wagons served lunches to people working in factories and offices who needed fast service because their lunch breaks were short. With the advent of the internal combustion engine, lunch wagons became self-moving, able to move faster and to more locations. Made out of stainless steel and with heating and cooling systems, these modern lunch wagons serve many working people in North America and around the world. In recent years, another form of lunch wagon has appeared on the world's streets: food trucks. In the early 21st century, food trucks have become one of the fastest growing segments of the dining industry. Looking like delivery vans and often highly decorated, food trucks serve every kind of food imaginable. In North America, these include Asian, Mexican, German, African, Jamaican, South American, upscale hot dogs, hamburgers, pizza, cupcakes, cakes and pies, and many mixtures of cuisines. In Europe, food trucks have followed the same trend, usually serving such ethnic foods as North African, Burmese, Nepalese, Indian, and others. Food trucks are increasingly popular the world over.

Trailers are another kind of portable food-vending venue. These come in two forms. One is basically a cart where the vendor stands alongside the vehicle, making and serving food. The other kind is like a food truck with cooking or heating and cooling equipment inside and sold through a window. Most of the famous New York food carts are actually trailers that are hauled away from their locations every night. The larger trailers are commonly seen at such seasonal locations as fairs and at some summer resorts. Virtually all food served at state and county fairs, such as ice-cream stands, corn dogs, caramel corn, cotton candy, saltwater taffy, and the many kinds of fried food come from trailers.

Fixed Sites

Street food merges with fast food when it is offered at fixed locations. Hot dogs and tacos, for instance, are among the world's first street foods, but in cities like Chicago, they are sold from fixed stands because of local regulations. The setups in walk-in stands are like food trucks in that the food is served from behind a counter; the customer going outside or standing in another small counter to eat it.

Other fixed stands are more rudimentary. European kiosks, essentially booths but somewhat larger, are located in and around public squares, railway stations, and shopping areas. They offer everything from sausages, to crêpes, fish, breads, and sweets and are heavily patronized. Similar kiosks are common in Asia's cities, especially in popular retail shopping centers. In Mexico and Latin America, fixed stands called *fondas* are features of every enclosed market and many retail food stores. These are simple counters with cooking apparatuses behind them on which food is prepared and served. They are among the world's best eateries because the food is always fresh and made by experienced cooks using home recipes.

One can consider the United States' drive-ins and drive-throughs as kinds of street food because the food is prepared and eaten outside, or at least eaten in vehicles. And many of the dishes are the same as in street stands and carts. Drive-ins are places where diners pull their cars into bays and place orders over speaker systems. The food is then delivered. These were once very popular though only a few chains still exist. Drive-throughs are locations where drivers pull up to a service window and pick up food that they have ordered via an intercom. These are very common; one of them, Taco Bell, sells one of the ultimate street dishes.

Semisedentary Machines

One very modern kind of public food service place is the vending machine that stands in one place but can be moved to another. Coin-operated machines are so universal that they are integrated into almost every country's food culture. Invented in England in the 1880s, they were adapted to chewing gum dispensers in the United States in the 1890s and soda machines in the 1920s. Modern vending machines usually sell such prepackaged, industrially made food as candy and sodas. However, many are highly sophisticated, especially in Asia, which has the world's greatest concentration. These can make such items as hot ramen noodles, rice dishes, fresh French fries, and many others, to say nothing of such hot drinks as coffee. Increasingly around the world, robots are replacing human vendors.

HOW IS STREET FOOD PREPARED?

Street foods are prepared in almost every way known to human beings. Cooking equipment is geared directly to the ways that food is cooked and so are ingredients. For instance, deep-frying requires a deep-frying pot, a high heat source, and lots of oil (which is almost always industrially produced). The same can be said for metal pots, pans, and griddles, most of which are made in factories.

Heat sources depend on locally available materials and legal regulations. The earliest heating fuel was wood, followed by charcoal, then coal and kerosene or paraffin. Wood is still used in many parts of the world, in Africa, for instance, in firepits, ovens, or simply set within a circle of stones over which a pot can be set. Charcoal is wood that has been burned under cover so that the carbon and some ash remain in it. Charcoal burns well and is a staple of backyard grilling. It is also widely used to cook street food even in some New York City carts, despite smoke pollution regulations. In the 17th century, coal began to replace charcoal in England (because England was running out of trees to cut) and the practice of using mined coal for heating and industry spread around the world. Coal-fired heating units are still used in such countries as China to create very high heat for street-food dishes even though coal is highly polluting. Kerosene, also known as paraffin, is a liquid fuel refined from petroleum. It was created in the 1850s and eventually became widely popular for food preparation at home, in restaurants, and on the street. It is still very popular in India and East Asia for cooking and also in camping stoves around the world. In India, a popular cooking fuel is *gobar*, dried cow dung.

Most purveyors in the Western world use gas, either in its natural state or as propane or butane. Propane gas tanks are universal in portable home gas grills and in street-food vehicles. It is relatively cheap and safe and can produce high heat depending on the kind of grill used.

Electricity is also used for street-food preparation. Mostly it runs machinery for confections. Popcorn makers, cotton candy spinners, saltwater taffy makers, ice-cream and ice-based mixers, shavers, and batter mixers are all electric devices. And, of course, electricity runs all the lighting in Asia's famous night markets.

Modern cold products depend on refrigeration or ice to maintain them on the street and other vending locations. The earliest cold storage was ice put into insulated boxes, but the ice in summertime had to be kept in large warehouses where they were stored in wintertime. Ice could also be made with refrigeration machinery. Portable refrigeration was developed in the early 1930s and made such vehicles as ice-cream trucks possible. These were run from gasoline engines in the trucks. During most of the 20th century, Good Humor, sold from trucks, was the most famous ice-cream company in North America.

The kind of vessels used to cook street food varies according to the dish itself and its culture of origin. For example, in East and Southeast Asia and anywhere Asian cuisine is made, woks of various sizes are commonly used. Flat griddles are used for tortillas in Mexico and for certain styles of hot dogs in the United States. Among the cooking gear are

- Woks (*hù* or *guō* in Mandarin, *kuali* in Southeast Asia) are used across Asia and everywhere Asian cuisine is made.
- In India, large flat or concave iron pans called *tawa* are used for shallow frying bread and meat.
- Stew pots are used across Africa and in Asia for many hot pot dishes.
- Frying pans—shallower than woks—are used for sautéing and lighter frying, such as south Chinese dumplings.
- Flat griddles are used universally for everything from tortillas to hot dogs and hamburgers.
- Grills come in many sizes and are fired by wood, charcoal, or gas. These are used for many skewered meat dishes and such vegetables as corn.
- Hot boxes are boxes with heating elements or steam vents beneath them to allow heating of such food as buns and sausages.
- Fryers are electric or propane-driven deep-fryer boxes that adjust the cooking temperatures of oil in which food is cooked.

Frying

Fried foods are the most popular street foods worldwide. They are sold at all kinds of fairs in North America, where everything from chicken and corn dogs to doughs, batters, candy bars, Twinkies, and even ice creams are fried. Fried foods come in two main forms: pan fried and deep-fried. The first requires only a shallow pan in which a small amount of oil or fat is heated and then used to cook the food. Deep-frying is used to totally immerse a food in hot oil (typically 330–350°F), thus cooking it and crisping the exterior.

Typical fried foods include the ever-popular French fries, or *frites* (Belgium's national street food), churros (in Mexico and Latin America), and other such fried sweet doughs and batters as funnel cakes and doughnuts, batter-coated and breaded foods like chicken and hot dogs, and even fried fruit pies and candy bars.

Open Grilling

Open grills are used the world over to make such foods as kebabs—meat and vegetables on skewers—and satays in Thailand and other Southeast Asian countries. Sausages are a natural for grills in Europe and the Americas. Vegetables are also cooked, often called roasted as with corn and tomatoes, though roasting usually means cooking in an enclosed device.

Boiling

Large pots of liquids set over heat sources are prevalent in the street-food world. Soups, stews, dumplings, beans, and other vegetables are all cooked this way. A great many African dishes are stews cooked in this manner in the open air as are dumplings made of cassava and other starchy plants.

Roasting

Roasting can be done in ovens, in pits dug in the ground, or in the open. Many street foods are prepared by roasting in ovens, and for festivals in many countries, whole animals are cooked in pits. Perhaps the best-known roasted food is shawarma—similar to gyros and *döner kebabs*—in which cut meats are compacted on a spit and then roasted before an open flame.

Baking and Toasting

Typically, baking means cooking in an enclosed oven. In some cases, enclosed ovens are used within shops to make such street food as pizza. Mainly, though, street-food baking is done on a heated flat griddle. Flatbreads are commonly made in this way, from corn- and wheat-flour tortillas in Latin America to cheese-filled *gözleme* in Turkey. Sandwiches and nuts are toasted, and even insects are roasted and toasted on flat metal sheets. On the Indian subcontinent, small portable clay ovens called tandoors are used to bake breads and meat.

Steaming

Dumplings and such foods as hot dogs are often steamed. A flat sheet or pan with a perforated bottom is set over boiling water so that steam filters upward.

Chinese dumplings such as wheat-flour buns called *baozi* are steamed in round bamboo trays and served hot.

TYPES OF STREET FOOD

Street foods appear in many forms but can be put into several general categories. Governments often arrange them in this way so that regulations can be better made and understood. The basic groupings can be defined in the following ways.

Single-Ingredient Food

Single-ingredient foods are the simplest kinds of street food. They are one product unadorned or unprocessed, such as grilled chicken, meats, fish, or vegetables. Roasted or grilled corn on the cob is probably the world's most commonly eaten single-ingredient food.

Combined Ingredients or Compound Foods

Compounded foods are the most common of street food. They are composed of two or more ingredients made of different textures and flavors in a single dish. Condiments on sausages, hamburgers, or tacos are examples. There are several general kinds of these foods.

Stuffed

Stuffed foods are ingredients that are processed in some way, usually chopped, mixed with seasonings, forced into an outer covering, and then completely encased. A great many street foods fit this category, notably sausages—chopped meats in a gut or artificial casing. Some casings can be made of vegetables or leaves; others use wheat or corn dough.

Cabbage, grape leaves, and such flowers as zucchini are all used to make famous dishes such as dolma (Mediterranean stuffed grape leaves), *golubzi* (East European stuffed cabbage), and *flor de calabasa* (stuffed zucchini flowers in Latin America). Corn husks or banana leaves are also stuffing casings, the most common dish being the tamale. Green and red peppers and tomatoes are also stuffed but more often served at festivals rather than as street food.

Corn flour dough is used for tamales, empanadas, and the ubiquitous Latin American arepa. Rice flour, sometimes mixed with tapioca starch, appears in almost all *jiaozi* (southern Chinese dumplings) and southeast Asian dumplings. Wheat flour has wider uses, from *baozi* (northern Chinese steamed dumplings), to Indian *momos* and samosas, Ukrainian German American runzas, to Cornish pasties, East European pierogis and *pirozkis*, and many Latin American and Spanish empanadas. Bean and pea flours are used in Indian dumplings (*muthia*).

Wrapped

Likely the most widely consumed complex foods are wrapped. Here, shells of various breads or vegetable leaves are folded around a filling with tops or sides left open. This technique allows flexibility in adding condiments to the food. Anyone who has loaded mustard, onions, or varieties of ingredients on a hot dog knows the method. So popular is wrapping that a whole category of sandwiches called "wraps" are now staples of North American dining.

Corn-based flatbreads, tortillas, are among the most popular wrappings, used in everything from tacos to enchiladas. Wheat flour is even more universal. The everyday sandwich, eaten worldwide, is basically a wrap, as is any food served on a bun. Flatbreads such as Middle Eastern *lavash* and pita, Indian naan, the chapati, and *kulcha* serve similar functions. Some breads are yeast-leavened and made in ovens, and others are baked on flat griddles. The Turkish *yufka* is a good example.

Stews and Soups

One way to serve many people is by extending a food by cooking it in water. Soups and stews of every variety appear in street-food venues and in great many festivals of every sort. They can be made of meats or meats and vegetables or vegetables and starchy tubers. Usually any soup or stew is accompanied by a bread or dumpling (noodles are types of dumplings).

Beverages

People need something to drink with their food, so individual vendors and stands serving freshly made or industrial soft drinks are common in markets. On the Indian subcontinent, tea stands are ubiquitous, often little more than a single vendor with a small grill, a kettle, a teapot, and cups. In tropical countries, freshly squeezed fruit juices and coconut water are an important source of vitamins and minerals. Aside from beer and wine, alcoholic beverages are not usually supplied by street-food purveyors.

EIGHT TASTIEST STREET FOODS IN EUROPE

1. St. Petersburg: Fried *pirozhki*
2. Amsterdam: *Kroketten*
3. Berlin: *Currywurst*
4. Bruges: *Frites*

5. Florence: Gelato
6. Paris: Crêpes
7. Rome: *Pizza al taglio*
8. Stockholm: Fried herring sandwich

Tom Meyers, "The 8 Tastiest Street Foods in Europe," *Huffington Post,* http://www.huffingtonpost.com/tom-meyers/the-8-tastiest-street-foo_b_714856.html#s139260&title=Stockholm_Fried_Herring.

PREMADE FOODS

In the modern industrialized world, plenty of foods sold on streets and from vending machines are made in factories. All of them are compounded foods with chemical preservatives and flavorings. Packaged candies in their considerable profusion are the best examples of industrial snack foods. Small baked cakes, cookies, and crackers are others. The most universal of this category are soft drinks. A good many of them are made by international beverage companies that have spread their brands everywhere. Cola companies are without question the best known.

HEALTH AND SAFETY

Many tourists shy away from eating street food because of its association with various digestive disorders, known variously as "Montezuma's revenge," "Delhi belly," or simply "traveler's diarrhea." These are caused by bacterial contamination, especially from *Shigella sonnei* and *Escherichia coli.* Food is susceptible to contamination at all stages of the food chain. Factors causing contamination include poor food preparation and handling practices, inadequate storage facilities, exposure to flies and rodents, vendors' lack of personal hygiene, and lack of adequate sanitation and garbage disposal facilities.

One of the most critical problems for vendors is the supply of water of acceptable quality and in sufficient quantities for drinking, washing, cleaning, and other operations. In tropical countries with high ambient temperatures and humidity, the problems are intensified, especially if the ingredients or the dishes are kept a room temperature for a long period of time, which turns it into an excellent culture broth in which bacteria thrive. One of the most effective ways of killing dangerous microorganisms is by proper cooking. Serving at or reheating food to 160°F (71°C) may eliminate many of the bacteria.

Because street food plays such an important role in the eating patterns of people in many developing countries, international organizations have been working to develop guidelines for its production and regulation. The two most prominent are the Food and Agricultural Organization (FAO) and the World Health Organization (WHO), both divisions of the United Nations.

WHO's Five Keys to Safer Food

1. Wash your hands often and always before handling and consuming food.
2. Make sure your food has been thoroughly cooked and remains steaming hot. Avoid raw seafood, poultry meat that is still red or has pink juices, and rare minced meat.
3. Make sure that cooked food is not in contact with raw food that could contaminate it and any uncooked food; exceptions are fruits and vegetables that can be peeled or shelled. However, avoid any fruits and vegetables that have damaged skin.
4. Avoid cooked food that has been held at room temperature for several hours, which means avoiding foods from street vendors if they are not kept hot or refrigerated or on ice.
5. If available, drink bottled water but always check the seal to ensure it has not been tampered with. When the safety of drinking water is doubtful, bring it to a vigorous boil. Other bottled beverages are usually safe to drink.

Regulations

Street-food regulations vary widely among countries and even among cities within the same country. Some entities have adopted legislation or ordinances to regulate the preparation and sale of food, others have no regulations at all, while in others, the regulations may exist but are not enforced or enforced haphazardly because of indifference or a shortage of inspectors. In some countries, street-food vendors have no legal status, which makes them vulnerable to harassment by officials. In others, licensing is required and enforced. In Singapore, for example, all vendors are licensed, and every vendor is required to be vaccinated against typhoid. North American and European countries all require and enforce regular health inspections.

Although the main purpose of regulations is to promote health and safety, often other factors come into play, such as opposition by the owners of brick-and-mortar restaurants who fear the competition and by real estate interests who want to use the valuable urban space occupied by vendors. One common rule is that no mobile food vehicle can be within 200 feet of a fixed restaurant. There are also concerns about vehicle and pedestrian traffic congestion. Moreover, street food is becoming an important tourist attraction throughout the world, but since some tourists may be squeamish about buying food from the street, cities have created food courts with clean facilities and tables and chairs.

Vendors usually look at regulations as onerous because they restrict their ability to make a living. Most street vendors stand at the bottom of the economic scale, so every dollar makes a big difference in their lives. In such cities as New York, where a cart is allowed to operate can make the difference in a vendor's income, and there is competition for the best spots that the police will allow. Street vendors have formed organization in cities across North America, from Toronto to New York, Chicago, and Los Angeles under the banner of social justice for the small entrepreneur and working people. They have been effective in changing some laws and certainly public attitudes toward street food. In India, street vendors have formed the Street Vendors Association of India to protect their interests, make available information about best practices and legal issues, and find "long-lasting and sustainable solutions to the problems faced by street vendors."

Rules and regulations governing street food focus on several aspects:

- Authorization and/or licensing to conduct the production and sale of street food
- Composition and presentation of food products
- Offenses and penalties
- Institutions and officials responsible for food surveillance and control

One approach has been to move vendors off the streets into sanitary—some would say sanitized—food courts with seating facilities, clean water, disposal, and other amenities. The entrepreneurs are registered and have premises allocated with access to telephone, water, and electricity and trained in community health practices. This has occurred in many Asian cities, including Singapore, Bangkok, Guangdong, Jakarta, Hong Kong, and Shanghai. In other cities including Quito, Ecuador, Dar Es Salaam, Tanzania, and Cebu City in the Philippines, urban authorities have developed programs to improve food quality and safety and find appropriate locations.

Elsewhere, there has been a more halfhearted effort. In India, many cities had restrictions on street-food vendors, but they were not enforced either through neglect or corruption in the form of bribes to the police. In 2007, prior to the Asian Games, the Delhi city government tried to enforce existing legislation by banning the preparation of food at street stands, a move supported by India's High Court. However, the order proved unenforceable and has not been implemented.

In North America, some cities, notably Chicago, Toronto, and Montreal, have stringent regulations on food trucks and street vendors, whereas others, notably Seattle, Washington; Portland, Oregon; and Austin, Texas, are famous for their bustling food truck scenes.

Despite, or maybe because of, regulations and modernization in cities and countries across the globe, street food is among the fastest growing food industries. People want inexpensive meals and snacks made by cooks who use fresh ingredients to make delectable and sometimes hearty dishes. In the underdeveloped world, street food is a necessity. In the developed world, sampling dishes from varieties of culinary traditions that use locally sourced ingredients provides gustatory adventures that are hard to replicate in restaurants or at home. Perhaps more than anything else, street food gives people a sense of community—among sellers and buyers in the open air among crowds—that is hard to replicate anywhere else. In cities everywhere, street food is at the core of peoples' common existence and identity.

CHAPTER 1

CHICKWANGUE
UGALI MATOKE
SUYA KOSHARY
BOCAILLO
KENKEY

AFRICA

AFRICA

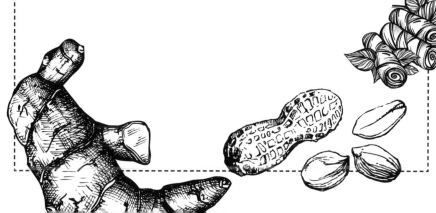

CENTRAL AFRICA

A LTHOUGH THERE IS NO TRADITION OF RESTAURANT CULTURE in Central Africa, street food is omnipresent and has a long history, dating back to at least several centuries. When Europeans first landed on Central African shores at the end of the 15th century, they encountered an active trading system with many local markets. On these markets, provisions ready for consumption could be bought. *Chikwangue*, for instance, was reported to be sold in 1698 at markets around Malebo Pool, a widening of the Congo River that separates the current capitals of the Republic of the Congo and the Democratic Republic of the Congo (DRC). Central Africa is a large geographical area that includes Cameroon, Gabon, Equatorial Guinea, the DRC, and the Republic of the Congo. Most of the mentioned countries border the equatorial rain forest, home to a highly diversified fauna and flora and crisscrossed by numerous waterways, of which the Congo River is the most important. In the era of colonization, most of Central Africa was French territory, still to be seen in numerous imported French foods, especially baked goods. The DRC, however, was Belgian, Equatorial Guinea was Spanish, and part of Cameroon was British.

Street foods serve different functions. Beignets or baguettes are purchased for breakfast, peanuts for a snack during the day, *chikwangue* for journey provisions, and roasted meat to accompany drinks at night. Street foods are found in markets and in strategically placed food stalls. Not only big cities like Brazzaville (capital of Congo) and Libreville (capital of Gabon) count numerous markets, but also in the countryside, markets are organized. Yafira, for instance, situated on the Lomami River, a tributary of the Congo River, is a village with a weekly market. People from distant places as far as Isangi and even Kisangani arrive there by boat for both trade and leisure. In towns and villages, street foods may also be purchased at food stalls. In Congo, food stalls are placed in village centers along the main roads, as well as near railway stations. Some foods, like fritters, are sold door-to-door. Women go around the village in the morning with a bucket or large bowl filled with fritters. Considering that the production of food is mostly a female activity, it is evident that food vendors are usually women. They do not even need to organize sales. Often, women prepare more food than needed, for instance, *chikwangue*, and sell the surplus on shelves near the road.

Food stalls are generally simple in structure, consisting of no more than a table and a roof. Foodstuffs may also be spread on a plastic sheet on the floor. Considering the sanitary issues of markets, having mostly dirt floors and lacking an organized garbage collection, selling food on sheets provides a serious health hazard. Certain street foods, like diverse wrapped foods, are prepared in advance and are displayed as such. Others are prepared on the spot. Such is the case of peanuts, which are roasted in front of the customers. Vendors of beignets also fry their goods in the market.

MAJOR STREET FOODS

Wraps

A popular Central African cooking method is to wrap ingredients in leaves and to boil or steam the package. Another cooking method is to bake the wrap on the ashes of the fire. The wrap may be formed with banana leaves, but more often, leaves of wild plants are used, for instance, from aroid species. Several street foods are wraps. The most important wrapped food in Central Africa is *chikwangue*, or *bâton de manioc*, a wrap of cassava paste. Not only can it be served as the starch component of the principal meal of the day, but it also has the advantage of being durable and easily transportable. Therefore, it is often a traveler's companion and may be purchased at food stalls in villages along the main roads. The preparation of *chikwangue* is an elaborate process, taking several days, sometimes even longer than one week. The bitter cassava tubers are first soaked in order to remove the toxins. The subsequent process varies. In some regions, the

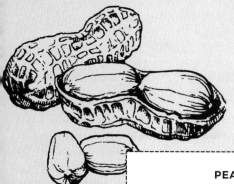

PEANUTS

Although treated as nuts in culinary practice, peanuts (*Arachis hypogaea*) are legumes that produce fruit underground. Peanuts originated in tropical South America and were introduced by the Portuguese in Central Africa as part of the Columbian Exchange. Because of their similarity to the local Bambara groundnut (*Vigna subterranea*), peanuts were quickly adopted. Curiously, Central African slaves brought peanuts and their use to North America. The denominations *pinda(r)* and *goober*, from *(m)pinda* and *nguba*, respectively, suggest that these slaves were Kongo. In Central Africa, peanuts are generally processed into peanut butter, an important seasoning of stews but today also spread on baguettes. Peanuts are also eaten raw, boiled, or roasted as a snack and are often paired with a cassava preparation to form a meal.

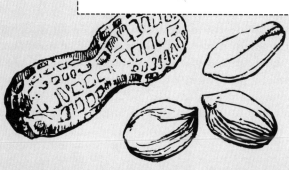

CASSAVA

Like peanuts, cassava (*Manihot esculenta*) is an American crop brought from Brazil to Central Africa by the Portuguese. The tuber was introduced in the third decade of the 17th century. No later than 1698, Italian travelers purchased the complex cassava product *coanche*, or *chikwangue*, on markets at the Malebo Pool. This cassava wrap was sold to supply the caravans that traded slaves, among other goods. Cassava thus was first transformed into a trade good. Only one century later did the tuber become a possible ingredient of the staple starch food, *fufu*, a thick porridge. The American plant has grown in popularity ever since. In Central Africa, cassava leaves are prepared as well, a use that is rare in the Americas.

---

tubers are pounded, wrapped, and boiled. In the west of the DRC and the south of the Congo, the preparation consists of different steps of kneading and steaming. Women often make more than needed for the household and sell their surplus to passersby or to their neighbors.

In the south of the Congo, another wrap is made with cassava. This wrap contains a mixture of bitter cassava paste, peanut butter, and optionally, chilies for a spicier version. It may be preserved several days and, therefore, is ideal for journeys. There are several variations on the recipe—for instance, using sweet instead of bitter cassava—and the dish carries various names. In Kunyi, it is called *mbala-mpinda*, literally "yam-peanut." A popular Cameroonian wrap is *koki*, a paste of cowpeas or other legumes, palm oil, and chilies. Wraps may also contain fish. To give a few examples, raw fish can be seasoned, wrapped, and baked on the ashes of the fire. Smoked fish can be added to a paste of gourd seeds, wrapped, and steamed. These wraps are known along the Congo River as *libóké*, a Lingála word for "wrap."

Beignets

Beignets or fritters are sold in markets throughout Central Africa. Women fry the beignets on the spot, seated on stools next to a pot of boiling oil placed over a fire. In the countryside, vendors may go around the village with a bucket of beignets. The ingredients vary. Beignets may be a mixture of wheat flour, yeast, sugar, vanilla sugar, and water. However, along the Congo River, beignets are prepared with cassava flour, plantains, and/or rice flour. Sometimes, they are seasoned with chilies. In the same region, beignets are fried in palm oil, giving them a distinct flavor. Other ingredients include maize and lemon. Beignets may be served alone or with peanut butter. In Cameroon, a common combination is beignets with beans.

Peanuts

Peanuts are a popular snack food throughout Central Africa. They may be eaten raw, boiled, or roasted. In markets, they are mostly sold roasted to serve as a snack. Peanuts are often paired with cassava preparations to form a quick meal.

OTHER STREET FOODS

Baguettes and Coffee

Breakfast is often a takeaway occasion. Food stalls in towns and villages sell baguettes, an inheritance from the ex-colonizer, which was France for most Central African countries. These baguettes may be sold with various spreads. Peanut butter is very popular, but baguettes may also be smeared with a portion of The Laughing Cow, a soft spreadable cheese. In Gabon, *pain chocolaté* is the name for a baguette with chocolate spread. These baguettes are often served with coffee or tea. Coffee is generally a mixture of coffee powder, milk powder, sugar, and hot water. Tea may be a herbal infusion, for instance, verbena, again mixed with milk powder and sugar.

Cabri or *Micopo*

A street food that is popular in the evening when people gather for drinks is roasted goat meat and onion served with chile powder and optionally slices of *chikwangue*. This snack is called *cabri* (French for "goat") in Kinshasa and *micopo* in Lubumbashi, the second city of the DRC.

A number of fruits are sold as a snack. Examples include oranges, which may be peeled for you, and (dessert) bananas. Coconut pieces form another small snack. European-style biscuits are sold in tiny plastic bags. A final example of street foods is skewers of shrimp that are sold on the beach at the Atlantic Ocean.

BIRGIT RICQUIER

EAST AFRICA

EAST AFRICA IS A WIDELY DIVERSE SET OF COUNTRIES that are located south of the Horn of Africa (Ethiopia and Somalia) in the northeast, down the Indian Ocean coast and interior regions to South Africa. Generally the countries include, from north to south, Kenya, Uganda, Rwanda, Burundi, Tanzania, Zambia, Malawi, Mozambique, Zimbabwe, Madagascar, and Mauritius. Among these countries, there are distinct groupings. For instance, Kenya and Uganda were under British rule from the later 19th century to the middle of the 20th century and have stronger British influences than other countries. Madagascar and Mauritius are island nations that have stronger Indian influences than the others. However, in all of East Africa's nations, British, Indian, and Arabic cultures are important in food culture.

East Africa has highly varied landforms and, despite its location along the equator, different climates. There are several broadly defined geographical regions within East Africa. One of them is the Great Lakes that include Lake Victoria with its spectacular falls, Lake Albert, and Lake Tanganyika (the world's deepest). Kenya, Uganda, Tanzania, Rwanda, and Burundi border on or include one or more of these lakes. Kenya, Tanzania, and Mozambique all border on the Indian Ocean to the east, though their interior regions differ in climate and landforms from the humid low-lying coasts. Madagascar and Mauritius are tropical islands to the south and east of the continent. To the north is the Horn of Africa, much of it subject to little, sporadic, or short-seasonal rainfall. Northern Kenya is part of that region. Portions of the region running from Kenya through Uganda into Tanzania are savanna lands, home to the wild animals that are world famous tourist attractions. Large swaths of East Africa's interior encompass agriculturally fertile highlands. This is one of the regions that exports food, but generally local foods are greatly affected by the lands and waters from which they come.

East Africa's dominant physical feature is the Great Rift Valley. Formed by movements of continental plates, the valley runs 4,000 miles from Ethiopia down to Mozambique. Within it are the Great Lakes and thrown up by its formation are such mountains as Kilimanjaro in Tanzania. Climates in the higher areas are temperate, but hot in the valley because of its equatorial location. Unlike the interior, East Africa's coastline is a mainly flat narrow strip of land backed by lands rising to the plateaus that compose most of the countries in the region. Though there are few major ports in East Africa, fishing is an important part of the economy, and fish from both seas and lakes is important part of peoples' diets. The coastal climate is legendarily hot and humid.

The peoples of East Africa possess varied physical characteristics, languages, ethnic groups, and national affiliations. The earliest peoples were hunter–gatherers, followed by herders who came in several waves from Sudan and other areas to the north. They are called Nilotic because of the language groups to which they belong and certain physical characteristics (the famous long-distance runners of Kenya and Ethiopia are Nilotic). Some peoples, like the Maasai, remain pastoralists, but most have settled into farms, towns, and cities. The largest numbers of people speak Bantu languages of which there are many. They migrated from West Africa over the last two millennia bringing their agricultural economy with them. Nilotic peoples lived on cattle and sheep, and Bantus brought yams, groundnuts, grains, probably bananas, and domesticated goats among other food sources. These provided some of the basics of today's East African cuisines.

Arab merchants had sailed down the Red Sea and along the African coasts to trade in gold, spices, and slaves for a thousand years before the Portuguese explorer Vasco da Gama arrived at the end of the 15th century. The Portuguese wanted to control the spice trade centered on the spice island of Zanzibar, now part of Tanzania. That event set off a series of conflicts that led to European control of East Africa. One consequence was the most widely used language in the region, Swahili, became the lingua franca of East Africa. Based on Bantu languages mixed with Arabic, English, French, Portuguese, Farsi, and others,

Swahili, or Kiswahili, is used officially in Kenya, Uganda, and Tanzania. It is commonly spoken in other countries, as well. Another consequence of Arab and European contact and conquest was the introduction of new foods to East Africa. Rice, corn, cassava, potatoes, chilies, pigs, and spices are a few of the major foods that are now part of the East African diet. Indians who came during British rule have been an especially important influence on food partly because they dominated commerce, such as owning and running a large percentage of food stores. The largest supermarket chain in Kenya, Rwanda, Tanzania, and Uganda called Nakumatt is run by Indo-Kenyans.

When colonial rule ended later in the 20th century, East Africa was divided into individual countries. All are different from one another in languages and customs. For instance, Malawi has one official language, Chichewa, but people there belonging to different tribal groups speak another six as their first tongues. In Mozambique, Portuguese is the official language, but at least half a dozen African languages are spoken. Most people in East Africa follow Christian religions and customs, but there is a sizable Muslim minority and many adherents of indigenous religious practices. Poverty is endemic among countries in this part of Africa. Malawi, Rwanda, Burundi, and Zimbabwe are among the poorest on Earth with low life expectancies. At less than a dollar a day for food, majority of people in the poorest countries rarely eat meat or even get enough nutrition to keep them healthy. In such situations, street food is not a luxury but a necessity that might be the main, or only, meal for half the population.

MAIN FOODSTUFFS

The most common kind of food sold on the streets of East Africa is starch. This calorie-laden kind of food is provided by starchy vegetables, legumes, fruits, and grains. Plantains, cassava (manioc), potatoes, beans, corn, and other grains are usually boiled into mushes or stews and served plain with some form of bread, especially Indian chapatis. When meats are affordable, goat and chicken are the most commonly eaten, sometimes in stews but also grilled. On the coasts and lakes, fish are very common, often grilled and made with spicy sauces. Some of the East African food traditions—Mozambique's, for example—value lots of spices while others do not. Whatever the specific food, it is usually sold by vendors who set up small stands or stalls near markets and on city streets where working people can get breakfast or lunch. Even along roads, travelers will see small stands selling mainly local produce or snacks such as roasted peanuts. Most of the sellers are women who also prepare the food at home. Vending is a major source of income for many families.

MAJOR STREET FOODS

Ugali

Ugali (also called *sadza, posho, sima,* and *upswa* among others, depending on the local language) is a staple dish made at home, in restaurants, and consumed on streets or as a takeout in people's places of work. It is basically cornmeal mush, that is, dried and ground corn that is cooked in water to either a soft or hard consistency. Corn is not native to Africa, but because it is relatively easy to grow, it became widely popular after Portuguese merchants brought it from the Americas in the 16th century. *Ugali,* as it is called in Uganda and Kenya, is made in large pots by women vendors who prepare it for lunches. It is rarely flavored, as polenta might be in Italy, but is usually eaten on a plate with other foods such as *matoke,* boiled cassava, cooked beans, rice, or a stew. When served with a meat or vegetable stew, some *ugali* is dipped out of the pot, formed into a ball, and then used to scoop up the liquid.

In truly impoverished countries such as Zimbabwe, where severe hunger is a fact of life, cornmeal mush is one of the few foods available. Mostly it is made from white finely ground corn donated by international aid agencies. Though having calories, the corn often lacks certain vitamins (niacin and tryptophan) that prevent the disease pellagra. Eaten everywhere, in public and in private homes, cooked cornmeal mush is truly an East African staple.

Matoke

One of Uganda's national dishes, *matoke* is widely eaten in Kenya and everywhere that plantains are grown. Plantains are peeled, wrapped in their leaves, and then steamed in pots for several hours until the flesh is soft. The bland dish is usually eaten with stew, vegetables, and in Uganda, with a groundnut sauce. Other versions can be cooked with chilies, tomatoes, garlic, or on the coast of Tanzania with smoked fish.

Fried Cassava

Cassava, or manioc, is another starch imported from the New World by Portuguese traders in the 16th and 17th centuries. It is widely eaten at home, but it is also served by take-out restaurants to be consumed with other foods as lunch to be eaten outdoors. The cassava is cut up and boiled, and put on a plate or cassava leaf. It is also grilled on open grills and quite good this way. In Tanzanian cities such as Dar es Salaam, *muhogo* is boiled cassava that is fried and served with cut-up tomatoes and cabbage with a chile sauce.

Roasted Corn, Roasted Peanuts

Anywhere street food is sold in East Africa, hungry diners will find corn roasting in their husks on an open grill. Depending on the country and region, ears of roasted corn are eaten plain, but mainly it is rubbed with lemon slices and served with spicy chile powders called *pili pili* or *piripiri*. Corn can also be served boiled. Peanuts and groundnuts are planted deep in African food culture, so it is no surprise that these are roasted and served in small paper cones almost everywhere as snacks and as sources of protein.

Mandazi

Mandazi is a kind of slightly sweet doughnut popular all over the coastal areas from Kenya to Tanzania. Made from wheat-flour batter, *mandazi* comes in many shapes, some round, but mainly as small pillows of fried dough. The dish can be made with milk or coconut milk or other ingredients to give different flavors. Cooks have large pans filled with hot oil ready to fry fresh batches for customers who like their *mandazi* warm to be eaten plain or as an accompaniment to a stew or soup. Most often, it goes with tea at breakfast or for tea breaks from work.

A similar dish in Madagascar called *mofo gasy* is made from rice batter. It is baked in molds on open grills. Malagasies, as people in the island are called, also have a form of *mandazi* called *menakely*. Both forms of cooked batter are widely as a breakfast street food.

Although made with lentils and chilies, fried balls of dough called *gateaux piments* are a common street food on the island of Mauritius. The dish has a French name, but it is Indian in origin.

Chapatis

Indians have exerted a huge influence on East African food through long-standing trade and settlement. In India, chapatis are flatbreads made from wheat flour (usually white, sometimes whole wheat) that are rolled out into rounds and baked on a flat griddle or pan. Some are finished by briefly cooking them over open flames. In East Africa, many chapatis are done in the local style, fried in oil. Chapatis are used as wraps and as scoops for other foods in almost every country in East Africa.

Nyama Choma

Nyama choma, or roasted meat, is sold up and down the East African coast and in such cities as Nairobi, Kenya, and Dar es Salaam in Mozambique. Although most East Africans eat very little meat because of its expense, it is highly prized and widely consumed. Goat is especially favored, though beef, chicken, and pork (except in Muslim areas) are also on the menu. Most of the time, meats are cooked over open charcoal fires, cut up, and served with perhaps a chapati. In Mozambique with its Portuguese and Indian influences, a hot spicy *piripiri* sauce will be served. Although *nyama choma* is not strictly street food because it might be prepared in a courtyard, in Uganda and Kenya, cooks set up long charcoal-fired grills and cook small split chickens seasoned only with salt and served with chapatis. Roasted chicken, made on grills, called *kuku* is also seen in such Tanzanian coastal cities as Dar es Salaam.

Mishkaki

Mishkaki is a popular meat dish throughout East Africa. It is chunks of usually beef or goat that are marinated with spices overnight, then skewered and grilled over charcoal. In most places, it is served with chapatis and, in such cities as Mombasa, Kenya, with an Indian chutney.

OTHER STREET FOODS

Rolex

This unusually named dish is also called *mugati naamaggi* (literally, "bread and eggs") or c*happo mayai* in Kenya. A common street in Kampala, Uganda, it is an egg omelet made with chopped tomatoes, onions, and green peppers wrapped in a chapati. Rolex is often available from street vendors in evenings as a snack while strolling the streets or going to movies or the theater.

Roti

A roti is the same as a chapati. *Roti chaud* (or "hot roti") is one of the classic street-food dishes of Mauritius. It is a flatbread that is filled and rolled up with cooked and chopped meats, fish, or vegetables and usually a spicy sauce. *Roti prata* is usually filled with chutney, *brèdes* (a kind of amaranth plant), or various tomato-based sauces.

Sambusa

Sambusas are really samosas, the famous Indian stuffed pastry that is found around the world. They can be stuffed with spicy chopped or ground meats or vegetables, especially potatoes. They are served with chutneys, sauces, or slices of lime. In Mozambique, where Portuguese is spoken, they are called *chamuças*.

Mutura

Mutura is a sausage from Kenya. It is made by stuffing a goat intestine with chopped meat, blood, and spices. It is first boiled, then grilled and sliced into rounds for serving. Like other dishes, it is served with chapatis and perhaps chopped vegetables.

Seafood

Grilled seafood is sold from open air stalls in many seacoast and lake coast areas. Grilled shrimp, squid, octopus, and local fish are the usual ingredients. Some are grilled whole, and others skewered and made into kebabs. In places like Tanzania and Mozambique, chopped vegetables such as onions and peppers accompany the fish. The food is seasoned with peppers, onions, and coconut.

Irio and *Githeri*

Irio, also called *mokimo*, is a typical Kenyan street food that is also eaten at home. Corn, potatoes, and greens of various kinds are cooked separately, then mashed together and put on a plate. *Githeri* is similar but simpler, but in Kenya, it is always made from corn, beans, and onions. It can be eaten with stews or soups, but often by itself.

Fruits

Many fruits grow in East Africa, each kind depending on the local climate. Mangoes, passion fruit, pineapples, papayas, oranges, papayas, pineapples, and, in coastal areas, coconuts are all sold by vendors on city streets and along roadsides. Bananas are especially important because of their nutritional value and because they are widely grown and available.

PASSION FRUIT

Kapuku (Rat)

One of the more unusual street foods is found in Malawi. The country is so poor that field rats have become a popular food. Also called cane rats, these rodents are trapped in fields, killed, and cooked. They are then dried, salted, and then tied to long sticks from which they are sold individually. As such, they are jokingly called "rat kebabs." Rats are a source of protein for people who desperately need it.

BRUCE KRAIG

EGYPT

E GYPT IS A TRANSCONTINENTAL COUNTRY. Most of its territory is in North Africa, while its Sinai Peninsula extends to Southwest Asia. For thousands of years, the Nile has supplied the nation's ever-growing population with the natural irrigation necessary to cultivate such crops as grains (mainly wheat and barley), legumes, cotton, and a variety of fruits and vegetables. The yearly flooding of the Nile was responsible for fertilizing the land naturally, but the building of the Aswan High Dam in 1970 put a halt to those yearly floods, and since then, Egyptian farmers have had to use fertilizers to keep the land fertile and productive.

Egypt's rich ancient Pharaonic (dating from the fourth millennium BCE) history has shaped many of the cultural and food traditions that many Egyptians observe until this day, such as Sham el Nessim, the celebration of the beginning of spring. During this feast, Egyptians have traditionally eaten *fesikh*, a fermented salted gray mullet, and green onions. Foreign influences may have had a more lasting impact on Egypt's current food culture. Egypt has been colonized by the Romans, Byzantines, Arabs, Ottomans, French, and most recently, the British, who were ousted in 1922. Egypt's food culture reflects all these influences as well as the use of spices from other Arab countries. Nowadays, this medley of cultural influences can be seen in the street food of the entire North African region, including Egypt. Turkish coffee and sweets, French-inspired white breads stuffed with herbed meats or spiced legumes, and traditional pastries like *kahk* made with Arabian dates are examples.

Egyptian street food is tasty and cheap, ranging from completely vegetarian items to hearty meat options and quick snacks and fruity drinks. Legumes like lentils and *ful* (broad beans or fava beans) are very popular, as are meat-based dishes like shawarma, kebab (or kebab), *kofta*, and *kibda*, which are often stuffed in a pita bread sandwich. Street food is generally the same everywhere in Egypt, with the exception of some resorts and beach towns. Here one finds more snacks and nibbles (like roasted nuts and bite-size desserts) than in major cities, where street food represents breakfast and lunch for a majority of working-class people.

MAJOR STREET FOODS

Koshary

Koshary is by far the most ubiquitous street food. It is a hearty mixture of protein and carbohydrates made of inexpensive ingredients: rice, lentils, and pasta. Street carts selling *koshary* are found all over Egypt, but college dormitories and lower-income rural and urban areas have the largest representation of *koshary* sales because of the dish's affordability. Also Coptic Christians in Egypt, who comprise 10 to 20 percent of the population, avoid animal products during Advent and Lent, eating vegetarian dishes that are filling.

During the Egyptian revolution in January 2011, *koshary* was served in liberal amounts to revolutionaries in Tahrir Square, giving the carbohydrate-heavy dish instantaneous worldwide recognition. Such Western food online publications as *Serious Eats* published an article explaining the role of *koshary* in the Egyptian revolution and credited the meal for fueling the demonstrators. The article explained *koshary's* significance to Egyptians accurately:

Koshary is a food of the people. Though associated with lower classes in Egypt, it would be tremendously ignorant to dismiss it as a "poor people's comfort food." Yes, koshary is very cheap to make and eat. But in a country with mass poverty, its very accessibility underscores the importance in its ability to feed everyone. Egyptians of all standing have fond personal memories of koshary. It is as close to a national dish as exists in Egypt and among the Egyptian Diaspora.

Ful Meddames and *Ta'ameya* Sandwiches

Ful, the fava or broad bean, is the most prevalent legume in Egypt. Of all Egyptian street foods, *ful* sandwiches are by far the most popular and comprise most workers' daily breakfasts. The *ful* mixture is often served either in a pocket pita or in a bowl when it is served at home. Members of the working class in Egypt, especially construction workers and others who have to wake up in the wee hours of the dawn, can be seen lining up in front of carts that sell *ful meddames. Meddames,* or *muddamas,* means "mashed" in Arabic. *Ful* is eaten because it's a cheap meal packed with complex carbohydrates and protein that supplies the working body with needed energy.

Typically, *ful* is bought as a dried bean, then soaked overnight, and slow cooked for a few hours. It is served mashed with lime juice and oil and seasoned with cumin, coriander, salt, and pepper, and sometimes a little bit of minced garlic. An Alexandrian version of *ful* features a hot sauce as well. Nowadays, most street vendors use canned beans to save the time and effort to soak and cook dried beans. Accompaniments to a hot bowl of *ful meddames* include fresh arugula and tahini, a sesame-seed paste mixed with lime juice and seasonings and made into a sauce. Sometimes hard-boiled eggs are added. Toppings vary among vendors and are individually chosen by the customer. The *ful* vendors also sometimes serve *bitingan ma'ly,* or fried eggplants, as a side to their bean dishes or in a separate sandwich.

A popular rendition of *ful meddames* is a fried version called *ta'ameya.* In the West, there is a version of *ta'ameya* known as falafel, but it is typically prepared with chickpeas (hummus) and not with fava beans as in Egypt. Street vendors all over Egypt sell sandwiches of *ta'ameya* mashed with tahini sauce and fresh tomatoes and arugula.

Meats on the Street, Egyptian Style

As in many other countries in the Middle East, many Egyptian street vendors sell shawarma sandwiches. Shawarma comes from the Turkish word *çevirme,* which means "turning," referring to the way the meat is grilled by turning the spit over a fire for several hours. The meat is usually stacked in alternating layers of fat and seasoned meat compressed together to form a thick block. A large knife is used to slice off layers of shawarma that fall into a circular tray underneath as the meat continues to be roasted. The meat used in shawarma in Egypt is beef, chicken, or lamb, with the most popular being beef.

Shawarma is not a cheap street food like *ful meddames* or *koshary* and thus is not as prevalent as the latter dishes. Many shawarma vendors also sell kebabs, which are pieces of grilled beef or mutton, and *kofta*, mini meat loaf balls seasoned with parsley and other spices and fried. Kebab and *kofta* are removed from their skewers and served in a sandwich or, with skewers intact, are laid on top of rice, with sides of tahini sauce along with fresh onions, tomatoes, and lettuce piled on for extra flavor. Beef shawarma is often paired with the tahini sauce, while chicken shawarma is served with an intense garlic-based sauce.

Another meat-based option served in curbside carts is fried *kibda* or liver (usually beef or chicken). It likely originated in Alexandria, because it is called *kibda iskandarani*. Thinly sliced beef liver is covered with lime juice and cooked in sizzling oil along with thinly sliced onions and green peppers, then topped with seasonings and spices, the most popular being cumin, garlic, and lime juice. A lot of people elect to add chile peppers on top for an added kick. *Mumbar*, cow or lamb intestines stuffed with rice and spiced ground beef, is another popular dish that features organs rather than just muscle meats. An Alexandrian version called *sogo'* is intestines stuffed with ground beef.

Many kinds of bread are used as sandwich casings for Egyptian meats. The most popular are whole-wheat pita breads, called *eish balady*, and white pita bread, or *eish shami*. (*Eish* means bread, *shami* refers to the Levant, and *balady* means country style.) Some vendors also encase the grilled meats in *eish fino*, or bread buns—a concept likely borrowed from American hamburger buns.

OTHER STREET FOODS

Nibbles, Snacks, and Drinks

Egyptians like to snack on different foods, especially while they're walking on the corniche along the Nile or relaxing at beachfront resorts. A few favorite snacks include roasted mixed nuts, *ful sudani* (peanuts), *leb* (pumpkin or certain melon seeds, dried and roasted), and *fishar* (popcorn). *Termis* (lupini beans) are another popular snack. They are typically soaked for several days and then boiled in salted water. Their outer layer is usually not eaten, so the beans are eaten by tearing a small piece of the skin with the teeth and popping the bean into the mouth, then discarding the skin. Other popular street snacks include *dora mashwi* (corn on the cob), which is served hot off the grill to passersby.

Dough-based snacks are also common. *Simit* is a dough shaped into a doughnut, but much wider, baked, and covered with sesame seeds. Sold along with the *simit* is a small newspaper cone filled with spice mixture called *do'aa*, a dry combination of ground cumin, coriander, sesame seeds, salt, and pepper. The hot *simit* is dipped into the spice mixture and eaten.

One of the most ubiquitous drinks in Egypt is *aseer asab*, or freshly squeezed sugarcane. Sugarcane juice has to be served freshly squeezed; otherwise, it ferments and becomes alcoholic. A popular specialty drink available during the hot summer months is *erq sous* (licorice), which is served cold, often by a wandering seller who has an *erq sous* jug strapped to his body with reusable plastic cups in his hand. Other specialty drinks served from a small juice store or street cart include *aseer manga* (fresh mango juice), *aseer rumman* (pomegranate juice), *aseer lamoun* (lemon juice), *tamr hindi* (tamarind juice), *karkade* (hibiscus tea—often served cold), *helba* (fenugreek tea), and the ever-present *shay* (black tea) and *ahwa* (Turkish coffee). However, the teas and coffees are most available in *ahawi* (cafés), rather than street carts.

Fruit and Sweet Treats

Batata (sweet potatoes) wrapped in foil, cooked on a hot roadside grill, and served hot are enjoyed by many people as a sweet snack or dessert after dinner. *Teen shouki*, a prickly pear cactus fruit, is a popular street food during the summer months. The fruit is often peeled by a glove-wearing vendor to avoid being pricked, and the flesh of the fruit is presented to passersby to eat on the spot. Fresh dates are widely available, especially when ripe and in season in late summer and early fall; otherwise, dried dates are sold from the same vendors who sell roasted nuts. *Kharroub* (carob) is another fruit that is dried and sold in street carts. *Asal eswed*, which means "black honey," refers to molasses, which is carried around by street sellers in large jugs. It is poured into smaller containers that many take home to eat with tahini, the unsalted sesame seed paste. The same vendor usually sells a chewy candy made with molasses called *asaliya*.

Egyptian street food does not heavily feature sweets, with a few exceptions that are often made with milk. *Roz bi laban* (rice pudding) is made of white rice, whole milk, sugar, and some cinnamon. A similar starchy dessert is *mahalabia*, a sweet pudding made by thickening whole milk with cornstarch and sugar and adding vanilla, rosewater, and pistachios for extra flavor. A liquid version of *mahalabia* is called *salep*, which is authentically made with orchid powder instead of cornstarch. Authentic *salep* is now very difficult to find: it has been replaced by a simple flavored starchy formula added to the milk.

Desserts that are not made with milk usually contain a lot of sugar and flour. *Fresca* is a sweet snack widely available on the shore that comprises two wafers with sticky sweet nuts sandwiched in the middle. *Basbousa*, a semolina-based honeyed dessert, is overly sweet to many, but enjoyed by those with a strong sweet tooth. Another dessert, called *kunafa*, is made with fried *she'reya* (vermicelli) sweetened with a syrup and sometimes stuffed with a creamy custard. *Luqmet el qadi* (which means "morsel of the judge," though it is actually an Arabic transliteration of the Greek *loukoumades*) is a semisoft dough with yeast that is poured into hot oil and deep-fried, resulting in irregularly shaped balls that are crispy on the outside and very soft on the inside. They are then dipped in sugary syrup; sometimes cinnamon is sprinkled on top. In some places, these sugary treats are called *zalabia*. These are similar in concept to *meshabbik*, another fried dough dipped in syrup, with the difference being one of shape and texture: the *meshabbik* is interconnected dough (similar to a pretzel but less uniform) and with a thicker, less puffy texture than *luqmet el qadi*. Finally, a traditional holiday dessert sold only during religious feasts and festivals is *kahk*, a cookie made with *samna baladi* (clarified butter or ghee), flour, and sugar, and sometimes stuffed with date paste or nuts.

HEBA SALEH

LIBERIA

The Republic of Liberia is a coastal country located in western Africa that shares borders with Sierra Leone, Guinea, and Côte d'Ivoire. Its coastline stretches 360 miles along the Atlantic Ocean and its capital, Monrovia, derives its name from the former president James Monroe, who supported the idea of creating colonies of free blacks in Africa. The population of approximately four million people is extremely diverse, including but not limited to Mende, Gola, Kpelle, Mandingo, and Bassa and a significant population of descendants of formerly enslaved Africans, or Americo-Liberians, who returned to the continent from the United States under James Monroe's initiative starting in 1822. Along with Ethiopia, the country boasts the distinction of never having been colonized by European powers. Like its neighbor Sierra Leone, it is the only other country on the continent organized specifically as a colony for African Americans (freedmen and escaped slaves) in the 1800s.

English is the official language, but because the country is so ethnically diverse, approximately 30 languages are also spoken. A creolized form of English is used by the majority of the population. The country's climate is warm and humid like the rest of western Africa. Historically, the country has been part of both the Mali and Songhai Empires and became a republic in 1847. During the 1990s, civil war raged throughout the country stunting economic growth and leaving millions of Liberians with the difficult task of rebuilding when the last conflict finally ended in 2007.

The primary staples in the Liberian kitchen are cassava cooked and processed in various forms, rice, palm oil, and butter, and dried, smoked, or fresh fish, and meat. Each meal consists of a combination of these ingredients and supplemented by such greens as sweet potato leaves, spinach, and cassava leaves. Leafy greens are usually finely chopped, pureed, and served cooked with meat as a sauce. Such vegetables as okra, eggplant, cucumbers, and pumpkin, a squash with a flavor and texture similar to kabocha, are usually stewed with meat or fish and served with a starchy staple such as rice or *dumboy*, the Liberian national dish, which consists of boiled, pounded cassava, either of which accompanies nearly every meal. Plantains, sweet (ripe) or green (unripe), are served fried as snacks or side dishes. Tropical fruits are also an important part of the Liberian diet. Like other western African cuisines, bitter flavors, slippery and oily textures, and spiciness are favored. One dish that embodies all of these characteristics is the very popular dish known as *palava sauce*, whose key ingredients are palm oil, chilies, and pureed leafy greens with a slippery, mucilaginous texture.

Rice is an important part of the Liberian diet and agricultural landscape. It is the foundation for many dishes including jollof rice, an iconic dish that also includes chicken, shrimp, and different types of vegetables. Such root vegetables as sweet potatoes and yams are important to the diet in addition to cassava. They are eaten roasted, mashed, fried, and often drizzled with palm oil or butter.

MAJOR STREET FOODS

Goat Stew

Small cookshops are found on the street of the country's capital, Monrovia. These are usually open fronted with cooking done in the shop or outside it. Customers can sit on small benches or stand and eat, all out in the open. One of the main dishes is a highly spiced (with chilies) goat stew. Served at every festival and when meat is available, at home, it is a favorite of people taking lunch or buying it to take home in evenings.

Cassava

Pounded cassava, the home staple called *domboy* or *fufu*, is also sold at cookshops as an accompaniment to stews. *Fufu* is the staple starch of West Africa and is consumed in many other parts of the continent. Cassava can also be sliced and fried into chips and as such a popular street food.

Fruits

As a tropical country, many fruits such as bananas, mangoes, coconut, and citrus fruits are popular. Of course, fried plantain chips stand alongside cassava as among the best-loved street snacks.

Peanuts

Peanuts are also a staple of the Liberian diet they are in the rest of sub-Saharan Africa. Roasted and boiled, they are sold by vendors in town and country. Alongside them are commercially made and packaged candies.

Drinks

Fresh fruit juices, coconut water, and carbonated beverages from such international companies as Coca-Cola are common beverages traditionally sold to accompany street foods.

RACHEL FINN

MOROCCO

T HE KINGDOM OF MOROCCO is located on the northwest coast of Africa separated from Spain by just eight miles of the Mediterranean Sea. Together with Tunisia, Algeria, Mauritania, and Libya, Morocco is part of the Maghreb region and shares cultural, historical, linguistic, and culinary ties with these countries. In 1912, it was divided into a French and a Spanish protectorate and regained its independence in 1956.

Moroccan street food is more distinguished and varies greatly in some respects, from food sold in carts across other countries in the North African desert, perhaps because it features dishes influenced by several food traditions, including African, Andalusian, Berber, Mediterranean, Middle Eastern, and Jewish. There are slight regional variations, but a common theme is the concept of preparing the meal in real time, with the customer involved in many steps of the process from selecting the meats to picking out the seasonings and bread type for a sandwich. Moroccan street vendors pioneered in involving the customer in the food preparation process, a model that many American fast-food chains have successfully adapted in recent years.

Though street food is plentiful in Morocco on roadsides and beachfront cities alike, there is a street-food epicenter located in Marrakesh called Jemaa el Fna in the form of an outdoor marketplace, or souk. Translated as "square of the dead," Jemaa el Fna is a large cultural center mainly attracting tourists by day and an outdoor food market at night for both tourists and locals. Because of the predominant presence of tourists in Jemaa el Fna, many of the vendors are dressed in traditional colorful costumes, including the water and juice sellers who keep the liquid cool in insulated water bags and serve the drinks in brass cups. Street food was not widely available in Morocco until the 1980s. Before that, food was closely tied with the home, and eating out was only reserved for the well-to-do. Over the past few decades when the margin of disposable income grew and many more women have chosen professional careers outside the home, a more robust eating-out culture has developed.

MAJOR STREET FOODS

Bocadillos

One of the most striking influences on Moroccan street food comes from Spanish and French cuisines. When street snacks started gaining popularity later in the 1980s, *bocadillo*, a Spanish word for sandwich, became used interchangeably for sandwich all over Morocco. A *bocadillo* is made differently depending on the region, but a common denominator is the type of bread, which is a French-style baguette. In more modernized cities like Tangier, the *bocadillo* can be stuffed with salad and thin layers of *jambon* (deli meat) and *fromage* (French for "cheese"). Other popular options include a Moroccan version of a Tunisian food called *fricassée*, a tuna sandwich that includes *harissa*, a spicy red pepper and caper mixture borrowed from Tunisian cuisine, as well as spiced mayonnaise, boiled eggs, and an option of adding *pomme frites* (French fries) on top. For those who like an uncomplicated sandwich, a *bocadillo* stuffed with an omelet is almost always available.

Boubouch

Though escargot is typically considered a French delicacy served in upscale restaurants, Moroccans have been serving it out of street carts for many decades. Named *boubouch* (or *b'bouch*) by the locals, snails—steamed or stewed—have a reputation for being a succulent snack in Morocco and are widely available all over the country. In Rabat, the capital city, many snail sellers have set up their stalls on roadsides or in the souk. Similarly, *boubouch* can also be found in Casablanca and along the shore, served steaming hot in little bowls with accompanying toothpicks.

Though the snail concept may be borrowed from the French, the preparation style is not. The Moroccan version of escargot forgoes the garlic butter sauce in favor of a more traditional concoction that is sworn by many to heal the common cold and other ailments. The aromatic, often spicy, broth served along with the mollusks includes at least a few of the following, the specifics depending on the vendor's recipe: cumin, ginger, licorice root, thyme, aniseed, sweet and spicy peppers, fresh mint, orange peel, and crushed Arabic gum (or mastic)—a resin obtained from the mastic tree and used extensively in Middle Eastern cooking. Sometimes it is made with a healthy dose of fresh garlic as well, but that depends on the region. Moroccan natives are used to *boubouch* and even those who do not like the texture of snails sometimes order the bowl of spicy broth for its health benefits.

Sfenj

Typical French-style pastries—*pain au chocolat, Napoleon, éclair,* and *petites tartes*—are more popular in Moroccan bakeries than on the street, though the occasional street vendor may carry a few of them alongside other more traditional Moroccan desserts. One dessert widely available all over Morocco is *sfenj*: basically small doughnut-shaped pieces of dough that are fried. The word *sfen* means "sponge" in Arabic and refers to the dessert's soft and absorbent composition. A simple mixture of flour, salt, yeast, and water is left to rise for a few hours. The batter is then made into doughnut shapes and dipped into hot oil to fry. They are pulled out of the oil with skewers, sometimes dusted with powdered sugar or honey, strung up in a thread similar to a Hawaiian lei, and sold to sweet-craving onlookers. *Sfenj* is typically eaten in the morning with coffee, as a midday snack or as a post-lunch dessert with mint green tea. (In Morocco, as in many Mediterranean countries, the main meal is served around two or three in the afternoon.)

Meat Sandwiches

In Morocco, "know the origin of your meat" is taken to another level, even for street food. Instead of serving customers ready-made cooked meats, many street vendors let the customer select a cut of raw meat and watch it grilled right in front of them. These roadside butcher stalls, which are especially popular at rest stops along well-traveled routes, often feature different meats—lamb, beef, and chicken—hanging from a pole, with bouquets of parsley and cilantro hanging in between them. The greens purportedly keep away flies, with the added bonus of imparting a pleasant smell that overshadows that of the raw meat. The same stand usually has ground beef available for purchase, sometimes already mixed with spices and ready to shape into *kefta* or meatballs.

After customers have picked their raw meats, they take their purchases to a nearby stall that specializes in grilling. Here too, customer involvement is encouraged: They can pick the spices and vegetables to be grilled alongside the meat, as well as the style of bread that will serve as the sandwich for the mixture.

Another popular street food is *raas* or lamb's head. As unappetizing as that may sound to some Westerners, the meat is incredibly tender as it is steamed and then served with a little side of salt and cumin for individual dipping.

OTHER STREET FOODS

Mehlaba

Largely a Moroccan phenomenon, the *mehlaba*, literally "the dairy place," is a word derived from the Arabic word for milk, *haleeb*. Found in many Moroccan cities, these milk bars are essentially smoothie-making stations that sell dairy concoctions and juices as well as other snacks such as ready-made *bocadillos*. Milk smoothies are made to order. The customer selects from a wide range of fruits and flavors to be blended in, the most popular of which include avocados, bananas, dates, and various fruits.

Moroccan Snacks

Snacks popular in Morocco, especially along the boardwalk, include grilled corn on the cob, called *kob'wal*, often eaten with a little bit of saltwater for added flavor. Freshly roasted and smoked, mixed nuts, peanuts, and chickpeas are wrapped in paper cones and sold in stands all over Morocco. Seasonal roasted chestnuts are especially popular in colder months. Dried figs and dates, native to the North African desert, are displayed in heaps in street stands. Often they are stuffed into various finger foods and pastries.

HEBA SALEH

NIGERIA

T HE FEDERAL REPUBLIC OF NIGERIA comprises 36 states and its Federal Capital Territory, Abuja. Located in West Africa, it shares borders with Benin in the west, Chad and Cameroon in the east, and Niger in the north. Its southern boundary is the Gulf of Guinea on the Atlantic Ocean. Its population of more than 260 million makes it the largest country in Africa and the seventh most populous in the world. Composed of more than 250 ethnic groups, the three largest are the Hausa, Igbo, and Yoruba. Half of Nigerians are Muslims, 40 percent Christians, while 10 percent follow indigenous religions. The largest city, Lagos, has a population of more than 10 million. Other large urban areas are the capital Abuja, Kano, Ibadan, and Kaduna.

Nigeria has a mostly humid, tropical climate, and a wide range of topographical features, including plains, plateaus, mountains, and desert. Each of these determines what crops are grown and what are available to the local populations. The original staples were rice, millet, groundnuts, yams, and lentils. The Portuguese, who came to West Africa in the 1400s, introduced cassava, potatoes, and peanuts—all New World plants—to the region. Later Europeans brought beans and corn, while the British, who controlled Nigeria from 1914 to 1914, brought pepper, cinnamon, and nutmeg from their Indian possessions.

A traditional Nigerian meal consists of a starch and a thick stew made with meat, fish, vegetables, or a combination of meats and vegetables. The best-known starch is *fufu* made from pounded yams, plantains, or cassava. There are wide regional variations in basic dishes. In the north, the staples of the largely Muslim Hausa population are beans and sorghum. Kebabs, called *suya* or *tsere*, are popular street foods. In the east, dietary staples are pumpkin, yams, and various dumplings made from cassava, while people in the south enjoy peanut-based stews and rice. The Yorubas in southwest and central Nigeria eat cooked *gari* (cassava root powder) with stews thickened with okra, yams, stews made with peanuts, mushrooms, and rice. Only the wealthy can afford to eat meat every day. The main cooking medium is palm oil, made from ground palm kernels. Fruit, including papayas, pineapple, coconut, plantains, and mangos, is abundant. Seafood is popular along the coasts and along rivers, the fish often made into hearty stews. Milk and milk products are not usually consumed in Nigeria except in the north, where the Fulani people are traditional cattle herders. However, because of the years of British rule, people take milk and cream in their tea. Hot chile peppers are used throughout Nigeria in stews, as dips and as condiment sauces.

PAPAYA

Street foods play a major role in the Nigerian economy. Traditional foods often take hours to process and prepare, so that some women buy street foods as a quicker way to feed their families. Women are also the main vendors of street foods, and many dishes they prepare are ones found in their customers' own home cooking. Students and small merchants are major customers, especially for breakfast. Household surveys show that more than 80 percent of people buy their breakfast from vendors between four and seven days a week. Almost everyone eats at least some of their meals on the street, and as much as half of all food expenditures is spent on street foods.

Some vendors are doorstep vendors, who set up a table and chair on the sidewalk in a residential district to sell to housewives. Others have carts that they push to the same location every day and remove at night, while others use bicycle carts or balance poles on their shoulders as they ride. Some women vendors carry the food in baskets on their heads. Bargaining in all Nigerian markets is expected, even with low-cost food. Although the initial asking price will be higher for foreigners, vendors have their true price; buyers who *ciniki* (bargain) will achieve a lower price.

Popular items include bananas, oranges, and peanuts (called groundnuts but not the same as the native groundnut, or *Macrotyloma geocarpum*), which are boiled or roasted and then sold in plastic bags that are filled and then twisted into round shapes.

MAJOR STREET FOODS

Pepper Soup

Pepper soup is served in most local restaurants and hotels and on the street. It is a spicy dish made with fresh or dried hot peppers and other local herbs such as utazi, a very bitter herb used widely, or ukazi, a dried leaf found in most southern Nigerian stews and soups. Pepper soup is commonly made with goat meat and, when done in fancier style, with crayfish. Chicken and fish can be substituted depending on the region such as rivers and coasts.

Other Soups

Other popular soups found in open-air dining spots include *ewedu* soup, made from a mucilaginous leaf (jute mallow) that gives a thick, okra-like texture to it. It can be served with *amala*, a thick brown paste made from dried, ground cassava. *Amala* can be made into a soup itself, perhaps mixed with vegetables. *Gbegiri* or black-eyed pea soup is also very popular throughout the country. As with pepper soup, these varieties usually have hot chilies in them. *Ogbono* soup is also a popular soup made from meats, vegetables, and greens and thickened with *obongo*, dried mango seeds.

Suya

Thin strips of beef are grilled on a metal stick over a charcoal fire on an iron grate. During grilling, the meat is seasoned liberally with groundnut oil squirted from a dishwashing liquid bottle. Spices, including paprika and cayenne pepper, are added. The beef is served in newspaper along with additional savory seasoning. The *suya* may be accompanied by masa, a spongy white dough made from fermented rice.

Jollof Rice

Popular throughout West Africa, jollof rice is basically long-grain white rice that is fried in oil (palm oil is common), then mixed with tomatoes and tomato paste, hot peppers, and other spices to make a hearty and hot accompaniment to meat and vegetable dishes.

Plantains

Plantains are a kind of banana whose texture is very firm, and they are not sweet in flavor. Plantains are used as a starch around the world, Nigeria being no exception. They are prepared as a street food in several ways. As snacks, plantains are sliced and fried until crisp. Called *dodos*, or when served with other foods such as stews, *boli*, plantains are a staple of the Nigerian diet.

Other Fried Treats

Hot oil is maintained at the roadside for immediate frying of street snacks. Favorites include puff puff, a light sweet dough that is rolled into 1¼-inch balls and then fried, and *kosai* or *akara* made from ground beans that are also rolled into 1¼-inch balls or made into small cakes and fried until crispy. Spices can be added to the batters to make them spicy.

Corn

Whole corn cobs can be found in markets on streets and along roadsides roasting on open charcoal-fired grills. The corn is chewed carefully with little residual left on the cob. One way it is served on the streets of Lagos, the capital city, is with fresh coconut. Corn is also used by grinding it into a pulp, then frying it into fritters called *mosa*.

OTHER STREET FOODS

Snails and Tripe

Snails are eaten throughout Nigeria. Usually they are boiled in salted water, then removed from their shells, fried, and covered in a spicy red sauce. Fried plantain slices are the usual accompaniment. Tripe is also very popular through all of Nigeria. It is the stomach of an animal that is cleaned, boiled, and then fried and served with typical stew ingredients.

Sugarcane

This is a popular snack, sold in cut segments of about five inches. The sugarcane is kept moist until consumption, then a mouthful is bitten off, the sweetness savored, and the starchy remnants spit on the ground by pushing them out of the mouth with the tongue.

Kunu

Kunu is a fermented millet drink sold in plastic bags and especially popular in the northern part of the country. The buyer cuts off a corner of the bag and sucks the contents into the mouth. Similar drinks are made from wheat and called *malta* from the German *malzbier*. Nonfermented drinks are made from mixing water with cornmeal and pounded cassava. They are very high in calories and carbohydrates, but filling for the many poor people of the country.

Nigeria is the largest consumer of sugar in Africa, much of it going to soft drinks. The usual international bottlers sell colas and other products familiar the world over. Local Nigerian companies make varieties of similar beverages. Fruit juices are popular though many of them are fortified with sugar.

BRUCE KRAIG AND COLLEEN TAYLOR SEN

NORTH AFRICA

Nᴏʀᴛʜ Aғʀɪᴄᴀɴ sᴛʀᴇᴇᴛ ғᴏᴏᴅ ɪɴ Tᴜɴɪsɪᴀ, Aʟɢᴇʀɪᴀ, ᴀɴᴅ Lɪʙʏᴀ has obvious similarities, but notable differences as well. The culinary landscapes of the three are similar in that the traditional ingredients that have been used for generations are incorporated into affordable dishes with a Mediterranean bent. For example, in both Tunisia and Algeria, the French influence is obvious in the prevalence of the French baguettes and pastries, which are used to encase everything from tuna and eggs to meats—all with traditional North African spices and mixtures. Libya's history as an Italian colony is reflected in many traditional Libyan foods that heavily feature pasta. *Rishda*, a thin handmade pasta, is one of the most popular, as well as couscous, which is made out of semolina flour.

Harissa, a spicy chile-based sauce, originated in Tunisia and Algeria but is now found in all North African countries of the Maghrib (in Arabic: the "West," referring to countries that lie West of the Middle East), including Morocco, Algeria, Tunisia, and Libya. Street vendors who sell sandwiches, whether on a French baguette or in pita bread, are almost guaranteed to have *harissa* on hand. It is typically made with hot chile peppers (serrano peppers are commonly used), as well as cumin, garlic, lemon juice, coriander, red chile powder, caraway, and olive oil. Sometimes, the sauce is also made to have a smoky flavor, but the specific ingredients used and their proportions depend on the region where the food is being sold, as well as the vendor.

MAJOR STREET FOODS

Fricassée, *Brik*, and *Kafteji*

One of the most popular Tunisian street foods is a rather sophisticated sandwich called the *fricassée*. The inspiration for the name is French, which literally means "fried and separated"—quite an accurate description for the sandwich itself. Rumor has it that the street vendors adopted the frying method in order to compensate for the lack of oven space needed to bake the coveted French baguettes. The dough is formed and fried in oil, then split and filled with boiled eggs, fish (usually tuna), green or black pitted olives, and figs. Of course, the composition of the *fricassée* varies based on the vendor making it, but the basic elements of the sandwich—eggs, fish, and vegetables—are usually the same everywhere. Other possible ingredients include peppers, mayonnaise, pickled vegetables (particularly carrots), and chile sauces like *harissa*.

Brik is yet another dough-based street food widely available in Tunisia and Algeria; it has a thin flaky dough that is wrapped in a triangular formation to cover a variety of stuffings—then the whole thing is fried in vegetable oil until the shell crisps up. Popular stuffings include a mixture of egg and tuna, mashed potato and celery, or halal ground beef. Regardless of the stuffing used, egg is almost always included in the mixture—mainly as a congealing agent, but it also imparts a subtle savory taste. Various spices are also used to complement the flavors of the mixture, but often include capers, onions, lemon juice, olive oil, and parsley.

Another sandwich eaten by the poor in Tunisia, making it a ubiquitous street food, is *kafteji*. It is made by frying various vegetables—usually potatoes, tomatoes, onions, peppers, and pumpkins—separately, then mixing them with a beaten egg, and chopping up the mixture and adding it to a baguette. As with most street foods in this region, *harissa* or some fried hot peppers are often added to the sandwich for an extra kick.

Karantita

The *karantita* is a typical Algerian street food that originated in Algiers. It is made of some of the most widely available ingredients in the country: bread and chickpeas. Cheap and filling, the sandwich is sold everywhere—in front of schools, in cafés, and on street corners. *Karantita* (or *kalinti* in Moroccan dialect) is derived from the Spanish word *caliente* meaning "hot" and *torta* meaning "pie." Chickpea flour (the unroasted variety) is mixed with eggs, water, oil, salt, and cumin and baked until the top is a golden brown. The mixture, seasoned with spicy *harissa* sauce and sprinkled with cumin, is eaten as a stand-alone pie in the west of Algeria, but in other parts of the country, the savory mixture is stuffed into a French-style baguette and served to hungry passersby.

Rishda

Libya's street-food presence is scarcer as compared with the other North African countries, largely because more than 90 percent of the country is covered in desert. It doesn't feature nearly as many pastries and French breads, but the Italian influence is obvious in the popular pasta dish known as *rishda*. Thin handmade noodles made of flour and water are cooked with tomatoes, onions, and chickpeas and flavored with paprika, cinnamon, and turmeric.

Bsisa (Ground Roasted Barley Cereal)

Bsisa, colloquially in Arabic meaning "mashed," refers to a North African dish made of out of roasted barley flour, which is ground with spices. Some of the most popular spices used with *bsisa* include fenugreek (in Arabic, *helba*), aniseed, and cumin. Popular in Tunisia, Algeria, and Libya, *bsisa* is usually eaten as a breakfast food or as a snack and has historically been used as a snack food by travelers and Bedouins, because it is packed with nutrition and doesn't spoil easily. In the east of Libya, sometimes wheat flour is used instead of barley flour to make *bsisa*. A version of *bsisa* called *howira* can be mixed with milk or water and made into a thick drink called *rowina*. Alternatively, the flour is mixed with olive oil and eaten with dried dates or figs as a snack. It is also paired with *halwa shamiya*, or sweetened sesame seed butter, on top.

Lablabi (Tunisian Soup)

Lablabi is a Tunisian stew available in street carts for cheap; it is made with the affordable base ingredient chickpeas in a strongly seasoned, aromatic soup flavored with garlic, cumin, *harissa*, salt, pepper, lime juice, and olive oil. Stale bread that has hardened is dropped into the hot soup to add a crunch to each bite. Sometimes, a raw or lightly boiled egg is added to the hot soup and stirred in. Other toppings include tuna, olives, and scallions.

HEBA SALEH

SOUTH AFRICA

T HE REPUBLIC OF SOUTH AFRICA encompasses the lower tip of the African continent. There are 11 climate zones in the Republic, ranging from snowy mountains to warm seacoasts, and the country ranks among the most world's greatest biodiversity regions. Since more than 60 percent of the nation's population lives in cities, South Africa's produce goes into the many street foods found there.

Portuguese explorers landed here in 1487, followed by the Dutch, who established permanent colonies on the southern tip of Africa in 1652. After the establishment of Fort de Goede Hoop, the colonist brought slaves from Malay, Indonesia, Madagascar, and India as workers. The fort later became the economically and culturally important Cape Colony and the South African city of Cape Town (or Kaapstad). Portuguese, German, and French also migrated here. The colonists eventually expanded into lands occupied by such peoples as the Khoikhoi (or Hottentots), Xhosa, and Zulu. A series of wars forced the native South African populations into the margins so they were not integrated into the new society.

During the 1800s, the discovery of diamonds, and later gold, resulted in the Anglo-Boer War(s), and eventually the British annexation of Cape Town and the Cape Colony. When slavery was abolished in the British Empire in 1839, Indians were brought in as workers. In 1909, the autonomous Union of South Africa was established. It obtained independence from the British crown in 1931 and became the Republic of South Africa in 1961. Because of strong racial segregation laws until the 1990s, known as the apartheid system, a small white minority controlled the vast majority of blacks, people of mixed ancestry, and Asians. The first official public elections ended apartheid, and today the country is a multiethnic nation embracing diverse cultures and languages. Almost 80 percent of the population is of (black) African ancestry, 9 percent white (European), 9 percent mixed ancestry, and 2.5 percent is of Indian/Asian origin.

South Africa is divided into nine provinces and is home to more than 50 million people. The largest part of the population lives in urban areas, and each province has a large city with at least one million inhabitants. The biggest cities are Johannesburg and Durban, with more than 10 million people.

RAINBOW CUISINE

Contemporary South African cuisine, nicknamed "rainbow cuisine," incorporates the culinary practices and influence of many cultures. The daily food of the majority of the population can be traced back to a blend of European, Asian (Malay), and indigenous cooking styles and practices. European foods and dishes such as *potjiekos* ("pot food" or stews, cooked outdoors in a round cast-iron, three-legged pot, or *potjie*), *melktert* ("milk tart," a sweet pastry custard tart), *droëwors* (dry sausage), *boerewors* (farmer sausage), and *biltong* (dried, salted meat) evolved and were popularized from the 17th century onward. Containing Asian spices (cumin, turmeric), the national minced meat dish *bobotie* is a spicy Malay version of the British shepherd's pie. Throughout the country, the *braai* (barbecue) is very popular. In conjunction with meat, many people rely on *millies* (corn or maize); corn is roasted on the cob and widely used to prepare a stiff *pap* (porridge) also known as *phuthu*. After its arrival from the Americas in the 1700s, corn rapidly replaced sorghum, traditionally a staple ingredient. Nowadays indigenous Xhosa, Zulu, Sotho, Tswana, and Swazi communities commonly use corn to prepare all sorts of foods. Similarly, a wide range of street foods can be traced back to nonindigenous populations.

At a national level, more than 10 percent of South Africans buy street foods from around 60,000 stalls officially counted nationwide. Most of the street foods are sold from stalls, stands, carts, and kiosks in informal settings in urban areas. The street vendors can be found on the pavement of busy streets and busy public areas such as the beaches, bus and railway stations, and school premises. Very often, the vendors (hawkers) sell only a few foods and drinks, often the same items.

MAJOR STREET FOODS

Corn on the cob (*millies* or *mealies*) are sold almost everywhere by mealie cookers that set up their drums or braziers on the pavement. Smoke from the wood fires often indicates the presence of a *mealie* facility. Traditionally, African women carry the lit braziers on the head, which is a Zulu specialty known as Bovine Head Cooking, and prepare, cook, and serve the meat of the heads of cow and goats and smileys (roasted sheep's head).

Townships' Street Meats

Grilled, deep-fried, and boiled chicken heads and feet, known as walkie-talkies, enjoy nationwide popularity, but are commonly purchased at stalls, taxi stands, and markets in townships. Walkie-talkies evolved during apartheid when people living in townships and workers received leftover parts of chicken from wealthy farmers and turned these into grilled, deep-fried, or boiled foods, seasoned with pepper and salt. Walkie-talkies are eaten with *pap* or corn porridge. Sometimes Walkie-talkies are boiled and prepared with salt and spices or stewed with onions, green peppers, and tomatoes. The skin and meat of chicken feet are scraped off with the teeth, and the meat is chewed up. Apart from the beak, the chicken heads are consumed whole. Other street foods with unusual animal parts include *amanqina*, the spiced and boiled hoof of a cow, pig, or sheep; the township staple *skop*, the braised head of a cow, sheep, or goat, which is eaten on the bone; *mala*, chicken intestines that are first boiled and then fried; and *mogodu*, boiled tripe that normally is served with *samp*, slowly cooked, dried, crushed corn kernels and beans. Zulu refers to *samp* as *isistambu*, but it is the traditional dish of the Nguni people, especially the Xhosa tribe. *Samp* was on record as the favorite dish of the most famous Nguni tribe member, Madiba, or Nelson Mandela.

Malay Influence

Sosaties, marinated skewers of meat, usually lamb (mutton) or beef, are a popular Malay-style street corner food and very similar to Asian satay and Middle Eastern–style kebabs. In South Africa, the meat is marinated in tamarind juice with such ingredients as fried onions, chilies, garlic, and curry leaves, put on skewers. *Sosaties* are either pan fried or cooked over an open fire or grill.

    Samoosas (or samosas), which are of Indian origin, are popular in Cape Town. The fried or baked triangular pastry is stuffed with a mixture of cooked potatoes, onions, peas, coriander, and lentils. Apart from a vegetarian *samoosa*, there are also variations with chicken, lamb, and beef. *Samoosas* are a favorite *padkos* (food for the road) that is either brought from home or bought at road stalls.

European Influence

Vetkoek (literally, fat or grease cake) are deep-fried dough balls made from a dough of flour, yeast, and salt. *Vetkoek* can be stuffed with sweet or savory fillings. Apart from filling the dough before deep-frying, South Africans cut *vetkoek* open and fill it with curried minced beef, cheese, butter, jams, and syrup. *Vetkoek* variations can include a stuffing from chicken fillet and mayonnaise, topped with cheese and bacon. At a traditional *braai*, it is served alongside *boerewors*, the farmers' sausage made from fresh meats, which is also turned into a popular street food. *Boerewors* is made from coarsely minced beef or pork with such spices as coriander, nutmeg, clove, and allspice. The sausage is not only grilled over an open fire but also cooked on a (gas) grill, in the oven or in a pan. Served on a bread roll, and known as the *boerie roll*, it is the South African equivalent of the hot dog, which as a *hoddog* also enjoys popularity. American-style hot dogs are commonly sold from carts, vans, and a chain of food shops called Wild Bean (owned by the British Petroleum Company). *Pap en vleis* (porridge and meat, beef, or chicken) is a traditional street food in Johannesburg. In addition, street vendors sell pies, fried fish, pizzas, chicken—and hamburgers, curries, *pap*, fish and chips, and the popular snack food slap chips, which are French fries drenched in vinegar and sprinkled with salt, Aromat (a mass produced seasoning), and chile powder.

Bunny Chow, *Kota*, and the Gatsby

Filled loaves and bread rolls are among the most popular street foods. Bunny chow, originating in the city of Durban and developed by working-class Indians, is a very popular hollowed-out loaf of bread filled with a meat or vegetarian curry. The removed soft bread is used to dip in the curry. Although traditionally Indians do not eat with cutlery, it is also often said that bunny chow was invented by Indian golf caddies, as they were not allowed to use cutlery during apartheid.

Kota is the Sowetan slang for a quarter loaf of bread with any type of filling inside. In slang, *kota* is also referred to as *spatlo,* indicating it is easily carried. *Kotas* evolved from the Indian bunny chow during the late 1970s and originally consisted of bread, mashed potato, mincemeat, and atchar (a spicy Indian condiment or pickle developed in South Africa). The older generation still eats this version accompanied by a cooked chicken's foot. The most popular *kotas* are a quarter loaf of white bread filled with fried chips (French fries), cheese, meats, sausages, fried eggs, and hot sauces. Popular among youngsters in Soweto and Johannesburg is the Sowetan quarter, a *kota* filled with French fries.

Gatsby, a long bread roll cut lengthwise, stuffed or filled with fish or meats, hot vinegary slap chips, masala (an Indian spice mixture), and hot sauce or pickles, enjoys popularity in Cape Town. The most popular Gatsbys are filled with *polony*, a corruption from British word "boloney," which are curled red meat sausages. Commonly, all sorts of salads are served on the side. According to the legend, the Gatsby was invented by a Maori chief who was passionate about rugby and owes its popularity to the popularity of the New Zealand rugby team in Cape Town. The invention is also claimed by a local fish-and-chips shop and brought in connection with the 1974 Hollywood movie *The Great Gatsby*, starring Robert Redford as Jay Gatsby.

Drinks

Throughout South Africa, drinking black tea is common practice. In recent years, South Africans started developing a taste for caffeine-free rooibos tea, from the oxidized leaves of the typical South African plant *Aspalathus linearis*. It is served black and either with lemon or honey.

Popular carbonated soft drinks, known as fizzy drinks, include bottles and cans of Appletiser (apple, pear, and grape flavors), Bashew's (since 1899), Coca-Cola, Fanta, Iron Brew, Soda King, King Cola, and Twizza.

Traditionally homemade by women and drunk straight after production are African beers, which are commonly known by their names in local languages such as *mahewu, mechow,* and *umqombothi.* These popular beers, with a relatively low alcohol content, are produced with corn or sorghum, malt, and yeast that is mixed with water. *Gemmerbier,* ginger flavored beer, is prepared by fermenting ginger, raisins, yeast, cream of tartar, and tartaric acid in water. The popular refreshing, slightly fermented drink Mageu, maHewu, amaRhewu, or amaHewu is made from corn porridge with flour and diluted with water, similar to *amasi* (sour milk) fermented milk with a yogurt taste. Mageu can be purchased as a supermarket product and on the streets.

KARIN VANEKER

WEST AFRICA

WEST AFRICA IS A VAST REGION bordered by the Sahara desert to the north and the Atlantic Ocean to the west and south. Several river systems run through the region, the most important being the Niger River and its tributaries. West Africa encompasses three climactic zones: desert in the north, savanna (grasslands) south of the desert, and tropical rain forest near the Atlantic Coast, roughly from Guinea to Nigeria. This ecological diversity led to the development of large-scale trade throughout the region and beyond.

Until the last half of the 19th century, European colonization in Africa was mostly limited to outposts along the coast. In 1885, the continent was portioned by the colonial powers, with France and England getting the lion's share and Portugal and Germany smaller areas. Only Liberia, established by the United States as a refuge for ex-slaves, remained independent. Portugal ruled Portuguese Guinea, now Guinea-Bissau. Togo and Cameroon were German colonies until the end of World War I, when each was split into two and administered as trust territories by France and Britain. French colonies were amalgamated into a vast French West African federation with its capital in Dakar, Senegal. The federation split up after the end of colonial rule into its constituent parts: Senegal, Mauritania, Mali (formerly French Sudan), Niger, Upper Volta (later Burkina Faso), and Guinea. British colonies included Gambia, Sierra Leone, Gold Coast (now Ghana), and Nigeria. English, French, and Portuguese remain the official languages of almost all these countries.

Before West Africa was colonized by Europe, caravan routes crisscrossed the grasslands, linking the desert in the north to the rain forests in the south. European explorers occasionally described the kinds of street foods they found in the larger trading towns. René Caillé, who traveled to Timbuktu disguised as a Moor in the 1820s, also passed through the great commercial hub, Jenne (in modern Mali), where he noticed that the butchers in the market "also thrust skewers through little pieces of meat, which they smoke-dry and sell retail." He also saw hawkers in the street, selling food from the countryside, as well as milk, honey, kola nuts, and vegetable and animal butter. Some 70 years later, Captain Louis-Gustave Binger witnessed similar scenes in the town of Kong (modern Côte d'Ivoire). The hawkers in Kong were young girls who, aside from honey and kola nuts, also sold sweets and a confection that Binger describes as "little ginger breads"—most likely fritters—made of millet, honey, and red peppers, alongside such fruits as bananas and papayas.

A different tradition of street food emerged in towns that sprang up along the Atlantic Coast as a result of the slave trade. A Dutch traveler, Pieter de Marees, described women along the Gold Coast (modern Ghana) in 1600 who sold *kenkey* in the marketplace, particularly to fishermen and others who could not prepare it themselves. *Kenkey* is a staple food prepared from fermented maize; it takes several days to prepare and so lends itself well to specialization and to sale in the marketplace or simply by vendors hawking along the street.

Most of these street foods—meat skewers, kola nuts, fritters, fruit, *kenkey*— are still sold today. Honey has been replaced by industrially produced sugar as the sweetener of choice. Kola nuts are not exactly foods; they are chewed but not swallowed. They grow only in the rain forest, but have long been a luxury item in the grasslands and were one of the major commodities traded along caravan routes. The taste is very bitter, but the nuts contain a high dose of caffeine, so that they act as a stimulant.

Though street foods have a long history in West Africa, their place in the African diet was, until relatively recently, entirely marginal. They were found mainly in larger urban centers, but the West African population was overwhelmingly rural. The growth of a modern rail and road transportation network in the 20th century permitted the movement of foodstuffs and of people, which contributed to a proliferation of the street foods in West Africa. New towns mushroomed, attracting migrants, many of them single men. Entrepreneurial women opened stalls in the marketplace—known as chop bars in Anglophone countries—where

ASIA IN AFRICA

Perhaps the most surprising street foods, evidence of true globalization, are the items sold in Dakar and other large cities of French-speaking West Africa. These are bite-size Vietnamese egg rolls (called *nem* in northern Vietnam), bits of meat in a fried wrapper that are sold in special stalls by women. Both Senegal and Vietnam were French colonies, and in the early 20th century, Senegalese men were sent to Vietnam as soldiers. Some married Vietnamese women who returned home with them and opened stalls and restaurants.

men with no woman to cook for them could purchase in inexpensive meal, particularly at midday.

Some vendors sell entire meals. Throughout West Africa, the format for such meals is standard, consisting of a large portion of starch supplemented by a soup or sauce; depending on the starch base, the sauce is either poured over it or a bite-size portion is dipped into it. The ingredients depend on local availability and food preferences. Oil palm kernels, a product of the rain forest, yield oil used for preparing rich red sauces. Cassava leaf sauces are popular in Guinea, Liberia, and Sierra Leone. Pepper soup is popular throughout the region. In Côte d'Ivoire, Ghana, and Nigeria, pounded yams—"foofoo" in English and "foutou" in French—form a popular dish. (Yams must not be confused with sweet potatoes, erroneously called "yams" in the United States; yams are longer and larger, white inside, and not particularly sweet.) Increasingly, rice has become the starch of choice, especially in market stalls. It has long been grown in parts of West Africa, but more recently, cheap imported Asian rice has become readily available. Cheap, easy to transport but also easy to prepare—unlike maize, sorghum, or millet, it has already been husked and winnowed—it is now served in marketplaces everywhere. A popular rice dish is *thiebou djeun* (with fish) or *thiebou yapp* (with meat).

Some modes of preparing staple starches have a more local distribution. These are typically foods that require labor-intensive preparation, often over a period of several days. This is most obvious in foods that require fermentation as part of the process of preparation. *Kenkey*—fermented maize balls wrapped in corn husks and steamed—are typical of southern Ghana. In the south of neighboring Côte d'Ivoire, the local specialty is *attieke*, cassava that has been grated, pressed, and fermented so that it has a consistency similar to couscous, with a pronounced sour kick. Both *kenkey* and *attieke* are easily sold on the street (the *attieke* is served in cones of plantain leaf) and are often accompanied with fried fish, another street food found only along the coast.

Traditional West African breakfasts usually take the form of porridges rather than stews. In the mornings, women may sell these porridges in the market or simply in front of their house as a means of earning a bit of extra cash. These porridges can be made with almost any starch: millet, sorghum, maize, rice, and even yams or plantains. They have the consistency of oatmeal and are sweetened (as liberally as possible!) with sugar and mixed with fresh, condensed, or curdled milk. Such curdled milk, not unlike yogurt, is often available on its own as a street food. Another similar kind of preparation found in Mali, Niger, and northern Côte d'Ivoire is *dègè*, a sweet paste traditionally made from millet mixed with honey and curdled milk. In Niger, alongside traditional *dègè*, one can find a modern variety flavored with ginger and mint. These pastes and porridges can be supplemented with boiled eggs or omelets, also available as street food in the mornings and sometimes throughout the day.

On the other hand, colonial cuisines have had a particular influence on African breakfasts, particularly served in street stalls, in this case run by (as well as for) men. In former French colonies, such stalls serve French-style breakfasts: baguettes, sometimes with butter or (as a substitute) mayonnaise, along with instant coffee mixed with a large quantity of sweetened condensed milk. Of course, in former English colonies, tea is served instead of coffee, and white bread in place of baguettes. Even though wheat does not grow in West Africa, bread is such a popular food that flour is imported in large quantities, and bakeries constitute a very common small-scale enterprise. A modern variety of this kind of breakfast is known in Senegal as *tangana* ("heat" in Wolof) and is typically prepared not by Senegalese, but by migrant men from Niger. Along with café au lait with bread and butter (or mayonnaise), such a breakfast includes boiled eggs or an omelet along with a meat stew. Such breakfasts have apparently grown so popular that they are now served throughout the entire day.

Different snacks tend to be associated with different times of day. There is no hard and set rule, of course, but different street foods tend to be available in the morning, the afternoon, and the evening.

Aside from boiled eggs and omelets, which can be eaten as snacks as well as part of breakfast, mornings are associated with millet and especially flour fritters. Millet fritters are more like cakes, regularly shaped and quite filling. They need to be prepared in advance and are generally served cold. However, flour fritters are far more common nowadays and can easily be prepared by young women outside their homes. These fritters are easy and quick to make by dropping large spoonful of batter into boiling oil. Vendors can prepare them to order so that customers can eat them fresh and piping hot, when they are best. Fried bean cakes—*akara*—are sometimes eaten in the morning as well, though they are more likely to be available throughout the day than flour fritters.

The greatest variety of snacks tends to be available in the afternoon. Some require no preparation, notably fruits: oranges, bananas, mangos, papayas, and more occasionally, guavas and pineapple. Boiled or roasted peanuts can easily be

BURKINA FASO'S ROADSIDE KIOSKS

Croissants and pastries inspired by Burkina Faso's history as a French colony are served from carts everywhere in the capital city of Ouagadougou. But the roadside kiosks, or *maquis*, where mostly women dish out fast, cheap, hot meals to mostly male patrons, take their inspiration from the country's natural vegetation and multiethnic tribal heritage. A common dish in every *maquis* is *tô*, a starch made from millet or corn flour and topped with sauces made from the fruit of the baobab tree, the seeds of the kapok tree, or chopped greens from the leaves of the kenebdo plant, all wild vegetation native to Burkina Faso.

Couscous with *niebe* beans and rice with sauces of stewed eggplant, yams, or tomatoes are cooked on open flames or atop propane tanks starting at dawn. *Gari*, or ground cassava, topped with a medley of fresh vegetables including peppers, onions, cucumbers, and a drizzle of palm tree oil is often served as a lighter alternative. Patrons quench their thirst with refreshing tumblers of ginger juice; *zoomkoom*, a punch made with millet flour, ginger, lemon juice, and tamarind; or *bissap*, a sweet herbal tea made from a hibiscus plant. Fried plantains served with a pinch of salt on the side satisfy the sweet tooth.
—*Manya Brachear*

prepared in advance to be sold and eaten cold. Other foods are roasted, fried, or boiled in the street and sold hot. Ears of corn on the cob are roasted when they are in season (generally from July to September in the grasslands); occasionally, they will be boiled. Plantains are also roasted whole, but more often are cut up and fried. Known as *alloko* throughout Côte d'Ivoire, they are among the most popular of all street foods and served with a very spicy red sauce made from crushed red peppers and oil. Fried yams are also appreciated throughout West Africa, although they do not grow too far north of the rain forest. They are sliced in pieces to make something that both looks and tastes somewhat like very oversized French fries. Yams as well as cassava can also be boiled, though in this case, they must be served with a little sauce or other condiment or else they will be too bland.

Evening is the best time for grilled meats, especially lamb. Such meat is sometimes also available during the daytime, especially in the close vicinity of bus and taxi stops—generally one of the best places, aside from the marketplace, to find any kind of street food. Virtually the entire animal, including organ meats, is cut up into small pieces that can easily be skewered. Men tend to congregate around these grills after dinner; this tends to be a man's snack, both in its preparation and in its consumption.

West African countries tend to have their own bottling companies that manufacture European- and American-style beer and soft drinks. These are sold on the street as well as in shops, but on the street, they compete with locally made beverages. Home-brewed maize or sorghum beer is sold in open-air stalls, served straight from a large pot into calabashes split into two, which serve as drinking vessels. Of course, such beer stalls are not to be found in areas that are overwhelmingly Muslim. Islam forbids the consumption of alcohol; Muslims who flaunt the rule prefer to do so in private. On the other hand, anyone, whatever their religion or age, can consume sweet drinks, also readily available on the street. These include *lemburudji*, lemonade; *nyamakudji*, a ginger drink that resembles West Indian ginger beer without the carbonation; *bissap*, a sweet hibiscus flower drink; as well as drinks prepared from baobab or tamarind seeds.

In all, in the course of the second half of the 20th century, there has emerged a West African street-food culture that has built on traditional African elements while incorporating European and even Asian foodstuffs. Of course, there remain regional and national differences, but the large-scale movement of people as well as of foods has led, in the long run, to relative homogeneity.

MAJOR STREET FOODS

Pepper soup—*pépé soup* in French-speaking countries—is a clear broth made from meat, vegetables, and (as the name implies) lots of black pepper. A sauce made from peanut butter is particularly popular in the grasslands. These sauces are often beef stews; beef can easily be cut into small pieces, so that all customers can enjoy a portion. In towns along the seacoast, such sauces are also often made with fish. In the interior, fresh fish is too expensive, though dried fish from the Niger River is a popular ingredient; because its flavor is so overpowering, a little goes a long way, and it is a cheap source of protein.

Thiebou djeun (with fish) or *thiebou yapp* (with meat) is a rice dish that has spread from Senegal throughout West Africa, a potent example of how regional dishes have been widely diffused along with migrants along modern transportation networks. The names for it in Ghana and Nigeria—jollof rice—or in Côte d'Ivoire, where it is simply called *riz sénégalais*—Senegalese rice—openly acknowledge its foreign origins. It is a fried rice dish with a red coloring (from tomato paste), cooked with either fish or meat as well as with whatever vegetables are locally available. As a one-pot dish, it is particularly easily prepared and consumed in the market.

ROBERT LAUNAY

Note: The author wishes to thank Issouf Binaté, Noah Butler, Aly Drame, Marie Miran-Guyon, and Bill Murphy for their invaluable information and suggestions.

CHAPTER

2

EMPANADA

MANDOCA
HOT DOG
BAMMY
CIVICHE
SALARA
BAKE N' FISH

TACO

THE AMERICAS

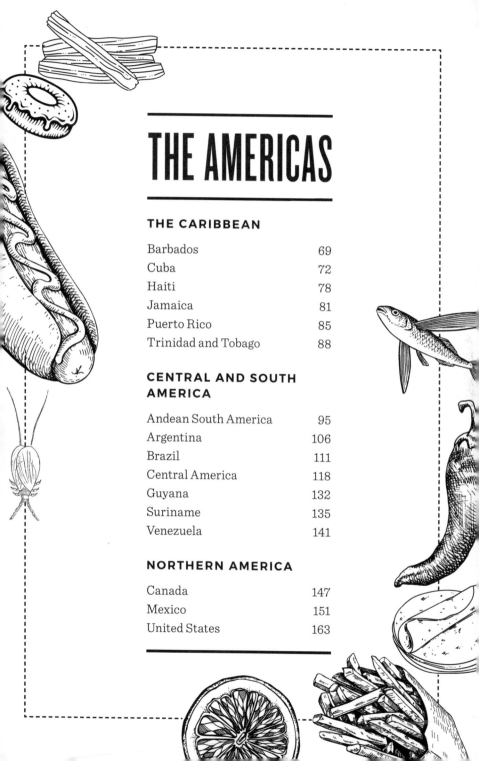

THE AMERICAS

THE CARIBBEAN

CENTRAL AND SOUTH AMERICA

NORTHERN AMERICA

THE CARIBBEAN

BARBADOS

BARBADOS is a small island nation in the Lesser Antilles with an area of less than 200 square miles and a population of around 300,000. Despite its small size, it has one of the Western Hemisphere's most interesting street-food scenes, combining influences from many different cultures, including Jamaica and Trinidad and Tobago.

Originally settled by the Caribs and the Arawaks, Barbados was claimed by the British in 1625. The introduction of sugarcane from Brazil in 1640 led to the building of large-scale plantations, the production of rum, and the introduction of slavery. Barbados won its independence from Britain in 1962. Today 80 percent of its population is of African origin while the rest are of Asian or European origin, including recent immigrants of Indian origin from Trinidad.

Street foods are sold from temporary stalls, vans, pushcarts, hawkers with trays, coal pots, and barbecues. A 300-year-old Bajan (the adjective for residents of the Barbados) institution is the rum shop. There are more than 1,500 rum shops on the island, including at least one in every village, and many of them sell not only rum (by the bottle) and beer but also local dishes prepared by the owners and eaten outside on tables and chairs. They are especially popular in the evenings and on weekends. (Trinidad and Jamaica also have rum shops, but they are mainly for drinking.)

As in other tropical countries, fresh fruit and fruit juices are sold at streetside stands and at markets. Local fruits include bananas, carambola (star fruit), citrus, guava, many varieties of mango, papaya, pineapples, sapodilla, and soursop and such seasonal fruits as ackee (See Jamaica), dunks (a small round yellow-orange tart fruit), fat pork (an astringent plum-like fruit), and tropical plums. Coconut water is available everywhere. Roasted corn is another streetside favorite.

MAJOR STREET FOODS

Flying Fish

Barbados's national dish is flying fish with *coucou*. Flying fish (marine fish belonging to the *Exocoetidae* family) is the national symbol of Barbados and appears on coins and official documents. The fish that is eaten is typically around eight to ten inches long. It is boned and filleted, soaked in lime juice, salted, washed, coated with a Bajan seasoning mix (salt, onion, chives, Scotch bonnet, thyme, marjoram), then dipped in flour, egg, and breadcrumbs and fried. Steak fish is the term for any larger fish that is cut into steak and fried or grilled. Fish fries are held on weekends in fishing villages, especially on Friday evenings. Hot sauce made with Scotch bonnets is a standard accompaniment.

FLYING FISH

To make *coucou*, a dish of African origin, the vendor boils chopped up okra, then gradually adds cornmeal and stirs it with a *coucou* stick until it thickens. It is poured into a bowl to set and then inverted onto a plate where it is served with stewed salt fish, flying fish, stewed pig or calf's liver (called *harslit*), or any kind of stew. *Coucou* can also be made from breadfruit and green bananas. All three varieties are sold from lunch vans, stalls, and at rum shops.

Bake n' Fish

A Trinidadian marine import is bake n' fish. Marlin is used instead of shark, and the bake is a popular Caribbean bread that is fried, not baked. Other Trinidadian imports are *buljol*, a mixture of boiled and shredded salt cod, tomatoes, onions, and hot pepper served with bakes or biscuits; *aloo* (potato) pie; rotis; and doubles.

Meat

The favorite street-food meat is barbecued chicken marinated in tomato, soy sauces, herbs, and spices. A uniquely Bajan specialty is barbecued pig tails that are pickled in brine, then boiled and barbecued with a spicy sauce.

Sandwiches

Cutter is the prototypical Bajan sandwich. A roll of oval-shaped crusty bread, called salt bread, is cut in half and filled with whatever the customers like: ham, cheese, corned beef, fried egg, fried flying fish, or breaded chicken. Two fish cakes sandwiched in salt bread is called a "bread and two." The fish cakes are made from boiled salted cod, flour, and onions beaten into a batter and deep-fried. They are one of the most widely available snacks at street-side stalls and rum shops.

Pudding and Souse

An extremely popular street food of British origin is pudding and souse. It is sold in rum shops throughout Barbados, but only on Saturdays. The souse is made from various parts of a pig that are boiled and pickled in lime juice, onion, cucumber, and parsley, while the pudding is a combination of grated sweet potato, green pepper, onions, thyme, and other ingredients that are baked. Traditionally, the pudding was stuffed into a pig's intestine.

COLLEEN TAYLOR SEN

CUBA

T HE REPUBLIC OF CUBA is an island nation in the Caribbean 90 miles off the coast of Florida. It is the largest island in the Caribbean both in size and in population (more than 11 million). In 1492, Christopher Columbus landed here and claimed the island for Spain. Cuba remained a Spanish possession until 1898, followed by four years as a territory of the United States. In 1959, Fidel Castro overthrew the previous regime, and in 1965, Cuba became a single-party Communist state.

The island was originally inhabited by the Taino (also known as Arawak), who were enslaved by the Spanish and virtually wiped out by hardship and disease. Starting in the late 18th century, slaves, mainly from West Africa, were brought in to work on the plantations and in the mines. After slavery was abolished in 1886, Chinese were brought as indentured laborers.

Before the revolution, Cuban cuisine was based on Spanish cooking, with elements of African, French, and Chinese cuisine. Haute-cuisine and peasant fare were often blurred. Ingredients included such indigenous American crops as tomatoes, corn, yuca, calabaza (a kind of squash), green chilies, sweet potatoes, and products from other parts of the Spanish empire, such as mango, sugarcane, rice, beans, coffee, coconut, plantain, and citrus fruits. Traditional food was seasoned but not spicy.

Havana streets have always been alive with street-food vendors. Early drawings and lithographs as early as the 17th century show *panaderos* (bakers) wandering through the crowds in Old Havana's most beautiful square, Plaza Vieja, carrying their wares on their heads in enormous turban-like baskets. Their street cries could be heard at all times of the day.

One of the most iconic was the peanut vendors (*maniseros*) who hawked their roasted salted peanuts in a paper cone through the streets of Old Havana. Female vendors who sold fritters in the streets were called *lucumisas* (Yoruba women) because of their supposed origin in West Africa. In the 19th and early 20th century, vendors were called *las bolleras*, since they served *bollos* (buns), tortillas, sausages, and *butifarras* (ham sandwiches) from their stands that had a little burner and a table. Everywhere there were walking vendors calling out their hot tortillas, which passersby would rush to buy.

For the first eight years of the Revolution, street food and ambulatory vendors remained part of the Havana streetscape, but in 1968, street vendors were put into the category of counterrevolutionary remnants of the private sector. They were referred to as "lazy persons in perfect physical condition who set up some kind of vending stand, any kind of small business, in order to make 50 pesos a day." The government took total control over food production, and street-food vendors in Cuba largely vanished for 30 years. An exception was state-run stands selling ice cream and snacks at amusement parks. The crackdown especially hurt Havana's Chinese community, who had entered the street-food vending market with delicious *bao* (steamed buns) stuffed with sweet pork.

The state monopoly on food distribution ended with the collapse of the Soviet Union in 1989–1990, which led to the collapse of Soviet economic aid and the massive food imports from Russia and Eastern Europe. In 1994, the government introduced measures to make the economy more flexible, including the creation of farmers' markets, and the conditional permitting of private restaurants, called *paladores*, often located in people's homes. (One paladar, La Guarida (The Den) in Central Havana, was the site of the shooting of some scenes from the award-winning movie *Fresa y Chocolate*.)

In April 2011, President Raul Castro announced a substantial "updating of the model" of the historic socialist economic arrangements permitted under the Cuban Revolution. In terms of street food, it allowed the formation of a category of worker that had not existed in Cuba since 1968: the self-employed worker (*cuentapropista*). Street-food vending is one of the more than 150 trades allowed under the new policy. Once the vendors buy a license and pay taxes on their profits, they can advertise and sell food on the streets. This is done either from stationary kiosks on house porches open to the street (cafeterias) or, less frequently, from ambulatory carts. They can employ workers (beyond immediate family members) and set their own prices. The proprietors come from all backgrounds, but many are professionals who have left their secure but unremunerative salaried positions.

Today, street-food vendors can be found throughout Havana, although most of them are on the main avenues near bus stops, schools, hospitals, around train and bus stations, and at concerts or sporting events. They sell their wares from stands, windows, wheelbarrows, and baskets. Once again, the peanut vendors in Plaza Vieja are announcing their wares with their full-throated cries, and thanks to its street food, Havana is coming back to life again!

The stationary cafeterias range from tiny mom-and-pop-run stands offering takeaway coffee and cookies in the owners' front yard to sophisticated operations with nonfamily employees and space for clients to sit down to a meal. They may be run out of purpose-built or renovated front yards or street-level porches of private homes. The one common characteristic of all cafeterias is that they advertise their wares via a menu-board, whether home-made and hand-lettered or professionally designed, and all food items are denominated, as a rule, in Cuban pesos.

The country operates with a dual-currency system: Cuban convertible pesos (called CUCs, commonly pronounced "kooks") are the default currency for tourists, and Cuban pesos are the default currency for Cubans, although there is nothing preventing either group from possessing both currencies. Though tourism is increasing rapidly, especially with the recent ending of US restrictions on trade and travel, the main consumers of food eaten standing are local residents.

MAJOR STREET FOODS

Sandwiches

Bread with (*pan con*) almost anything is the most popular food sold at kiosks: a fried egg in a soft bun (*pan con tortilla*) is emblematic of this category. Other options are *pan con bistek* (pork cutlet), *pan con chorizo* (pork sausage), and *pan con lechon* (suckling pig). In this last, a sprinkling of *chicharrónes* (pork cracklings) can be added. A very popular dish is Cuban pizza—a thick piece of dough with a thin layer of seasoned tomato sauce and cheese.

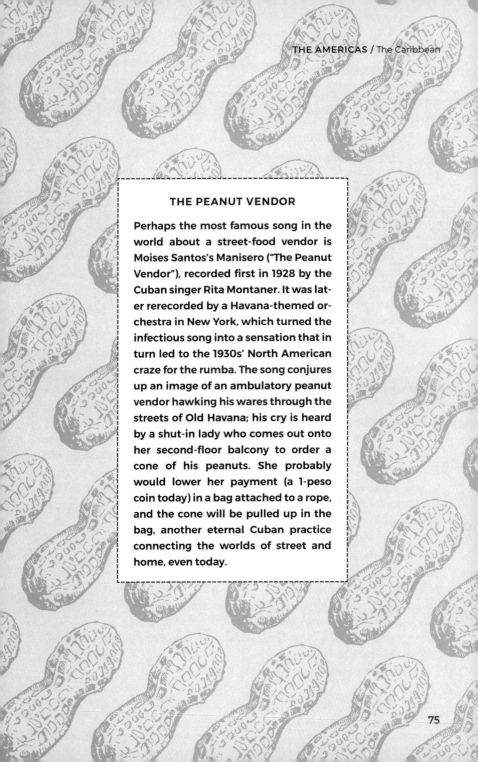

THE PEANUT VENDOR

Perhaps the most famous song in the world about a street-food vendor is Moises Santos's Manisero ("The Peanut Vendor"), recorded first in 1928 by the Cuban singer Rita Montaner. It was later rerecorded by a Havana-themed orchestra in New York, which turned the infectious song into a sensation that in turn led to the 1930s' North American craze for the rumba. The song conjures up an image of an ambulatory peanut vendor hawking his wares through the streets of Old Havana; his cry is heard by a shut-in lady who comes out onto her second-floor balcony to order a cone of his peanuts. She probably would lower her payment (a 1-peso coin today) in a bag attached to a rope, and the cone will be pulled up in the bag, another eternal Cuban practice connecting the worlds of street and home, even today.

Fried Foods
All manner of fried foods are sold on the street. The main ones are

- *papas rellenas*, balls of mashed potatoes filled with ground pork and deep-fried
- *croquetas*, small roll coated with bread crumbs and filled with ground pork.
- Cuban *tamal*, which unlike the Mexican *tamal* is a cylinder of pork-flecked rice seasoned with ground corn, garlic, onion, tomato, and cumin, wrapped in corn husks, then steamed
- churros, deep-fried dough cut into finger-size strips
- *chicharitas de planate*, thin slices of plantain fried in oil
- *frituras de malanga*, grated taro mixed with egg and crushed garlic
- *tostones*, fried pieces of plantain with a soft interior and crispy outside

CHURROS

Beverages
Any of these street delicacies may be accompanied by a cup of Cuban coffee, typically black espresso, which is sipped by most Cubans with industrial quantities of sugar. An alternative is a glass of natural fruit juice in season or a delicious *batido* (milk shake) made with mango, guava, pineapple, *mamey* (mamey fruit), or *guanabana* (sapote). Sometimes you find a stand, perhaps run by an *oriental* (a person from Eastern Cuba) offering *pru* (a specialty drink of Santiago de Cuba made with fermented plant, cinnamon, and sugar) or *guarapo*, fermented sugarcane juice.

Sweet Dishes
Sugar was for centuries the basis of the Cuban economy, and sweet dishes are very popular in Cuba:

- guava pastries, small tarts with guava or coconut filling
- *turron de mani*, a hard candy made with roasted peanuts mixed with honey and caramel
- *turon e ajonjoi*, sesame seed nougat

- *boniatillo*, mashed sweet potato cooked in syrup and sprinkled with powdered sugar
- *tartaletas*, little tarts filled with grated coconuts in syrup
- Cuban ice cream may be served in cones, cups, or between two cake slices. Another version is *duro frio*, ices and glaces made of fruit juices, sugar, and water.

Cajitas

Cajitas ("little boxes") are small boxes of the size of a thick wallet that contain the equivalent of a meal featuring a classic *comida criolla* ("Creole cuisine"), consisting of rice—plain white rice *(arroz blanco)* and black beans *(frijoles negros)* or *congri* (rice with bacon fat, oregano, and cumin, mixed with black beans)—a *vianda* (a root vegetable such as cassava, potato, sweet potato, plantain, or taro); a green salad (lettuce, cabbage, sliced cucumber, and/or tomato), and a portion of meat, usually a pork chop or fried or roast chicken, less often fish.

IAN MARTIN

HAITI

T HE REPUBLIC OF HAITI, which shares the island of Hispaniola with the Dominican Republic, has a unique history and culture. Christopher Columbus landed here in 1492 on his first voyage to the New World and claimed the island for Spain. After the Spanish wiped out the native Taino, they brought slaves from Africa to work on the gold mines and sugar plantations. In 1697, Spain ceded the western part of the island to the French, who called it Saint Dominique, and brought another million African slaves. In 1791, the slaves revolted; in 1804, having defeated the armies of Napoleon, they created the independent republic of Haiti (a variation of what the Taino called their homeland). In the late 19th and early 20th centuries, Syrians and Lebanese came as traders.

Today, Haiti has a population of nearly 10 million in an area of 10,000 square miles, making it one of the most densely populated and poorest countries in the world. In 2010, Haiti, and its capital Port-au-Prince, was devastated by a 7.0 magnitude earthquake that killed between 200,000 and 300,000 people and left a million homeless.

The Haitians have a distinctive cuisine, called *manje kreyol* in the local French Creole, which reflects French, African, Middle Eastern, and, more recently, American influences, with a dash of Spanish and Amerindian for good measure. The basic flavoring is *épis,* a spice mixture made from local chilies, which are moderately hot, garlic, green onions, thyme, and parsley. The most popular sauce is *ti-malice,* a spicy mixture made from tomatoes, onions, and local chilies. Tomato sauce, sometimes made from imported tomato paste, is used both as an ingredient and as an accompaniment.

Street food is popular, especially for breakfast and lunch in the cities. A common sight is Haitian women elegantly balancing bidons (pots) full of hot *mayi bouti* (boiled corn) or *akasan* (a drink made from corn flour) on their heads as they peddle their wares. Young boys carry baskets of popcorn or fried plantains and sell soft drinks, including a local, very sweet orange soda called Juna. Vendors with wheelbarrows or portable carts on wheels line the sidewalks and cluster together at street corners. They cook the food on small metal charcoal or propane stoves and display it in round woven trays, metal bins, or wooden trays or sometimes simply on clothes spread on the ground. The customers eat standing or sitting on plastic chairs. A common breakfast sandwich is fried egg with slices of tomato and hot sauce.

MAJOR STREET FOODS

Rice and Beans
As it is elsewhere in the Caribbean, the staple dish of Haiti is rice and beans (*diri kole ak pwa*)—brown rice with red kidney or pinto beans lightly flavored with onions and garlic. It is often accompanied by barbecued meat or fish and topped with tomatoes and onions or served with *bouyon,* a stew made of potatoes, tomatoes, and goat or beef.

Patties
Staples of parties in Haitian homes, these celebrated appetizers are also sold by some street vendors. Delicate layers of puff pastry are filled with beef, chicken, cod, spinach, cabbage, and other vegetables. Unlike Jamaican patties, the filling is not usually spiced with curry powder, and the crust is not colored yellow.

Griot
Cubes of pork are marinated in a dressing of sour orange, onions, and garlic and then deep-fried. The dish is often served during festivals.

Fried Plantains

Ripe plantains are cut into slices, fried in oil, and smashed a bit after cooking to soften them. They are served with a side dish of *pikliz,* a spicy pickle made from carrots and cabbage.

Corn

Mayi, Creole for "corn," is boiled or made into *akasan,* a sweet thick drink made from milk, corn flour, and spices that may be drunk hot or cold, especially at breakfast. Nearly every Latin American and Caribbean country has its own version, since corn originated in the region. Another nutritious dish is cornmeal mush (*mayi moulen*) cooked with kidney beans, coconut, and peppers.

COLLEEN TAYLOR SEN

JAMAICA

A POPULAR TOURIST DESTINATION, Jamaica is a small island nation with a population of three million. The indigenous people, the Taino, were wiped out, but their culinary legacy lives on in such ingredients as cassava, corn, sweet potatoes, callaloo (a green leafy vegetable), superhot Scotch bonnets (a key ingredient in Jamaican sauces), allspice (pimento), and papaya. Later African slaves working on the sugar plantations brought yams, pigeon peas, and pumpkin. After the abolition of slavery in 1833, the British brought in Indian and Chinese workers as indentured laborers, later joined by Lebanese traders. These ethnic groups contributed to Jamaica's rich culinary traditions that reflect the country's motto: "Out of many, one people."

Street vendors are everywhere on the island. Some sell fresh fruits, fruit juices, sugarcane juice, or coconut juice (as in the popular Jamaican-based song, "Coconuts have iron—they'll make you strong as a lion"); others cook dishes to order. Breakfast and lunch are the busiest times for vendors who sell complete meals called "box food." The most popular lunch boxes have fried, baked, or curried chicken with white rice or oxtail stew with peas. Some vendors have been organized into parks to serve tourists, including the Harbour View Roundabout near the airport in the capital, Kingston.

Jamaican street-food vendors are colorful characters, and some invent jingles about their products. An example, "Chips, chips, banana chips. Give the girls nice hips." Many are housewives who sell baked goods, chutneys, sauces, and other items in order to supplement their income.

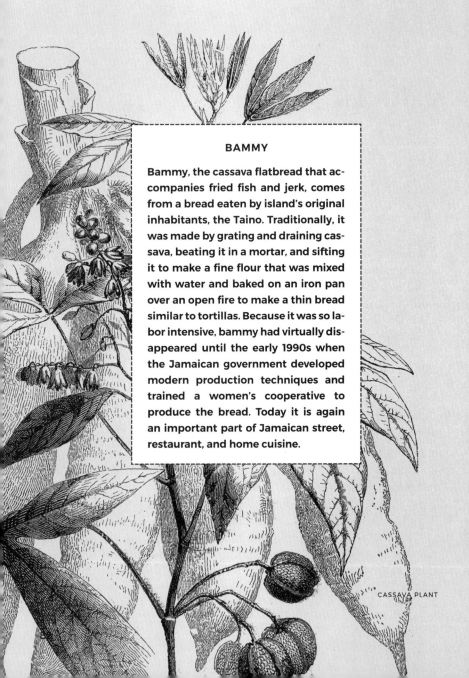

BAMMY

Bammy, the cassava flatbread that accompanies fried fish and jerk, comes from a bread eaten by island's original inhabitants, the Taino. Traditionally, it was made by grating and draining cassava, beating it in a mortar, and sifting it to make a fine flour that was mixed with water and baked on an iron pan over an open fire to make a thin bread similar to tortillas. Because it was so labor intensive, bammy had virtually disappeared until the early 1990s when the Jamaican government developed modern production techniques and trained a women's cooperative to produce the bread. Today it is again an important part of Jamaican street, restaurant, and home cuisine.

CASSAVA PLANT

MAJOR STREET FOODS

Jerk

The most famous Jamaican street food is jerk (derived from the Taino word *charqui*, or dried meat), which is the local version of barbecue (another word of indigenous origin). Meat (traditionally chicken or pork but today fish, beef, even tofu) is rubbed with a very hot spice mixture and grilled over charcoal in a steel drum. The seasoning contains allspice and Scotch bonnets and other spices that are the vendor's secret ingredients.

Jerk may be served with a flatbread called bammy made from cassava flour; Johnny cakes, fried wheat dumplings; or with festival, a fried hot dog-shaped piece of sweetened dough. A standard accompaniment is a piquant sauce made of garlic, ginger, pimento berries, Scotch bonnet, and cinnamon. Another popular dish is pan chicken: chicken marinated in onions, garlic, Scotch bonnet, and spices that is grilled slowly over an open flame, then chopped up, doused with hot pepper sauce, and served with hard dough bread.

Fried Fish/Fry Fish

"Fried fish" means large whole fish such as parrot and snapper that are eaten using utensils; "fry fish" are little fish eaten whole with one's fingers. The fish are wrapped in foil or paper and served with festival or bammy and the usual hot sauce.

Patty

A relative of the empanada, the Jamaican patty is a small semicircular savory pastry with a spicy meat, fish, seafood, or vegetable filling. The flaky crust is tinted golden yellow from turmeric or an egg yolk. The colored dot on the crust indicates the filling: no dot means ground beef, red dot chicken, and a green dot a vegetable filling. Jamaican immigrants have taken patties to the United Kingdom, Toronto, and New York.

Ackee and Saltfish

Known as Jamaica's national dish, this is a popular street breakfast food. The ackee fruit (*Blighia sapida*; sometimes called soapberry) was brought in the 18th century by Captain Bligh of the book and movies *Mutiny on the Bounty* fame. The dish is made by sautéing salt cod with boiled ackee, onions, Scotch bonnets, tomatoes, and spices. Side dishes include bammy, festival, fried plantain, boiled green bananas, or breadfruit (brought from Tahiti by the same Captain Bligh). Wedges of breadfruit are another popular street-food dish that are fried or roasted.

Soup

Cauldrons of boiling soup are a common sight on Jamaican streets. A popular hangover remedy is fish tea prepared by gutting small fish, boiling them with garlic and thyme, and crushing and straining them to make a boneless broth into which finely cut yams, carrots, and other vegetables are added. No two fish teas are alike, since each vendor has his own special recipe.

Cow cod soup is prepared from the genitalia of a bull simmered in a broth with vegetables, dumplings, vinegar, garlic, pepper, pimento, and thyme. This dish is popular with men because of its alleged aphrodisiac properties. A cousin is mannish water, a spicy soup made from goats' heads and penises, garlic, scallions, chayote, Scotch bonnets, and sometimes white rum.

Seafood

Land crabs are a popular street food. Live crabs are cleaned, then thrown into a pot of boiling water flavored with scallion, thyme, black pepper, butter, and lots of Scotch bonnets. The cooked crabs are placed in a basket so that customers can choose their own and take home in a plastic bag.

COLLEEN TAYLOR SEN

PUERTO RICO

P UERTO RICO is one of the Antilles Islands, lying to the east of the Dominican Republic and Cuba. The main island of Puerto Rico proper has a number
of smaller and mostly uninhabited islands located in the Caribbean Sea off its
shores. With a warm bi-seasonal climate (dry and wet), Puerto Rico was once a
sugar-growing area that is now home to a number of small manufacturing and
service companies. It also has a large tourism industry catering to North Americans who are attracted to the island's flat beaches. In actuality, Puerto Rico's geography is mostly a low mountain chain covering the middle, with flat coasts and
only about 4 percent arable land.

Puerto Rico's earliest peoples were Tainos, who came from nearby Central
and South America. Living in villages, they farmed yuca (also known as manioc
or cassava—a starchy root that needs a great deal of processing to get poisons
leached out of it), beans, some chilies and corn, pineapples, and other fruits, and
they ate a good deal of fish. The Spanish conquest added rice, plantains, and coconuts (from southeast Asia via Africa), a kind of taro called *yautía*, wheat, onions
and garlic, sugarcane, many herbs such as cilantro, and domesticated animals—
cattle, pigs, chickens, goats, and sheep. West Africans were brought to the island
in the Colonial period and influenced Puerto Rican food. The main cooking
technique introduced from Europe and Africa was frying, now the most common
method of cooking street foods. Together, all these ingredients form the basics of
Puerto Rican cuisine. Rice and beans are at the basis of many meals, and Puerto
Rican dishes are heavy on pork and chicken. One important element is sofrito, a

mixture of finely diced vegetables such as onion, garlic, tomatoes, and peppers, cooked with spices and herbs. It is used in many dishes to add delicious flavors to otherwise bland foods.

Since 1898, Puerto Rico has been officially a commonwealth, a territory of the United States, when it was ceded by Spain after the Spanish American War. Naturally, North American influence has been strong. American fast-food chains selling hamburgers, fried chicken, and pizza are everywhere as are soft drink companies and candies. Yet Puerto Ricans savor their own cuisines, and street foods are often traditional dishes.

MAJOR STREET FOODS

Street-food stands abound in cities, near airports such as in the capital, San Juan, and at beach resorts. The most characteristic street food—and one made at home as well—is *mofongo*. Originating in Africa, the dish is made from green plantains or yuca that is fried and pounded into a paste with oil or fat, garlic, and pork cracklings or bacon. It can serve as a kind of dumpling in soups or stand on its own. When stuffed with shredded meat or vegetables, the dish is called *mofongo relleno* and then it resembles the other great Puerto Rican street food, *alcapurria*, a kind of empanada. *Yautía* is cooked and mashed, sometimes with plantains, formed into cakes, and stuffed with many kinds of fillings that range from meats or fish—often crabs on the resort beaches—to vegetables. The small cakes are then deep-fried. In an area where there are many vendors, such as the famous beach area of Luquillo in the north, each of the 60 or so stands has its own special type of *alcapurria*.

There is a wide range of savory fried street foods in addition to *mofongo* and *alcapurria*. They include *pastelillos* or arepas, fried stuffed pastries made from wheat flour; *bacalaitos*, fried dough made with salt cod; fried stuffed potato balls; *piononos*, mashed ripe plantains stuffed and fried; and *taquitos*, small tacos rolled up tightly and fried. Perhaps the most widely known Puerto Rican fried food is the *tostone*, thinly sliced plantain chips that are fried twice to a crunchy crispness. *Tostones* are now eaten universally in the Caribbean and in Central America.

Grilled foods and sandwiches are also featured in food stands. *Pinchos* are like kebabs in other parts of the world. Cubed meats—mainly beef, chicken, or pork—are skewered, seasoned, and cooked over open grills. The diner can dip the cooked meats into a spicy sauce before eating. Sandwiches of all kinds are popular, one of which is the *tripleta*. This is usually a roll filled with three grilled meats and slathered with mayonnaise, mustard, and ketchup. Other simpler sandwiches such as ham or fish are also popular.

Small open-air restaurants called *fondas* serve larger lunchtime meals for working people in towns and cities. Rice and beans, sometimes with cooked meats and seasoned with sofrito and a condiment called *sazón*, are common. Soups, some made with tripe, or pig's feet, and many accompanied by *mofongo* are also found. On the coasts, a great many seafood dishes are served, from octopus to shellfish and such local fin fish as *chillo*, or red snapper.

Street food in warm Caribbean climates always includes many fruits and frozen treats. Large bananas (*cavendish*) and small red ones, guavas, mangos, passion fruit, pineapples, and melons are refreshing treats on warm, sunny days. Ice cream and frozen ices are widely enjoyed. Flavors run from the standard vanilla and chocolate to fruit flavors including berries and passion fruit. The most famous ice-cream place is in Lares, a town in central Puerto Rico, where the Heladería de Lares serves some 1,000 flavors that include corn, beer, rice and beans, and codfish among other unusual ingredients. Common drinks are the usual international soft drinks, but Puerto Rico has its own soft drink with guava, orange pineapple, and passion fruit among favorite flavors.

BRUCE KRAIG

TRINIDAD AND TOBAGO

T HE STREET FOOD OF THE REPUBLIC OF TRINIDAD AND TOBAGO is one of the liveliest in the Caribbean and mirrors the ethnic diversity of the two islands. More than 40 percent of the one million Trinidadians and Tobagonians are of South Asian origin; another 40 percent are Afro-Trinidadian, while the remaining 20 percent are of Chinese, European, and Middle Eastern descent. Trinidadian cuisine combines elements of all these culinary traditions, although the food of the Indian subcontinent is the dominant influence, especially in the street-food sector. Trinidad has been called a "callaloo culture," a reference to the popular stew that combines South Asian and African ingredients, including a local green, leafy vegetable by that name (also known as dasheen).

Originally inhabited by the Caribs and Arawaks and discovered by Christopher Columbus on his third voyage in 1498, Trinidad and Tobago was at various times controlled by the Spanish, the Dutch, the French, and finally the British. It gained its independence in 1962 and became a republic in 1976. When the abolition of slavery in the British Empire in 1833 created labor shortages in the Empire's sugar and coffee industries and plantations, the British government recruited Indians and some Chinese as indentured laborers for a fixed period. Between 1834 and 1917, nearly 1.5 million Indians emigrated to other parts of the British Empire, including 240,000 to British Guiana (now Guyana), 144,000 to Trinidad, and 36,000 to Jamaica. The majority came from Northeastern India with a smaller group from South India. Most elected to stay after their tenure was over and purchased land or set up small businesses. Some entrepreneurs set up small roadside stands selling versions of popular Indian street food.

Although Trinidad and Tobago is one of the richest countries in the Caribbean because of its oil and gas reserves, unemployment is high, leading many Trinidadians to enter the street-food sector. Most vendors are men. Street-food stalls and trucks are ubiquitous in residential neighborhoods and are especially popular next to schools, universities, and offices. Everyone eats street food, from laborers and students to company executives. The leading street-food areas include the town of St. James, just west of the capital Port of Spain, especially its Western Main Road that is open around the clock; the Savanna, a large park in the center of Port of Spain; Maracas Beach, an hour's drive south of the capital, famous for its shark n' bake; and Store Bay on the southeast coast of Tobago, known for its curry crab.

Street foods are popular for breakfast and lunch as well as in the late evening among people who spent a night on the town. They are also an essential part of Carnival, the local version of Mardi Gras. More recently, Trinidadian immigrants have taken their street food to North American cities, especially Toronto and New York.

Bread is a staple of Trinidadian street food and is similar to Indian breads, with some important differences. Whereas most Indian breads, such as roti, are unleavened, in Trinidad and Tobago, bread is always leavened with baking powder and sometimes a little yeast and left a few hours to swell. Moreover, unlike most Indian breads that are made mainly from whole wheat flour, almost all Trinidadian breads are made from white flour. One explanation is that wheat was not grown in the immigrants' home regions, and the flour they first encountered would be the white flour used in Calcutta, the embarkation port for many. Popular varieties sold as street food are *sada roti* (plain bread), *paratha roti*, also called buss-up-shut, doubles, and *dhalpuri*. Roti is also the name for what may be the most famous Trinidadian street food, a thick bread filled with meat, vegetable, or fish curry.

Curries are another Indian transplant. Trinidadian curries are often made with ready-made curry powders. Their chief ingredients—cumin, coriander, fenugreek, and turmeric—are very similar to those that would be used in a rural household in Northeastern India. For coriander leaves, people substitute a local herb called shado(w) beni (from the French Creole *cha(r)don béni*, called Vietnamese coriander in the United States) that grows wild. The chile pepper used in Trinidadian curries is the very fiery Scotch bonnet (locally known as *congo pepper*).

Another popular category of street foods is crunchy sweet and savory snacks that came from India. Many are made from ground spit peas or lentils, flour, curry powder, and other spices. The best known are *phulorie*, a small ball that is deep-fried and served right out of the pot; *saheena*, the same mixture rolled in a dasheen leaf, steamed, and then sliced and deep-fried; and *kachouri*, the same filling without the leaves. They are eaten freshly made and hot with some mango or tamarind chutney on the side. A popular sweet is *kurma*, strips of deep-fried dough soaked in sugar syrup and sold in little plastic bags by street vendors and in roadside shops.

The most common meats used in curries are goat and chicken, since Hindus traditionally avoid beef while Muslims as well as many Hindus shun pork. Today younger people are less likely to observe these restrictions.

Street-food vendors offer their patrons a range of accompaniments, including mango, cucumber, or tamarind chutneys that can be sweet or sour; *chokha* (tomato, eggplant, or even potato roasted over a fire, or under a grill, then mashed, seasoned with oil, chopped raw onion, and hot pepper); *mango kuchela*, a mango and mustard oil pickle made with ground spices roasted black; and "mother-in-law," a hot vegetable relish. They also serve a variety of hot sauces made with red chilies that fall into three categories: slight, medium, and hot—which means mouth searing!

Vendors called "juice men" sell fresh fruit, such as mangoes, sour cherries, and tiny sweet or sweet-and-sour bananas; freshly squeezed fruit and coconut juice (coconut water) drunk straight from the shell; shelled and lightly roasted peanuts and cashew nuts (popular at cricket matches).

The small island of Tobago north of Trinidad is known for its crab curry and raw oysters that are served with a spicy tomato/vinegar sauce.

MAJOR STREET FOODS

Bake

A popular and uniquely Trinidadian street food, especially for breakfast, is bake (a word used for both the singular and plural), although the dish is not necessarily baked. The word *bake* refers both to the bread itself and to a sandwich containing meat or, more commonly, fish that is cooked over an open flame, on a griddle or on a cooking stone on the stove top. It is served on or between slices of different varieties of bread: a flat heavy baked white bread (called a Johnny bake), fried bake (also called float) that is deep-fried to golden brown, and coconut bake, made with grated coconut. Bake may be served with *buljol* (from the French *brûle-gueule*), shredded salt fish seasoned with tomatoes, onions, and sweet peppers; smoked herring; *chokha* (tomato, eggplant, or even potato roasted over a fire, or under a grill, then mashed, seasoned with oil, chopped raw onion, and hot pepper); or even standard breakfast items such as sausages and eggs.

The most famous bake is shark n' bake (sometimes called bake and shark), believed to have been invented at Maracas Bay, a popular beach around an hour's drive from Port of Spain. The beach is lined with a dozen shacks serving shark n' bake, which consists of deep-fried, battered, and seasoned young shark meat stuffed into a fried unleavened bread. It's eaten with plenty of hot sauce and often washed down with cold beer.

Doubles

A street food that ties with rotis for the honor of being Trinidad's national dish is doubles, sometimes called "channa hamburger." This is a sandwich made by filling two pieces of fried bread, or bara, with curried chickpeas and topped with chutneys made from tamarind or cucumber and with chile sauce of varying degrees of hotness. Its invention is often attributed to Mohammed Deen, who in the mid-1930s started selling fried chickpeas in a paper cone and later in a piece of bread. His customers would ask him to "double up" on the bread, which led to the name. Doubles are eaten for breakfast and lunch and sometimes as a late-night snack. The doubles man selling doubles from his bike is a popular figure in many neighborhoods. Famous street-side vendors include Deen's Doubles in San Juan, Ali's Doubles in San Fernando, Sauce Doubles in Curepe, and Johnny's Doubles in La Romaine and Golconda.

Roti

Roti is the ultimate street and take-out food, sold by vendors and small shops, especially in the St. James district of Port of Spain. In Trinidad, the word *roti* (from the Hindi word for bread) denotes both bread in general and a specific dish that shares with doubles the reputation as the country's national dish. It consists of a large, thick, round, and slightly fried bread coated with ground yellow peas and wrapped around a goat, chicken, seafood, or vegetable curry. It is enclosed in wax paper or foil and eaten on the run. Popular condiments include mango, cucumber, or tamarind chutneys; *chokha*, mango kuchela, a mango and mustard oil pickle; and "mother-in-law," a hot vegetable relish.

Varieties of roti include *paratha roti*, also called buss-up-shut, supposedly because it looks like a "busted-up shirt." The starting point is a plain roti made from white wheat flour, salt, water, a little leavening, and sometimes butter or oil that is rolled into a flat circle and cooked in oil until it has a crispy exterior. When it is almost finished cooking, the cook wraps it in a kitchen towel and beats it with a wooden paddle or his hands until it opens and crumbles into pieces. It's eaten with curry and various side dishes and is a popular lunch meal.

Another variety is *dhalpuri* or *dhalpuri roti* made by filling a round of white flour dough with mashed boiled yellow split peas flavored with roasted cumin powder, garlic, and pepper. After cooking on a lightly greased flat pan, it is folded into four and served with curry and mango chutney. It is the subject of a film by Richard Fung called *Dhal Puri Roti,* which traces its journey from Bihar, India, to Trinidad. Novelist Peggy Mohan gives the following description of the *dhalpuri* experience in her book *Jahajin*:

> We parked the bike and walked through the market. We got two Carib beers and strode around drinking straight from the bottles. Then Fyzie headed for a dhalpuri stall and before I knew what he was doing, he bought two dhalpuris and handed me one. I bit into the paper thin roti, bursting with split pea stuffing, and lapped up the spicy, juicy curry shrimps wrapped inside it, and shrugged off obsessive thoughts of eating light that belonged in another world of idleness.

OTHER STREET FOODS

Aloo (Potato) Pie

This is a soft fried piece of dough made from flour and water, filled with boiled, spiced mashed potatoes and other vegetables such as green peas or channa dal. It is sometimes compared with an Indian samosa but is much larger and more closely resembles a calzone. It is served with a tamarind chutney. *Aloo* pies are often sold by doubles vendors and are popular among students.

Corn Soup

This popular Trinidadian street food reflects Indian, Chinese, and African influences. Medallions of corn several inches thick are simmered in a giant pot with dumplings and assorted vegetables, especially roots or tubers to thicken the mixture and seasoned with garlic, shadow benny, and onions. It is served in Styrofoam cups and is a favorite of people after a night on the town. Boiled corn (called boil corn) and roast corn are other popular street-food snacks.

Curry Crab

This is the quintessential street food of the small island of Tobago and is especially associated with Store Bay on the little island's southeast coast. Locally caught crabs are cooked with cumin seeds, shadow beni, and curry powder and served with a large boiled flour oblong-shaped dumpling, which may be of African origin. The dish is sold in legendary stalls with names like Miss Jean and Miss Esme. Patrons eat them in benches or a covered pavilion.

Oysters

Oysters are a popular street food in Trinidad and Tobago, especially among men who believe them to have aphrodisiac properties. In Trinidad, the species *Crassostrea rhizophorae* are harvested from the Claxton Bay Mangrove System as well as from the west coast. They are typically served raw in a small glass or Styrofoam cup in a mixture of lime juice and a spicy tomato sauce, a dish called oyster cocktail. Oyster vendors have distinctive setups: a table, often blue in color, with a few scattered shells, glass bottles for sauces of different degrees of hotness, and a torch made from a bottle, twisted paper, and fuel.

Pholourie

This is a small golden ball made of ground split peas, curry, and turmeric (which Trinidadians sometimes call "saffron") that is deep-fried and best eaten freshly made. It is served with condiments, including mango or tamarind chutney. *Pholouries* are sold everywhere and at any time: on the street, at football matches, and at festivals. They are usually served in little paper bags with an accompanying spicy sauce in a plastic bag.

COLLEEN TAYLOR SEN

CENTRAL AND
SOUTH AMERICA

ANDEAN SOUTH AMERICA

(Colombia, Ecuador, Peru, Chile)

THE COUNTRIES ON THE WEST COAST OF SOUTH AMERICA—Colombia, Ecuador, Peru, and Chile—are situated between the Pacific Ocean and the Andes Mountains, the longest mountain range in the world (4,300 miles) and the highest mountain range outside of Asia. This region was home to many indigenous civilizations, the last of which, the Incas, arose in the early 13th century in the highlands of Peru and conquered much of western South America between 1438 and 1533. In the latter year, the Inca Empire was conquered by the Spanish, who extended their rule over much of South America, with their capital in Lima.

The region has a wide variety of climates and soils and an extremely rich biodiversity. The Incas used an already ancient sophisticated system of agriculture based on terracing, storage, and distribution of foods. Their dietary staples were maize and quinoa, supplemented by potatoes, yuca, sweet potato, and the ají pepper. Protein came from guinea pigs, llama, and fish and seafood. The Spanish introduced crops from other parts of their vast empire in Asia and Europe, including bananas, cattle, pigs, chickens, wheat, and rice. Slaves from Africa and immigrants from Asia, Europe, and other parts of South America later added their own ingredients and dishes to this fabulous culinary stew.

The region has an especially lively street-food life thanks to deep-rooted traditions of making, selling, and serving food outside the home. Some dishes are common to the entire region, including empanadas, ceviche, and tamales (called *humitas*), but others are regional or local specialties.

COLOMBIA

Located in the northwestern corner of South America, Colombia is bordered by five countries, the Pacific Ocean, and the Caribbean Sea. It is a county of considerable topographic and climatic diversity, all of which affect local foods. Mountains run along the west side of the country down into Ecuador and Peru, and rivers cut through much of Colombia. The west coast is flatter with a very warm climate. Fishing and commerce through the main port of Cartagena are located here. As the land rises toward the mountains, the temperature moderates, allowing Colombia's famous coffee to be produced on small farms and large plantations. Across the mountain range with its cool temperatures lie the vast Amazonian jungles that Colombia has in common with Brazil and the *llanos* (plains) that it shares along its long border with Venezuela. Colombia produces bananas—it is the world's third largest exporter—corn, yuca, rice, wheat, potatoes, and cattle. All are staples of the Colombian diet.

Colombia has a variety of ethnicities in its population. The majority are of mixed European and indigenous descent, but as a partly Caribbean country, there is a minority of people of African or mixed African heritage. Colombia's street food reflects all these influences: Spanish, indigenous, and African. Colombia is also regional so that street food in the coastal city of Cartagena might differ from the capital located in the highlands, Bogota. Nonetheless, there are universal dishes.

Major Street Foods

AREPAS
Like neighboring Venezuela, thick-fried corn cakes that are split and filled are the standard street fare. In Cartagena, they tend to be flaky made with butter and often filled with melted cheese. In Bogota, they are drier and filled with cooked meats of various kinds with sauces.

EMPANADAS

Filled savory pastries, empanadas are standard street food across Latin America. Colombian versions often use corn flour instead of the usual wheat flour. They come with many fillings, often meat and potatoes or cheese, and can be toasted on a griddle or fried.

PERROS CALIENTES (HOT DOGS)

The American hot dog is very popular in the countries of northern South America. In Colombia they are usually grilled or steamed, put on large buns and then loaded with mustard, ketchup-like sauces, tomatoes, beans, cheese, chopped cabbage or lettuce, pickles, bacon, and other toppings. They are literally meals on buns.

FRUIT

Fruit vendors are everywhere in cities, towns, and along roadsides. Various kinds of bananas, of course, are common as are pineapples, melons, papaya, *carambola* (star fruit), mango, guava, and others and are peeled or cut into fancy shapes and sold from carts. The Caribbean region is particularly rich in tropical fruits eaten as street food. Young coconut is also popular. As a drink, one end is cut open, a straw placed in it, and the milk consumed. It can also be cut into chunks and eaten out of hand.

JUICES

Fruit juice stands are ubiquitous. Various types of fruit are squeezed with hand-operated presses directly into individual glasses. Juices can also be blended, sometimes with milk, into frothy drinks. One special Colombian drink is *avena*. Cooked oats are mixed with milk, sugar, and cinnamon and heated. It is served warm and often with rice. *Limonada* is made from local limes that are mixed with lots of sugar to make a super sweet, but refreshing, drink.

Other Street Foods

In the Caribbean region, street stands sell ceviche, fish that is cut up, placed in a container with chopped onions, garlic, and herbs, and then covered in lemon juice. Within a few hours, the juice cooks the fish, and it is ready for eating. It is usually served with a pink sauce made of ketchup and mayonnaise.

CANDIES

Columbians love sweets. Candy stalls and vendors selling it from baskets are common sights in cities, towns, and at public events. *Dulce de leche* or *coco de leche*—milk caramels, plain or with coconut—are especially liked. Filled hard candies and many others made from plain sugar or with fruits such as tamarind are also very popular.

BRUCE KRAIG

ECUADOR

A country in western South America that straddles the equator (hence its name), the Republic of Ecuador is bordered by Colombia to the north, Peru to the south, and the Pacific Ocean on the west. The region was home to many ancient cultures, the last of which was conquered by the Incas in 1463. They were subsequently defeated and ruled by the Spanish from whom Ecuador won its independence in 1809. A quarter of Ecuador's population are indigenous Amerindians belonging to a number of groups; two-thirds are of mixed Spanish and Native American heritage.

Indigenous starchy staples include potatoes, which were domesticated in the Andes, corn, quinoa, and cassava, as well as bananas and plantains, which originated in Asia and are now a major Ecuadorian export. As in Peru, guinea pig is a popular meat. The country, especially its capital Quito and its central market, has a lively street-food scene that features such dishes as empanadas and shawarma found in other countries as well as some uniquely Ecuadorian dishes.

Major Street Foods

POTATOES

Llapingachos, which originated in the city of Ambata in the central Andes but are now popular nationwide, are balls of mashed boiled potatoes filled with cheese, then flattened and cooked on a griddle. They are served with a peanut sauce and sausage, slices of roasted suckling pig, or a fried egg on the side. *Papas con cuero*, often sold at football games, are small potatoes served in a stew with bits of pork skin and fat.

PLANTAINS

Slices of starchy plantain are fried and eaten as a popular snack, called *chifles*. *Bolon de verde* are dumplings made by frying green plantains, mashing them into dough, filling them with cheese or pork, and then frying them again until crispy.

CEVICHE

In Ecuador, unlike in Peru, the seafood in ceviche is cooked briefly before marination, a policy adopted after a cholera outbreak in the early 1990s. Shrimp ceviche served with a tomato sauce is especially popular. *Ceviche de chochos* is a vegetarian version made with broad beans, onions, tomatoes, cilantro, limes, oranges, and tomato sauce and served with a corn tostado, *chifles*, avocados, and hot sauce.

CORN

Many Ecuadorian street vendors sell grilled corn served with a cheese and cilantro sauce. The Andean version of Mexican tamales, *humitas*, are packages of ground fresh corn mixed with milk and fat, wrapped in corn husks, and steamed. Served with a mild chile sauce, they are popular breakfast dishes. In Chile, basil leaves are added to the corn filling. To make *tortillas de maiz con queso*, a small ball made from corn flour and water is stuffed with a pinch of grated fresh cheese, then flattened into a patty and fried until crisp.

CORN

TORTILLAS

MOTE CON CHICHARRÓN (HOMINY WITH PORK SKIN)

A specialty of Quito, the capital, is *mote con chicharrón*. It is usually sold by women walking around with a cook-pot containing *mote*, or hominy (corn kernels soaked in an alkali solution) and *chicharrón*, or fried pork rind. It is sold in little plastic bags, with the *mote* on the bottom and the *chicharrón* on the top.

COLLEEN TAYLOR SEN

PERU

The third largest country in South America, the Republic of Peru, extends from the Pacific Ocean to the Brazilian jungle, with borders on Ecuador and Colombia on the north, Bolivia on the southeast, and Chile to the south. Although situated near the equator, Peru has enormous climatic and geographical diversity. Potatoes play an important role in the diet: more than 3,000 varieties are produced. A key ingredient in the local *salsa criolla* is the ají pepper—a mild red pepper with a smoky fruity taste. A popular meat is the guinea pig (cuy)—more than 65 million are consumed in Peru each year—fried or roasted with rice and corn on the side.

Peru was home to many ancient cultures, the most recent being the Inca Empire, which existed for 100 years before being conquered by the Spanish in 1532. Starting in the 16th century, African slaves were brought to work in construction and domestic service. The 19th century saw the arrival of Chinese, Japanese, and European immigrants. Today about two-thirds of Peru's 30 million people are Amerindian or Mestizo (mixed European and Indian). This melting pot of cultures and traditions has created one of the most vibrant culinary cultures in South America.

Street vendors, many of them women, have been plying their trade in the plazas of Peru's capital Lima since the 16th century. Many famous Peruvian dishes, such as *anticuchos* and *chicha morada*, were first sold on the streets, and today some are incorporated into what is known as *Nova Andino*, or New Andean, cuisine. Vendors park their carts at markets, bus stops, or places where manual workers congregate and serve either single dishes or sometimes entire meals. Cities are dotted with bakeries and mobile carts selling pastries.

GUINEA PIGS AS DELICACY

Guinea pigs play such an important role in Andean culture and cuisine that an 18th-century painting even shows Jesus and his disciples at the Last Supper about to eat a platter of guinea pig instead of the traditional lamb. The painting by Marcos Zapata hangs in the cathedral in Cuzco, Peru. Guinea pig was a sacrificial animal in Inca agricultural festivals, and incorporating it into Christian symbolism was part of the Spanish strategy of conversion.

Major Street Foods

ANTICUCHOS

Sold at food stalls called *anticucheras*, this Peruvian version of kebabs has become popular throughout South America. Small pieces of meat marinated in vinegar and spices (including garlic, cumin, and ají pepper) are roasted on skewers, often with a boiled potato or piece of bread. Dating back to Inca times, *anticuchos* were originally made with llama meat and, later, starting with the Spanish, beef, especially the heart. Today they are made from various cuts of beef and sometimes chicken. A standard accompaniment is a sauce made from garlic, onion, vinegar, lemon juice, and beer.

CEVICHE

Ceviche—fresh raw fish or seafood marinated in citrus juice—is probably the most emblematic Peruvian dish; it even has its own national holiday! There are an estimated 11,000 cevicherias—from market stalls to gourmet restaurants—in Lima alone. Ceviche stalls and shacks are especially common near fish markets or along beaches.

The citric acid in the lime or lemon denatures the protein in the fish, which has the same effect as cooking. Some historians say that ceviche dish originated in Peru 200 years ago when local coastal people marinated fish in fermented passion fruit juice.

In a standard Lima version, fish, often sole, flounder, or sea bass, is marinated in fresh lime or bitter orange, onions, ají peppers, salt, and pepper and served with roasted corn, a seaweed called *yuyo*, and cooked sweet potato. Often a small glass of the piquante marinade, called *leche de tigre*, or tiger milk, is served as an aperitif. Other ingredients include black clams, mixed fish and seafood, octopus, crayfish, black conch, even duck, and mushrooms. In a modern Japanese-Peruvian version called *tardito*, the fish is sliced into paper-thin slices.

The Spanish took ceviche to other parts of their empire, including Mexico, Central America, Ecuador, Chile, and Spain, all of which have their own variations.

BUTIFARRA

This popular sandwich is made from slices of *jamón del país* in a roll of French bread topped with *salsa criolla*, mayonnaise, and lettuce. *Jamón del país* is a local ham or pork loin seasoned with ají pepper, garlic, vinegar, and spices and served with the omnipresent *salsa criolla*, a spicy blend of thinly sliced onions, ají peppers, lime juice, and cilantro leaves.

EMPANADAS

Introduced by the Spanish, empanadas became a popular breakfast dish in Peru. The most popular filling is ground beef, but chicken and cheese are also used. Often hard-boiled egg, onions, olives, and raisins are added to the filling. The dough is usually sprinkled with icing sugar, and the empanadas are always topped off with a dash of fresh lime juice.

CEREALS

A popular breakfast dish is made from quinoa, a highly nutritious indigenous grain boiled with apples and mixed with hot milk. Another cereal is made from maca, a plant that grows in the Andes, which is mashed and boiled to produce a sweet, thick liquid mixed with milk. They are usually sold by the same vendor and sometimes served with bread or cake.

POTATOES

Potatoes, native to Peru, are a staple of the Peruvian diet. *Papa rellena* is a dish of ground meat, egg, and vegetables coated with mashed potatoes and fried. Another popular dish, especially along the coast, is *causa*—mashed potatoes flavored with lime juice, onion, and chilies and layered with such ingredients as avocado, chicken, canned tuna, or shellfish. It is served cold with hard-boiled eggs and olives. French-fried potatoes are a standard accompaniment to many items, such as *salchipapa*—sliced sausage that is mixed together with the fries and served with ketchup or mayonnaise.

DRINKS

Chicha morada is a sweet beverage made by boiling local purple corn with pineapple, cinnamon, clove, and sugar. Sold in the evenings, *emoliente* is a traditional herbal drink made from roasted barley, various medicinal herbs, sugar, and lime. The actual ingredients vary by region and family. The drink is usually served hot. One of the most popular drinks is Inca Kola, a yellow-colored sweet soda flavored with lemon verbena.

COLLEEN TAYLOR SEN

CHILE

The Republic of Chile occupies a narrow 2,600-mile strip along the west coast of South America between the Pacific Ocean and the Andes. It is a country of enormous geographic extremes, including the Atacama desert, the fertile Central Valley where Chilean wines are produced, and the glaciers of Patagonia. About 85 percent of Chile's 16 million people live in the Central Valley, and almost a third of them reside in the capital Santiago. The country's oldest cooking traditions come from the Incas, who ruled north and central Chile, and the Mapuche, who lived in south central Chile. The Spanish ruled the country until 1818 when Chile won its independence. The 19th century saw the arrival of immigrants from Spain, France, Italy, Great Britain, and other European countries and, more recently, from neighboring countries in South America. All these groups contributed their eating habits and some foods to Chilean cuisine.

Not surprisingly, in view of its long coastline, seafood plays a central role in Chilean cuisine, which has its own versions of ceviche made with sea bass (Patagonian toothfish), lime, grapefruit juice, and cilantro. Beef is imported from Argentina, but pigs and sheep are raised here. Chilean cuisine is generally quite mild: although ají pepper is a common ingredient, it is used in small amounts. A popular sauce in restaurants and on street stalls is *salsa pebre* made from chopped garlic, chilies, onions, cilantro, salt, oregano, vinegar or lemon juice, and tomatoes.

CEVICHE INGREDIENTS

Street food is regularly found in open fairs, stadiums, and streets throughout Chile. Street carts provide an essential part of the diet for many Chileans, especially university students. Carts are either parked in fixed locations or moved throughout the city in search of customers.

Major Street Foods

SÁNGUCHE DE POTITO

When Chile's first railroad was built from Santiago to Valparaiso in 1851, the early travelers had to eat whatever the white-gowned salespeople with their wickerwork baskets offered at the train stations. The food had to be fast and practical to prepare, easy to eat, and delicious. The result was the "traveling sandwich," prepared with a round, flat, unleavened loaf cooked directly over the fire or embers (*tortilla de rescoldo*), cheese, and ham. Different versions were created, and in the mid-1930s, the *sánguche de potito* was born. Potito means "backside," and the name came because of the meat, fried beef or pork intestines or the terminal end of the animal's rectum. The sandwich was served with a sausage and onion and *salsa pebre*. Today these sandwiches are sold at stadiums or public events and are especially popular in Santiago.

SOPAIPILLAS (PUMPKIN FRITTERS)

A *sopaipilla* is a fried pastry traditionally made from leavened wheat dough or a mixture of wheat and corn flour and shortening or butter. It is traditionally made and eaten during cold or rainy weather. In central Chile, boiled pumpkin called *zapallo* is added to the dough. After rising, the dough is rolled out and cut into circular, square, or triangular shapes that are then deep-fried in oil. The frying causes the shapes to puff up, forming a hollow pocket in the center. If eaten as a pastry, *sopaipillas* can be dipped in *chancaca*, a sweet syrupy sauce made of brown sugar, orange zest, hone, and cinnamon. In warmer weather and in southern Chile, they are often served with *manjar*, a thick caramel custard, ketchup, and mustard, or *salsa pebre*.

MOTE CON HUESILLOS (POACHED DRIED PEACHES AND PUFFED WHEAT DRINK)

Mote con huesillo is as Chilean as the *huaso* (the proud horseman), and its preparation can be traced back to the pre-Columbus native populations. It is a sweet, clear, nonalcoholic drink made from with dried peaches (*huesillo*) cooked in sugar or honey, water, and cinnamon, mixed with fresh cooked husked wheat (*mote*). The sugar is caramelized to give the drink a rich orange color. The drink is served chilled, in a tall glass with a long spoon for easy serving. Occasionally, it is served with dried prunes.

EMPANADAS

Chilean empanadas can have a wide range of fillings, but three types are the most popular. One is baked and filled with *pino*, a mixture of beef, onions, raisins, black olives, and a hard-boiled egg. The second is filled with seafood and fried. The third kind contains cheese and may be baked or fried. There are many variations on these basic types: for example, *pino* can be made without raisins and olives or all kinds of seafood may be used, such as mussels, crab, prawns, or *locos* (similar to abalone), or shrimp may be mixed with the cheese. Chilean empanadas are considerably larger than Argentinian empanadas, so that usually one is enough for a meal.

CHURRO

The dessert staple of Chilean street food, churro, is basically long thin pieces of ridged dough that are deep-fried and coated with sugar, sometimes both granulated and powdered. They are sold plain or filled with *manjar*. They are best served very hot.

JORGE PÉREZ

ARGENTINA

T HE ARGENTINE REPUBLIC is the second-largest country in South America by land area. Before the arrival of Europeans at the beginning of the 16th century, the area was settled by colonies of the Inca Empire and by Indian tribes living in semi-sedentary styles. Argentina became a colony of Spain in 1580 and won its independence in 1815. An estimated 60 percent of the population has some Italian descent, thanks to large-scale immigration in the 19th and 20th centuries and more than half have some level of indigenous ancestry. Argentina is divided into several culinary zones, each distinguished by its own distinctive gastronomic characteristics. In the central region and the Pampas (the great Argentinean plains), dishes with a strong Italian influence, such as pizza, pasta, and polenta, are consumed on a daily basis. Pre-Hispanic dishes and ingredients, such as corn, potatoes, and chilies, are common in the northwestern provinces, while Welsh and Central European immigrants have influenced the gastronomy of the cool Tierra del Fuego region in the far south.

Most major cities have vendors who walk the streets with small carts, or park their carts in strategic locations, selling everything from local specialties to staple fast food. At first glance, Argentina's capital, Buenos Aires, like other big cities in the country, does not appear to have a large street-food culture. Argentine lunches are traditionally more leisurely affairs than in many of the world's cities. Rather than grab a quick lunch from a street cart, people often go to little restaurants or fondas and sit for an hour or two. Another reason for the lack of large numbers of street-food vendors are that some consider it rude to eat while standing. Moreover, many streets in the business districts are so narrow that parked carts block traffic. They are highly regulated for health and traffic reasons. The ubiquitous Argentine *parrilla*, or grill, is allowed only in certain places, and the varieties of what they serve are limited. Despite the apparent scarcity of street food, intrepid diners can find and eat fast food on the street if they know where to look.

Parks, green areas, and squares are the first place you can spot vendors selling street food. Sandwiches are popular. The *pebete*, a tender bun sandwich with ham and cheese, is the most famous combination in Argentina. But also worth trying is the pepperoni and cheese *pebete*. Around train stations, commuters can find hot dogs called *panchos* or *súper panchos* (meaning average size and large ones), *milanesa* (breaded cutlet) sandwich, and the regular Buenos Aires snacks: *garrapiñada* (caramelized nuts), salty or sweet popcorn, and orange juice squeezed to order.

The Costanera boardwalks are also good spots to find Argentine street food. On the city banks of the Río de la Plata, small mobile food stands called *carritos* sit by the riverside. They serve cheap simply grilled meats, *choripán*, and drinks. The Costanera Norte, near the metropolitan airport, is where many taxi drivers lunch on their *choripán*. In 1966, the military dictator Juan Carlos Onganía banned the authentic *carritos*, painted in white and with wheels, and then cleared out those who tried to resist the move with bulldozers. But the carrito has lived on in the form of fixed stalls made of sheet iron and relatively permanent wagons with odd names like El Puestito del Tío (Uncle's Little Place), El Parrillón (the Griller), El Cocacolero (the Coca-Cola Man), and others. Many have been dodging municipal inspections for years. In Costanera Sur, business executives from Puerto Madero (the newest and upscale neighborhood in Buenos Aires) blend with taxi drivers and families on weekends at the famed *carritos*.

Fútbol (soccer) is very popular in Argentina, and the stadiums and surrounding streets are good places to find street food. Inside the bigger stadiums, only hamburgers, *panchos*, popsicles, and occasionally *choripán* are sold. Outside the stadiums, varieties of sellers offer everything from empanadas and *chorizos a la pomarola* (in tomato sauce) to pizza. The word *canchera* refers to a stadium, and a *canchero* or eater is used to describe somebody with street credibility.

MAJOR STREET FOODS

Choripán (or *Chori*)

Choripán is Argentina's most recognizable street food. It is one of those ubiquitous cultural icons that unites a country, regardless of peoples' socioeconomic status. The *choripán* or *chori* is said to be the product of the mid-19th century when gauchos (cowboys) used to eat sausage on bread that was toasted on open grills. This new form of sandwich is a chorizo-style sausage served on French bread. The bread can be whole or split vertically into two parts and grilled again. The dish later moved to the cities where it became popular. Two centuries later, it is now a key part of street food, a delicious Argentine classic. The usual Argentine dressing for *choripán* is chimichurri, a sauce made with garlic, marjoram, red pepper, oil, and vinegar, according to the traditional recipe. One story claims that the name comes from Jimmy McCurry, an Irishman sympathetic to the cause of Argentine independence who is said to have first prepared the sauce when marching with General Belgrano's troops in the 19th century. As his name was difficult for the native people to say, the name was corrupted to "chimichurri." More likely it is the local pronounciation of *salmoriglio*, a common Sicilian sauce brought by Italian immigrants.

Grilled Meats

But the real tradition in Argentina has always been, and will be, the grill. In several working-class neighborhoods in Buenos Aires, like La Boca or Mataderos and also near the big meat-packaging plants, there are many little hole-in-the-wall *parrillas* where standing to eat is commonplace. These spots are little more than stand-up lunch counters, where workers on a quick break can cram in a *choripán* (sausage sandwich), a *vaciopan* (flank steak sandwich), or a huge slice of pizza. *Pizza canchera*, along with others, is more like a calzone, that is, a flat dough filled with cheese or meats, then folded over and baked. Another favorite is Buenos Aires classic *fainá* (a baked flatbread made with ground chickpea flour often used as a base for pizza). For larger meals, the *gauchos* (cowboys) of the Pampas invented the *asado*. These are large wood-fired grills on which all sorts of meats, including intestines, are cooked. It is considered to be Argentina's national dish and can be considered as street food only when it is served at festivals. Today riverside *carritos* offer a quite sophisticated range of *parrilla* options: from sandwiches to small plates, including the different types of sausages: chorizo, *morcilla, salchicha parrillera*, as well as various cuts of meat, both beef and pork. The most recent development that now rivals *parrilla* and *choripán* in popularity is the *bondiola* sandwich or *bondipan*. It is a slice of roasted pork shoulder served in bread and accompanied by lemon juice. Some carts have a few plastic tables and chairs, but most people eat standing up by the bar, in public benches, or inside their cars.

Sweet Breads

Carritos are also found in different parts of the sprawling Parque Tres de Febrero and handicraft fairs like Recoleta, where they often share space with coffee vendors (the coffee is very sweet). Aside from serving sandwiches, they offer mixtures of Spanish and French patisserie, among which are *vigilantes* (long shaped, with custard), regular butter croissants and sweeter ones dipped in sugar syrup, *tortitas negras* (sweet dough baked with milk and covered with brown sugar), at relatively low prices. They can also be found at the entrance of hospitals and train stations. At the amusement parks, the vending stalls and vendors offer treats for children: snowflake sugar, caramelized apples with popcorn, figs in syrup on brochette sticks, ice creams, and a local specialty: *alfajores* (two round sweet biscuits joined together with mousse, dulce de leche, or jam and coated with black or white chocolate).

Chipás

The *chipá* comes from the Mesopotamian region between Northern Argentina, Brazil, Bolivia, and Paraguay. These cheese buns or cheese breads are a variety of small, baked manioc flour and cheese-flavored rolls, an inexpensive snack that is often sold from street-side stands or by vendors carrying heat-preserving containers. A relatively new kind of street dish is grilled bread similar to the Indian chapati that is prepared mainly by women vendors near the city's railway stations. Mostly women vendors grill this white bread by the railway stations that dot the city. Early in the morning, the vendor uses a grill built from half a 200-liter barrel and a barbecue-like rack over a burning coal fire to make a delicious comfort food that is not especially healthy.

Salsa Criolla and Other Toppings

Although not a separate street food, almost all vendors serve *salsa criolla* with their dishes. It is basically chopped onion, tomato, red and green pepper with vinegar, and oil. Other toppings for street dishes include mayonnaise, mustard (American style), ketchup (sweet, not hot), salsa golf (thought to be a local invention that is made by simply mixing ketchup and mayonnaise), pickled vegetables, *lluvia de papas* (crumbled potato crisps showered as a topping on such dishes as *súper panchos*, or hot dogs and hamburgers), tomato and lettuce, chopped canned mushrooms, and crumbled bacon.

OTHER STREET FOODS

- Churros are fried rods of sweet dough filled with dulce de leche (milk caramel sauce).
- *Colaciónes, caña* sweets, and *rosqueta* are sweet doughs made with milk and boiled before being cooked in the oven, like a bagel. These, too, are a north Argentinian specialty.
- Doughnuts and *bolas de fraile* or *berlinesas* are fried and tender doughnuts, sprinkled with sugar.
- Empanadas, savory filled pastries, are especially popular in the northern part of Argentine.
- *Pastelitos* are made of puff pastry and filled with quince or sweet potato paste, dipped in sugar syrup.
- Tamales are also popular in the north.

MARCELA MAZZEI

BRAZIL

WITH 190 MILLION PEOPLE and an area of 3.3 million square miles, Brazil (officially the Federative Republic of Brazil) is South America's largest country. Its variety of geography and climates, ranging from green mountains along the Atlantic Ocean to the Amazon forest in the north and a central plateau cut with hundreds of rivers, is reflected in its cuisine.

The Portuguese explorer Pedro Álvares Cabral in 1500 was the first European to visit Brazil; he called it Ilha de Santa Cruz (Saint Cross Island.) At the time, it was inhabited by around 5 million people with different cultures and languages. For many years, the Portuguese made little attempt to move inland or colonize the vast territory. But in the mid-16th century, the king of Portugal decided to install a central government and divided the territory into hereditary captaincies. New arrivals cut down vast swathes of forests, initially for brazilwood, later sugarcane, cotton, and tobacco plantations. Coffee and cocoa beans were introduced and grown for export. Other products from Portugal's vast overseas empire included rice, bananas, and coconuts. The colonists in turn were introduced to native products, including corn, manioc, chilies, peanuts, sweet potatoes, pumpkins, and various beans. Today rice, beans, and manioc flour are the main staples of the Brazilian diet.

To work on the plantations, the Portuguese brought slaves from Western Africa. In 1850, the transportation of slaves was banned, and in 1888, slavery was abolished in Brazil. Today around 47 percent of Brazilians are of European origin (mainly Portuguese, Spanish, German, and Italian), 51 percent are of

African or mixed descent, plus a small percentage of Asians and indigenous people.

Street food first appeared in the villages of the southeast, where modern São Paulo and Rio de Janeiro are located, and the northeast, where Brazil's first capital Salvador in Bahia State was located. It was initially sold by the *negros de ganho*, slaves who had expertise in cooking. Usually they would have to give all their profits to their owners, but eventually, it became a way of social advancement that could even lead to freedom if the slave managed to save enough money to buy his manumission.

After slavery was abolished, selling street food became a major source of employment for freed slaves. The first Brazilian street food was *angu*, boiled and mashed cornmeal seasoned with salt if the latter was available. Other dishes sold outdoors were fried fish with mashed fruits (a staple among indigenous peoples); stews made with local vegetables, boiled and mashed cassava, and palm fruits, such as the *pupunha*; fresh fruits, including banana and pineapple; and *sonhos* ("dreams" in Portuguese), round sweet deep-fried treats made from sugar and flour (mainly cassava). Dishes from the African repertoire became the quintessence of street food in Salvador and throughout Brazil. The most famous is *acarajé*, a fritter made from peeled black-eyed peas formed into a ball and then deep-fried in palm oil.

Today everyone can be seen eating street food in Brazil, although its major appeal is for low-salary workers. For people who live in the poorest areas in big cities and work far away from home, it is the only way to eat, since they have to have lunch in the city centers close to their jobs. Moreover, as in many other countries, selling street food provides employment for immigrants and new-comers who do not have regular jobs.

In cities like São Paulo and Rio de Janeiro, street food is sold mainly during lunchtime and rush hours. For breakfast, Brazilians stop by the *padarias* (bakeries) and *botequims* (informal snack bars) that for many years were run by recent Portuguese immigrants. Here customers drink coffee and eat bread, snacks, and sandwiches. *Botequims* are a trademark of Rio, serving coffee and bread for break-fast, beer and typical appetizers all day long, such as *bolinho de bacalhau* (codfish fritters), boiled eggs, fried fish, and pastel (thin pastry folded like a paper, filled with meat, ham, cheese). Many of these are officially sanctioned, unlike the vendors who sell without licenses in the poorer parts of cities.

Street-food stalls were built informally in city markets, at bus and subway terminals, and at street fairs. Early in the morning, one can see a vendor selling *mingau de tapioca* or *mingau de maizena* (tapioca and cornstarch porridge) in train stations in many big cities. In São Paulo, Brazil's largest city, there is no law protecting street-food vendors, who are harassed by the police. Food trucks are prohibited by the public health sanitary code. Meanwhile, street food is becoming trendy, and many chefs occasionally become street-food vendors, trying to help to legalize the activity.

Brazil's street-food culture is so rich that a person would have to travel all over the country to appreciate it. The most important street-food scenes are located outside of the capital São Paulo and Rio de Janeiro. A famous street-food venue is the Ver-o-Peso Fish Market and streets around it in Belém in the State of Pará. It is known for its *açaí com peixe*—açaí berries pulverized into a porridge and served with toasted cassava flour and grilled fish. Mercado Modelo in Salvador is famous for its *comida de santo*, African inspired dishes such as *acarajé* and *cuscuz* (couscous), which are dedicated to African deities on worship days. Japanese *sobás* are popular dishes in street fairs in Campo Grande, capital of Mato Grosso do Sul. The coastal cities of the Northeast are famous for *queijo de coalho* (curd cheese) melted on a skewer that is sold by ambulatory vendors.

MAJOR STREET FOODS

Acarajé

Originating in West Africa, the local word for this dish is *akará*, which roughly means food with beans or ball of fire. It is made with cooked and mashed black-eyed peas seasoned with salt and chopped onions, then molded into the shape of a large scone and deep-fried in palm oil in a wok-like pan in front of the customer. In the variation called *abará*, the same ingredients are boiled instead of deep-fried. Many authors trace its origins to Middle Eastern falafels, which were brought to Africa by Arabs.

Customers waiting in the line to buy an *acarajé* must tell the vendor whether they want it "hot" or "cold." In Bahia, the seasonings are quite heavy: Locals always order "hot," which is slang for "lots of pepper," usually a hot sauce made with *pimenta-malagueta* or *piri-piri* and palm oil.

Acarajé is a fixture in the Afro-Brazilian religious traditions of *Candomblé*.

The presentation is theatrical even when it is not part of a religious ceremony. Many vendors are *baianas*, women born in the state of Bahia, who wear white shawls and turbans, round starched skirts, bracelets, and colorful necklaces. Their image often appears in local artwork.

Inexpensive and rich, *acarajé* is the most popular street food in Salvador, the original capital of Colonial Brazil, where many African slaves lived. It is sold in stalls near historical churches and street fairs, in Pelourinho, the old historic center, and beaches like Itapuã and Praia do Forte. It is also eaten in almost every city in Bahia State and some parts of Rio de Janeiro, where it has a sweeter taste thanks to the addition of coconut milk. *Acarajé* also has different flavors depending on the filling. The most common is *vatapá*, a yellow porridge made with palm oil, bread, coconut milk, okra as a thickener, and coriander, topped with dried shrimps and dressed with pepper sauce.

Milho verde / pamonha

These two dishes made from sweet corn are found everywhere in Brazil except the North, where the cassava culture dominates. *Milho verde* is an ear of corn cooked in boiling water and eaten off its cob, usually sprinkled with salt and butter. It is sold near train stations, factories, and commercial centers of São Paulo year-round (even on the elegant Avenida Paulista, the core of businesses' headquarters) but is especially popular in autumn and winter.

Pamonha resembles a Mexican tamale: fresh corn is grated and juiced to make a paste, which is wrapped in fresh corn husk, tied with a string, and cooked in boiling water. *Pamonhas* can be savory or sweet, and filled with cheese, sausage, minced meat, or served plain.

Like many other dishes made from sweet corn, *pamonha* and *milho verde* are popular in a traditional Catholic festival in June, called Festa Junina.

Pastel

Pastels are thin pastry envelopes wrapped around assorted fillings, then deep-fried in vegetable oil. They are sold in every street market in cities in southeastern and central Brazil. The usual accompaniment is *garapa*, sugarcane juice crushed in an electric mill served by itself or mixed with pineapple juice or lemonade.

Pastel is commonly filled with savory ingredients: mozzarella cheese or *queijo prato*, a local soft cheese, and tomatoes; ham and cheese slices; ground meat with sliced boiled eggs and parsley; chicken with Catupiry (an industrial cream cheese with low acidity); or even small cooked or fried shrimps. Recent years have seen the appearance of sweet pastels with fillings made from banana and chocolate, *goiabada* (thick guava jam) and cheese from Minas Gerais, and *doce de leite* (a caramel-like sweet made with sugar and milk).

As the pastels are fried, they fill with air, but customers can never tell if the vendor has really filled the envelope. Street-food stalls in markets are known for their *pastel de vento* (with just air inside, no filling), which should be cheaper than the filled ones. There are various explanations of its origin. One is that pastels were introduced by Japanese and Chinese immigrants in stalls and *lanchonetes*, small establishments that serve sandwiches and snacks. A variation that may be of Italian origin is the *fogazza*, a calzone-like pastry made of wheat flour, stuffed with cheese and meat, and fried or baked.

Tacacá

This thick rich soup is popular in northern Brazil, especially cities in the states of Acre, Amazonas, and Para. It is one of the last indigenous foods available in urban surroundings and is sold mainly by women. The broth, called *tucupi*, is made from fermented cassava juice, gum starch (also from cassava), and dried shrimp stock mixed with *jambu* (paracress), a green vegetable that makes lips and tongue tingle. The soup is served hot in bowls and is especially popular on torrid afternoons and at sunset. *Tucupi* is used as a broth for many dishes in northern Brazil, including duck.

OTHER STREET FOODS

Tapioca

A kind of pancake made from cassava (manioc) starch and water, tapioca is a staple street food in markets in the north and eastern Brazil. A culinary heritage from the indigenous people, the starch is made by pulping, filtering, and centrifuging the tuberous root. The flour ranges from a fine powder to coarser granules or pearls. The tapioca dough is spread in a thin layer on a frying pan; filled with dried shrimps, jerky, cheese, coconut chips, chocolate, fruits, or *doce de leite*; and then folded over like a crêpe.

According to local lore, the *tapioqueiras* (tapioca women vendors) must use a charcoal fire and frying pan instead of stoves and flat grills. The city of Fortaleza in the state of Ceará has Center of Tapioqueiras, with dozens of stalls. In Olinda city, good tapiocas are sold in front of the Cathedral Church (Sé). In Recife, capital of the State of Pernambuco, tapioca can be found at city central streets like Dantas Barreto, Guararapes, and Conde da Boa Vista, near the 13 de Maio Park entrances, or around soccer stadiums on match days.

Soba

The second largest Japanese community in Brazil lives around Pantanal biome, one of the most impressive wetlands in the world, in the State of Mato Grosso do Sul in western Brazil. They came mostly from the Okinawa archipelago and brought with them soba, a thin noodle made with buckwheat. The noodles are served in a bowl with dashi, a characteristic Japanese soup stock made from fish shavings and kombu, topped with seaweed; seasoned with soy sauce and mirin (rice wine); and sometimes topped with a raw egg. Since there is no buckwheat in Brazil, cooks adapted the recipe to wheat flour. In Campo Grande, the capital of Mato Grosso do Sull, vendors make soba with imported noodles in Feira Central, the city's central market.

Cocada

Cocada is a traditional Brazilian sweet made with coconut milk, egg yolks, and sweetened condensed milk that is sold by walking vendors. It is associated with poor neighborhoods in large cities. In Bahia, it is traditionally paired with *acarajé*. Usually *cocada* is prepared indoors, particularly the hard chewy version that has a fudge-like texture and is filled with coconut chunks. However, a few vendors cook the mixture on the spot in gas stoves and large pans to make a version that is eaten like a creamy pudding. Another variety is made with toasted coconut that gives it a brownish color and called *quebra-queixo* ("jaw breaker") because of its thickness.

Hot Dogs

Over the last four decades, some street foods have been imported from outside, notably the hot dog, which has been transformed into a rich sandwich with all kinds of fillings and toppings. The meat is industrial sausages made with pork, poultry, and leftovers. A plain version consisting only of bread and sausage is found in cities of the northeast. In São Paulo, street vendors add cheese, corn niblets, canned peas, mashed potatoes, shoestring potatoes, and condiments such as vinaigrette, mayonnaise, ketchup, and mustard.

Queijo de Coalho (Cheese on Skewers)

A firm but light cheese is threaded on wooden skewers, much like a kebab and semi-melted in portable charcoal ovens. It is sold by walking vendors on the beaches of northeastern Brazil. It is often topped with *melaço*, reduced sugarcane extract.

Espetinho (Kebabs)

Skewers of meat grilled over a fire are available everywhere in Brazil. The meat is usually beef seasoned with salt, but sometimes the skewers are threaded with vegetables (corn, tomato, carrot, and broccoli), sausages, or cheaper cuts of chicken. They are served with vinaigrette and a slice of French bread.

OLÍVIA FRAGA

CENTRAL AMERICA

ENTRAL AMERICA IS THE LONG, THIN LAND BRIDGE that connects the North and South American continents. An isthmus, it stretches from southern Mexico to Colombia, is bounded by the Pacific Ocean and the Caribbean Sea, and includes the countries of Guatemala, Nicaragua, Honduras, El Salvador, Costa Rica, Belize, and Panama. The land is filled with mountains, interspersed with fertile valleys, and is volcanically active. Climates vary in the isthmus depending on altitude, but most of it is tropical with a number of forests and amazingly diverse biosystems. Ecotourism in the tropical areas has become a large industry, especially in Costa Rica.

Central America was part of the ancient Mesoamerican civilizations. Guatemala, for instance, was the heartland of the ancient Mayas. When Spain conquered the whole region, these civilizations disappeared, but the peoples speaking many native languages did not. Today, almost all the countries have large indigenous populations. Most also have peoples of African descent that date from the days of slavery between 1500 and the mid-19th century. Mixed together by proximity to one another and intermarriage, Central American peoples created Creole cultures including their foods. Based on native corn, and beans, to which imported rice has been added, along with Asian bananas (plantains) and native yuca, fish, and European food animals, the cuisines of the region are truly mestizo. The classic *pupusa* of El Salvador and neighboring regions is one of them.

BELIZE

Belize (once called British Honduras) is the second smallest country in Central America in landmass, the smallest in population, yet is one of the most diverse in several ways. Subtropical in climate with a wet and a dry season, the country is located on the Caribbean Sea with Mexico to the north and Guatemala to the south and west. Most of Belize is low-lying country. The long coastline is often swampy with lagoons and many small islands (cays). A coral barrier reef, the world's second longest, protects the coast from high sea tides, but not from frequent destructive hurricanes. The northern region is also lowland and heavily forested with old-growth hardwoods such as mahogany. These have been harvested for many years and have been a staple of the Belizean economy. For such a small country, there is surprising biodiversity. From drier low mountains and plateau in the south to the northern and coastal forests, there are broad ranges of flora and fauna. Belize is recognized as one of the world's ecological treasures, and as a result, ecotourism is a growing part of their economy.

Although small in numbers, around 350,000 people, Belize has as varied a population as any in Central America. Originally most of Belize was part of the Mayan culture sphere, the largest center being Caracol in the southern Maya Mountains. The longest occupied center is Lamanai in the northern Orange Walk area dating from about 1500 BCE to 1650 CE. The Spanish who arrived in 1540 never conquered all of Belize, leaving the coastal areas open to British pirates, merchants, and settlers in the 17th and 18th centuries. Baymen, as the sailors were called, brought African slaves, both settling in coastal towns and villages, and mixing together with native peoples into new ethnic groups. In the 19th century, British Honduras became a Crown Colony and became fully independent in 1981.

Belize comprises several major ethnic groups, and each has contributed to the country's street food. About a quarter of the population are Kriols (or Creoles), who are mixtures of the English Baymen and Africans or people of African descent who came from nearby Caribbean islands such as Jamaica. Their language, a version of English, is the most widely spoken dialect. Garingu (the singular is Garifuna like Belize's neighbors in Nicaragua and Honduras) are peoples of African, Carib, and Arawak (natives of the Caribbean islands) ancestry. Their language comes from the latter groups with French, English, and Spanish thrown in. Their food is more closely related to Caribbean cuisine than others. Mestizos are mixtures of Spaniards and native Indian people and are about 30 percent of the population.

Many came from neighboring Guatemala to escape long civil wars fought there. Other peoples include English, Germans, East Indians, Chinese, and four different Mayan-speaking people. Although English is the official language, most people also speak two or three languages according to their ethnic group.

Like other countries in Central America, beans (red beans rather than black) and rice form the core of Belizean cuisine, but with much more seafood and a lot more spice. Chicken, pork, and beef are widely eaten, cow's foot stew being a Belizean specialty. Festival foods eaten in public celebrations can also include iguana, peccaries, and even large wild rodents—gibnut and agouti (called *hicatee*). Gibnut and agouti are often fried and served from food stands in many places in the country's interior towns. Stews and barbecued meats are also sold from stands in every town and city. Curried chicken, brought from India via the Caribbean islands, is also a standard dish. On the coast, fried conch fritters and *escabeche* (fresh fish cooked in lime juice or vinegar) are very popular. For seafood at public events, there is a national lobster festival held every year where massive numbers of crustaceans are boiled and grilled. Plantains and manioc, mashed and made into flatbreads or dumplings (*bundiga*), are a Garingu addition to the food scene. In all cases of food, a very hot sauce is served, usually made from habanero peppers.

Street vendors almost always have *panades*, or small meat pies, and tamales. Some tamales are like those in Mexico and Central America: corn dough stuffed with cooked meats, wrapped in corn or banana leaves, and steamed. Others, called *dukunu*, are often meatless and made with fresh corn. Tacos, made with corn or flour tortillas, are common and made with chicken or other meats and topped with vinegar-laced cabbage, just as they are in North America. *Garnaches*, another import from Spanish Central America, are corn tortillas that are fried and loaded with fried beans and shredded cheese.

In a subtropical country, fruits are abundant on the streets. Mango, guava, *craboo* (a small yellow fruit with a strong smell), sapote, oranges, pineapples, and lots of coconuts—from meat to milk—are always to be found on vendors: stands, carts, and baskets.

Warm weather calls for beverages. *Horchata*, a rice drink, comes from the Mestizo tradition. Tamarind is widely used in a nonalcoholic beverage as are soft drinks. Beer is very popular, much of it Jamaican. Being a former British colony, tea is a staple drink as is coffee since Belize and its neighbors produce high-quality beans.

BRUCE KRAIG

COSTA RICA

Costa Rica is a Central American nation that shares many geographical and ethnic characteristics with its neighbors. Nicaragua borders the country to the north, and Panama is the southern border. Like these two countries, Costa Rica is subtropical in climate and has highly diverse ecological zones. On the east, the Caribbean coast was always low, swampy land while the Pacific area of Guanacaste Province is a tourist destination because of its excellent beaches. The center of Costa Rica rises from open grasslands to mountains, some of which are spectacular, potentially active volcanoes. The interior valleys are fertile farmlands, while the grasslands support cattle ranching. Some of the country's ancient forests have been cut to make more pasture for cattle, much of that for American fast-food chains. Yet Costa Rica has become a world leader in preserving its pristine ecosystems with their great varieties of flora and fauna through large national parks. Ecotourism is now a major part of the economy.

Most Costa Ricans are of European or mixed European and indigenous heritage. This began with the Spanish colonization in the mid-16th century and was followed by more European immigrants in the succeeding centuries. There are some native peoples living in the country and a number of people of African descent who are found on the east coast. Most of these came from the Caribbean islands in the 19th and 20th centuries to work in construction and agriculture. Many of them speak English as well as the national language, Spanish. Refugees from political wars in Nicaragua have settled in large numbers in the northern part of the country. Each group has contributed to Costa Rica's cuisine.

Costa Ricans' characteristic dish is *gallo pinto*, or rice and beans. Only in the north, among Nicaraguans, does corn play a significant role in most people's food. Versions differ from region to region. In most of the country, the beans are black and in equal measure to the rice, but among the coastal people with ties to the Caribbean countries, red beans are used, along with coconut milk and spicy red peppers. In other parts of the country, the rice and beans are toasted or cooked with lots of oil. No matter how it is cooked, *gallo pinto* appears as street food, in restaurants, and in home kitchens.

Many Costa Ricans eat street food, especially in such cities as San Jose, the capital, from small open-fronted restaurants called *sodas*. There, such dishes as *gallo pinto* are accompanied by a picadillo made from shredded vegetables such as cabbage, chayote, carrots, and even green mangoes. *Gallo pinto* in most of the country might have finely sliced sweet peppers, onions, and lots of cilantro on top. A version of this dish called *casado* ("married man") has beans and rice served side by side. Since diners like fried foods, fried plantain slices, or *patacones*, are very popular. *Barbudos*, string beans coated in an egg batter and deep-fried, is a Costa Rican specialty. *Pejibayes*, or peach palm, is an important food that is used in soups and stews. Diners might also find *mondongo* (tripe soup), *olla de carne* (beef stew), chicken stews and soups, and on the coasts ceviche. Tortillas often accompany dishes, and in cities, corn dough-based dishes such as *pupusas* and tacos can be found. Tamales are a customary holiday dish, prepared at home and served to the public at events.

Fruits are among the most common foods sold by vendors. The country produces mangoes, papayas, melons, pineapples, guavas, and bananas. Fruits are sweet, but a special sweet dish is made for the holidays from squash. Called *chi verre*, the squash is cut up and dried, and the pieces are then cooked down with sugar to form a very sweet jelly, called *miel de chiverre*, that is eaten on rolls and used in sweet pastries, especially around Easter.

As might be expected from a famous coffee-producing country, coffee is sold everywhere and is widely consumed. Costa Ricans use a drip technique, in which a cloth bag containing the coffee is set in a wooden frame, hot water is poured over it, and then allowed to drip into a pot.

Refrescos are usually fruit juice-based drinks that are found everywhere in the country. They are made by blending fruits with either water or milk, often with sugar. The most popular flavors are mango, blackberry, carambola (star fruit), papaya, tamarind, and watermelon among others. Bottled soft drinks are also widely drunk, especially colas.

Carambola (star fruit) is a popular flavor for refrescos.

Because of foreign tourism and changing tastes among young people, international fast-food chain restaurants have expanded greatly in Costa Rica, causing some to worry that traditional street food will disappear. Fried chicken chains such as the native Rostipollos and Pollo Campero from Guatemala now compete with Kentucky Fried Chicken and Popeyes. McDonald's (which serves *gallo pinto*), Burger King, Wendy's, Applebee's, Quizno's, and others have all entered the market and are becoming more popular.

BRUCE KRAIG

EL SALVADOR

In territory, El Salvador is one of the smallest countries in Central America, yet its population of 6 million it is comparable with its bigger neighbors. Unlike others, the country has no outlet to the Caribbean Sea but faces westward toward the Pacific Ocean. El Salvador has been called "the land of volcanoes" with good reason. Most of the country is mountainous with extinct and some potentially active volcanoes covering the interior. The spectacular region is where the country's protected biodiversity areas are located, and thus attracts an increasing number of tourists. A narrow strip of fertile land along the coast is where much of the country's population lives, where most of its economic activity is located and where its cities and largest towns are located. The climate is tropical in the lowlands with a bi-seasonal rainy and dry season, but it is more temperate in the uplands.

Before the Spanish arrived in the 16th century, the land of El Salvador was occupied by indigenous peoples, mainly the Pipil who spoke a Nahuatl language (related to the Aztecs of Mexico). Only a small fraction remains because so many native people were killed during the conquest and civil wars in the last century. Most Salvadorans are of mixed European and indigenous ancestry, and their language (Spanish) and culture reflect this varied heritage. El Salvador's food is a mixture of imported and native ingredients, all of which go into what is sold as street food. Corn is the basis of most Salvadoran food, along with beans and rice, yuca, plantains, *loroco* (an edible flower bud that is important in local cuisine), many fruits and vegetables, pork, chicken, seafood, and some beef.

Pupusas

Corn tortillas are eaten at all meals, but one form of them is El Salvador's most famous dish. *Pupusas* are thick tortillas made from cornmeal dough and almost always made by hand on the spot. Once toasted on a flat griddle, the pupusa is cut horizontally and stuffed with variety of fillings. The most popular is *quesillo*, a semisoft melting cheese, and *chicharon*, a ground pork mixture. Other fillings range from fried beans, cheese, and *loroco*, to chopped vegetables such as chayote. The *pupusa* is usually served with a shredded pickled cabbage and chile salad called *curtido*. Two variants are made from rice and mashed plantains. Salvadorans who have migrated to other countries in the region and to the United States brought *pupusas* with them. They are now popular in all of these places, and in North America are sold in food trucks and Hispanic markets.

Other common Salvadoran street foods are *yuca frita* and *panes rellenos*. *Yuca frita* is composed of slices of yuca that is deep-fried (sometimes just boiled) and served with *curtido* and sometimes ground pork, or fried pork cracklings, and fried sardines. *Panes rellenos*, or stuffed breads, are sandwiches made with marinated spiced turkey that is shredded and packed into the rolls. Other street foods include empanadas (stuffed pastries that can be savory or sweet), tamales, plain fried yuca, and fried plantains. Because of its location on the Pacific Ocean, Salvadorans eat a lot of seafood cooked in many ways. It is often prepared in soups and stews that are sold in small open-fronted restaurants and by some street vendors.

Fruit

Fruits are widely available, especially bananas, papayas, mangoes, pineapples, and others. Salvadorans also like fruit drinks. Some are bottled soft drinks, others are *minutas* (milk based and mixed in blenders with fruits), *refrescos* (such as limeade), and *horchata*. *Shuco* is like Mexican atole, corn dough mixed with water and flavors such as fruits. Coconuts are very common and, when punctured for the insertion of a straw, make for a highly nutritious and refreshing drink. Of course, coffee is universal because El Salvador has long been a major coffee-producing nation.

BRUCE KRAIG

GUATEMALA

Guatemala lies in Central America, or Mesoamerica, the region located between Mexico to the north, Honduras and El Salvador to the south. It is a mountainous country with only small coastal plains along the Pacific Ocean and the Gulf of Mexico. With a tropical climate in the lowlands and cooler temperatures in the highlands, Guatemala is a perfect place to raise bananas and among the world's best coffees.

In pre-Hispanic times, Guatemala was within the Mayan culture zone. Today, some of the world's most famous Mayan archaeological sites (e.g., Tikal) are found in the northern parts of the country. When that civilization collapsed in the 9th and 10th centuries AD, the people did not disappear. Instead, they remained in villages scattered across the country. Mayan speakers are still there, mainly in the highlands, and represent about 40 percent of the population. Most of the rest are mestizos, or people of mixed European and indigenous heritage.

Guatemala City is the capital, and it is here that visitors will find the greatest numbers of street-food vendors. Antigua, near the capital, is also well known for its open-air food scene. Like other emerging nations, the vendors come from the lower economic levels of society, many of them indigenous people who have come to the city to find employment. Street food certainly serves to nourish poor people, but it is also enjoyed by all Guatemalans and the large numbers of tourists who visit each year.

Guatemalan food resembles Mexican cuisine in many ways, but it is far less spicy. For instance, *elotes*, or grilled corn on the cob, are the most common food sold by street vendors, but unlike Mexico, they are not eaten with chile powder sprinkled on them but with a mild salsa. Tortilla-based foods are also popular, like tacos in Mexico. Here, they are often deep-fried and then stuffed with chopped meats or beans. Black beans are a staple and can be eaten whole, or *revueltas* (meaning mixed and fried), or even liquefied in a blender. Most of these dishes are topped with chopped cabbage, cheese, and often guacamole. A smaller version of tacos, called *garnachas*, is made this way, only with meats and cheese.

Most people agree that locally made cheeses are one of the best things about Guatemalan food, and they are commonly served in tortillas. Cheese and meat are also fillings for the *pupusa*. This is a dish imported from neighboring El Salvador, a thick tortilla that is split and stuffed with various ingredients, especially cheese.

Since Guatemalan cuisine has a good many meat stews in it, tortillas accompany a bowl of beef, chicken, or pork stew. Of meats, chicken is the most popular, though a turkey stew called *kakik* from the north can also be found in markets and at stands.

Drinks always accompany street food. The most Guatemalan of all are atoles. Similar to Mexican atole, they are made from corn dough mixed with water; only the Guatemalan versions often have ground beans added. Atoles come in many flavors, since fruits can be mixed in, and are a favorite hearty breakfast beverage. Varieties of local fruits are sold by street and market vendors ranging from mangoes, to sapote, papaya, guavas, and melons. If these are not sweet enough, then candies are also available.

Wrapped hard candies are sold cheaply by vendors from trays, the most famous being *canillitas de leche*, or "little milk legs." These are made from milk and sugar with vanilla flavoring, boiled down and set out until hardened. Guatemalan candies and desserts are super sweet and include *tamarindos*, small red balls made from tamarind, marzipan, and *buñuelos* (sugared fried dough), among many others.

BRUCE KRAIG

HONDURAS

Honduras is one of the more beautiful countries of Central America. It has a long coast along the Caribbean Sea and a much smaller outlet to the Pacific Ocean at the Gulf of Fonseca. Like its neighbors, Guatemala, El Salvador, and Nicaragua to the south, Honduras has a subtropical climate with a long autumn rainy season. The central part of the country is mountainous, and here temperatures are more temperate. Because of its location and climate, its forested highlands, and swampy southern coastline, Honduras is designated as one of the world's biodiversity centers. Most of its neighbors share that honor. Unfortunately, deforestation for agricultural purposes is rapidly destroying the country's old ecological system.

Before the Spanish arrived in the 16th century, Honduras was partly within the Mayan culture zone and also occupied by other tribal groups. One of the greatest Mayan ruins, Copán, in the northern part of the country is a major tourist attraction. Honduran people are mainly a mixture of Spanish and native people, but other groups are important. Among them are the Garifuna, a mixture of Africans and native peoples, and at least seven Indian peoples. Each has influenced Honduran food, though the country's food is not as complex as other places such as Mexico. Because Honduras is one of the Central America's poorest countries, cheap street food is very important to its peoples.

Honduran cuisine is best known for its many delicious soups and stews, but not for much spiciness. A standard meal, called a *plato tipico*, consists of beans, rice, fried plantains, grilled meat or fish (on the coast), and plenty of flour tortillas. These same ingredients are the basis of street foods.

The most popular street foods are *baleadas* (literally, "shots"). They are large hand-made flour (not corn) tortillas that are often lightly grilled until soft, covered with fried and mashed beans, grated dried aged cheese, or meats, then folded in half and eaten on the spot.

Pastelitos de carne are flour-based dough stuffed with meat and rice or potatoes that are deep-fried. *Burritas* are another favorite, only they are not like the burritos familiar from North American–Mexican foods. Instead, they are two flour tortillas stacked with some meat, fried beans, grated cheese or onions, and avocados on top. The fillings are separated into each tortilla, folded in half, and eaten by hand.

Enchiladas in Honduras resemble Mexican tacos, fried corn tortillas filled with shredded meats but more often fried beans and cheese. These are usually served with chopped hard-boiled eggs on top and dosed with ketchup. Tamales are large and often filled with bits of meat with some bone in them (which have to be picked out) and steamed in banana leaves.

Tajadas are probably the most widely eaten food in the country. They are nothing more than thinly sliced plantain slices that are deep-fried until crisp. They can also be made from unripe sweet bananas, and even ripe ones. *Tajadas* are not only street and snack food but commonly accompany main dishes served at home and in restaurants. One special dish is served more often in restaurants than on the street, but the ingredients are the same: beans and melted cheese in a clay pot served with tortilla chips.

Its climate and land make Honduras a fruit-producing country, all of which are sold by street vendors. Pineapples are very popular as are bananas, guavas, coconuts, and mangoes.

In recent years, fast-food chains have opened in Honduras, especially in the capital, Tegucigalpa. They serve both Honduran dishes and others from North America such as hamburgers, fried chicken, and pizza. All serve soft drinks that are popular across the world, from colas to fruit flavors. Visitors can still enjoy traditional street foods, though many young people will frequent the international chain restaurants.

BRUCE KRAIG

NICARAGUA

Nicaragua is the largest country in Central America and one of the most ecologically diverse. Situated between Honduras to the north and Costa Rica on the south, Nicaragua has three major ecological zones. Most of the almost six million Nicaraguans live in the fertile western Pacific Ocean coastal region where the climate is warm with a long rainy season. The capital, Managua, is located here as is a scenic wonder, Lake Nicaragua. The largest lake in Central America, it has become a major tourist attraction. Central Nicaragua is mountainous with a temperate climate, forests and even active volcanic and seismic activity. On the east, the tropical Caribbean coast differs from the rest of the country. Most of it is known as the Mosquito or Moskito Coast, a good deal of it swampy and forested with thin populations. Fishing and timber have always been important industries, yet this is the poorest part of Central America's poorest nation.

Nicaragua was occupied by peoples related to either Mayan or Nahuatl (Aztecs) cultural and linguistic groups. Other groups lived along the eastern coast. The Spanish conquest saw the founding of the hemisphere's oldest Spanish city, Granada (1524), and a mixing of peoples. Today, a majority of the population is of mixed European and indigenous ancestry with Spanish the official language. The Caribbean coast differs because of the presence of Africans originally brought in as slaves and because of English trading ports and influence. About 9 percent of Nicaraguans are of African or mixed African-indigenous ancestry and many speak English. Alongside them are native peoples such as the well-known Moskito Indians. Each contributed to Nicaragua's cuisine. Nicaraguan cuisine is heavy on beans, corn, rice, grilled meats and fish, plantains, and bananas, plus many fruits and vegetables.

Like most of Central America, south of Mexico spicy hot foods are not traditional. *Gallo pinto* is the national dish, eaten at home, in restaurants, and on the streets. It is a simple combination of cooked rice and red beans boiled with garlic then mixed together, often with strips of sweet peppers, and fried in oil. It is eaten at all times of the day, a filling and fairly nutritious, if oily, dish.

Nacatamal is the Nicaraguan version of the tamale. A dough made of ground corn and butter is spread on a banana leaf and filled with chopped meat—pork or chicken usually—chopped tomato and onion, and perhaps rice or potatoes. Folded into packets, they are steamed or boiled for several hours before serving.

Vigorón is a popular national dish that was invented in the old city of Granada. It is one of Nicaragua's few spicy hot dishes. A banana leaf is spread on a plate and then covered with thick slices of boiled yuca (also called cassava), *chicharrónes* (fried pork skin, or cracklings), and a salad made of shredded pickled cabbage. A chile-infused vinegar sauce is usually available for sprinkling. There are also nonmeat versions.

Quesillo is a common street food. This is a fresh string cheese that is wrapped in a thick flour tortilla with pickled onions, sour cream, and some salt sprinkled on top.

Tostones are like those in nearby Honduras. Slices of plantains that are fried, pounded flat, and fried again until browned. They are often served with salt and garlic sauce. *Vaho* is another food wrapped in a banana leaf and steamed. The filling is thickly sliced yuca and meat covered with a vinegared cabbage and tomato salad.

Indio viejo (literally, "old Indian") is made by boiling meat with onions, garlic, sweet peppers, and tomato. Once cooked, some tortillas are put in the water and mixed until well broken up and soft. The meat, vegetables, and tortilla pieces are then shredded and fried with the vegetables and some orange juice. On Sundays especially, food stands sell *mondongo*. This is a very hearty stew or soup made from beef tripe and bones that are slow cooked with yuca, peppers, cabbage, chayote, tomatoes, and other vegetables and finally thickened with ground rice. Fresh fruits are always available from street vendors, including papaya, mango, jocote (something like a cherry), pineapple, and the ubiquitous banana and plantain. Drinks also reflect the country's tropical nature. Fresh fruit drinks mixed with milk or whipped into slurries are everywhere. And, as a country with international connections, worldwide soft drinks are common, especially colas. One very local, traditional beverage is called *pinol* or *pinolillo*. It is made from ground cornmeal mixed with cacao (chocolate) and then diluted with water or milk. *Pinol* can be served warm or cold and is often taken at breakfast time because it is so hearty and filling.

BRUCE KRAIG

PANAMA

Panama is the southernmost country on the long isthmus that connects North and South Americas. It is a narrow country with long coastlines along the Caribbean Sea on the north and the Pacific Ocean on the south. The climate is tropical with a long rainy season, making for tropical forests and fauna that are unique to the country—its 900 species are the world's highest number. Only about 7 percent of the land is arable because Panama is mostly mountainous with some rolling uplands and fairly flat coastlines. The varied landforms make for different economic activities: cattle ranching on the meadowlands, coffee in higher elevations, fruit production, and lots of fishing on both coasts. Panama supplies North Americans with bananas, coffee, and fish, especially shrimp.

Panama's nickname is the "Crossroads of the Americas" because of its location and history. Various indigenous peoples occupied Panama and nearby Colombia for at least 10,000 years. Living in villages with sophisticated pottery and weaving techniques, they practiced small-scale agriculture and hunting-collecting ways of life.

Today, about 10 percent of Panama's population are indigenous peoples, some of whom live traditional ways of life. Most Panamanians are of mixed European-indigenous heritage with a good number of Afro-Caribbean descent. Spaniards arrived in the early 16th century, the most famous of whom was Vasco Núñez de Balboa, the first European to have seen the Pacific Ocean from the New World side. Africans were first brought to Panama to work in agriculture—sugarcane and banana plantations—and soon mixed with native and Europeans to form a mestizo population.

Today, there are strong ties between Panamanians on the Caribbean coast and other countries such as Trinidad and Tobago, Barbados, and Jamaica. There is also a large Chinese population, most of who came to work on the economic engine in the country, the Panama Canal. The canal, started in 1903, is one of the greatest engineering feats in human history and has been responsible for a good deal of Panama's ethnic mixture.

Panamanian street food is heavily influenced by both indigenous foods and those brought by immigrants. Grilling is very popular, often done over old metal barrels or small grills set up on stands. *Carne en palito* (meat on a stick) are pieces of beef, pork, or chicken threaded on wooden skewers and roasted over an open fire. They are served with a fresh green sauce. Some vendors make a more elaborate version called *brochetas*, really kebabs with onion, green peppers, and tomatoes skewered with the meat. Steamed or fried yuca is often an accompaniment. Other items can be grilled, especially plantains or even ripe bananas that are cooked until the skins blacken and the interiors are succulent. Grilled fish is a standard in coastal areas, especially on the Caribbean side where people use a spicy hot sauce as a condiment.

Taco vendors sell all kinds of these tortilla-based foods. Toasted on a flat griddle, large tortillas are filled with grilled and fried meats, shredded cabbage, and dosed with vinegar-based or spicy sauces. *Bollos*, a kind of boiled tamale, is a Panamanian specialty, though steamed tamales are almost always served at festivals.

The best places to get street food are at the many small open-fronted eateries called *fondas*. For urban working people, these are the usual lunch places. Most of the foods are fried, but soups and grilled meats are common. *Gallo pinto* (rice and beans), covered with onions and culantro (a strongly flavored kind of cilantro), is the standard Panamanian dish.

A chicken soup called *sancocho* also flavored with onion and *culantro* is very popular, as are stews (one made with pork tails). Hojaldres, or puffy fried breads, are much enjoyed. Most dishes are accompanied by thinly sliced deep-fried plantains. These are also sold by vendors who carry small bags of them on trays.

Meat- or vegetable-filled empanadas are widely consumed. One type, called *carimañola*, is made from mashed yuca, which is then filled with cooked meats and fried. As one might expect, much Panamanian street food is quite greasy, but delicious.

Fresh fruits are everywhere on Panama's city and town streets. Pineapples, cut melons, mango, passion fruit, papayas, and many more make for a refreshing snack in a hot climate. Panamanians usually eat them with vinegar and salt, very much in the old Spanish style. Naturally, drinks are ubiquitous. Panamanian drink a good deal of *chicha*, fresh fruit drinks made from varieties of fruits, and sometimes rice. One variation, *chicheme*, is made from corn dough mixed with sugar and cinnamon. Fresh coconut milk is widely available, made from coconuts cut on the spot by vendors. All the international soft drink companies sell beverages in Panama either from shops, on the street, or in the growing number of international fast-food chains that are well established in Panama City, the capital, and other cities.

BRUCE KRAIG

GUYANA

G UYANA IS SITUATED on the northern coast of South America and is the only English-speaking country in that continent. It shares much common history and culture with the Caribbean Islands and is considered part of the Caribbean from a cultural point of view. The country was first charted in 1499 by Spanish explorers and was originally known by the name that the native Indians used: Guiana, which means "land of many waters." Guiana was passed back and forth among several European powers and was a bone of contention between the Dutch and British for several centuries. By the early 19th century, the British had gained a firm foothold and were to remain there until 1966 when the country went from being a British colony to an independent country and the name changed from British Guiana to Guyana. It was declared a Republic in 1970.

Guyana was valuable to the Europeans as a producer of sugar. Native Indian tribes such as the Arawaks kept to themselves and were not part of the labor force. African slaves kept the sugar industry running, and after the abolition of slavery in 1837, laborers were brought from China and India. Indians were accustomed to agricultural work in hot conditions and were soon arriving in increasingly large numbers. Most of them stayed on after their contracts expired and now make up almost half of the country's population, closely followed by those of African descent. Native Indians (known as Amerindians), descendants of the Chinese and Portuguese, as well as a small number of other Europeans form the rest of the population. Street food shows many of these varied influences.

Street food is sold at the side of busy roads, in and near ferry and bus terminals or taxi stands, at markets, and outside schools. Although guidelines are issued with regard to public safety and hygiene, they are difficult to enforce and small stalls can appear overnight. They are usually stocked with a few home-style items cooked in a domestic kitchen.

MAJOR STREET FOODS

Bakery Items

Salara, a yeast bread with a spiral of sweet red coconut filling, is sold in slices, and plain sweet buns are also popular. Pastries show British and Asian influences. The three most popular are pine tarts (triangles of shortcrust pastry with a filling of pineapple jam); cheese rolls (a thin round of shortcrust pastry with a spicy cheese filling rolled into a cylinder before being baked); and Chinese cakes, made from a Chinese-style flaky pastry that is filled with sweetened black-eyed pea puree. Some vendors buy tennis rolls (sweet round yeast buns flavored with lemon oil) from bakeries and resell them, split and buttered and filled with cheese.

Sweets

Coconut drops (a kind of coconut ice also known as sugar cakes) are widely sold. They are made from finely grated fresh coconut cooked in syrup and shaped into small cakes. When the coconut is cut into tiny chips instead of being grated, they are often known as chip-chip. Tamarind balls are sweet, sour, and spicy all at once. Tamarind pulp is mixed with sugar, garlic, and chilies and shaped into tiny balls. Cassava pone is a dense, chewy cake made from manioc; a touch of black pepper is often added.

Savory Snacks

Plantain chips (crisply fried, salted green banana slivers) are to Guyanese what potato chips are to Americans. Fried salted peanuts are sold in small packets. Tiny savory dough sticks called "salt-seo" are made primarily with flour and a little chickpea or split pea flour. They are the economical local take on the snack sticks known as *sev* in India.

Chickpeas are a popular item and are prepared in two ways. One way (fried channa) is to soak the dried peas overnight, then rub off the skins and split the peas before frying them, and seasoning them well with salt and chilies. In the second method (boiled channa), the soaked peas are boiled until tender, then fried with sliced onion, cumin, and other spices. The latter is served with hot pepper sauce or sour green mango sauce known locally as "sour."

Bara and *phulourie* are both snacks of Indian origin, made from ground split peas, seasoned with chilies, garlic, and green herbs, and then deep-fried. *Bara* is flatter and palm-sized with a heavier texture, while *phulourie* is a soft walnut-sized puff. They are also served with sour mango sauce or spicy green mango chutney. Potato balls are deep-fried balls made from highly seasoned mashed potato.

Salt-fish cakes are an even more delicious treat. They are similar to potato balls, with the addition of small flakes of rehydrated salted cod to produce a pronounced flavor. Black pudding is made the local way: cooked rice is seasoned with herbs and spices before the blood is added, and the mass is stuffed into well-cleaned intestines to be boiled. It is served in thick slices together with a relish made from bilimbi, a tart fruit that looks like a tiny cucumber. Schoolchildren are very fond of sliced green or half-ripe mangoes that are seasoned with salt, vinegar, and chilies.

Beverages and Coolers

Sugarcane is pressed through a small machine with rollers to extract the refreshing sweet juice. *Mauby* is a drink with a slightly bitter undertone made from the bark of a kind of buckthorn, boiled with sugar and various spices. Coconut water drunk straight from an immature green coconut is a great thirst quencher. After the water has been drunk, the vendor splits open the shell so that one can scoop out the flesh, which is so young that it is transparently white and gelatinous. Snow cones start off solid and quickly turn into liquid in the tropical heat. They are made by producing finely shaved ice by hand with metal shavers or by using a special machine. It is packed into a paper cup and topped with the buyer's choice of sweet fruity flavored syrups and/or sweetened condensed milk. It is eaten like an ice-cream cone and then drunk from the cup as it melts.

GAITRI PAGRACH-CHANDRA

SURINAME

THE REPUBLIC OF SURINAME is the smallest independent country on the South American continent. Historically and culturally, Suriname is part of the greater Caribbean Basin. On the north the country borders the Atlantic Ocean, on the east French Guyana, on the west Guyana, and Brazil to the south. In the 17th century, the first Europeans settled in the area. After a short period of British rule (ca. 1651–1667) from 1667 until 1975, Suriname was a Dutch colony, a plantation economy, with a strong focus on growing such cash crops as sugarcane, cacao, and coffee. During this period of almost 300 years, the country became a melting pot of cultures and religions that include indigenous peoples, Brazilians, Creoles (West Africans), Javanese, Dutch, Lebanese, Portuguese, Germans, Chinese, Indian Hindustanis, Jews, and French Huguenots. Suriname's official language is Dutch, but Sranan Tongo, a Creole language, is the lingua franca and commonly spoken. The vast majority of Suriname's population of around 520,000 people live on the coast in the capital city of Paramaribo. Following independence in 1975, a third of the population migrated to the Netherlands, where at present approximately 350,000 Surinamese are living. Historically, the contacts between Suriname and the Netherlands were always close, therefore, and at present, the community consists of populations (Surinamese people) living on both sides of the Atlantic Ocean.

Surinamese cuisine is a melting pot. Ingredients, dishes, cooking techniques, and eating habits reflect the many different ethnic and religious groups of the population. The majority is of Asian Indian descent, Creoles or Afro-Surinamese, Javanese, or Maroons (descendants of runaway slaves who intermarried with indigenous peoples). Other minorities include Jews, Chinese, Lebanese, Syrians, French, Dutch, and Germans.

Food, food preparation, and selling play a very important role in the daily and social life of the Surinamese community. A typical Surinamese meal consists of a variety of dishes, all of different ethnic origin. Overall, it is popular belief and custom that dishes of different ethnic origins are best prepared by individuals of that ethnicity. Traditionally, cooking is learned at home, and it is still common to measure the skills of women through the quality of her cooking. Thus most Surinamese women have their own secret recipes and ingredients.

Although traditionally cooking and entertaining is done at home, Surinamese are used to buying takeaway foods and to snack in public. Cakes, fruits, sweet and savory snacks, bread rolls, sausages ice, and drinks—almost everything edible—are available as street foods. Stalls and vending to make a livelihood is a common phenomenon, and many women make a living by street, selling all kinds of homemade foods. At the Central Market on Paramaribo's Waterfront, numerous stalls and vendors sell street and snack food items, reflecting their rich and dynamic multicultural society. In addition, Surinamese love to party. No festivity or festival is complete without plenty to eat and drink. The *bigi jari* (a birthday ending in zero) is a big event, and Keti Koti, the abolition of slavery in 1863, is a national celebration with a display of the great variety of street foods in the Surinamese community on both sides of the Atlantic Ocean.

Within the Surinamese community, street selling is considered an art. The stalls are often decorated with the national flag and lively Surinamese music from speakers. Male vendors and Creole women vendors, dressed in a colorful Koto (the traditional dress with a headpiece), lure pedestrians by promoting their merchandise in all sorts of verbal fashions, varying from shouting slogans to singing about the good quality of the food on sale to offering samples to passersby.

MAJOR STREET FOODS

Telo

One of the major street-food items is *telo*, strips of (precooked fresh or frozen) indigenous cassava that are rubbed with garlic and deep-fried in vegetable oil. The crispy (French fries–style) cassava strips are served sprinkled with salt and most often accompanied by *bakkeljauw*. This is dried and salted cod fish, desalted in water, braised in oil, together with small pieces of onion, tomatoes, garlic, and chilies, until it is tender and falls apart. *Bakkeljauw* is also popular on *puntjes*, white bread rolls.

Sandwiches

Filled bread rolls are popular. The French baguette-style Surinamese bread roll is filled with almost everything, including potatoes, noodles, minced meat, steak, chicken, shrimps, tofu, and tempeh (Indonesian pressed soy cake). Even the very typical *kousenband*, a yard-long (green) bean, is put in the bread roll, which is always eaten accompanied by *zuurgoed* (pickles). Very often, a baguette is filled with leftovers from hot meals.

Broodje pom is the national festive dish and one of the most popular bread rolls. *Pom* is a Jewish/Creole oven dish with three central ingredients: chicken, citrus juice, and *pomtajer* (also known as *malanga* in many parts of the Caribbean). It became a Surinamese tradition, at celebrations and festive occasions, to serve both *pom* and *pastei*, a savory chicken pie that is available in many sizes and always contains cooked peas and carrots.

Hindustani Foods

Toward the end of the 19th century, Indian (Hindustani) contract workers arrived in Suriname. Lacking traditional atta flour, they started to use wheat flour (and *roti soda*—sodium bicarbonate) to produce roti, their daily bread. In Suriname, the result is a soft flat wheat bread, often stuffed with potatoes or yellow split peas and closely related to the Indian *paratha*. In Suriname, roti is one of the best-known street foods. Other popular Indian street foods include the *bara*, a fritter made with self-raising wheat flour, ground *urdi* (black split peas), taro leaves, and cumin, which are eaten with a chutney; *phulouri*, small deep-fried balls prepared with boiled yellow split peas, garlic, and cumin; and all sorts of samosas, savory pastries with a vegetarian potato and curry masala fillings.

Condiments

Surinamese love condiments, and most foods are accompanied by pickles and hot pepper sauces of multiple origins. The popular condiment *gekruide ketjap* (spiced soy sauce) can be traced back to the Javanese migrants bringing with them Indonesian *ketjap* (soy sauce). Deep-fried spring rolls, *kroepoek* (Javanese prawn crackers), and *lemper*, sticky rice filled with braised chicken wrapped in banana leaves, are common. Satays are marinated meats cooked on skewers over an open flame with a peanut butter sauce called *satésaus* or *saté met pinda*. The same sauce also accompanies *baka bana*, slices of plantain that are dipped in a batter and deep-fried. Also well known is *spekkoek* (literally "bacon cake"), which is an Indonesian sweet cake with thin layers in different colors.

GINGER

Chinese migrants introduced the use of ginger and the stir-frying technique, which over the years resulted in numerous typical Surinamese street foods varying from stir-fried noodles, Chinese cabbages, smoked pork, beef, and duck.

Plantain chips (or crisps) and potato chips are common. The indigenous people's contribution to the Surinamese street-food repertoire is flat cassava bread (from shredded and dried cassava) and *casripo* (or *casiri*), a thick boiled cassava juice or syrup that has multiple uses. It's often served as a condiment or used as a cooking liquid.

Sausages

Sausage sellers are a common phenomenon along Paramaribo's waterfront, on street corners, and in the Dutch Surinamese communities. Several Creole Surinamese families are famous for selling the spiced sausages *vleesworst* (a beef sausage with a coarse structure) and *bloedworst* (a dark, fine-structured beef blood sausage). The long sausages, in a bovine intestinal casing, are boiled in a spiced broth, cut into pieces, and served in a plastic tray, the pieces eaten warm (pushed out of the casing) with a relish. Most often, the sellers offer boiled *fladder* (beef tripe) and *beré*, the boiled large intestine of a cow, and chicken-blood sausages.

Surinamese Pickles

Almost every Surinamese woman has her own recipes for *zuurgoed*, pickles and relishes that accompany almost every meal. Apart from being eaten with hot foods and bread rolls, *zuurgoed* is consumed as a snack. The pickling of fruits and vegetables is a widespread domestic activity and a Surinamese tradition. They are made with cucumbers, peppers, red onions, and bilimbi (the small, round, light-green fruit of the bilimbi tree), which are pickled in vinegar with herbs and spices. These pickles are widely on sale in stalls run by pickle sellers.

Cakes

Surinamese women are known to raise their children alone. During the slavery period (1667–1873), families were torn apart by the Dutch. Ever since, it is very common for Afro-Surinamese women to raise their children alone and sell cakes and food to support their families. The cake sellers carry plates of cakes on their heads and often sell *bojo* (flourless shredded cassava coconut cake), *keksi* (yellow cake), *fiadu* (cinnamon roll or Danish), or *bolo pretu*, a "black cake" moistened with rum or amaretto that is a distant cousin of Britain's moist Christmas or plum pudding. Popular cookies are *maizenakoekjes* (corn flour cookies) and *pindakoekjes* (peanut cookies). Both are commonly sold in small, transparent, and round plastic containers.

Beverages and *Schaafijs*

Many Surinamese love color. Red, yellow, blue, and green liquid colorings are frequently used for the decoration of pastry and the flavoring of soft drinks. Sugar syrups made from almonds, roses, tamarind, ginger, and tropical fruits such as passion fruit, pineapple, and coconut are highly popular. Selling *schaafijs* (shaved ice) is a Surinamese specialty, and cart vendors sell the treat flavored with sugar syrups. A fresh green coconut, with a straw, is a popular thirst quencher. The most popular Surinamese-Indonesian drink, *dawat,* is prepared from palm sugar and coconut milk, most often with rose syrup added, giving the cold drink a pink color. *Skrati*, made from bars of pure cacao beans, is diluted with water and flavored with sugar and condensed milk. *Zuurwater* is the Surinamese equivalent of American lemonade. *Gemberbier* (ginger beer) is a popular nonalcoholic drink made from fresh grated ginger, sugar, clove, lemon acid, and water. Local brands sell bottled ginger beer, regular (malt) beer known as *parbo bier,* and colored soft drinks.

KARIN VANEKER

VENEZUELA

VENEZUELA is a country located on the northeastern shoulder of the South American continent. It is bordered by Guyana and Brazil to the south and Colombia on the west. Venezuela's long coastline along the Caribbean Sea gives its main population centers a decidedly Caribbean character. Venezuela has a diverse geography and climate. The northern extension of the Andes Mountains covers much of the southeastern part of the country, while other mountains border the northwest. In between are broad grasslands called *llano* and low areas that are hot, humid, and tropical. Major rivers run through the country, the best known being the huge Oronoco, which runs just under the southern mountains. Venezuela has one of the world's most varied ecosystems that includes large tropical forests, mountain forests, rivers, and coasts. It has species of plants and animals that are found nowhere else and is a destination for ecotourism. Foodstuffs, as well, come from each of the regions—grazing animals from the high plains, fish from rivers and coasts, and plenty of tropical fruits and vegetables. All of them go into street food.

The name "Venezuela" is thought to mean "Little Venice" from the Italian city of the same name. Spaniards conquered Venezuela in the 16th century and mixed with the indigenous peoples. Today about half the population is mestizo, or mixed, along with a sizable number of Europeans, people of African descent, and a small number of native people (who live mainly in the Amazon jungle area of the country). Spanish is the country's official language, but English is widely spoken because of long-standing contacts with English-speaking Caribbean nations. Venezuela's food mirrors this mixture of peoples and cultures and the many international contacts.

MAJOR STREET FOODS

Arepas

Arepas reveal both the history of Venezuela's food and its regional character, although they are also popular in neighboring Colombia and other Central and South American countries. The basic arepa is a thick cake made of finely ground cornmeal that is made into a dough, toasted on a griddle, split horizontally, and filled with various ingredients. It is often griddled in butter and, to be done properly, should be placed in a hot oven to give it an outer crust. Another version, made in the upland areas of the country, is made with wheat flour. There are many kinds of arepas. The most popular are *arepa de queso* (filled with various cheeses, especially a soft white cheese), *arepa mechada* (filled with cooked shredded chicken or beef), *arepa pelua* (with shredded beef and cheddar cheese), *arepa de chicharrón* (with crispy fried pork skin), *arepa de perico* (eggs scrambled with finely chopped vegetables and white cheese), *arepa de dominó* (with black beans and cheese), *arepa con molida* (with spiced ground beef), *arepa de coco* (with coconut), and even *arepa dulce*, which are sweet. Venezuelans eat other varieties, some with fish, others with yuca (manioc or cassava) or vegetables. Arepas are quite delicious and have made their way to North America where they are served in Venezuelan restaurants and a growing number of urban food trucks.

Pepito

The *pepito* is a sandwich that is one of Venezuela's most popular street foods. It is made with a soft roll, similar to a baguette, split down the center, and then filled with any of a variety of ingredients. The most popular are grilled chicken dipped in sauce, beef in a sauce, fried eggs, cheese, or mixtures of these ingredients. The *pepito* is heavily garnished with shredded lettuce, sliced or chopped tomatoes, avocado slices, *guasacaca* (similar to guacamole), ketchup, tomato-based sauces, mayonnaise, and lots of other sauces. Customers typically tell the vendor what they want from the long list of possible fillings.

THE NATIONAL DISH

The Venezuelan national dish is called *pabellón criollo*. Not only is it good to eat, but it also illustrates the history of the Venezuelan people. The base is beef boiled in water with onion. Cattle were not native to the Americas but were brought by Spanish settlers, as were the onions we use today. Bell peppers, tomatoes, plantains, black beans, and rice also compose the final dish. Peppers are native to the Americas, but sweet bell peppers were not developed on that side of the Atlantic. Rather, hot peppers were taken to Spain and bred by monks into the sweet varieties we now know and were then returned to the Americas. Tomatoes come from South America as do almost all the beans we eat today. Plantains originated in South India. Rice came from Southeast Asia, was imported to the Mediterranean region, including Spain, in Roman times, and eventually made its way to Venezuela and elsewhere. The word *criollo* means someone of European descent born in the Americas. This classic dish is exactly that.

Mandocas

Similar to doughnuts, these are fried cornmeal dough rings. They are popular for breakfast and snacks. Though they are made at home, the thick fried rings are also sold by street vendors. The most famous *mandoca* is prepared with plantains, but the original version appears to have been a soft cheese variety. Typically, a plantain is cooked and mashed together with finely ground cornmeal and a local molasses called *papelón*. Formed into rings, it is deep-fried and served warm often with fresh cheese or butter.

Patacones

Patacones are fried plantain chips universally known in other parts of Latin America as *tostones*. Ripe plantains are sliced, dried, and then fried in hot oil. On the street, they are fried once, but in restaurants and by commercial food processors, they can be fried twice in the manner of French-fried potatoes. *Patacones* can be served as accompaniments to other dishes, but usually are just salted and served in small bags for snacks. Venezuelans love baseball, and there is hardly a ball game at which spectators do not happily munch on *patacones*.

OTHER STREET FOODS

Hot Dogs

Imported from North America, hot dogs are now sold on the streets of many Venezuelan cities. They are usually made of pork, steamed, placed on steamed buns and then loaded with all kinds of toppings to make almost a full meal on a bun. Toppings can be chopped potatoes, shredded cabbage, mustard, or a pink sauce made from mixing ketchup and mayonnaise, and often the ensemble is topped with crisply fried potatoes.

Empanadas

Fried triangular pastries similar to those found throughout Latin America, empanadas have long been sold as street food in Venezuela. They can be made from wheat flour or corn flour and filled with everything from cheese to shredded meats and vegetables. Vendors will often have spicy sauces on their carts and stands because Venezuelans love their street foods heavily sauced.

Shawarma

Middle Eastern immigrants, mainly Lebanese, brought skewered meats to Latin America in the 20th century. Today, vendors cook skewered beef or chicken chunks threaded with onions, green peppers, and tomatoes on open grills.

Fruit

Due to its climate and geography, Venezuela produces a huge variety of fruits that are often sold fresh on the streets. Mango, papaya, sweet bananas, coconut melons, pineapple, and guava are but some of them. They can be cut up and eaten plain, but a squirt of lemon juice is also a favorite way to eat them.

Drinks

In a warm climate, refreshing drinks are always ready at stands and small open stalls. Fresh fruit juices are always popular as are *batidos*, fruit juice thickened in a blender, and *merengada*, or milk shakes. Sugarcane juice, or *papelón*, and coconut milk are widely consumed.

BRUCE KRAIG

NORTHERN AMERICA

CANADA

A LTHOUGH IT IS THE WORLD'S SECOND LARGEST COUNTRY in area after Russia, Canada is also one of the least densely populated with only 35 million people. The original settlers came from the British Isles and France, but since the 1960s, the government has pursued an active immigration policy with the result that Canada is one of the most ethnically diverse countries in the world. In the 21st century, the main immigrant groups are South Asians, Chinese, Caribbeans, and Filipinos. The largest concentrations of immigrants are in Toronto and Vancouver, where nearly half of the residents are born outside of Canada.

Since many immigrants come from countries with vibrant street-food cultures, Canadian cities might be expected to be beehives of street-food activity. But until very recently, this was not the case. Stringent local and provincial regulations have long prevented or restricted the selling of food on the streets.

TORONTO

The largest city in Canada and the fourth most populous city in North America, the Greater Toronto area has an ethnically diverse population of around 6 million people. The largest ethnic groups are South Asians (12% of the population), Chinese (11.4%), black (8.4%), Filipino (4.1%), and Latin Americans (2.6%). This diversity is reflected in the large number of restaurants, food courts, and malls featuring their cuisine but not to the same extent in Toronto's street food. Until relatively recently, the only street foods that could be legally sold from carts were hot dogs and sausages served in buns.

In 2011 and 2012, a number of gourmet food trucks appeared on the scene. However, the regulations put in place that determined where they can vend and what they can serve were rigorous and complex and driven in part by opposition from restaurant owners. Today, trucks can operate on private property with the permission of the owner. To operate on public roads requires a permit that costs around $5,000 a year and requires them to stay at least 30 meters from brick-and-mortar restaurants. In 2014 the city council eased the regulations somewhat and more changes are being considered.

However, so many of Toronto's ethnic eateries feature street food items on their menus that street food lovers can easily find their favorite kathi rolls, pho, crêpes, *döner kebab*, laksa, bhelpuri, many kinds of dumplings, tortillas, empanadas, rotis, doubles, and much more.

Hot Dogs

Most of the hot dogs sold by Toronto vendors are all beef, many of them made by Champs or Shopsy's, a company founded in 1922 to feed garment workers. The large wieners (usually five or six to the pound) are griddled until brown, placed on a yellow bun, and topped with condiments that sit on a rack at the side of the hot dog cart. They include mustard, ketchup, corn relish, sliced mushrooms, bacon bits, olives, and sometimes sriracha sauce.

VANCOUVER

Vancouver is a success story when it comes to street food, with more than 100 carts and trucks now in operation. Vancouver's only legal street foods used to be chestnuts, hot dogs, and popcorn, but in 2009, things changed in response to a growing interest in street food, motivated in part by the coming Winter Olympics in February 2010 and the expected influx of tourists. A panel of food professionals, members of the public, and city council members identified suitable sites for food carts and invited proposals that were then peer reviewed. They were judged not only on taste but also on their healthfulness, making Vancouver perhaps the first city in the world to impose healthy food regulations for vendors.

In a pilot program in 2010, the city held a lottery for 17 licenses, which drew some 800 entries from about 400 vendors. The program continued to expand, and regulations were put in place in 2013. Trucks can not be closer than 100 meters from city parks, except downtown, and they must be at least 25 meters away from an open restaurant (except with the owner's permission). By mid 2016, there were 103 stationary food carts, most of them concentrated in a five-square block area of downtown. The vendors range from mobile handcarts to converted ice-cream vans and full-fledged trucks. The city also hosts an annual Street Food Showdown at its YVR Food Fest.

The food served at these carts and trucks reflects Vancouver's diversity: Mexican, Korean, Vietnamese, Ukrainian, Greek, Middle Eastern, Chinese, Indian, Salvadoran, Thai, and more. The most famous among them are JAPADOG, which serves fusion hot dogs with Japanese ingredients; Soho Road Naan Kebab; and Vij's Railway Express, where one of Canada's leading chefs serves such Indian fusion dishes as blueberry lassi, coconut ginger green beans, and halibut cheek curry.

MONTREAL

Although it is the largest city in French-speaking Canada and famous for its sophisticated restaurants, Jewish delis, and—thanks to more recent immigration—restaurants serving North African food, Montreal has had no street food since 1947 when its mayor banned them outright (along with chicken coops and newspaper boxes) because he considered the carts ugly. The only exception has been hot dogs.

The ban was finally lifted in 2011 but with a lot of regulations. As of this writing, only owners of existing retaurants can own a food truck. The Association des Restaurateurs de Rue du Québec (ARRQ) has the final say on what types of foods can be sold by local food trucks and auditions candidates for membership in their association. Several licenses are required. As of mid 2016 there were over 50 food trucks operating in Montreal at 16 designated locations. They offer a variety of dishes ranging from grilled cheeses, pulled pork, and bacon to mobile haute cuisine such as gras poutine and lobster truffle cappuccino by well known chefs.

OTHER CITIES

In 2011, the city of Calgary launched a pilot street-food program that was so successful the city streamlined the process of licensing food trucks and created a website announcing their locations. Today there are 40 food trucks serving such dishes as gelato, smoked brisket sandwiches, pad thai, pho, pierogi poutine (a Polish-Canadian hybrid), naan, and tacos. However, the city subsequently tightened regulations, banning trucks in any business revitalization district that asks and forbidding more than one truck from operating on the same street.

Ottawa, Canada's capital, has taken a cautious approach. At one point, there were 100 spots for vendors in downtown Ottawa, but in the mid-1990s, the city began refusing to issue new licenses and the number declined to 44. In 2012, the city council approved the New Street Food Vending Program to encourage new, convenient, and culturally diverse fare on city streets. There was also a push to limit the food served to healthy items. As of this writing, there are around 60 street-food vendors.

COLLEEN TAYLOR SEN

MEXICO

EXICO HAS A GREAT STREET-FOOD TRADITION that has influenced the whole world's food. Public squares in the mornings and evenings are filled with food carts, stands, and strolling vendors with trays and baskets. Anywhere a traveler goes, in cities and towns, in markets and festivals, the person is bound to find these colorful scenes with interesting and delicious foods.

Mexico is a diverse nation, whose geography, topography, climates, and peoples and local cultures vary greatly. Naturally, these elements make for varieties of food traditions. For instance, dishes made along the tropical coastlines will not be the same as those in the mountainous interiors. There are, however, many similarities among these traditions so that a distinctive Mexican cuisine exists. Tacos are the best example of the most famous national street-food dish and enchiladas are found in almost every Mexican restaurant.

Called either Mesoamerica or North America, Mexico's territory runs a thousand miles from its northern border with the United States south to Guatemala and Belize and other Central American countries beyond. The northern regions tend to have a drier climate with large desert areas, while further south, the climate is tropical and has jungles. Between these climatic extremes, there are diverse landforms and climatic zones. Each has a different climate depending on latitude and altitude. Large parts of Mexico are covered by mountains. Between them lie fertile plains and basins, some cut by rivers. The best known is the southern altiplano, or high plains, which includes the capital, Mexico City. Temperatures in the higher mountains of the north and center are temperate, as are high plains through much of the year. Mexico also has long flat coastlines: the Gulf of Mexico and Caribbean Sea on the east and the Pacific Ocean on the west. Many of these coasts are warm year-round, hot and humid in many places, and have become vacation resorts since the 1950s. Cancun in the Yucatan, Acapulco and Puerto Vallarta on the Pacific coast are among the most famous and popular for North Americans.

For the pre-Hispanic peoples of Mexico, the most famous being Mexica (or Aztecs) and Mayans, corn was the most important edible seed. Pre-Hispanic peoples had many different kinds of corn, ranging from sweet to hard. Sweet corn could be boiled up and served on the cob flavored with chile powder. Hard corn was usually boiled with calcium limestone to release the full nutritive value of the grain, then mashed into a dough to be used in many ways. Everyone ate plenty of tortillas and Mexicans still do—it is the staple of their diets. Made into round disks and baked on a griddle, tortillas can be filled with anything: when folded over they are called tacos. The dough can be made into other shapes such as fatter gorditas, or chalupas, flat shapes with raised edges. Dough can also be filled, wrapped in corn leaves, and steamed into tamales. Tamales remain as one of the most popular handheld foods especially at religious and other festive times.

Aztecs ate cooked beans and squash, often in the form of stews, as well as some meat stews on special occasions. The only domesticated animals at the time were turkeys (the ancestors of all today's domesticated turkeys), a kind of duck, dogs, and the cochineal, an insect used for coloring. All other animal proteins, such as deer, rabbits, rodents, fowl, and grasshoppers (called *chapulines*), were hunted in the wild. Many would later be replaced by new animals.

In 1519, a small force of Spaniards led by Hernan Cortez landed on Mexico's east coast. Within two years, aided by native Mexican allies, the Spanish destroyed the Aztecs, took over their empire, and soon conquered the rest of the country. Not only did they install Spanish as the official language and Catholicism as the religion, but they brought many new foods, ones that today are integral to Mexican cuisine. Cows, pigs, chickens, sheep, goats, milk and cheese, wheat, barley, rye, citrus fruits, grapes, cilantro, olives, lettuces, oregano, and many spices were established in Mexico and Latin America. Modern Mexican cuisine is a fusion of native plants, animals, and cooking techniques and new ones brought from Europe and Asia.

The dishes considered as Mexican street food appear in several kinds of

---

INSECTS

Insects have always been a part of Mexican cuisine. Water beetles and their larvae, mosquito eggs, ant eggs, moth larvae from maguey plants, and grasshoppers were eaten in pre-Hispanic times and still are. Some are found in street food. In markets such as those in Oaxaca, heaping mounds of dried and marinated grasshoppers (called *chapulines*) are sold to eager eaters. They are toasted, put in tacos, and served with a spicy sauce. Not only are grasshoppers tasty, but they are healthier than other meats because they eat only wholesome grain and have very little fat. As many diners say, insects are all protein and, with grasshoppers, their spiky legs serve as built-in toothpicks.

---

places. One is on streets where it is sold from carts, trucks, and semipermanent stands. Some may be year-round, for instance, as food carts on public squares or in front of churches. Another kind is found in the many indoor markets, a permanent stand called *fonda*, where customers can get breakfast, quick snacks, and even full take-out meals. A third kind of food vending is done at weekly markets or flea markets called *tianguis*. Mexican street food has also migrated to restaurants both at home and abroad, mainly in the form of tacos.

Street food has always been served thought of as cheap food for the poorest people in Mexican society. This was true in the past, and is still to some degree now, but street food has also become popular among students and tourists. Guidebooks, newspapers, magazines, and blogs routinely talk about which eating places are good and what to buy there. In part, this appreciation comes from the fact that a large percentage of food sold on streets and markets is made at home. Women are the chief cooks and vendors in many, if not most of the street—fast-food venues. The food they make often comes from their own home recipes, so there is variety in preparations from stand to stand. Stews (*cocidos*) or meats and vegetables for tacos will come straight from home kitchens. The best cooks are always popular among a broad cross section of the population. Certainly tamales are homemade. In many places where there is space, *fondas* for instance, women vendors make tortillas on the spot from fresh corn dough. Other shapes such as gorditas and chalupas are almost always made by hand on site. Outdoor stands usually buy their tortillas and stack them up for use during the day.

COCHINEAL

One of Mexico's most valuable insects is used for coloring in fabrics and for food. The cochineal is a small insect that feeds on cactus plants. What makes it special is its coloring, a deep red called carmine. Cochineals have been domesticated and harvested for many centuries, especially in the state of Oaxaca. The females settle on a cactus leaf and cover themselves with a thin whitish-gray or silvery shell—they look like silvery specs on the green leaves. When mature, the shells are scraped off the leaf, killed in boiling water, and then dried. They are ground into a red paste. Cochineal is used in traditional rug weaving and fabric dying in Oaxaca, but its widest use is as a food coloring. Many processed food products use it, and though government regulations ensure that it is listed as an ingredient, most consumers do not know that they are eating insects.

Such conditions are ripe for pathogens and so are other prepared foods. Mexican authorities and tourist guides issue regular warnings about food-borne illnesses—they are fairly common. Mexicans have a jokey name for gastric distress brought on by eating tainted, or at least unfamiliar, food: *tourista*.

The basic ingredients of street food include cooked meats—pork, beef, chicken, lamb, or goat. These are usually cooked by grilling, by frying, or in stews. In the case of goat and lamb, it may be roasted. Common items are corn served either on the cob or cooked into stews; grilled onions, potatoes, cabbage, carrots, greens, jicama, sweet potatoes, zucchini, cactus leaves (thornless, cut into strips and marinated in vinegar), chayote, and both sweet and hot peppers, among many others. Such grains as amaranth, legumes—beans and lentils—and fruits like melons, apples, quince, berries of all kinds, citrus, pineapples, mangoes, papaya, guava, sapotes of several kinds, tomatoes (they are fruit), and tomatillos (a green fruit that looks like small tomatoes) are all widely used in Mexican dishes. Cheese is another common ingredient. These are often cheeses that melt, especially panela; Chihuahua, which comes from the state of that name; and Oaxaca, a braided cheese used in central and southern Mexico. Queso fresco is a fresh cow and goat milk mixture that is crumbled over many tortilla-based dishes.

Almost all foods are flavored with dried and fresh chilies. Chilies come in many varieties, each with its own flavor and level of spicy hotness. Each region of Mexico favors certain kinds of chilies. Generally, the further south one goes, the hotter the chilies. Jalapeños, named for a town in Veracruz, are used all over Mexico, as is the hotter *chile de árbol*, but in the Yucatan, the superhot habanero is often used in sauces. Dried chilies are highly flavorful and are the glory of Mexican cookery. Moles are rich sauces composed of dried chilies and many spices. The red, mildly spicy guajillo chile is widely used in central and northern Mexico, while in places like Guerrero, the small round cascabel is favored. Three chilies, the ancho, pasilla, and mulato are used to make the famous mole poblano, while in the state of Oaxaca, this classic black mole uses the chilhuacle negro. There are dozens and dozens of specific chilies used in Mexico, from state to state, town to town, and even home to home. The sauces in street foods can vary in just the same ways.

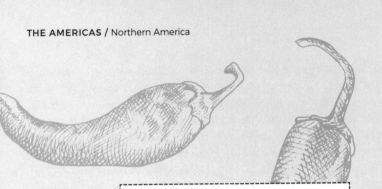

CHILIES

Everyone knows that chile peppers have reputations for being spicy hot. In fact, these fruits vary greatly in heat and flavors. The word "chile" comes from the indigenous Nahuatl word "chilli." They were critical in pre-Hispanic food, as they are today, because they are full of vitamins C and A. The name "pepper" comes from Europe, where it referred to black pepper that came from India. When hot chilies appeared, people likened their spiciness to black pepper and the name stuck. People domesticated chilies at least 5,000 years ago and changed their qualities. The sweet peppers, most popular today, were bred in Spain, after they were imported from Mexico.

MAJOR STREET FOODS

Tacos

Without question, tacos are the leading street and fast foods in Mexico. These ancient dishes were consumed by thousands in the markets of Aztec Tenochtitlan. The name is Spanish for a "wad" or "plug" and means a handful of wrapped food. Tacos are composed of thin flat cakes made from dough that are toasted on a griddle, topped with various fillings, then folded over and eaten out of hand. Tortillas vary by region. In most of the country, they are made of corn, but in the north, wheat flour is more common. Tortillas range in size from small white ones (*blancas*) to the most common four-inch, and up to six inches and more, such as those made from blue corn in markets in the states of Guerrero and Puebla. Most tortillas are soft and are often doubled to hold wet ingredients, though some are fried until crispy (tostadas). So popular are tacos that they are eaten at all times of the day and night.

People going to work or out to shop in the morning often pick up a taco or two for breakfast. They are often sold by women from baskets (*tacos de canasta*) along the streets. Because the tacos are premade and kept warm in cloth or paper, they are called "sweated" tacos (*tacos sudados*). Fillings are simpler than others and might include chopped meats, chopped potatoes, and some with cheese. Early morning tacos include some fillings that North Americans might find unappetizing. *Tacos de cabeza* come from a cow's head that is cooked over steam for a long time. Customers can choose from slices of cheek, tongue, lips, ears, brains, or eyes. Since the cow's head is leftover meat, it is cheap and thus popular with lower-income people and those with adventurous tastes. Barbacoa is another kind of taco often eaten in the morning, especially in market fondas where the more elaborate cooking can be done. Barbacoa is traditionally made by placing a goat or sheep in a pit with heated charcoal and then cooking it overnight. Alternately, pieces of meat are wrapped in banana leaves or the skin of maguey plant leaves with sauce and cooked. A visitor to almost any large market will be able to enjoy this treat.

In the evening hours, after work, and on weekends, taco stands appear in all sorts of public places. Standard preparations are the usual ground or shredded meats, cheese, and legumes or potatoes, and vegetables, each usually topped with chopped onions and cilantro. Stews are also prepared and dished up in doubled tortillas. There are a number of specialized ones that are native to different states, but are now popular throughout the country. One is the *taco de carne asada*, meaning grilled meats. Associated with the cattle-raising country of the north, the meat is usually thinly cut slices of beef—often skirt steak—that has been marinated and then quickly cooked on an open grill. In northern Mexico, grilled whole knob onions and perhaps a small guero (yellow) pepper accompany the taco. Salsas of varying hotness are also available for pouring on the taco. Carnitas are a specialty of Michoacán and are now served everywhere. They are chunks of pork that are deep-fried in large copper kettles for long periods until they are crispy on the outside but with tender interiors. The pork is then pulled apart, sauced, and served. All of the pig is used, and many people prefer the fatty and gristly bits because of the texture.

Michoacán is also home to a kind of chicken dish called *pollo placero*. A wide copper pan with a deep well in the middle is set over a heat source. Oil is placed in the well, chicken pieces set in it, and cooked until fried. When done, the chicken is placed on the pan's wide rim, cut up, and put into tacos. Similar pans are used in other parts of Mexico to fry chicken and other meats. One special taco cannot be made on streets but appears in fondas and restaurants. *Tacos al pastor*, meaning shepherd tacos, are very much like Middle Eastern shawarma: only these are made of pork. Layers of meat are built up on a spit, which is then cooked upright, while turning over an open fire. The cook slices off thin slivers and serves them in tacos. The dish was introduced by Lebanese immigrants who made the dish in their homeland with lamb. In the city of Puebla, these are called *tacos árabes* when they are served on a form of pita bread and liberally dosed with guajillo sauce. On the Pacific coast, fish tacos have become popular because freshly caught fish is widely available. Often fresh fish fillets are batter dipped and then served, though fish can be grilled whole, then placed in a taco with sauce. Fish tacos have spread to the United States.

Tamales

Tamales are one of Mexico's greatest food preparations and come in many regional varieties. They are not only eaten on the street, but also served at almost all special occasions, prepared days in advance of the event by women of the household. Tamales are usually called *tamales rojo* when they are filled with shredded

It is no exaggeration to say that hot tamales are a singular identifier of Mexican culture.

pork or beef in a red chile sauce. *Tamales verde* have similar meats but are mixed with a green slightly sourish and tangy tomatillo sauce. *Tamales dulce* are made with such dried fruits as raisins or berries, fillings, and are meant for desserts. Tamales vary by region. In Oaxaca and other southern states, larger tamales with red, green, and sweet fillings steamed in banana leaves are specialties. Fancier tamales have complex moles in them, even the famous huitlacoche, a black fungus, found on corn. It is no exaggeration to say that hot tamales are a singular identifier of Mexican culture.

Enchiladas, Gorditas, Sopes, and Tortas

North Americans are used to eating enchiladas in restaurants where they are covered in lots of sauce and melted cheese. The originals are street food, composed of larger tortillas rolled up and dipped in sauce between bites. The name, enchilada, means "to dip in a chile sauce." Some may have simple fillings such as green onions, cheese, chopped fried potatoes, strips of grilled green peppers, poblano peppers, or strips of meat as in the plaza style of Michoacán.

Varieties of open corn-dough-based foods are also abundant on the street-food scene. Sopes are small disks of dough baked on a comal (a flat metal griddle used in making tortillas) that are topped with different ingredients. The cheapest are bean preparations, sometimes with grated hard cheese on them, or cooked meats with chile sauce, among others. Chopped potatoes and cold salads such as finely diced tomatoes, garlic, onions, peppers, and cilantro are among other kinds of sopes. Tostadas, or crisply fried tortillas, can be considered a kind of sope.

Gorditas, or "little fat ones," are thicker cakes made from corn dough (or wheat dough in northern Mexico) that are fried, split along the side or down the middle, and filled. Ingredients are much the same as in tacos, but are usually wetter stews made from various meats. One variation is *chicharrónes*, fried pork skins that are further cooked in sauce to make them soft. Rajas, cheeses, potatoes, eggs, and more are very common. Like other snacks, gorditas are usually served with chile sauces or salsas.

Tortas are somewhat different in that they are really sandwiches. The base is usually a *bolillo*, a long, hard-crusted roll with pointed ends. This is cut in half and filled with cold ingredients that range from lunch meats—cold sliced tongue, for instance—to cheese, lettuce, tomatoes, or even tuna and chicken salads in modern versions. Tortas are very popular as lunch standards.

Guisados

Guisados, or stews, are considered by Mexicans to be the most flavorful and filling of all street foods. Usually they are made at home by women and sold by them or their families on the street and in fondas. The kinds of stews vary by region, the differences based mainly on what kinds of chilies are used in the preparation. Meats, such as pork, chicken, and beef (beef more in the north) and tripe (sliced animal stomach), are usually on the menu. On the coasts, fish, shrimp, and octopus are often used for stew. There are also vegetable stews, some with greens, which provide a healthier alternative. A large pot stands on a heat source to keep warm, and the vendor scoops out a portion with a big ladle onto a plate or into a tortilla. The *guisado* can be garnished with sour cream, chopped onions, chopped tomatoes, and cilantro. This hearty dish often serves as a dinner for people coming home from work.

Drinks

Drinks are almost as important as the food itself in Mexico. Vendors selling soft drinks are everywhere: some serve from baskets, and others from carts, trucks, and even trunks of cars. Major international brands like Coca-Cola and Pepsi Cola are universal, but their formulas differ from their products in North America. Sugar, rather than high fructose corn syrup, is preferred by Mexicans, so Mexican colas have a special flavor that others do not have. Jarritos ("Little Jars") is a popular brand of carbonated drinks made with more carbonation than American sodas and natural flavors that appeal to Mexican tastes. They include guava, hibiscus flowers, lime, tamarind, and mango, among others. The flavors in Jarritos replicate those in another popular drink called *licuados*. These are made with a milk base, placed in a blender with fresh fruits, and whipped into a thick drink. *Licuados* are sold on streets, in special open storefront juice bars, and plenty of other places. The most traditional drink of all is atole. It is very ancient, dating back to the earliest civilizations. It is composed of corn dough mixed with water, sugar, and other flavorings such as cinnamon, vanilla, and chocolate, which is then heated. Atole is very filling and thus it is a prime breakfast drink, often eaten with a roll of taco by people going to work each day. It is found on streets and in markets and is almost always homemade by the vendor.

ATOLE SPICES: VANILLA AND CINNAMON

OTHER STREET FOODS

Mexico has a large sugar production industry, so it is not surprising that people love sweets of all kinds. In any neighborhood and public venues, *raspados* vendors ply their trade. These are treats of shaved ice placed in cone-shaped cups and then covered in sweet fruit-flavored syrup. The flavors are the same as in soft drinks and *licuados*: only these ices are favored by children. *Paletas* are similar in that they are ices flavored with fruit formed into popsicles around a stick. Mexicans are also great candy makers. Among favorites sold on the streets are hard candies of all kinds along with a favorite, dulce de leche (milk sweets). There are several kinds of this candy, the best known being something like a soft caramel. *Jamoncillo* has several regional variations—in the north it is a hardened milk-and-sugar mixture, but in south central Mexico it is made of ground pumpkin seeds mixed with sugar. *Camotes* are candy made from sweet potatoes mixed with sugar, the best known of which is made in the city of Puebla. While candy is a big industry in Mexico, most are considered treats and are not eaten on a daily basis.

BRUCE KRAIG

UNITED STATES

THE UNITED STATES IS A HIGHLY VARIED LAND. Its geography ranges from low-lying eastern and southern coasts, mountain chains in its eastern (the Appalachians and Adirondacks) and western (the Rockies and Cascades) regions, huge fertile river valleys (the Mississippi and its many tributaries), vast deserts (the Southwest), immense plains (the Midwest), and the world's greatest inland seas (the Great Lakes). Climates range from tropical and subtropical in the south to cool and temperate in the north. United States' food comes from these lands, and local street foods, to some extent, still reflect their geographical origins.

Even more important to United States' street food is the history of the country's people. The United States is one of the world's greatest immigrant countries. Naturally, the people who came brought their own food preferences with them and adapted what they found in their new country. Native Americans themselves were immigrants, most of who came during the last Ice Age, as long ago as 20,000 years. Over time, the Native Americans came to raise corn, beans, and squash, hunted wild game, and gathered many wild plants for food. Though some had complex societies with settlements large enough to be called cities and states, they seem not to have had street food, as far as we know. But at gatherings where different peoples met, food was shared. The first Thanksgiving at Plymouth Plantation in 1621 was one of them. Stews, made of meats, or especially seasonal vegetables, would have been common. One of these, a mixture of corn and beans called "succotash" (*msíckquatash* in its original Narragansett form), passed down to later European settlers and is still served at community festivals around the country.

Starting about 1500 CE, peoples from Europe, Africa, and Asia poured into the continent later known as North America. Spaniards settled in Florida and the Southwest, while France sent people to modern Canada, the Great Lakes, and the whole Mississippi Valley. Most important of all were British immigrants, Africans (most of whom came unwillingly), and, beginning in the 19th century to the present, Irish, Germans, Europeans, and people from Latin America. Today, descendants of these groups number in the millions: about 50 million people of German descent, 17 million with Italian roots, 10 million of Polish origin, and more than 5 millions Jews mainly of east European origin. Mexican Americans constitute a large percentage of the American population, numbering at least 38 million. All these groups contributed a great many items to North American street food, and some are more regional than others, especially in the Southwest where Mexican influences are strong.

Immigrants brought most of the basic ingredients of United States' street food. Pigs, cattle (including dairy products made from cows' milk), chickens, sheep and goats, wheat, barley, rye, and many others are imports from the Old World. Native American corn, however, is one of the most important ingredients of most American food. From animal feed, to corn oil, cornmeal, corn starch, corn syrup, high-fructose corn syrup, and even popcorn and its variants, such as caramel corn, this seed (it is not a vegetable) is found everywhere. As one expert on food production puts it, even chicken nuggets are mostly corn with a little animal protein in them.

Native American corn is one of the most important ingredients of most American food.

The reason for corn's universality is that it is so useful in United States' industrialized food system. Centralized food processors, such as meat and poultry producers, milling companies, and confectioners make many of the products sold by vendors of all kinds. Few American food sellers make their own sausages, raise their own beef cattle, keep poultry for eggs, grow sugarcane or sugar beets, or make their own chocolate. Certainly, the food sold in vending machines all comes from factories. Nevertheless, most street food is prepared on the spot by sellers from as fresh ingredients as they can get. A taco from a vendor (as opposed to a large fast-food outlet) loaded with freshly cooked meats and vegetables and coated with home-made sauces is as close to home-made and locally sourced food as one can find.

American street food is most popular in its cities, at fairs, and at places of amusement and vacations, such as beachside boardwalks. It is stronger in ethnic communities, especially those that are home to more recent immigrants, such as those from Latin America and Southeast Asia. Most street vendors who operate carts tend to be new immigrants—in New York, roughly 70 percent are from South Asia—or people who are at the lower levels of the economic scale. Street food has always been an entryway into higher economic strata. Street vendors' organizations have sprung up in a number of cities, allied with social justice groups, asking for licenses to be granted and better treatment by local authorities. Other kinds of vendors such as operators of food booths or wagons at fairs tend to be part-time, seasonal sellers who have other jobs in the food industry or do it as a family enterprise. Food trucks have become popular in the early decades of the 21st century, and many are run by chefs who see them as good ways to make a living and to give themselves visibility, since the best trucks are highly publicized in the local and national media. Today, about 28 percent of Americans have seen or patronized food trucks.

Legal street-food venues (some, called "gypsy," are not), such as carts and trucks, are regulated by local governments. Vendors must obtain licenses and are regularly inspected by health authorities to ensure food safety. Overwhelmingly, street food in North America is safe from food-borne diseases, though much of it is not exactly nutritionally healthy fare. Americans consume street food during the whole day. Early morning coffee trucks are very popular in cities, while lunchtime is the busiest time for vendors. Since Americans like to snack, street food is eaten all through the day, depending on the food. Television programs and movies shot in New York, for instance, often show characters snacking on food from the many stands that dot the city's streets. Some trucks serve what amounts to dinner entrees, so people can pick up evening meals on the street. Though large quantities of street foods are eaten, unlike a number of African countries, it is not the main source of calories in the American diet.

Mobile food vending has always been part of the American street food scene. Motorized food trucks appeared at about the same time that automobiles became popular in the early 1900s. Some served only sandwiches, soft drinks, and coffee for breakfast and lunch: trucks that served factory workers acquired the joke name, "roach coaches." Others had portable kitchens to cook up simple dishes quickly such as tacos, hot dogs, hamburgers and egg dishes. Taco trucks began in Los Angeles in the 1970s to serve the city's large Mexican population and became so popular that there are now 3,000 to 4,000 taco trucks in and around the city. Many of the tacos use recipes from different regions of Mexico and so are the other dishes that the truck operators make: tamales, cemitas (sandwiches), and other griddled corn-dough based dishes such as sopes and huaraches. Taco trucks spread to cities across the country as Mexican food became one of the nation's most popular cuisines.

Upscale food trucks really took off in the 1990s when trained chefs found that they could operate trucks more cheaply than owning a fixed location restaurant. Chef Roy Choi's Kogi truck set the trend with fusion Korean barbecue tacos and Korean hot dogs. Others followed such as Los Angeles' Jogasaki Sushi Burrito and Komodo which serve southeast Asian-Mexican fusion dishes. Nammi Truck in Dallas, Texas, has Vietnamese fusion in its bánh mí, taco, and rice bowl while Roti Rolls in Charleston, South Carolina has Caribbean-Indian-southeast Asian mixture dishes and Cucina Zapata in Philadelphia creates Thai-Mexican dishes like Thai short rib tacos covered in veggies and topped with avocado.

New York, Philadelphia, Boston, and Portland, Oregon, are all famed for their food trucks, many of which feature ethnic cuisines. Greek gyros, Middle Eastern shawarma and falafel, Jamaican jerk, Indian street-food dishes, Thai, Vietnamese, Chinese, South American *pupusas*, artisanal sausages with international toppings and similarly dressed hamburgers are to be found in urban food trucks. So popular are food trucks that there is an annual contest called the Vendy Awards held in New York and Philadelphia to which the public is invited. The idea is to promote street food vendors and the prizes are highly coveted. There are currently about 20,000 in the United States which serve as examples of America's culinary melting pot.

The most popular street foods are those that are served in a wrapper made of wheat or corn flour. The wrapper may be made of leavened bread, usually white bread in the form of buns, or flatbreads, such as pita (which may be raised) or tortillas. Sandwiches, including hot dogs, hamburgers, submarines (or hoagies), meatball sandwiches, cheese, and many others have been staples of American street and fast food since the 19th century. Tacos and wraps (food wrapped in flatbread) and sweet crêpes are also common on the streets on stands, in trucks, and at fairs. Some prewrapped tacos or burritos are also available in vending machines. Stuffed dishes that can be reheated at a stand or cart are also popular. Small meat or vegetable turnovers such as empanadas, tamales, and knishes are among the best known, though some are regional specialties, such as Cornish pasties in the Upper Midwest and runzas in Nebraska. The rising popularity of Asian foods has brought dumplings and egg rolls of many kinds to trucks and a few carts.

Baked goods are common in street-food venues. Cinnamon buns, bagels, croissants, muffins, and scones often appear on carts and trucks that serve morning coffee and tea. Cupcake trucks, following the fad for these small cakes, can now be found in a number of cities. Waffles, and to a lesser extent pancakes, are almost always found in stands at fairs and in some street trucks. Savory baked pies, pizza mainly, are also mainstays, especially of the truck business.

Fried foods, from savory to sweet, are staples of fairs and some street-food vendors—deep frying is difficult to do on street carts, but often found in trucks. Fried potatoes and other vegetables, corn dogs, fried cheese curds, fried chicken, chicken wings, bacon, and tortilla chips (for nachos) are among many savories. Fried doughs such as funnel cakes, doughnuts, elephant ears, bunuelos, and churros are ubiquitous at fairs and in many stands. In recent years, fried food on sticks have become features of public dining, including fried candy bars, fried ice cream, bananas, and even beer and lemonade. None of these can be considered a healthy part of a diet; instead, they are snacks eaten for pleasure.

POPULAR BAKED GOODS AND FRIED FOODS

Sweets have always been elements of the street-food scene. Ice creams and other frozen products have been on the scene since the 19th century. Confections such as sweetened popcorn—today's caramel corn, saltwater taffy, fudge, toffee, cotton candy, and a host of commercially manufactured candies—have long been popular as public foods. Sweet beverages are found on almost every food cart, truck, and fair stand in the United States. Except for coffee, most sweetened drinks include sodas/pops, lemonade, sweet tea (mainly in the South), and fruit drinks. They are served usually with food, but often alone as refreshments for customers who are on the move.

MAJOR STREET FOODS

Sandwiches

Far and away, the most widely consumed types of food are those wrapped in bread. Sandwiches are made with wheat-flour breads. The earliest kinds were simply slices of bread filled with sliced meats or cheese and sometimes peanut butter when it became popular around 1900. The famous ham and cheese, BLT (bacon, lettuce, and tomato), tuna or chicken salad, and melted cheese are examples. They were served by lunch wagons who serviced factory and office workers in United States' cities. Now from breakfast and lunch trucks, these sandwiches are still sold to people who usually work in urban industrial areas across the United States. The submarine sandwich, called a hoagie in Philadelphia, is one such sandwich that was probably invented by Italian street vendors near industrial shipyards around 1900. It is a long crusty Italian-style roll, cut lengthwise down the center, and filled with sliced cold meats and cheeses, shredded lettuce, and drizzled olive oil that was common in Italian American communities. The "sub" has become the center fast-food chains, but remains a feature of lunch trucks and some food carts throughout the United States.

HOT DOGS

Of all sandwiches, hot dogs are the most popular and iconic street food. Hamburgers are more common, but are not usually served as street food. Hot dogs are sausages, specifically frankfurters (supposedly from Frankfurt, Germany) and wieners (originally from Vienna, Austria)—all the names are used interchangeably. Modern hot dogs are made in two basic forms, cased and skinless. Cased hot dogs are made in the traditional sausage maker's way, by stuffing very finely ground meat and other ingredients into a tube made from animal intestines or casings made from plant fibers. Natural casings give cooked hot dogs a crunchy snap texture that many fans of the dish prefer. Skinless sausages are meat stuffed into casing, cooked, and smoked, and then the casing is stripped off. By far, skinless hot dogs outsell natural casing ones because they are much cheaper to make and sell.

Hot dogs are a prime example of United States' ethnic food history. As the names say, they were introduced by German immigrants beginning in the 1850s and then taken up by makers and vendors of other ethnicities, namely, East

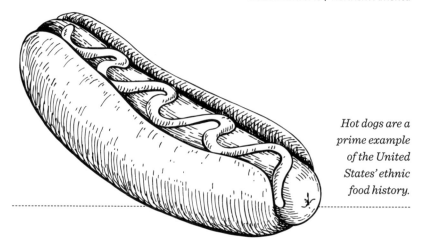

Hot dogs are a prime example of the United States' ethnic food history.

European Jews, Greeks, Italians, and later Latin Americans and South Asians such as Pakistanis and Bangladeshis. Hot dogs have been served as street food in American cities and at amusement areas, such as seaside boardwalks, since at least the 1860s, and have been associated with sports events, especially baseball, for more than 100 years. There is hardly a public event at which hot dog vendors do not appear.

The basic hot dog found on street stands or carts or served from roller grilling appliance is a heated sausage, mostly pork-based, placed on a slit bun, and topped with mustard and perhaps ketchup. New Orleans's Lucky Dogs is one, though other toppings appear. Sometimes a thick cheese food sauce or shredded cheese is added as a topping. But many hot dogs are heated and dressed in a number of regional styles in the United States and around the world as well. In some places such as New York City and Chicago, all-beef dogs are preferred, but elsewhere, sausages made of pork and beef are common. New York City has more hot dog street carts than any other American city. Most of the hot dogs are called "dirty water dogs" because they are heated and held in water just under the boiling point. The New York style is a small 1½- to 2-ounce sausage set in a heated bun and topped with yellow mustard, chopped raw onions, or chopped onions that are griddled and mixed with a light tomato sauce mixture. Sauerkraut might also be a condiment. Some hot dogs are griddled until browned on a hot metal sheet (griddled) and served with the same condiments.

In other parts of United States' East Coast and the South, other styles are favored. One of these is a hot dog covered in a meat sauce, usually called "chili." The chili is usually ground beef mixed with seasonings and a tomato-based liquid. Chopped onions and shredded cheese are also added to these kinds of hot dogs. Chili dogs are found from Rhode Island down to Florida, but in West Virginia, North Carolina, Georgia, and some other parts of the South, chili is accompanied by a coleslaw to make the famous "Slaw Dog." Coleslaw is shredded cabbage (and sometimes carrots) mixed with either a vinegar or mayonnaise dressing. The result is a messy, but filling dish.

In the Midwest, two basic styles are common, the Chicago-style hot dog and Coneys. Chicago dogs are all-beef sausages, water bathed, placed on a heated bun, and topped with mustard, bright green relish, chopped fresh onions, tomato slices, pickle spears, and small spicy hot "sport peppers," and never with ketchup. Coneys are associated with the Detroit, Michigan area, and are flat-griddled beef and pork sausages, set in buns and topped with mustard and a thick or thin meat sauce made with beef hearts. Both styles are served as take-out dishes, and no ballpark or amusement area is without them.

One hot dog style is a fusion of ingredients used in tacos and the American hot dog. In the American southwest, Arizona in particular, a new style of hot dogs appeared in the 1980s. The Sonoran Hot Dog is also known as the Mexican Hot Dog, or Tijuana Dog, and even "danger dog" in Los Angeles. When made "all the way" it is a griddled or grilled hot dog, wrapped in bacon—or covered in cooked bacon bits—then loaded with cooked pinto beans, chopped onions, chopped tomatoes, mayonnaise, crumbled or shredded cheese, Mexican red or green salsa, mustard, sometimes ketchup, and it can also have sliced radishes or cucumbers and a roasted Mexican pepper alongside it. An estimated 200 Sonoran Hot Dog carts and stands are in Tucson, Arizona, and more in Phoenix. Across the United States, many hot dog restaurants that serve different styles from around the country also serve some version of this Mexican American specialty.

BRATWURST

Bratwurst is a German word meaning "cooked." When Germans began migrating to the United States in large numbers beginning in the 1850s, they brought their favorite foods, especially sausages and beer. Bratwurst was one of them. Bratwurst is usually prepared from its fresh, raw state, but some versions are also smoked. Fresh bratwursts are almost always cooked on grills; for tailgating and in street festivals, open charcoal fires are used. In North America, especially Wisconsin, the sausages are either cooked directly or first simmered in water or beer—usually the latter—and then heated on the grill. Smoked brats are most often flat griddled or cooked quickly on a grill. When served, these kinds of bratwursts should be put on a special bratwurst bun that is larger, crustier, and chewier than a hot dog bun. Toppings are traditionally a brown mustard made in the style of the German city of Düsseldorf, and onions, with sauerkraut, an option depending on the region and state.

In Wisconsin, there is not a public event that does not have bratwurst stands, and many have sprung up around the Midwest. One of the most famous is in Bucyrus, Ohio, where an annual Bratwurst Fest has been held since 1967. In this area that has been heavily settled by Germans, at least a dozen vendors sell grilled brats, some on buns, others on rye bread, and all with mustard, onions, and optional sauerkraut and horseradish.

POLISH SAUSAGE

Polish sausage is an alternative to hot dogs in many places. Named for various sausages made in Eastern Europe, the Polish sausage is a pork and beef, or all-beef, coarse-grind sausage, thicker in dimension than a regular hot dog, heavily seasoned with garlic, and naturally cased. It is almost always grilled on an open fire or flat griddled. The sandwich is topped with mustard and freshly chopped onions. In Chicago, the home of Maxwell Street Polish, a third-pound sausage is striped with mustard and loaded with a thick layer of grilled and caramelized onions. Customers can add the other usual Chicago-style toppings, including hot sport peppers, but never ketchup. Maxwell Street Polish became very popular in the city, and many hot dog stands also serve it.

FUSION AND GOURMET SAUSAGES

Newer fusion styles of hot dogs have arisen in urban areas across the United States, many of them served from food trucks. Now popular Asian ingredients are staple toppings in these places. Asia Dog is a portable stand that started in Brooklyn, New York, and now appears at various festivals around the city. Their hot dogs have become popular for toppings that range from Korean to Thai. One is a barbecued pork belly with scallions and cucumber, another a Thai-style sauce made of mango, onion, peanuts, and fish sauce, among other ingredients. Korean toppings are used in several street trucks in Los Angeles, Seattle, and other cities.

Bulgogi and Galbi, marinated strips of grilled meats, and kimchi, spicy hot pick-led vegetables, are among the characteristic Korean preparations put on these hot dogs. So-called Japanese hot dogs originated in Vancouver, BC, Canada, and have migrated to the United States. Here Japanese teriyaki-grilled strips of meat in a sweet marinade, seaweed, savory pancakes, and spicy noodles are included in the toppings. All these versions show how flexible hot dogs can be as platforms for the integration of ethnic cultural tastes.

Wrapped Foods

Mexican food traditions have greatly influenced North American traditions, none more so than in wrapped foods. These are like sandwiches except that they have thin outer shells that enclose fillings of various kinds. Wraps do not have to fully enclose food, but can be partial. Tacos are the most widely consumed such dish. Tacos shells are tortillas, made of dried corn that is soaked in lime water, then ground into dough, flattened into thin rounds, and toasted on a hot flat metal sheet, or griddle. Wheat-flour tortillas are a common variation in North America. The vendor takes a tortilla in hand, fills it with a usually cooked filling, and serves it forth. Fillings are usually made from shredded meat, pork, beef, or chicken (less common) mixed with chile pepper-flavored sauce and often topped with shredded cheese, chopped tomatoes, chopped onions, and cream cheese. There are many variations on the basic theme, including newly popular fish tacos (usu-ally fried catfish, tilapia, or shrimp), Korean-style tacos (with grilled beef and kimchi, the famous Korean spicy pickled vegetables), and many vegetarian op-tions available in upscale food trucks. In areas with newer Mexican and Central American immigrants, some specialties such as brains, eyes, tongue, and tripe tacos are popular. One variation more acceptable to most Americans is the fajita, a marinated skirt steak that is grilled and served with spicy sauce, cooked sliced green peppers and onions, and sometimes shredded cheese on a taco. Street carts and stands with flat griddles usually serve some type of fajita.

North American tacos originated on the Mexican-American border that runs from Texas west to California, though they are very ancient in Mexico proper. The word *tacos* is slang for handheld food and implies a filling dish meant to be eaten "on the run." Until the 1970s, tacos were mostly confined to the American Southwest, California, and wherever there were concentrations of Mexican Americans. Gradually, and with the spread of taco fast-food chains from Califor-nia, such as Taco Bell, this dish became very popular. Tacos are now sold from stands, carts, and trucks across the country. They are so popular and numerous in Los Angeles, for example, that truck owners have been cleared from streets by local authorities.

Enchiladas are based on the same principle as tacos, only they are larger and often served as main courses in restaurants covered in a Mexican-style sauce. Burritos, literally "little burros," is a food born in California in the 1930s. In its original form, the burrito is a large wheat-flour tortilla wrapped in a package with a filling, usually shredded meat cooked in sauce and mixed with beans and rice. The burrito is now widely found on breakfast and other food trucks, at take-out places, and even in some vending machines. They are also common in chain fast-food restaurants with various fillings, such as scrambled eggs for breakfast.

Flatbreads such as pitas can be thought of as sandwiches, but they are usually more fully wrapped around their fillings than a normal cut-in-two bread sandwich base. Flatbreads for wrapping are soft thin wheat-based breads that are oven baked before use. Shawarma (Middle Eastern), gyros (Greek), and *tacos árabes* (Mexican) all appear as fillings for flatbreads of various kinds. They are all large cones of layered meats, normally lamb, put in a long spit and roasted over an open flame. The meat is cut from the core in thin slices and served on flatbread that is usually rolled up, served with a dressing or sauce, and eaten out of hand. Presliced gyros and related meat preparations are served from street stands, sometimes cooked on a flat griddle, while some specialized food trucks cook the meat on the spot. Kebabs that are so common in the Middle East also make appearances as street food in the United States. Meats—lamb, beef, or chicken—are skewered with onions and other vegetables and cooked over an open flame. Kebabs are served with sauces and often eaten on a flatbread.

One kind of flatbread is now a standard American dish served in all kinds of eating places including street-food vehicles. Brought by Italian immigrants before 1900, and found only in their mostly urban communities, pizza began to spread across the United States in the late 1950s and 1960s. It morphed into many styles with many toppings, but basically it is a flat dough round covered in a tomato sauce ("white pizza" is just cheese), with cheese, chopped vegetable, and optional sausage toppings. As street food, it is sold from carts, and some upscale food trucks make fancy versions with exotic toppings. Pizza is probably United States' premier fairly healthy snack food, unlike packaged snack chips.

Stuffed Foods

Stuffing means a wrapper, usually pastry, which totally encloses a filling and then is baked, fried, or steamed. Tamales comprise a kind of Mexican food that is widespread, though not to the same extent as tacos. They are long rolls of corn dough that are filled with shredded meats cooked in sauce or sweet fruits, then wrapped in a corn or banana husk, tied into a bundle and steamed. Two kinds of tamales exist in North America: the standard Mexican style made with corn dough and the Mississippi Delta tamale. The latter comes from the region for which it is named but can also be found on street stands, carts, and fairs as far north as Chicago. These are made with coarse cornmeal, filled mainly with cooked pork and a spicy sauce composed of different ingredients than its Mexican counterparts.

Dumplings of various kinds are a major form of stuffed foods, ranging from Chinese steamed dumplings to Italian raviolis. Many of the world's dumplings migrated to the United States, and some have become street food, as they are in their native lands. Chinese dumplings that go under the name *dim sum* or "snacks" come in many varieties. *Jiao* are made from thin rice wrappers, filled with chopped meat or vegetables and then steamed. *Bao*, from northern China, are either thicker wheat- or rice-flour wrappers, made into large balls and also steamed. Lightly poached and fried *guotie*, or pot stickers, and *shaomai*, small steamed dumplings, can all be found in American street-food venues, mostly in food trucks and fairs. Thai and Vietnamese dumplings similar to their Chinese cousins usually accompany other dishes in food trucks. Of all Asian dumpling-like dishes, deep-fried *cheung yun*, or spring/egg rolls, remain the most popular.

European and Latin American dumplings have places in the street-food scene. Empanada is a generic name for a wide range of foods made from a flour dough, rolled out thinly, cut into circles, filled with chopped meat, or cheese, or vegetable fillings, sealed, and then baked or fried. There are literally hundreds of types of empanadas, most of them sold from food trucks and at fairs. Wherever vehicles display food from Ecuador, Columbia, Argentina, or Brazil, to name the most popular, empanadas will be sold. Polish dumplings, pierogi, are also found as street and fair foods. There is even a massive Pierogi Fest held in Whiting, Indiana, where thousands are gobbled down by throngs of vistors.

More specialized dumplings include two foods often thought of as meat pies and the other as a fruit pie. In upper Michigan, Wisconsin, and parts of Minnesota, Cornish pasties are local specialties served at fairs and festivals. They are thick pastries, filled with ground meat, chopped potatoes, often carrots and root vegetables, formed into squares or rounds and baked. The runza is the Nebraska State dish, also a meat and vegetable dumpling, but originating in Russia. Fried pies are thought to be southern in origin, but can be found at fairs almost everywhere. These are square-shaped pastries filled with dried fruit that are deep-fried until crispy.

Deep-Fried Food

For more than 200 years, Americans have loved fried food. It is everywhere on the food landscape, in most corporate fast-food restaurants and in street food. While most portable food carts and stands cannot do deep frying for technical reasons, food trucks and fair food are loaded with fried products. Of these, two types predominate, savory and sweet. French-fried potatoes top the list of favorite deep-fried food, either alone or an accompaniment to another food. Fried chicken might be United States' best-known fried meat dish. It can be done in a number of styles, from Chinese to American southern. Buffalo wings is a recent addition—seasoned chicken wings, deep-fried and served with sour cream and a spicy hot sauce.

FRENCH-FRIED POTATOES

Other foods in this category are fried cheese curds, nachos-fried tortilla wedges swerved with a soft cheese food topping, and, at the Wisconsin State Fair, a bacon and cheese hamburger served on a fried Krispy Kreme doughnut.

Fried stick foods are state and country fair favorites and can be found on street trucks, as well. Corn dogs are the oldest and best-known fried food on a stick. Dating from at least the 1920s, these are hot dogs that are impaled on a stick, dipped in a cornmeal batter, and then deep-fried to a golden brown. At the Illinois State Fair, for example, there are a dozen stands, many serving the famous Cozy Dog. Many other savory stick foods followed, among them bacon, batter-dipped fish, patty sausage dipped in batter, pizza, macaroni and cheese, pickle slices, and battered spam. Nothing escapes the batter bowl!

Sweet fried foods have also long been favorites. Doughnuts in numerous forms, filled and plain, and crullers are sold from street stands and trucks, especially for breakfast. Fried batters, especially funnel cakes (poured into hot oil in strings and served with powdered sugar) and elephant ears (flat, round pastries), appear at almost all fairs and amusement parks. In recent years, Latin American *buñuelos* (fried dough balls) and churros (fried dough sticks sprinkled with sugar and cinnamon) have spread to carts, trucks, and fairs. Fried Coke is one recent creation, made by mixing Coca-Cola syrup with batter, deep frying it, and pouring more syrup on top of the final product. Sweet stick foods are common in many fairs. Among them are battered deep-fried chocolate cake, S'mores, banana splits, fresh fruits, Oreo cookies, Twinkies, and candy bars, especially Snickers, Milky Way, Three Musketeers, Reese's Peanut Butter Cups, and Tootsie Rolls.

Sweet Foods

Sweet foods are iconic street and fair foods. Some were introduced at World's Fairs, such as caramel corn in 1876, Cracker Jacks in 1893, and ice-cream cones and cotton candy in 1904. Others, such as candy apples after 1908 on the Jersey Shore, appeared as snack treats at amusement parks. Sweetened popcorn and spun sugar cotton candy can be found in every fair and amusement area. Cold treats are even more popular. In the late 19th century, ice cream was sold by "hokey pokey" men from mobile carts. In the 1920s, small motorized trucks led by the Good Humour Company sold the newly invented chocolate covered ice-cream bars, and ice-cream trucks have roamed American streets ever since. Popsicles, shaved ices, coarsely ground and syrup flavored ices, and other frozen treats are sold almost everywhere people gather for fun.

Commercially made candies are the most widely consumed street food if newspaper stands, kiosks, and vending machines are considered. They are produced in many varieties by major companies such as Mars, Hershey, and Nestlé. However, one candy is almost completely associated with seaside resorts, saltwater taffy. Taffy is a semisoft candy made from sugar, cornstarch, corn syrup, and flavorings. Taffy originated in England about 1800, but by the 1880s, shops in Atlantic City were selling it packaged in souvenir boxes as "Salt Water" because it was made at a seashore resort. Today, saltwater taffy trucks can be found at most fairs where it is pulled by machines in customers' view, adding to its universal appeal.

BRUCE KRAIG

AFRICAN AMERICAN STREET FOOD

Since the 18th century, African Americans have been a vital part of the U.S. street-food scene. Anywhere a lakeside city, river town, seaport, or transportation hub sprouted up in colonial United States, African American vendors were likely to be there roaming the streets in search of customers. African Americans have a deep history of selling beverages, fruit and vegetable produce, and prepared foods all over the country, including diverse places as Charleston, South Carolina; Chicago, Illinois; New Orleans, Louisiana; New York, New York; Philadelphia, Pennsylvania; and San Francisco, California.

Slavery and racism loomed large in the street vendor's life. Prior to the Civil War, African American street vendors tended to be recently freed slaves or aged or disabled slaves who could no longer perform the arduous tasks required of domestic servants and field slaves. Some plantation masters saw an opportunity to make additional income by allowing their slaves to sell goods in nearby towns. These goods were often surplus crops from the plantation and eggs, poultry, and vegetables the slaves raised themselves. Municipal officials were wary of having a large influx of African American vendors, so they regulated the practice. Even with the attempts to restrict this commercial activity, African American street foods proved tremendously popular with people of all races. Most earnings went to the master. Yet, in some circumstances, the slaves got a portion and could save enough money to eventually purchase their own freedom and that of other slaves.

In the antebellum North, street vendors successfully formed a profitable, secondary economy with Native American suppliers and poor white customers. White elites sought to stamp out these vending relationships because they operated outside of the established public market system that the very same elites created for profit. By 1740, African American women were so successful at selling boiled hot corn and fruit in New York City that a municipal law was passed to specifically prohibit their livelihood. Violators were publicly whipped.

Despite the hostile environments they often encountered, the street vendors carried on many West African cultural expressions that were characteristic of the market sellers in their ancestral homes. They wore colorful outfits and bandanas as they sold food. They sang rhythmic, musical street cries in falsetto to attract their customers. They also balanced their food baskets on their heads as they traveled from place to place. Not surprisingly, these urban characters fueled a fountain of folklore within African American and mainstream popular culture. Some scholars have argued that ragtime, the progenitor of jazz, was inspired by a New Orleans street vendor who sold rags in the late 1800s. African American vendors also permeated high culture when George Gershwin spotlighted their street cries in his 1930's opera *Porgy and Bess.*

After Emancipation, street vending offered African Americans one of the few opportunities to be entrepreneurial. Women particularly prospered in the street vending trade. As millions of African Americans left the South and settled in other parts of the United States, street food played a critical role in nourishing poor migrants who didn't have the resources, physical space, or cooking equipment to recreate traditional southern food in their new homes. Vendors thrived where the grocery stores were either too expensive or didn't have enough inventory to meet the demand of working-class African Americans. Though many rudimentary restaurants known as "ankle joints (selling pig's feet)," "fish houses," and "chicken shacks" were open for business, customers counted on the street vendors for cheaper prices. As early as the 1890s, street vendors sold fried chicken, boiled pig's feet, roasted possum, baked sweet potatoes, watermelon, and other southern favorites in the black neighborhoods of major urban centers.

Around the turn of the 20th century, African American street vendors had become adept at successfully selling the street foods associated with other ethnic groups. In Chicago, African Americans did a brisk trade in hot dogs. In New York City and San Francisco, African American vendors were known for their specialty of spicy chicken tamales. In Philadelphia, the boiled corn dish called hominy was associated with African Americans despite its clear Native American provenance. Philadelphians also patronized African American street vendors to get a taste of a Caribbean soup called pepper pot.

Major Street Foods

FRIED CHICKEN WITH HOT BREAD
Often the street foods offered were tremendously provincial, yet the combination of fried chicken and hot bread has endured as a universal and popular menu item. Many vendors were former Big House plantation cooks who gained years of culinary expertise in making this popular plantation breakfast pairing. The most famous vendors were the African American women who sold fried chicken along

with a biscuit, hot roll, pancake, or waffle at train depots throughout the South, particularly the train station at Gordonsville, Virginia.

SWEET SNACKS

Sweet snacks form the next biggest category of popular street food. Foremost in reputation were the enchanting confections of Charleston, South Carolina, and New Orleans, Louisiana. The Charleston vendors sold candies with a strong West African heritage. Groundnut cakes were made from peanuts (associated with the slave trade), molasses, sugar, and butter that were boiled together and then cooled. Similarly made was a coconut and molasses confection called "monkey meat," and a soft sesame seed candy called "benne cakes." The word *benne* is a close approximation of a West African dialect word for sesame seeds. Drawing upon two rich culinary traditions from France and West Africa, New Orleans vendors sold traditional French candies and desserts that they gave their own culinary and cultural spin. The French candied almonds called "pralines" came to Louisiana, but in the Creole kitchens of New Orleans, they were transformed into sugary nougat patties that contained almonds or pecans. The vendors renamed the traditional French rice beignets they sold "calas," using a dialect name for a rice fritter that is a longtime popular treat in West Africa.

Today, African American street-food purveyors are experimenting with traditional foods by reinterpreting them with upscale ingredients, fusing them with other cuisines, or by changing ingredients to make it vegan. Still, some version of fried chicken and hot bread, usually waffles, remains a popular choice. Aside from food trucks, street vendors continue to sell traditional foods at African American cultural events.

ADRIAN MILLER

CHAPTER 3

DÖNER KEBAB

TAHO

RAMEN

PHỞ

PAKORA

SATAY

CURRY

BAOZI

STINKY TOFU

ASIA

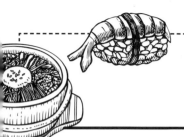

ASIA

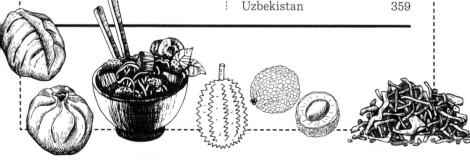

EASTERN ASIA

CHINA

W ITH MORE THAN 1.3 BILLION PEOPLE, the People's Republic of China is the world's most populous country. This situation is not new, since China has been the world's most populous political entity for more than 2,000 years. China is also the world's fourth largest country in area, covering 3.7 million square miles. Its territory encompasses the most diverse landforms and climates on the planet. Climates range from cool with cold winters in the north to tropical in the far south. On the east, running down the coastal areas, are alluvial plains with dense populations and major cities. Further west, the land rises into hills and mountains, cold in the north as they approach the Himalayas in Tibet and very warm in the south near neighboring Vietnam, Laos, and Burma. Sichuan in the southwest is one of the world's great biodiversity centers. North China has a vast desert, the Gobi, dry steppe lands along the Mongolian border, and subarctic areas near Siberia. Great rivers cut through China, the most critical being the Yellow in the north and the Yangtze running from the western mountain through the center of the country. Each area has many subregions because of China's complex topography, and each one has its own culinary traditions.

The Chinese people are mainly one ethnicity, called Han, but within the country are nearly 60 ethnic groups, all speaking different languages. Even within the Han, there are multiple languages and different customs. Because so much of Chinese culture is centered on food, differences among peoples are often expressed in that idiom. Northern Chinese, who come from regions less rich in diverse foods than the south, say that the Cantonese will eat anything with four legs except a table.

Chinese food traditions are often divided into four groups: north, east, west, and south. The northwest has been added to the list as Chinese interests, and settlements have spread out to the regions near the Mongolian and Central Asian borders. Each area is usually defined by the main foods that are indigenous to it. Rice in the south and millet and wheat in the north are major distinctions. There is considerable diversity within each region as well. Although major geographical divisions are commonly used in Chinese food, food experts in China and abroad recognize eight major culinary traditions. These are characterized by foods and preparation techniques—spicy hot pots in Hunan, for instance—and also fit the regional model.

Due to a cooler and drier climate, the earliest domesticated foods in north China where the earliest states began were millet, vegetables such as cabbages, and fish and pigs as main protein sources. Around the 12th century BCE, soybeans became domesticated. Soy sauces, made by fermenting beans, and soy curds are absolute musts in Chinese cookery. Much later, probably in the first millennium CE because of Central Asian contacts, wheat became much more important than millet. South of the Yangtze River, rice was domesticated by at least 7,000 BCE. In their richer environments, southerners raised many more fruit and vegetable crops, though pigs and fish were equally important food sources. Ginger, a key ingredient, grew in the south. Today the warmer regions of China still have the most sophisticated cuisines. For historical and ecological reasons, pastoralism never played an important role in the Chinese economy. Milk and milk products were never used, and many Chinese remain lactose intolerant. However, when China's economy opened to the West in the late 1970s, cheese-topped pizza became a popular fast food in cities everywhere.

Chinese farmers have always been open to new ideas and food. When European merchants introduced new foods in the 16th and 17th centuries, they were readily adopted. Chilies, peanuts, corn, potatoes, sweet potatoes, and even tomatoes were incorporated into the food system. Chilies are fundamental flavorings and important vitamin sources in Hunan and Sichuan. Chinese cuisines are products of local conditions and history, and the same applies to street foods.

Medicine and religion have also played a role in what Chinese eat. In traditional Chinese medical thought, the body is divided into four humors: wet, dry, cold, and warm. The four stand alone or are mixed depending on the season and on the human body's response to illnesses. Foods are assigned properties according to the system. When eating street food, Chinese diners often have these principles in mind. Buddhism, once the national religion, influenced cuisine because it recommends vegetarianism and spread the use of soybean curd. Muslims are an important minority, especially in the north and northwest. Since Muslims do not eat pork, lamb and mutton are the meats of choice. In Xi'an's famous night market where there is an old Muslim community, Han vendors line one side of the market while Muslim stands are on the opposite side. Each serves its own cuisine, and both are very popular.

HISTORY AND DEFINITION OF STREET FOODS

China's street food is the most varied and complex in the world. It has been since the first evidence of street food in the cities of the Han Dynasty (206 BC–220 CE). A famous painting from the Southern Sung period (1127–1279 CE) called *Qing Ming Shang He Tu* ("Along the River during the Qing Ming Festival") is a complex representation of the everyday hustle and bustle of a capital city with many street-side stalls or ambulant food vendors that remain recognizable today. Marco Polo, who visited Hangzhou in this period, would have seen this amazing scene.

For all its long history, there is no generally used word to express the idea of "street food" in the Chinese language. Instead, there is a somewhat different notion: *xiaochi*, usually translated into English colloquially as "small eats" in the sense of "snacks" or a minor meal. *Xiaochi* refers to the food eaten outside the context of main meals. It is food to stave off hunger between meals and might range from a few nibbles to a full bowl of food. *Xiaochi* such as dumplings may be prepared in one's own kitchen, but it is usually associated with streets and markets where the most varied and abundant selection can be found.

METHODS OF DELIVERY AND PREPARATION

The sheer variety of Chinese street food is astonishing: sometimes it seems as if the challenge in describing street food in China is identifying a food item that could *not* be found on the street. Until very recent modernization, a constant stream of hawkers on foot would still be seen making regular rounds with seasonal fruits on a basket slung against his back or a tray of pastries and sweetmeats balanced on the head. Each delicacy would be announced by the singsong calls of each vendor that identify his specialty as he wanders through the neighborhood.

The most iconic image of street food in China is that of a man balancing two loads on a bamboo shoulder pole. The shoulder pole is rarely seen today in big cities, but in times past, it was not uncommon to see two evenly balanced large stands made of lightweight bamboo or wood with shelving to hold a brazier of coals for cooking, ingredients, and water for washing, as well as a surface for bowls of condiments arrayed for the customer's enjoyment.

Portability—not just of food but of the fire source for the preparation of food—is a hallmark of street food in China. Quite elaborate loads that include griddles and burners might be balanced today on the two sides of a motorcycle or bike. Often they are transported on small wooden carts or wheelbarrows very much like those shown in the Sung Dynasty scroll. Bread-baking tandoors, small charcoal grills, and pots of simmering water over which steaming baskets can be stacked are still seen on the street. This economy of space is also remarkable. At the most, there might be a long worktable and perhaps several plastic tables for the client to enjoy his food. In simpler arrangements, food is eaten standing up or in a typical deep squat. Mobile vendors might even bring along low stackable plastic stools to make eating a bit more comfortable. A makeshift cloth or plastic tarp hung on portable bamboo poles provides protection from scorching sun or rain.

For all its association with convenience, street food represents a distinct form of urban pleasure. There is a sense of immediacy in going out to search for a favorite vendor. There is enjoyment and gratification in watching the preparation of one's food. The virtuosity and grace required to make many types of street food often rise to the level of street performance or theater. Street food also presents a variety of distractions throughout the day: the constant comings and goings of ambulatory peddlers and the changing parade of roving food carts mark the passing hours of a neighborhood. Carts offering different types of congees or holding vats of hot oil to *youtiao* for breakfast start the morning. By midday, these early vendors would have given way to sellers of noodle soups (*tang mian*) or dumplings (*jiaozi*) or different kinds of sweet or savory pastries. Carts with sweet puddings or iced desserts offer treats to end the day. Street food tends to be very local, and delicacies that can be acquired on a particular street or a corner at specific times of the day become part of the fabric of that neighborhood's everyday life and come to define its local flavor and character.

Small open-sided shacks such as those around the bridge in the Sung painting, or even stalls in dense marketplaces, are also sources of street food. But many permanent storefronts open out to the street with an "invisible fourth wall" that could be shuttered at night by sliding movable wooden slats in place (or the shop could be open all night and day). In many such places, food preparation takes place not in some back kitchen but on tables set up on the sidewalk in front. Like tea gardens or coffee shops that are also sources of street food, such places are characterized by a continuity of inside and outside and provide a constant sense of the passing city.

CATEGORIES OF STREET FOOD

Noodles (*Mian*)

Pasta is made when an unleavened mixture of starch and water is transformed into a solid edible product through contact with heat. This product might be a malleable sheet, which can be folded, rolled, or cut and broken down into strips. Or it could end up by various means as the strands that we call noodles.

China is famous for its hundreds of varieties of pastas, and every city or region boasts a distinctive shape or form. Historians stress the importance of wheat flour and rice in the food culture of China, but in fact, pastas are also made from a range of other starches: mung bean, tapioca, pea starch, beans, sweet potato, buckwheat, millet, oat, and even the root of bracken fern. In Fuzhou, noodles are made from pounded fish paste. Specific processing methods as well as the addition of ingredients like egg or lye affect variations in taste and texture. Pastas can be stir-fried or served as a cold salad (*liang mian*), or simply tossed with a dressing of one's choice. Noodle soups are accompanied by a seemingly infinite range of toppings: cabbage and pork in one region, cuts of beef or mutton in another, a few pieces of pickled vegetables in a third. Different combinations of aromatics (ginger, garlic, star anise, or the spicy and numbing Sichuan peppercorn) and condiments (black vinegar, sesame oil, soybean paste, chile) add even more permutations to the balances of sour, sweet, and spicy flavors.

In the northeastern city of Shenyang, pasta made of mung bean starch (*da la pi*) serves as the base for the beautifully composed salad of precisely cut vegetables that are dressed at the table by tossing with a mixture of pungent mustard and thick sesame paste. Thick sheets of steamed rice flour are studded with bits of meat, scallions, or dried shrimp to be folded into the rolls called *cheong fun* in Cantonese. Among the Hakka people of the east coast, wheat-flour dough is flattened, rolled like a log, and cut thinly across to form long strips called *ban mian* or *dao qie mian* (cut noodles). *Dao xiao mian* (knife-sliced noodles) are "shaven" from a block of dough with a curved knife made for the purpose right into the cooking water with breathtakingly rapid and dexterous motions. *Lamian* is made by pulling a piece of dough and doubling it continuously with repeated folding and stretching until seemingly hundred thin elastic strands of noodles have been formed. *Lamian* is a specialty of the Uyghur minority group of northwestern China. Through internal migration, the noodle soup vendors of the city of Lanzhou in Gansu province are now found in almost all the big cities of China preparing *lamian* right on a street-side stand with show-stopping skill. The spectacular process of making *lamian* raises the preparation of a street food to the level of virtuosic performance and entertainment.

There are yet other ways of making noodles: a dough of buckwheat flour can be pushed with a wooden press through holes and extruded into hot water to form *qiao mian*. The province of Shanxi claims to have a hundred forms of pasta, including the so-called cat-ear pasta (*mao er duo*) or tubes made of oat paste called *youmian kao lao lao*. Noodles might be as fine as the *misua* of Xiamen in Fujian province, or they could be the thicker round rice noodles called *mi fen*, so beloved in Yunnan, Guizhou, and elsewhere. Noodles can be chewy or slippery in texture. They can be opaque or translucent like the delightful noodles made from sweet potatoes. Noodles can even be made from bean curd skin or a jelly like the *liangfen* of Sichuan crescent dumplings (*jiaozi*).

A sheet of pasta can be cut into smaller pieces to form wrappers for dumplings. In many regions of northern and western China, thick chewy dumplings made of wheat-flour pasta might be eaten at main meals as a staple. These dumplings are related to a whole family of dumplings ranging from Russian *pelmeni* to Korean *mandoo*. The Uyghurs of Xinjiang make the lamb-stuffed dumpling called *manti*, a word also used throughout Central Asia and Turkey. But dumplings are also a beloved street-food with countless variations throughout China. Each region boasts distinctive shapes and preferred stuffings: chive, cabbage, radish, pickled vegetables, finely minced beef, mutton, duck, fish, and even such luxurious ingredients as crab roe and dried scallops. Local mushrooms or foraged herbs might be used. For instance, in Shanghai and the bordering province of Jiangsu, a dumpling stuffed with finely minced pork and the herb called shepherd's purse (*qi cai*) is much beloved. Dumplings need not just be savory. They might contain fillings of lotus seed, peanuts, sesame, jujube, or osmanthus flower and sweet bean paste.

Zheng jiao are dumplings steamed inside an enclosed bamboo or metal basket set over simmering water. Steam rises through each tray cooking each layer. It is this efficiency of fuel economy of space (some trays can hold several dozen dumplings at once) that make even large-scale dumpling preparation possible on a portable street-side heat source. Steamed dumplings with a base allowed to brown and crisp in a bit of oil are called *guo tie*, or "potstickers." Dumplings can also be boiled in broth or in water to make *shui jiao* (water dumplings). An exceptionally thin wrapper called *yan pi* (swallow skin) encloses the beloved wonton of Guangdong, often cooked in

ZHENG JIAO DUMPLING

a soup with roast pork or duck and egg noodles. Chengdu boasts a form similar to the wonton called *chao shou* (which means "crossed hands" because of the way it is formed). A few of these *chao shou*, boiled, drained, and served in a small bowl with a typical dressing of red chile oil, vinegar, sesame oil, and the numbing Sichuan peppercorn are one of the most beloved street-food snacks in this city.

Apart from wheat-flour pasta, many other starches might be used to form the wrappers. Glutinous rice flour is a very common wrapping ingredient and is used in the meat-stuffed *yuanxiao* dumpling balls eaten on special occasions in the Beijing area. The Hakka people are well known for the inventiveness of their wrappings, which are made using dough flavored with taro, pumpkin, and different medicinal or foraged herbs to produce intriguing colors and flavors. Arrowroot flour mixed with wheat starch produces the pearly translucent wrapper for the Cantonese shrimp-and-bamboo-shoot dumplings called *har gow*.

Dumplings might be simple half-moon forms or the rim of the wrapper could be gathered up like a bag and sealed with elaborate pleats to form the familiar chrysanthemum pattern. Sometimes, the edges of the thin wrapper barely reach the top to enclose the stuffing as in the open-faced *shaomai*. A high level of connoisseur culture distinguishes fineness and delicacy of form, the laboriousness of construction, the fragrance, and the deliciousness of the filling. A celebrated example of such specialist items is the time-consuming *xiaolongbao* of Shanghai. These are simply called "soup dumplings" because a cube of meat aspic is placed in the dumpling before it is pleated closed.

A dumpling is a civic symbol and a source of pride in its city or region of origin. Dumplings and other street foods can also be tourist attractions. In Xi'an, tourists are often urged to enjoy dumpling banquets featuring dozens of local varieties. In all the major cities, many shops with the *lao zihao* (Old Trademark) designation started as humble shacks a century or more ago serving a unique or an especially delicious street food. Many are now prosperous (often quite luxurious) restaurants or even chains far removed from the hustle and bustle of the street.

XIAOLONGBAO

Stuffed Buns (*Baozi, Mantou*)

These steamed dumplings made of yeast-raised wheat flour are a staple of northern cuisine. *Bao* means "to bundle" and *bao zi lai* means "to bundle up." These are two basic techniques: bundling the dough up on top and then pleating it closed. Or the bun can be inverted, and the seamless part becomes the top (the seam on the dough having been worked away).

Bao is prepared by steaming or baking. Steaming is more important and common in northern preparations. In a way, steamed stuffed *baozi* can be seen as an extension of dumplings. Many of the *bao* forms are the same as southern dumplings and steamed in exactly the same way. In fact, steamed buns often share the same basket with dumplings as they are being prepared. The difference is in the dough: one uses a *mantou* dough, and the other is made with an unleavened pasta. Some *mantou* doughs are so thin and fine, especially on tinier buns, that one could almost confuse them for pasta wrapping.

Like *jiaozi*, there are a number of ways to make and use *bao*. In some versions, buns can be steamed, then fried and crisped at the bottom in the very manner of potstickers. Such buns are called *shengjian baozi*. A very common Shanghainese snack is small *mantou* pieces that are deep-fried and served with condensed milk on the side as a dip. Of baked buns, the most famous example is the *char siu bao* of Guangdong.

Soups and Stew

Stews are standard street foods, especially if hot pots are counted. Hot pots are usually thought of as hot broth into which food is dipped and cooked by individual diners. But the term also applies to southwestern dishes from Sichuan and Hunan, where food is steamed in clay vessels in broth or made into soupier stews. Meat, fish, vegetables, and fungi are all stew ingredients.

Soups of every variety are sold by street vendors. A good many are eaten with dumplings and noodles, and others have additions that make rich meals. Some are specific to regions. For example, a sweet soy-milk soup made with pickled vegetables, vinegar, and bits of pork is a classic northern soup. In Xi'an, *hulatang*, a chile-laced broth, is a favorite. In Hunan, a special covered clay pot with a tapered chimney in the center is used to make spicy hot pots. Some soups, like *hulatang*, are so thick that they can be thought of as soup–stews. Soups, like stews, are regional and made from meats, fish, or vegetables mixtures. Flavorings vary greatly by region; Shanghai and southern styles use five-spice powers, dried meats, fungi, and vegetables for flavoring.

Crêpes, Flatbreads (*Bing*), and Griddled Items

Dough made with a different ratio of flour and water and prepared with other cooking methods, including the use of leavening or the addition of oil or fat, yields different kinds of cakes and breads, which are quite distinct from pasta.

A thin batter of wheat flour and water is brushed on an extremely hot griddle to form a fine round pancake, or crêpe, which is used as a wrapper to form spring rolls. In Fujian province and in the various countries throughout Southeast Asia with Fujianese immigrants, *popiah* (*baobing* or *runbing* in Mandarin) is a very thin rice flour crêpe filled with a tender mix of finely shredded cabbage, carrot, turnip, strips of dried bean curd, pork, and omelet strips. A sprinkling of coarse peanut powder before the crêpe is rolled adds flavor and texture.

Jianbing is a very common breakfast street food throughout China. A balled-up towel dipped in very wet batter is used to cover a round, high-heat flattop grill in a rapid circular motion. The batter (made of wheat flour and corn or mung bean flour depending on the vendor) sets instantly because of the intense heat. An egg is broken over and brushed over the setting crêpe. The foot-and-a-half diameter crêpe—thin, crispy, but malleable—is brushed with bean paste and chile sauce, sprinkled with chopped green onions or cilantro, and rolled up with a whole savory cruller (*youtiao* or *baocui*). The result is stuffed into it to make a fat breakfast roll to be eaten on the go.

For *cong you bing* (scallion pancakes), a wheat-flour dough is rolled flat, brushed with lard or oil, sprinkled with chopped scallions, rolled into a log that is in turn curled into a snail form, and then flattened again to griddle until golden brown. There are many recipe variations for *cong you bing*, including one that uses two doughs (an oil dough and a water dough or an oil dough and a yeast-leavened dough) to achieve alternating effects of flakiness and rise.

A process that includes both steaming and crisping produces the *mo* of Xi'an, a round white flatbread with a hard shell and a soft, chewy interior. *Mo* is torn at the table into small pieces to soak in a bowl of mutton soup in *yangrou paomo*, one of the most famous examples of the halal cookery of the large Muslim population in Xi'an. *Mo* is also slit open and stuffed with either lamb or pork to make the sandwich *roujiamo*, the most famous street-food item of this city.

Yeast or sourdough leavening is used to make such baked flatbreads such as the many forms of *shaobing*, a fairly fat round that nestles easily in one hand and is usually studded all over on the outside with sesame seeds. *Shaobing* is also often slit open to sandwich various kinds of meat including smoked meat (*dong rou*) or braised beef (*hong shao niu rou*). Or it could enclose a layer of sweet sesame paste such as in *tang huo shao* of Beijing.

Traditionally, baking in China is done in a tandoor, a large clay urn. As in tandoor bread-making, the prepared dough is pressed on the inside of the urn to bake. Among Uyghurs and Han Chinese who are Muslims in northern and western China, a tandoor bread called *nang* serves as a staple food. *Nang* is typically quite large, much thicker than the Indian naan, and is closer in form to Central Asian equivalents. It is always intricately stamped on top with distinctive decorative patterns. It is very common to see tables set out on the street stacked high with these hefty bread rounds in the old and rapidly disappearing *hutongs* (back-alley neighborhoods) of Beijing. As a tandoor is relatively portable (modern versions encased in metal and set on wheels are often seen today), it is still possible today even in some big cities to see *bing* of various sorts not just being peddled but actually being baked right out on the street.

Skewers (*Chuan*)

Skewers, called *chuan*, are a very ancient food. Although central to the food culture of China, skewers, especially those of lamb or mutton (*yang rou chuan*), are usually associated with the food cultures of the steppes beyond the Great Wall. They are the most prominent street food throughout northern and western China but can also be found in the Muslim quarters of big cities such as Kunming in Yunnan. Typically, such grills are set out right on the street where the fragrant, wafting smoke lures the passersby. Patrons can choose between skewered chunks of meat and delicacies such as skewered lamb liver or kidney. Lamb skewers are much beloved in Beijing.

The character for skewers in Chinese is a very visual image: two small rectangles crossed ("skewered") with a vertical line. Stalls selling skewers are among the most typical nighttime street food throughout the country. Typically, such stalls would have a display of two or three dozen raw items already on skewers, ready to be grilled. Each skewer holds a few mouthfuls of food and costs a few cents. The idea is to select a range of different items and take it to the grillmaster to be prepared. There is seemingly no limit to what might be on offer as skewers: offal, green vegetables, mushrooms, kelp, fish balls, lotus root, shellfish, bean curd, bamboo shoots, quail egg, and more.

Skewers need not be grilled. They can be used to hold fish balls while deep-frying out on the street. Fish paste balls (*yu yuan*) are an important part of Fukienese food culture.

Another skewered street food can be found in the *malatang* ("hot and numbing soup") stalls. *Mala* (numbing and spicy) is considered a typical flavor combination in Sichuan, and *malatang* itself refers to a typical hot pot with these flavors. In recent years, *malatang* stalls have become very popular throughout the country. Instead of having a selection of grilled skewers, one would dunk and cook them in a large vat of flavored soup. This kind of communal hot pot bolsters the notion that there is virtually no food in China that could not be found out on the street. *Malatang* setups are also typically found at night as a little snack to end the day.

Candies, Brittles, Pickles, Nuts, and Fruits

Candymakers are the most colorful of food peddlers. The *tanghulu* man sells candied hawthorn (*shan zha*) in long skewers of eight to ten little bright red fruits. These skewers are inserted diagonally into holes on a stand that allow the display to flare out decoratively. The stand is usually raised on a high pole so that it looks like a headdress ornamented with red beads or like some fantastical animal were gliding above the crowds. Artisans of dragon beard candy (*long xu tang*) repeatedly stretch and fold molten sugar to create hundreds of very fine silklike candy strands. Other candymakers (called *tang ren*) entertain hordes of fascinated onlookers by drizzling hot caramelized sugar with flamboyant calligraphic strokes to create fragile dragons or phoenix forms. Candy sculptors blow into molten sugar balls to create little glass candies resembling dogs, rabbits, or other animals. As with the making of noodles like *lamian* or *dao xiao mian*, virtuosity becomes street performance and spectacle. Such breathtaking displays as these turn the preparation and peddling of street food into theater.

There is an endless procession of nibbles the entire day: malt sugar candies, *mahua* (sesame sweetmeats), brittles made from different seeds and nuts, candied ginger or winter melon, fried broad beans, honeyed fruits or sour fruit pickles, and pressed, sundried persimmon fruits (*shi bing*). There might be iced sweets or noodle-like jellies swimming in sweet syrup on hot days. Roving carts offer freshly roasted chestnuts or hold beautiful samovars dispensing herbal tonics and jellies, such as *guilinggao*, or a sweet soup made with lotus root powder (*ou fen*) for cold winter days.

By nighttime, carts offering all kinds of sweet dessert soups or puddings can be expected in the same semipermanent spot. One might find *tang yuan*, round glutinous rice dumplings swimming in sweet soup. Or soups with jujubes, lotus seeds, white ear fungus, grass jelly, or goji berries. Or a hot, sweet congee of purple glutinous rice (*zhi nuo mi*). The famous eight-treasure congee (*ba bao zhou*) is a fortifying mix of red rice, barley, beans, nuts, dried fruit, and so forth. Then there are various sweet puddings called *ni*, which might be made of pounded taro root or sweet potato. A famous pudding of Chengdu is called *san he ni* (three harmony pudding) and is made from pounded sticky rice, black beans, and sesame seeds. These are all treats to mark the end of the passing day.

REGIONAL SPECIALTIES

WESTERN AND CENTRAL CHINA

This region includes Sichuan, Hubei, Hunan, and to the south east, Yunnan. The provinces of Sichuan and Hunan are the centers of western Chinese cuisine. With good rainfall and varied landforms, Sichuan has ingredients ranging from river fish to such forest products as bamboo, mushrooms, and nuts. It is famous for its peppercorns, which are not black pepper but belong to the genus *Zanthoxylum*.

They come in several varieties with different flavors and give a unique, spicy bite to food. When dried chilies (introduced in the 17th century) are added to the pot, Sichuan cooking becomes extremely hot. Garlic and spices such as star anise, cassia, and ginger are often used. Hunanese cuisine is famous for its hot pots and steamed spiced chicken dishes.

Because of their relatively remote locations, other provinces have had little impact on this school of cuisine. Long winters make food preservation techniques important, such as pickling, smoking, and salting. Sichuan cuisine is composed of seven basic flavors: sour, pungent, hot, sweet, bitter, aromatic, and salty. Beans, including mung and soybeans, play an important role as do bamboo shoots.

Chengdu, the capital of Sichuan, is the most representative of the Western school of cuisine. In 2011, the United Nations Educational, Scientific, and Cultural Organization (UNESCO) declared it a World City of Gastronomy because of its sophisticated cuisine. Among the areas famous for their street food are Wadancang Street, the areas near Wenshu Monastery and Sichuan University, Jinli Road, and Shuhan Dongjie. However, the city government initiated a campaign to remove street vendors from its roads and some have disappeared, at least in the center of the city. Three of the most popular Chengdu street foods are noodles, tofu, and foods prepared and served on skewers.

Yunnan is a mountainous area in southwest China bordering on Burma, Laos, and Vietnam. Around a third of the population are ethnic minorities, which contributes to an extremely varied cuisine. Unusual street-food items found here include fern fronds, tree bark, various flowers, lichens, and bugs, including bamboo larvae.

MAJOR STREET FOODS

Noodles/Dumplings

By far, the most popular noodle street food, *dandan*, also called peddlers' noodles, was first introduced in the mid-1800s. Historically, the vendors carried cooked noodles and condiments in baskets hanging from a pole across their shoulders. The pole itself was called *dandan*, hence the name. Today, the noodles are either sold in stalls or carts located on street corners or neighborhood night markets.

To eat *dandan*, the freshly boiled wheat noodles are placed in a bowl covered with a thick, slightly sweet sauce containing ground pork, pickled mustard greens, chile oil, then garnished with chopped scallion and topped with a quick shake of the tongue-numbing Sichuan pepper.

Chengdu boasts a dumpling with very thin wrapping called *chao shou* (crossed hands) because of the way it is formed. In typical Sichuanese fashion, a small bowl of three or four dumplings is sold by street vendors dressed with chile oil, vinegar, sesame, pungent peppercorn, ginger, and garlic.

Mápó Dòufu

A very traditional and readily available dish found in street markets, *mápó dòufu*, is also called "pockmarked woman's tofu" because the white cubes of tofu become speckled with ground pork and black beans. This subtle but potent dish is made by braising squares of tofu in a mixture of ground pork, fermented black beans, chile oil, garlic, soy sauce, sugar, sesame oil, and a generous amount of ground Sichuan pepper and garnished with chopped scallions or coriander leaves.

MÁPÓ DÒUFU

The name of the dish *mápó dòufu* originates from a story about an unattractive spinster who was "mápó:" *má* meaning "pockmarked" and *pó* meaning "old lady." She was selling the most delicious tofu dish in the region. Since then, this unique dish has carried her name and has spread across the province. The speckled pieces of the cooked tofu also resemble the age spots on the face of the old woman.

Dòufu Nǎo

Street vendors travel the city streets on bicycles hawking this very soft, silky bean curd. *Dòufu nǎo* can be translated as either "bean curd brains" or "bean curd flower." It is typically served warm in the winter and chilled in the summer. After scooping the silken tofu from large wooden tubs into plastic or paper bowls, patrons select from a variety of savory toppings, which include preserved vegetables, chile sauce, black vinegar, soy sauce, chopped green onions, and Sichuan pepper powder or from sweet toppings such as sugar and chopped nuts.

Skewered Foods

A very common sight when browsing night markets in the entire region is crowds of people surrounding a street vendor's car, picking out skewers of meat from a communal cauldron of hot red broth. Vendors also grill meat, vegetables, and even potatoes on skewers on small charcoal stoves.

Malatang

Malatang literally means "numbness of the mouth." Vendors prepare a highly seasoned broth with copious amounts of dried and fresh red chilies and sesame oil. Patrons then cook their skewered food, including raw squid, sausages, crabs, tofu cubes, coagulated pork blood, fish paste dumplings, chicken or pork cubes, mushrooms, and scallions, in this broth. Once cooked to the desired degree of doneness, a personal touch is added by a variety of condiments: oil, soy sauce, oyster sauce, and chopped fresh garlic.

Reganian

These hot dry noodles are a traditional dish of Wuhan, the capital of Hubei province, where they are eaten for breakfast. They are sold by street vendors in residential neighborhoods from early in the morning to late at night. *Reganian* is made by mixing cooked noodles with oil and then drying them. Before eating, the noodles are scalded in boiled water and mixed with such condiments as soy sauce, sesame paste, pickled vegetables, chopped garlic chives, and chile oil.

Guòqiáo mǐxiàn

Translated as "crossing the bridge noodles," this is Yunnan's best-known dish. The vendor pours the rice noodles, not quite cooked, into the diner's soup, to which the customer adds his or her own selection of thin meat slices, vegetables, and spices.

Yunnan Lijiang Pancakes

Pieces of dough made from unleavened wheat flour are stuffed with shredded pork and minced green onions, rolled up, brushed with butter, and baked in a simple firepit oven on a street corner. All it takes is a skilled wife-and-husband team, and they are cranking them out at a pace of a dozen nearly every 15 minutes.

SOUTHERN CHINA

The South centers on the province of Guangdong and its major city Guangzhou (Canton). Chinese consider this region to have the greatest of all culinary traditions. The South is subtropical, giving three crops per year. As a result, Cantonese cooks use a wide variety of ingredients. Many kinds of vegetables, fruits, dried and fresh fish (dried squid and jellyfish are specialties), and meats are made into a profusion of dishes. Cantonese prefer fresh flavors under the theory that a food should taste like the thing itself. If a fish is consumed, then it must be a lightly cooked fresh fish, perhaps seasoned only with the typical Cantonese black beans, light soy sauce, slivered green onions, and cilantro. The same theory holds for street food, including the many delicately flavored and textured dumplings.

In Guangdong, as in Hong Kong and Fukien, the expression "dim sum" is used in a way that corresponds to *xiaochi*. However, this term is not to be confused with the Hong Kong institution of dim sum, which is well known in the West. The latter is the type of restaurant that specializes exclusively in a compendium of items associated with *xiaochi* and with street food: *baozi* of all sorts, congees topped with salted fish or different cuts of offal and meat, *jiaozi* of different shapes and forms, and even such European-influenced items as the beloved egg custard tartlets. Restaurant dim sum is a semiregular, almost ritualistic occasion (during the morning, particularly Sunday morning or as afternoon tea) among family and friends.

Many of the street foods in Guangdong are the same as those in Hong Kong. Note that in the following section, the food names are written in Cantonese, not Mandarin.

MAJOR STREET FOODS

Lo Mai Gai

Glutinous rice is filled with such savory ingredients as chicken, black mushrooms, Chinese sausages, green onions, bamboo shoots, and sometimes dried shrimp or scallops, then wrapped in a lotus leaf and steamed. The leaf is not tied but rolled up and stacked with other packets in a steamer.

Cheong Fun

A mainstay of dim sum as well as the street, large thin noodles are rolled around

---

THE ISSUE OF LANGUAGE

The Chinese language is actually 17 or 18 languages, depending on how they are classified. Some are mutually intelligible, but many are not. The official language is called Pinyin or Mandarin in the old style because it comes from north China and was spoken in the old royal court in Beijing. Mandarin speakers do not understand Cantonese, which is spoken in Guangdong. Fortunately, all Chinese languages are written in the same symbols so that when Mandarin speakers go to a Cantonese restaurant, they know what's on the menu—they just cannot say the dish in Cantonese. In the United States, where most Chinese restaurants are Cantonese, Mandarin speakers have to use English.

---

a filling of bits of meat or shrimp, then folded into rolls and steamed. A sweet soy or savory sauce is poured over the dish; it is just cut and served. Another variety (*zaa loeng*) has a crispy vegetarian filling made out of fried dough.

Siu Mai

Sometimes translated as "pork and mushroom dumplings," these translucent, cup-shaped dumplings have a wrapper made of arrowroot and tapioca starch that is usually filled with ground pork, small shrimp, black mushrooms, green onions, and ginger seasoned with rice wine, soy sauce, sesame oil, and chicken sauce. Other ingredients can include bamboo shoots and water chestnuts.

Tingzai Porridge

This famous rice porridge is cooked with pork, fried peanuts, squid, fish, and ginger. *Tingzai* means "small boat," and it is sometimes called "sampan porridge." In the old days, poor fishermen would row up to people walking along the bay and offer them a bowl of porridge filled with fresh shrimp and fish. Today it is sold to passengers on boats and is even served in upscale restaurants.

Fried River Snails

One of the favorite snacks of Cantonese, these freshly caught snails are associated with the mid-autumn festival. They have thin shells and thick meat and are fried with perilla leaves, which accentuate their delicate flavor.

Siu Laap

Siu laap is a category of Cantonese cuisine that includes all meat dishes. It is divided into *siu mei* (barbecue) and *lou mei* (delicatessen). Depending on the item, it may be cooked on- or off-site. If it is an entire pig, it is roasted in a vertical oven at a location close to the market. Smaller items like ducks, pork butts, and chickens may also be roasted in these ovens. Charcoal grills in the market may be used to crisp up the meat for the patron.

Siu Mei

This is the generic Cantonese name for meats roasted on spits over an open fire or in an oven. The meat is coated with a sauce (a different sauce for each kind of meat) before roasting. Popular ingredients include pork, duck, beef, and chicken. Goat and lamb are rarely used in Cantonese cuisine.

Lou mei dishes are simmered in a soy-based sauce (*lou*) that is flavored with aromatic spices, including star anise and dried orange peel. *Lou mei* can be made from meat or fish, internal organs, and entrails. It is served hot or cold. Cold *lou mei* is often served with a side dish of hot *lou* sauce.

Char siu is pork seasoned with honey, five-spice powder, soy sauce, and hoisin sauce and roasted in an oven. For all these meats, the exterior should be crispy and sweet, and the interior soft and juicy.

Char Siu Bao

A puffy white leavened dough with a yeasty aroma is filled with barbecued pork seasoned with soy sauce, shallots, oyster sauce, and sesame oil and steamed or baked. The bun is wrapped in such a way that the dough splays open to make several petals. *Mak yue* are boiled or roasted cuttlefish or squid that are colored orange.

Hao Jian (Oyster Omelet)

Originating in Fujian, one of the most popular street dishes is oyster omelet made on-site by vendors. An egg batter is thickened with starch, filled with small oysters (or sometimes shrimp), and fried in lard. Sometimes a hot and sour sauce is added. Variations can be found in Taiwan, Malaysia, Singapore, Thailand, and the Philippines.

NORTHERN CHINA

Despite low rainfalls and cold, dry winters, Northern China has a grand food tradition, especially in its noodles, dumplings, baked cakes, and filling soups and stews. Northern cuisine is characterized by boiling, stewing, and braising of meats and vegetables. Mutton and beef are far more common than the south. Steamed buns made from wheat flour are one of the most popular street foods, heartier than southern varieties. Northern food is considered to be oilier than other regions with strong flavorings based on garlic, green onions, soy sauces, and vinegars. Noodles of all sorts are made in markets as street food, usually served in clear soups with these kinds of flavorings.

In Beijing, entire neighborhoods and streets are devoted to the sale of street foods. The best known are Jiumen, where more than 200 varieties are sold; Wangfujing (Donghuamen) night market, where you can find such exotic items as deep-fried insects, scorpions, and snake; Guijie (Ghost Street), specializing in hot and spicy shrimps; Niujie, selling Muslim meat dishes; and Fucheng, where upscale restaurants serve dishes from all over China. Typically, these areas do not have tables or chairs; the food is eaten on the go.

MAJOR STREET FOODS

Baozi

These steamed filled wheat-flour buns are found throughout China but are especially popular in the north as a breakfast dish. They are usually filled with pork, but sometimes vegetables are used. They are accompanied by vinegar or soy sauce and chile paste.

Roujiamo

China's answer to the hamburger is this street food that originated in Shaanxi in northwest China and is now popular across the country. Its origins are said to go back to the third century BCE. Meat, usually pork but in some regions beef and lamb, is stewed for hours in a broth made from 20 spices and seasonings. The meat is shredded, mixed with coriander and mild peppers, and stuffed in *mo*, a type of flatbread, or sometimes a steamed bun.

Liangpi

This noodle-like dish also originated in Shaanxi but has become popular throughout northern and central China. The word means "cold skin." The skin refers to the dough that is made from rice or wheat flour that is mixed with water and washed until only the gluten remains. The dough is formed into a large pancake and steamed for a couple of minutes. It is then cut into strips and put a bowl with julienned cucumber and bean sprouts. The dish is then covered with a hot, salty, and sour sauce, each vendor having his own recipe. The sauces typically include vinegar, chile oil, garlic, and salt. One famous variety of sauce is *majiang,* which includes black sesame paste. The diner can also add vinegar, salt, and chile peppers to his or her taste.

Jianbing

This thin, crispy breakfast crêpe originated in Beijing but is now sold all over China. A thin batter made from millet flour is poured in a circle on a hot plate, spread with eggs, sprinkled with parsley, and lightly fried until it is crispy. It is removed from the fire, coated with red sauces made from tofu bean curd and chile sauce, and then folded over a piece of crispy dough and lettuce. Some vendors have motorized cooking plates that turns to speed the cooking process.

Shaobing

Another popular breakfast dish, this baked, layered round bread sprinkled with sesame seeds can be either filled or unfilled. Fillings can be savory, such as red bean paste, black sesame paste, or stir-fried mung beans with egg and tofu, or sweet. There are many local varieties. Traditionally, *shaobing* are served with warmed soy milk or, in the winter, with hot pot. Unfilled *shaobing* are eaten with steamed eggs.

EASTERN AND SOUTHEASTERN CHINA

The east is usually considered to mean the delta of the Yangtze, including such cities as Shanghai, Hangzhou, and Shaoxing. It has been called "the land of rice and fish" because of the numerous rice paddies and lakes located along the valley and its flood plains. Fish, rice, and vegetables are the base of eastern cuisine. Foods are more delicately flavored here, often slowly cooked in soy sauce and sugar-laced broths. Shaoxing is so famous for its rice wine that the city's name is given to the product. Numerous rice vinegars are also a feature of the region. Street food bears the same characteristics; buns, for instance, are lighter with sweet-flavored fillings. Fried batter-dipped foods are also lightly done and usually accompanied by a light sweet-sour sauce. The region includes Shanghai (the largest city in the world), Zhejiang, and Anhui.

MAJOR STREET FOODS

Xiaolongbao (Soup Dumplings)

The most famous of all Shanghai street foods, these steamed buns are also called soup dumplings because a cube of meat aspic is inserted before the skin is pleated, and it bursts into one's mouth when the dumpling is eaten. They are made with partially leavened flour, which makes their skin tender and translucent. The heat melts the aspic into soup.

Shengjianbao

A famous Shanghai specialty, also called *shengjian mantou*, is a small pan-fried *baozi*, usually filled with pork, that has a firm bottom and a soft top. Chopped green onions and sesame are sprinkled on the buns during cooking. *Shengjianbao* is usually eaten at breakfast and purchased from corner stalls that sell pork buns and other snacks.

Zongzi

These rectangular or cylindrical packets of glutinous rice are filled with various meat and vegetable stuffings, then wrapped in bamboo leaves and steamed or boiled. They are traditionally eaten during the Dragon Boat Festival in the late spring. Variations are found throughout China as well as Southeast Asia and the Philippines. Other leaves used for wrapping may include corn, banana, shell ginger, and pandan leaves. The filling also varies and can include azumi bean paste, salted duck egg, pork belly, taro, shredded pork or chicken, Chinese sausages, and mushrooms.

Beggar's Chicken

A famous and very old dish, beggar's chicken originated in the city of Hangzhou, the capital of the coastal province of Zhejiang. A whole chicken is stuffed with mushrooms, sometimes pork, and seasonings, wrapped in lotus leaves, covered in clay, and baked at low heat for hours. Today it is usually prepared in an oven, though originally it was cooked in the ground. Legend has it that it was invented by a Hangzhou beggar who stole a chicken, but because he had no stove, wrapped in clay and baked it in a hole in the ground.

THE ORIGINS OF STINKY TOFU

The inventor of stinky tofu was Wang Zhihe, who came to Beijing in 1669 to take the examination to enter the civil service. After he failed, he stayed in the city to make a living by selling tofu. To preserve the tofu that hadn't been sold, he cut the leftovers into small cubes, put them into an earthen jar . . . and forgot about them. When he opened the jar several months later, the tofu pieces smelled terrible but tasted great. So he started selling it, and the business was a great success. He opened a store, Wangzhihe, which became the Beijing Ershang Wangzhihe Food Company. According to the *Global Times*, the company has opened a museum dedicated to tofu, which includes a model of the original store and tofu-making equipment.

Xie Ke Huang (Yellow Crab Shell)

Named for an entirely different food, *xie ke huang* is a pastry and one of the iconic snack and street foods of Shanghai. The filling can be either sweet—sweet bean paste or date paste and roses—or savory—shallot oil, pork, and crab meat. The pastries are round, slightly flattened, yellow in color, and sprinkled with sesame seed. Its name comes from its resemblance to a crab.

Stinky Tofu (*Chou Doufu*)

This fermented tofu has a very strong odor but a taste that aficionados consider delicious. It is sold at night markets and roadside stands or as a side dish in lunch bars, but rarely in restaurants. It is an iconic street food of the province of Hubei, although versions are sold all over China and Taiwan, where it is roasted on skewers. A traditional method of preparation is to make a brine from fermented milk, vegetable, meat, and spices in which the tofu ferments for up to three months. It can be eaten cold, steamed, stewed, or fried and is often accompanied by a sauce, which may be sweet or spicy hot.

RICHARD TAN, BRUCE KRAIG, AND COLLEEN TAYLOR SEN

HONG KONG AND MACAU

Hong Kong (Chinese for "fragrant harbor") is a city state on the south coast of China enclosed by the Pearl River Delta and the South China Sea. It is one of two special administrative regions of the People's Republic of China, the other being Macau. With a population of 7.3 million people in an area of 426 square miles, Hong Kong is one of the world's most densely populated areas. Its population is 95 percent ethnic Chinese, mainly from neighboring Guangdong. Many of Hong Kong's iconic street food dishes come from this province. The British made Hong Kong a colony after the First Opium War (1839–42) and later extended its territory to Kowloon and the New Territories. It was returned to Chinese sovereignty in 1997 but has autonomy in most matters except foreign relations and military defense. Hong Kong citizens have the world's seventh longest life expectancy—perhaps a tribute to its fabulous variety of food ranging from street food to international haute cuisine.

Though operating on Hong Kong for hundreds of years, many food stalls remained unlicensed until after World War II, when the government issued licenses to the families of deceased civil servants. These so-called *dai pai*, or big licenses, led to so many small street stands that traffic was soon disrupted. Traffic problems, plus concerns about hygiene, led the government to limit such licensure. This old-age trade has also been threatened by property developers. In 1980s, the government started buying back the licenses to control and regulate the spread of street vendors in Hong Kong. Today a few of the old-style food stalls (called *dai pai dong*) remain.

Because today many street-food vendors in Hong Kong operate out of permanent buildings, the perceived safety of this food is much higher than it might be in other countries; thus, these vendors serve tourists as readily as locals. Many vendors offer large tables for use by the general public, and it's common to share a table with strangers. Patrons can also order items from different stalls: noodles from one and drinks from another. Moreover, Hong Kong has a large number of restaurants, many of which offer street seating. Unlike the street markets in many other Southeast Asian cities, these seating arrangements in Hong Kong make the bustling markets seem somehow less hectic.

The 2015 edition of the Michelin Guide for the first time listed 23 street food stalls in Hong Kong and Macau as worth visiting. Though there are smaller pockets throughout the booming metropolis, street markets in Hong Kong are largely collected into three major areas:

- Temple Street Night Market is a market that comes alive as the sun goes down. It is popular among tourists, and many of the vendors operate out of permanent structures.
- Tsim Sha Tsui is located on Haiphong Road in the Kowloon Peninsula. Here street food is sold amidst fashionable boutiques offering glamorous clothing and electronics.
- Mong Kok, known as the "ladies market," not only specializes in women's wear, but also has a sizable and wonderful market in prepared foods.

Because many vendors at Hong Kong's major markets operate out of permanent structures, they have the flexibility to prepare food in a number of different ways, including wok- and deep-frying, open grill, and stove top. This also means that they are likely to have hot and cold running water and other amenities that meet Western expectations regarding sanitation.

HONG KONG

Major Street Foods

Hong Kong has been a trade center for many centuries, and its central location in Asia made it very attractive to the British, who won the territory in concessions granted by the Chinese after the Opium Wars. Now, this central location benefits lovers of street food by allowing them to sample products that arrive from all over Asia.

EGG WAFFLES (*GAI DAAN TSAI*)

Somewhat surprisingly, waffles have become a very popular street food in Hong Kong. Made from egg, evaporated milk, flour, and sugar, these Asian waffles are unlike the dimpled flapjacks found throughout the West; instead, these simple pastries are of semispherical shapes, a little smaller than golf balls, that are cooked in a custom-made waffle iron and look like an upside-down egg carton. Often a waffle maker has three or four skillets steaming away at the same time. Because they are relatively bland, they may be dressed with sweet sauces or honey as well as hot sauces.

SEAFOOD

Given Hong Kong's location, it's not surprising that seafood has a major presence at street markets. Squid and octopus are especially popular at night stalls, with different items more prevalent in specific markets. The squid is first cooked in boiling water, then roasted or deep fried and served on a wooden stick.

In the Temple Night Market, crab is a big seller. It's offered by many large restaurants with street-side seating and frequently served with a heavy complement of garlic and hot chilies. Often prices are not published, and the price of menu items is sometimes based on the whim of the server, so bargaining may be in order.

NOODLES

Noodles are popular in Hong Kong, and because they're usually eaten in a bowl, many street-side restaurants serve a wide range of noodle preparations, sometimes fried and topped with meat, fish, or vegetables; steamed; or added to soups. Some common noodle preparations include:

NOODLE SOUP

- Wonton noodle soup with beef brisket, a very hearty bowl
- Fish ball noodle soup, which is lighter and in no way fishy
- BBQ pork noodle soup, which combines

Asia's favorite animal with what is certainly one of Asia's favorite starches (second only to rice)

- Pig intestine noodles (*cheong fun*), a name that comes from the noodles' appearance and slippery texture. Served in a Styrofoam cup and eaten with wooden sticks, *cheong fun* is made from steamed sheets of rice noodles. It is served with a sweet sauce, peanut sauce, sesame oil, and sometimes hot sauce.

FISH BALLS

One logical way of using the meat of an animal, such as fish, is to grind it up, shape it into balls, and string several on a stick. Stick-mounting makes these balls very easy to eat while walking on the street. Since the 1950s, one of Hong Kong's most iconic street foods has been fish balls, made with ground fish or seafood and often flour. Especially popular are curry shrimp balls, which are threaded on a bamboo skewer and served in a spicy curry sauce, reflecting the influence of the city's large South Asian population. A relatively new type of street food is noodles in a bag. Customers choose their preferred toppings—corn, fish balls, and fried squid are pouplar—and a sauce is mixed into a bag of prepackaged noodles.

PINEAPPLE BUN (*BO LO BAAU*)

A popular breakfast dish listed by the Hong Kong government as a part of the city's intangible cultural heritage, these crunchy sweet buns are made of a dough of sugar, eggs, flour, and lard served over a soft sweet bread. They contain no pineapple; the name comes from the checkered top that looks like a pineapple. Often they are served with a pat of butter inside. A pineapple bun may be stuffed with red bean paste, custard cream, peanut butter, barbecued pork, coconut, or even pineapple (in which case it is called a pineapple pineapple bun).

CONGEE

Though not an ideal street food to eat while walking, congee is served at most Hong Kong markets, especially by vendors that offer seating. Congee is a porridge made of grains such as rice, cornmeal, millet, barley, and sorghum and is eaten with sweet or spicy condiments, such as fresh crab, fish, 100-year-old eggs, fermented bean curd, or chicken with ginseng. Its easy digestibility is very good for the stomach, especially after eating more adventurous foods.

STINKY TOFU (*CHOU DOUFU*)
A Hong Kong classic especially associated with the Mong Kok market, *chou doufu* is made by fermenting tofu, milk, fish, and other ingredients for as long as a couple of months. The skin on the outside is crispy, but it has a soft, creamy center and is usually served with a sweet or spicy sauce.

Other Street Foods

OFFAL
As is the case at markets throughout Southeast Asia, Hong Kong markets sell a lot of offal, frequently grilled. Mong Kok has several stands selling pig intestine deep-fried to a chewiness that somewhat minimizes the funky taste, though a blast of hot sauce definitely helps. A common sight is a vat of boiling entrails, including stomach lining, lung, kidneys, and other organs cut into pieces and mixed with peppers, radish, and sometimes curry powder.

ROASTED SWEET POTATO AND CHESTNUTS
Usually sold together from mobile carts that are half-wooden potato baker, half steel chestnut roaster, these are very popular in the winter

DIM SUM
Though popular in Hong Kong, dim sum, the small dumplings with a huge range of fillings, are seen only sporadically in markets. Because such items require steaming immediately before serving and are consequently quite hot, they are best enjoyed sitting at a table.

FRIED CHICKEN
Often at the Mong Kok market, the longest line is for a fried chicken vendor. Such a fried food item is ideal for small vendors who lack seating; it's very easy to eat a piece of fried chicken while walking through the market.

PRETZEL PREPARATIONS
Many vendors offer pretzel fish, pretzel pork chop, and other items that may not actually contain any pretzels in the Western sense of the word. Rather, the word *pretzel* seems to refer to a light brown breading that contains neither pretzel nor salt.

EGG TARTS

A legacy of Hong Kong's colonial period, these small pastries are filled with a rich custard and are often sold outside cafés and restaurants. They probably originated in neighboring Macau, but unlike the Macau version, the top is not browned. Today they come in different flavors, including ginger, chocolate, and green tea.

VEGETABLES

Though not as flashy as grilled and skewered food items, many stalls that sell meat or fish also offer fried eggplant and peppers, which add color to street food and can provide a healthy balance to what might otherwise be rather rich fare. Many times, however, the vegetables are breaded and fried, mitigating the health benefits.

DAVID HAMMOND AND COLLEEN TAYLOR SEN

MACAU (MACAO)

Macau, also spelled Macao, is located on the western side of the Pearl River Delta across from Hong Kong. Like Hong Kong, it is one of the two special administrative regions of the People's Republic of China. A former Portuguese colony, it was administered by Portugal from the mid-16th century until 1999 when it was transferred back to China. Its economy is heavily dependent on casino gambling and tourism. The 30 square kilometer area consists of a peninsula and two small islands.

Macau's cuisine is a blend of Portuguese and Chinese influences. The basis is Portuguese, especially stews, enhanced by local ingredients. The territory has not only many restaurants and cafes but also a vibrant street-food life in the city's markets. Along the beachfront, many sell fresh seafood including prawns, squid, scallops, and abalone that is grilled or deep-fried. An extremely popular specialty is jerky made from dried smoked beef, pork, or chicken.

Major Street Foods

FISH BALLS

As in Hong Kong, skewered balls are a common sight in Macau. The customer selects one of the skewers in the stall, and the vendor cooks it in a flavored broth.

They are served in a small paper cup and usually topped with a yellow curry sauce. Some vendors also sell beef balls, hot dogs, and even skewered vegetables.

PORTUGUESE EGG TART

Sold in bakeries and street stalls, Portuguese egg tart (*pastel de nata*) is a small baked pastry tart filled with egg custard. Popular in Portugal and former Portuguese colonies, they were invented more than 200 years ago by the Catholic nuns who lived there. The most famous vendor is Lord Stow's Bakery on Coloane, one of Macau's two main islands.

PORK CHOP BUN

Probably the most famous Macau street food, this consists of a bun that is crisp outside and soft inside filled with a freshly fried pork chop.

JERKY

Macanese jerky—a version of Chinese *bakkwa*—is sold in large square sheets. Hawkers cut off small samples of delicious beef and pork flavors. Unlike Western jerky, it is moist, salty, and sweet all at the same time.

ALMOND COOKIES

Probably Macau's most popular souvenir, these almond cookies have a delicate flavor and a soft, crumbly texture. They are made by hand from a mixture of flour, sugar, shortening, and ground almonds that is pressed into wooden forms, baked in a charcoal oven, and slapped upside down onto tables in order to release the cookies.

COLLEEN TAYLOR SEN

JAPAN

J APAN HAS A FAIRLY HOMOGENEOUS CULTURE; residents of Korean and Chinese origin form less than 1 percent of the population. Throughout the country, there are many local customs and, because of the wide range of climatic conditions, many different agricultural products. Nevertheless, when it comes to street food, there is a remarkable congruity throughout the country. In the past, the coastal areas had greater access to fresh fish than the extensive mountainous areas, which had vegetables unavailable to coastal dwellers. However, with modern transport, this difference is largely a thing of the past, and the more popular items of street food are much the same throughout this nation of 128 million people.

There are numerous occasions in Japanese life when food is eaten out-of-doors, although even when food is prepared in the street, it is considered very bad manners to eat it in the street. It is just not done. If seating under some kind of roof or shelter is not immediately available, then people will take such food to an appropriate place, such as a picnic area, or even back home. Even eating at a bus stop or railway station platform while waiting for a bus or train is not considered acceptable. In a well-known article, a scholar from England describes an incident where newly arrived in Japan he was roundly criticized by one of his students for eating a piece of chocolate while waiting for a bus to set out on a pleasure trip! The informality and fun of the situation were no excuse.

There are, however, many occasions when food may be eaten out-of-doors, notably picnics on certain socially specified occasions and at religious or cultural festivals. Picnics include cherry blossom viewing in spring and enjoying maple and ginkgo leaves in autumn. Festivals include Buddhist temple and Shinto shrine visits in midsummer and at New Year's; university, school and city festivals; and rice-planting and harvest festivals.

Street food packed in boxes is also eaten on trains. The outcome of the chocolate incident related earlier was that the moment the teacher and his student were riding on the bus (a moving vehicle), it was alright to eat the chocolate.

Eating in the street is one thing, but preparing and selling food in the street is quite another. Buying food from street stalls is extremely popular in Japan, but more often than not, a covered area with seats will be provided nearby, or the food will be taken elsewhere to be eaten.

The first festival of the year is the New Year festival, commencing on New Year's Eve and running for the first three days of the new year. This is very much a family celebration at home, but Shinto shrine or Buddhist temple visits are a must. At this time, stalls are set up in the approaches to the shrines, selling *amazake*, a hot, sweet alcoholic beverage flavored with ginger.

Spring arrives and the cherry trees come into bloom. *Hanami* (cherry blossom viewings) offers the excuse for great fun, often with song and dance, under the cherry trees in parks. *Yozakura* (night viewing of cherry blossom) is a favorite activity. Although many groups bring their own home-made food, restaurants, department stores, and street stalls sell special *hanami bento* (boxed foods) containing rice and a variety of delicious tidbits. Summer brings opportunities of picnics, in the country or by the sea, and again food from home or the ubiquitous bento, often bought at a convenience store, provides the eats.

Many towns and cities have summer festivals at which the *yukata* (informal summer kimono) is worn, and on these occasions, the streets and shopping malls will be lined with stalls selling all kinds of street food, preferably to be eaten under an awning of some kind with seats, benches, boxes, or upturned cans to sit on.

With autumn comes *momijigari* (maple leaf viewing), the food being the autumn equivalent of the *hanami* of spring, though there will be no night viewing as it may already be a bit too chilly to eat out-of-doors, and there will not be so much jollity with song and dance, since the autumn mood is lower than that of spring.

On November 3, Culture Day, schools, colleges, and universities all celebrate the day with stalls set up on campus staffed by the students. Here not only will all the usual street foods be sold from stalls, but also there will often be quite innovative items based on foreign food, such as the French dog, a hot dog on a stick fried in batter.

Other occasions for eating bento are train journeys. Every major railway station has several different styles and prices, as well as its own local specialty. Finally, at any time of the year, any night of the week, in cities and large towns, stalls will be set up near railway stations for cheap and convivial eating and drinking. Seating, screened off from public view, will be provided for six or so people. The emphasis is on drinking, with all its conviviality, and street food will be served as an accompaniment. Often men on their way home after a night's drinking will drop in to such a stall (*yomise*), for *chazuke*, a bowl of rice sprinkled with flakes of salted salmon or some such topping and/or pickles, and flooded with tea. It is supposed to be sobering, a fitting end to a night's drinking.

MAJOR STREET FOODS

Most of the street foods are prepared on the spot by grilling or pan frying. Some, usually foreign ones such as corn on the cob, hot dogs, and frankfurters, are boiled, while *jiaozi* are steamed and then fried. This is inconvenient, since it is not easy to provide stalls with a ready supply of water. The source of heat is bottled gas. There is always a ready supply of disposable chopsticks to avoid eating with one's fingers.

The most traditional street foods are *noshi ika*, flattened slices of dried squid, often basted with soy sauce, and skewered on bamboo sticks; and tempura, food deep-fried in batter that was introduced by the Portuguese in the 16th century. Large shrimp is the favorite tempura ingredient. Also popular are squid; slices of sweet potato; green peppers; shishito, a very mild, green chile pepper; eggplant; pumpkin; onion; shiitake mushrooms; and lotus root. Stalls for tempura are nowadays not as popular as they used to be.

Sushi

By the early 19th century, nigiri (or *Edomae*) sushi had become the street food par excellence. *Nigiri* means "squeezed" and refers to the way this kind of sushi is made by squeezing a lump of rice in the palm of the hand. The rice is topped with wasabi and a slice of fish. This kind of sushi originated in Edo, now Tokyo, hence the expression *Edomae*. Nigiri is a true finger food, and it is a mistake to try to eat it with chopsticks in polite company, even when sitting at a table. Good sushi is extremely expensive, and only the most meager sushi, with cheap toppings such as squid, octopus, shrimp, or omelet, is sold as street food.

SHRIMP
NIGIRI

Wasabi is an essential between the rice and the topping (*neta*) and is an expensive ingredient. This has led to the extensive use of fake wasabi, especially abroad, when sushi is served to unsuspecting non-Japanese. This fake wasabi is prepared from powdered horseradish colored green and is much more pungent than true wasabi.

When eating nigiri, it is usual to dip the topping side in soy sauce, which is almost impossible to do when using chopsticks. On the other hand, it needs both hands to manage soy sauce in one hand and sushi in the other. There is nothing for it but to sit down at a table, pick up the sushi with the fingers, and dip the top corner into the soy sauce.

Bento

Bento means both a box-shaped container for carrying food and the food itself. The boxes come in all shapes and sizes and can be very elaborately decorated. For everyday use, it is a simple lidded box, usually with separate compartments for rice and tasty morsels. In the *Hinomaru* (name of the Japanese flag) bento, the box is filled with rice and decorated with a single, salt pickled *umeboshi* (red Japanese apricot). Children take their packed lunch to school in a bento box. Adults take their lunch from home to workplace in a bento box, and those traveling by train either take one from home or buy one at the station, where there is usually a wide choice. On the platform of Kyoto Station, they even sell one containing the vegetarian food eaten by the Buddhist priests, Kyoto being a major center of Buddhist temples. Traditionally, one eats bento during the interval at Noh and Kabuki, traditional styles of Japanese theater.

Normally the rice in bento is cold, but in recent years, enterprising convenience stores have added hot rice to the box at the time of purchase. This is called *hoka hoka bento.* The variety of foods to go with the rice is endless. Pickles are a must, and there might be a shrimp, pieces of fish, or fried oysters, some pieces of chicken, meatballs, pieces of tempura, all sorts of fish preparations such as *kamaboko* and *chikuwa.* The choices are endless.

Okonomiyaki

Okonomi means "your choice," and *okonomiyaki* is a pancake filled with the items requested by the customer. Shredded cabbage is a must, and there is usually a choice of thinly sliced beef or pork, squid, shrimp, or octopus. When ready, the pancake is brushed with a thick version of Worcester sauce and sprinkled with various savory toppings.

Takoyaki

Octopus (*tako*) is the main ingredient in these balls of batter cooked in a cast-iron mold and served with thick sauce and a sprinkling of chopped seaweed.

Ramen

The consumption of ramen, Chinese-style wheat noodles, is restricted to seating inside the stall, since they are served in a bowl of hot soup made from pork or chicken bones, flavored with salt, soy sauce or bean paste (miso), along with various such additions as bamboo shoots, spinach, spring onion, grilled pork, and slices of boiled fish paste. The stalls are most often in the vicinity of a railway station and are very popular with people returning home from work.

Other popular noodles are soba (buckwheat or groat noodles), usually served on a bamboo mat, and udon (soft wheat noodles) that are served in a broth.

Yakisoba

These noodles are made of regular wheat (not buckwheat), which are steamed and served with such vegetables as Chinese cabbage, bamboo shoots, mushrooms, and carrot, with the addition of shrimp, squid, and pork. The ingredients are fried together and served with a rich sauce.

Oden

A medley of popular snack ingredients, *oden* is prepared in a seaweed (kombu) stock. Because it takes time for the ingredients to reach their peak of flavor, the stall must have a stock bath big enough for all the ingredients to simmer in for some hours. Typical ingredients are daikon (long white radish); tofu; *chikuwa* (sausage shaped fish paste stiffened with starch and egg white and grilled on a skewer); peeled potato; hard-boiled egg; octopus tentacles; *ganmodoki* (tofu mixed with various chopped vegetables, formed into balls and deep-fried); and *konnyaku* (blocks of fairly tasteless jelly made from konjac root paste, enjoyed for its chewy texture). The customer's choice is served on a plate with the hottest English-style mustard imaginable and a pair of disposable chopsticks.

Taiyaki

A great favorite with children, *taiyaki* is a sweet snack cooked in an iron mold shaped like a sea bream (*tai*). *Yaki* refers to the direct application of heat, as in grilling or baking. The mold is lined with batter, placed over heat to set the batter, filled with adzuki bean paste, and finished off over heat. Innumerable Japanese confections have a filling of bean paste, of which the Japanese are very fond.

Ishiyaki-imo

Roasted sweet potatoes (*satsuma-imo*) are much loved by children. Children coming home from school love to see the *ishiyaki-imo* vendor waiting for their customers. *Ishiyaki* means "cooked over hot stones"; in this case it's pebbles. The vendor drives the streets in his van and has the sweet potatoes roasting over hot pebbles in a suitable container. The customer chooses a potato, pays for it according to weight, and takes it home wrapped in newspaper for a mid-afternoon snack.

Kuri

Kuri are chestnuts, greatly enjoyed in winter when roasted over hot pebbles. In some busy places, such as a shopping street or railway station, the vendor sets himself up with an empty kerosene can filled with pebbles heated from underneath and roasts the chestnuts on top. They are bought in a paper cone and cannot be eaten with chopsticks, so the fingers must be used.

Kakigori

Shaved ice, *kakigori*, is a traditional summer treat. The ice is shaved in a machine, placed in a bowl, and covered with bright syrup of strawberry, melon, or lemon, or with a sweet red kidney bean jam.

Watagashi

Wata means "cotton wool," and *gashi* means "confection," so *watagashi* is widely familiar spun sugar on a stick, much loved by children as "candy floss" in Britain and "cotton candy" in the United States.

RICHARD HOSKING

MONGOLIA

MONGOLIA IS THE WORLD'S LARGEST LANDLOCKED NATION, covering approximately 604,000 square miles of northeastern Asia, wedged between China and Russia's Siberia. A population of only about 3 million makes it among the most sparsely populated countries in the world. Called Mongol Uls in Mongolian, it is also known as Outer Mongolia, to differentiate it from the Mongol-inhabited region of China known as Inner Mongolia.

Almost 95 percent of the country's population is ethnic Mongol, and Mongolian is the country's official language. The dominant religion is Tibetan Buddhism, usually blended with traditional shamanistic/spiritist beliefs. However, due to the efforts of the Soviets to eradicate religion, about 40 percent of Mongolians now identify themselves as not being part of any religion.

Almost 80 percent of the land is steppe pastureland, which supports huge herds of grazing livestock. The remaining 20 percent of the country is divided almost equally between barren desert and forested mountains. Less than 1 percent of the land is arable.

Mongolians have traditionally been nomadic herders, but both freedom from the Soviet Union and the more recent discovery of large deposits of coal, copper, and gold have both boosted the economy and drawn more people into urban environments. Still, about half the population is nomadic.

Among the nomad population, the amount and types of food vary with the season. In summer, the consumption of dairy products is the heaviest. Everything that can be milked is milked: yaks, camels, horses, goats, sheep. Meat is more heavily consumed during the rest of the year. Cooking is generally done once a day, unless there are guests. Breakfast and lunch are the biggest meals of the day and generally consist of *boortsog* (fried bread), salty milk tea, boiled mutton, broth with noodles or other starch, and dairy products, depending on what is available—fresh milk, sour clotted milk, yogurt, cheese, curds, or *airag* (fermented mare's milk, the national drink of Mongolia).

In urban settings, meals vary only slightly from this, with the major differences largely relics of Russian occupation: borsch occasionally replaces mutton broth, and a salad of shredded beet, carrot, and/or cabbage is common. However, as more people move to cities, Mongolians are experiencing a far wider range of foods (though not always with positive results, as more sugar enters the diet).

Dumplings are tremendously popular, in both rural and urban settings. Sizes vary, but usually not composition. The dough is flour and water, and the filling is chopped meat (usually mutton) with onion and garlic. *Buuz* (pronounced "boats") are two-bite dumplings that are similar to, though fatter than, pot stickers. *Buuz* are steamed. *Bansh* are much smaller and are boiled. *Hushuur* is much larger—about five or six inches on its longest side. Because it is fried, *hushuur* is more portable than the other two dumplings, and it often appears at outdoor venues and festivals, where it is eaten out of hand.

Mongolians happily celebrate anything that marks a milestone in life or the year. They also have a strict code of hospitality. Anyone can approach a *ger* (the round, wool-felt tents of the nomads) and ask for food and drink. For special events, white foods (dairy products) are served first and are considered pure and noble. Then red foods (meat) are served.

MAJOR STREET FOODS

The culture of Mongolia does not historically include a lot of street food—largely because the history of Mongolia has not generally involved streets. However, even in traditional culture, there has always been a need for portable food, from picnics to festivals, with *hushuur* and grilled meats topping the list here.

Today, as more and more Mongolians find themselves living urban lives, they rely on street vendors to supply them with foods that were once part of their daily diets. An almost ubiquitous feature of the both urban and rural landscapes is the *guanz*, a generally modest establishment that offers Mongolian comfort food, including soup, salty milk tea, and either *buuz* or *hushuur*. A *guanz* can be located in a building, a *ger*, a small hut, or even a railway car.

CYNTHIA CLAMPITT

SOUTH KOREA

T HE KOREAN PENINSULA juts out from the north Asian continental landmass into the Yellow Sea on the west and the East Sea (or Sea of Japan) on the east. It is highly mountainous, its lowlands mainly along the west coast with pockets of fertile areas scattered across the country along its slow-flowing rivers. With its northern latitude and mountains, the Republic of Korea (popularly known as South Korea) has long, cold winters and brief, hot summers. However, the surrounding seas mitigate an inhospitable climate. The peninsula's southernmost tip and especially such islands as Jeju have warmer climates that make them tourist resorts.

Climate and landforms profoundly affect Korean cuisine. Seafood of every variety is a staple. In fishing areas, long lines of drying cuttlefish are ordinary sights, and seaweed is a standard dish consumed at many meals. The country's mountain pine forests grow many varieties of mushrooms used in all kinds of cookery and even attract Japanese tourist groups who come to pick them. The cold climate and relatively short growing seasons mean that food preservation for long winters has always been important. Pickling is an art form for Korean cooks, the most famous being pickled and spiced vegetables called kimchi. So famous are the hundred or so varieties that Seoul has a whole museum dedicated to kimchi, and it is now found in grocery stores in many parts of the United States.

Many of the foods prepared, sold, and eaten on the street in South Korea represent its most internationally recognized dishes. This is notable for the fact that the varied street-food culture that thrives now on city streets and highway rest stops didn't widely exist before the 1960s. Up until then, the great majority of the unified country's population was rural, working on land near home. Food was produced and eaten at home, and eating out was not a part of the culture. Apart from simple taverns that existed during the period of Japanese occupation, even fixed restaurants and drinking establishments did not exist.

At the end of the Chosun Dynasty (1392–1897), about 3 percent of the Korean population lived in cities. That began to change during the period of Japanese Occupation (1910–1945), especially during the Korean War (1950–1953) and its aftermath, when Seoul became host to a vast population of refugees with no home to go to. The population surged further in the 1960s, during a period of intense industrialization spearheaded by the president at the time, Park Chunghee. Street food was an essential component in that growth, offering cheap, easily accessible meals to the poor, working class, and displaced.

It was during this period of rapid growth that the iconic street-food venue *pojangmacha*, or tented wagon, first began to appear on city streets to serve huge populations of displaced urbanites. The *pojangmacha* is a mobile kitchen that appears on city streets in larger numbers at night. The vendors frequently provide benches or small stools for customers to eat in heated spaces enclosed in plastic curtains.

Initially, *pojangmacha* were drinking places. Soju, the lightly fermented rice brew *makgeoli*, and later beer were accompanied by *anju*, snacks meant to be eaten with alcohol. Roasted sparrows, being cheap and easy to procure, were common and remained so up until the early 1990s, when a more diverse and varied mix began to appear.

Today South Korea is one of the world's most densely populated countries, and it is the 15th largest economy. Street food thrives on its city streets and highways. In 2007, the Korean Street Vendors ConFederation estimated the number of street-food vendors—encompassing smaller carts, stands, and *pojangmacha*—between 40,000 and 50,000, while the government put it at 12,351. A March 2012 CNN Travel article placed the number of *pojangmacha* at 3,100. Today they cater to a broad customer base of office workers, students, late-night revelers, and tourists and provide a wide array of foods in settings both humble and elaborate, from small, stand-alone carts to large, full-service, semipermanent structures with varied menus.

The food offered at *pojangmacha* is cooked in full view of the customers and is often served on plastic plates encased in disposable plastic bags. Customers are seated at benches or small tables, and plastic curtains protect them from the elements. Interior spaces are heated in winter months. Often a roll of toilet tissue hangs from above to provide self-serve napkins. Some large *pojangmacha* feature water tanks filled with live octopus, sea cucumber, seas slugs, snails, and other sea creatures, and customers have the opportunity to choose those they would like the vendor to prepare.

The number of *pojangmacha* has declined in recent years, due to the efforts of government officials seeking to clear city space or regulate hygiene. In response, some vendors have organized. In 2011, the government corralled some 76 vendors operating in the tourist-heavy central Seoul neighborhood of Insa-Dong into designated areas. In 2010, the Seoul-based Korean Street Vendors ConFederation protested a government crackdown on street vendors and migrant workers in advance of the G20 summit, the annual meeting of leaders from 20 major world economies. Three years earlier, they organized against attempts to restrict them to certain zones and operate within prescribed hours.

On the other hand, some *pojangmacha* operators have become so successful that they have franchised their operations. Recently, operators of permanent nonmobile establishments have begun calling themselves *pojangmacha*, taking on the name to conjure up nostalgic associations. These often serve as meeting places for young singles.

The variety and diversity of food available on the street in South Korea today have multiplied since the days of roasted sparrows. Rice cakes, *kimbap*, kimchi pancakes, skewered meats, and fish cakes are universal, but a global influence is increasingly apparent, particularly in Seoul and other large cities. One can find everything from hamburgers and hot dogs to Chinese dragon's beard candy, Turkish ice cream, and *döner kebab*. While Korean food itself has established its own international profile, so has its street food. In the United States, the neo-food truck movement in the first decade of the century was sparked in part by the Kogi BBQ truck in Los Angeles, a food truck serving a Korean–Mexican fusion of short rib kimchi tacos. This has come full circle as some enterprising vendors have begun selling kimchi tacos on the streets of South Korea.

MAJOR STREET FOODS

Ddeokbokki

A dish that ironically originated in the royal palace during the Chosun Dynasty, this is perhaps the most popular food found on city streets, often served along-side other common dishes. Long, chewy cylindrical rice cakes called *garaetteok* are stewed in a fiery chile-based sauce alongside fish cakes (*odeng*) and vegeta-bles. Other such items as hard-cooked eggs, dumplings (*mandu*), noodles, and meats are sometimes added. Sometimes *garaetteok* are grilled and sold plain.

Odeng or Eomuk

Similar to the Japanese *oden*, *odeng* are fish cakes pro-cessed with wheat flour, threaded onto skewers, and cooked in a steaming, savory broth. As they simmer over hours, the broth becomes more flavorful. A complimentary cup of the broth is often offered on cold nights.

Kimbap

The ubiquitous *kimbap*, adopted during the Japanese Occupation and derived from *maki-mono*, is composed of thin layers of pressed, dried seaweed (*kim*) rolled around steamed rice (*bap*) and various fillings such as bulgogi, fish cakes, egg, imitation crab, cucumbers, or kimchi or other pickled vegetables. Sliced into bite-sized disks, they are portable and easily eaten with the hands. It is not only the ideal street food, but a typical lunch or light travel snack as well.

Kimbap *is easily portable, making it an ideal street food.*

Sundae

Sundae are deep-purple, steamed blood sausages. Pig or cow intestines are stuffed with blood and cellophane noodles and seasoned with garlic, green onion, or chile powder. Often served with other dishes such as *ddeokbokki* and *odeng*, or other offal such as liver or lungs, they are cut on the bias and eaten with toothpicks. Recipes vary from region to region and vendor to vendor, and in some areas, regional seafood-based versions are prepared. *Sundae* can also be incorporated into other dishes or used as an ingredient in soups and stir-fries. There are restaurants that specialize in *sundae* that are frequently concentrated in particular areas.

Dakkochi

These are skewered chicken chunks, glazed in a variety of sauces, including sweet honey based, salty soy based, or spicy chile and ginger. Grilled over coals, *dakkochi* are among the most popular foods on the street in Korea, partly due to their portability. Other chicken parts—feet, gizzards, and hearts—are commonly sold.

OTHER STREET FOODS

Beondegi

Beondegi are silkworm pupae boiled or steamed, served in cups, and skewered with toothpicks. They are a high-protein snack commonly eaten with alcohol. They emit a powerful, shrimplike, nutty aroma that can be smelled from a distance, sometimes before they come into view. Their brown exoskeleton softens when cooked, and when chewed, they emit a burst of hot briny liquid. With their insectoid appearance, they can seem startling to tourists from countries where the consumption of insects is not common. Eating *beondegi* for the first time is often viewed as a rite of passage for tourists and expatriates living in Korea.

Jeon

Jeon are crispy pancakes, griddled from rice or wheat flour, water, and sometimes eggs, served with a variety of add-ins. They are common appetizers in restaurants, along with other *banchan* (side dishes). But *jeon* make endlessly variable appearances on the street as well. The green scallion pancake *pajeon*, sometimes incorporated with seafood, is the most common, but other popular varieties include *kimchijeon*, made with kimchi; *yukjeon*, made with beef; and *haemul pajeon*, which can include any combination of fish, shrimp, squid, or octopus. A relative, *bindaetteok*, is made with coarsely ground mung bean batter, which rises thick and fluffy and takes on an extra crispy exterior due to the crunchy beans. *Jeon* are eaten with chopsticks and often served with a dipping sauce of soy, vinegar, garlic, and chilies.

Twigim
Analogous to Japanese tempura, *twigim* refers to items that are batter-dipped and deep-fried; these can include meat, seafood, vegetables, and even *kimbap*.

Other Sausages
A variety of sausages made from meat and fish appear on city streets skewered lengthwise and wrapped in all manner of foods, such as seaweed or bacon. Others are stuffed with rice cakes or cheese. Corn dogs and hot dogs encrusted with French fries are among the most popular, reflecting a growing Western influence on Korean street food.

Dried Seafood
Cuttlefish, squid, filefish, or other species of sea life are pressed and dried. When ordered, the vendor heats the item on a grill to soften it. These are common drinking snacks.

Other Roasted Foods
Corn on the cob, sweet potatoes, chestnuts, and ginkgos are all common items, roasted over coals.

BIBIMBAP

Bibimbap
This popular Korean rice salad is more common as a restaurant item or a dish eaten at home, but in certain markets, such as Seoul's Gwangjang Market, vendors set up elaborate stands lined with deep bowls of ingredients and build the salad to order. The dish starts with a bowl of rice and may include bulgogi, pickled vegetables, sprouts, cucumbers, mushrooms, spinach, and carrots, and it is often topped with a fried egg and a spicy sauce made from chile paste (*gochujang*).

Hotteok
This sweet pancake is made from wheat flour, water, milk, and yeast and filled

with a mixture of brown sugar, cinnamon, and nuts. It is a popular wintertime street food. The raw dough is stuffed with the filling, which is then pressed flat on a grill. As it cooks, the sugar on the inside melts.

Bungeoppang

Bungeoppang, or "crucian carp bread," is named for a specific species of fish. The bread takes the form of that fish and is filled with a sweet red bean paste. Batter is poured into a heated cast-iron mold, the bean paste is added, and then more batter is added before the mold is closed. The resulting pastry is light and fluffy, the interior hot and soft. Sometimes the cakes are made in other shapes such as flowers, eggs, and in reference to a popular children's cartoon character, piles of excrement.

Haeynyo

One unusual expression of street food can be found along the beaches of South Korea's island province of Jeju. There a fishery run by the island's women has been well established for decades. The *haeynyo*, or literally "sea women," represent a matriarchal society in which the women developed a thriving fishery, while men—who would otherwise be taxed—stayed at home and cared for the children. These wet suit–clad mermaids dive deep into the ocean holding their breath for long minutes and return to the surface with sea urchins, abalone, seaweed, and other products. In some beach areas, *haeynyo* set up tables and swim right up to the shore with their catch, serving sea urchins, snails, or small fish at plastic tables. This is a slowly disappearing way of life, as many of the *haeynyo* became so prosperous that they were able to afford to send their daughters to school on the mainland, and few remained to take after them.

MIKE SULA

TAIWAN

T AIWAN (OFFICIALLY THE REPUBLIC OF CHINA) is an island nation located across the Taiwan Strait 110 miles off the southeastern coast of China. It consists of the island of Taiwan (formerly known as Formosa), which forms more than 99 percent of its current territory, as well as several smaller islands. About 98 percent of the 23 million Taiwanese are of Chinese ancestry; the rest are Taiwanese aboriginals. Nearly half of the population lives in five cities: Taipei, New Taipei, Kaohsiung, Taichung, and Tainan. Between 1895 and 1945, Taiwan was a dependency of Japan. All these influenced its cuisine.

Some of the finest food in Taiwan can be found in the night markets, which have seen tremendous popularity over the past 30 years or so. Formerly, street food was sold from moving carts, but now many vendors are consolidated into specific areas. These markets, which do most of their business after hours, usually sell more than just food. In Taipei and Kaohsiung, night-market vendors are sometimes owners of regular brick-and-mortar restaurants that extend their selling area during the evening hours by putting stands on the street or unfurling awnings to create small and separate eating and serving spaces. The customers represent a broad cross section of Taiwanese society, especially young people for whom night markets are places that are well-lit, safe, and fun. There is more of a balance between male and female vendors than in Southeast Asia.

In Taipei, Shilin Night Market is a well-established destination for locals and tourists, with designated train stops, a tourist office, and other encouragements to increased traffic. In Kaohsiung, Liuhe Night Market offers a spectacular array of *xiaochi* (small eats) and a number of exotic food items, including snake meat. Although it's a regular city street by day, at night there are barriers set up to block autos.

An important part of night markets' offerings are *xiaochi*, which are actually substantial snacks along the lines of Spanish tapas. These are often innovative blends of local and foreign cuisine, and some night markets are famous for their special *xiaochi*.

Breakfast is an experience that Taiwanese people take seriously. You are never too far away from savory goodness on the street, especially in cities like Taipei. A typical Taiwanese breakfast may consist of *youtiao* (translated literally as "oil stick" or "twisted cruller"), warm soybean milk, *shaobing* (wheat cake, sometimes wrapped around various fillings of meats and vegetables), *luo bo gao* (turnip cake), and a number of buns (steamed or deep fried with meat and vegetable fillings). It is not uncommon to leave breakfast completely full.

MAJOR STREET FOODS

Stinky Tofu
The most memorable of the foods sold in Taiwanese night markets is stinky tofu. Fresh firm bean curd is fermented in a brine solution of meat and/or vegetable juices for as long as several months until the preparation turns a white, relatively flavorless and odorless substance into a brown, intensely smelly mouthful. Usually grilled or fried, stinky tofu is sometimes served with hot sauce or pickled cabbage that stands up to its flavors. The inside is surprisingly fluffy and soft.

Beef Noodle Soup
Many Taiwanese, when asked to name their favorite foods, will likely list beef noodle soup. The soup is predictably simple and satisfying. To enjoy it as the Taiwanese do, take a bowl at the midpoint or end of the meal rather than the beginning.

Skewered Meat
Many street stands in Taipei and Kaohsiung serve rolled pork, chunks of beef, and organs such as chicken hearts on skewers. Frequently, the meat is uncooked until it's ordered; buyers select the items they want by placing them in small baskets that they hand to the vendor who grills them to order.

Pig's Blood Cake
Served on a stick or in individual patties, this sometimes rather mild-tasting street-eat is composed of sticky rice soaked in pig's blood, steamed, bathed in a pork soy broth, rolled in crushed peanuts, and perhaps sprinkled with herbs. These magenta-colored cakes are cut into rectangles (or sometimes served on popsicle sticks) and benefit from a dash of hot sauce.

Fried Oyster Omelette
After a long night out, it is hard to find another dish that hits the spot more than an oyster omelette, fried to order with fresh oysters. The saltiness of the oyster adds umami to the dish, which is already rich in fat and spiciness. The omelette is usually cooked in pork lard and pairs well with Taiwanese beer.

Minced Meat Pork over Rice
Food stalls scattered all over Taiwan specialize in *lu rou fan* (minced pork over rice). The dish is a simple yet complete meal that can be consumed quickly. It consists of minced pork meat that is fried and then braised in soy sauce, rice wine, and local variations of spices. Often, the *lu rou fan* is accompanied by bok choy and served over a bowl of rice. A successful *lu rou fan* restaurant has perfected the flavor, texture, and consistency of the sauce in which the minced pork is served. As of 2016, a small, medium, or large bowl may cost 1, 2, and 3 U.S. dollars respectively.

Tea
Though alcohol is an uncommon sight in street markets, it is served at permanent restaurants that have extended their presence into the streets. More popular than alcohol, however, is tea, which is a major product of the island. Taiwan currently produces a range of teas, including somewhat surprisingly, Assam, an Indian variety brought to the island by the Japanese who encouraged its production, believing it to be more competitive than green tea in Western markets. The signature leaf on Taiwan is oolong, and the wide range of geographical variation on the island permits the cultivation of many different varieties of this tea.

OOLONG,
TAIWAN'S SIGNATURE
TEA LEAF

OTHER STREET FOODS

Bubble Tea

Also called pearl milk tea, this beverage originated in tea shops in Taichung in the 1980s. It generally contains tea, some fruit juice, milk or nondairy creamer, and the all-important tiny balls of chewy tapioca. Usually served cold rather than hot, the namesake bubbles are sucked up through oversized straws specially designed to accommodate them.

Fatty Pork Sausages

Sausages are a common sight in many Asian food markets. In Taiwan, the most popular are fatty pork sausages, which are just what their name implies: chunks of pork with a hefty dose of pork fat. Fatty pork sausages are frequently grilled and served on a stick pushed lengthwise through the sausage.

Quail Egg with Shrimp

Taiwanese street markets are open to such innovative food offerings as quail egg and salty shrimp, with a sprinkle of herbs, sharp Japanese-style pickles, and a squirt of cream served in a small pastry shell. A chunk of fresh pineapple can be added for sweet-savoriness, and this dish is a good example of some of nontraditional, highly imaginative minor offerings available at Taiwanese food markets.

Fruit

Travel literature issued by Taiwanese tourism agencies tout the country as the Kingdom of Fruit, and there's no doubt that Taiwan is home to a vast range of fruits, sold whole or in cut-up sections in markets throughout the island. Some of the more popular and distinctive varieties include

- Though not unique to Taiwan, durian is popular on the island. Durian is one of those foods that, like stinky tofu, is challenging for Westerners to appreciate (and perhaps even harder to eat). The fruit emits what is for many an off-putting scent of sweetness and sulfur. Though it may be an acquired taste, those who have pushed past the smell seem almost addicted to the fruit.

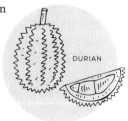

DURIAN

- Buddha's head, also called cherimoya, is native to the Americas. This large green fruit has thick flesh that's similar to papaya or mango, very tasty, and refreshing. The name derives from the artichoke-like layers of leaves that are reminiscent of the way the Buddha's head is sometimes portrayed in Asian art.
- Though it's likely they were brought to Taiwan by the Japanese, lychees are now eaten in the street and in restaurants. Their popularity attests to the extraordinary ability of the people of Taiwan to accept, assimilate, and make the products of other countries their own.

DAVID HAMMOND

SOUTHERN ASIA

AFGHANISTAN

T HE DIVERSITY OF AFGHANISTAN'S CLIMATE, geography, ethnicity, and agriculture has given rise to a rich and varied street-food culture. A landlocked
country, Afghanistan is situated at the crossroads of four major cultural areas:
the Middle East, Central Asia, the Indian subcontinent, and the Far East. Afghanistan played a vital role linking East and West along the ancient Silk Road,
where ideas, religion, trade, foods, and plants were exchanged.

Afghanistan, one of the poorest countries in the world, has had a turbulent
history, which continues to the present day. It has an estimated population of between 28 and 33 million, including 4 million in the capital Kabul. The population
is a mosaic of ethnic groups, the main ones being Pashtun, Tajik, Hazara, Uzbek,
Turkmen, and Baloch. While the majority (99 percent) are Muslims, there are
small pockets of Hindus and Sikhs. Many Afghans who fled to Iran, Pakistan, and
India during the Soviet occupation and the subsequent Taliban era have returned
home and brought back new dishes and ways of cooking.

Afghans love to snack, especially on outings, picnics, special holidays, feast
days, or on their way home from work. Despite the ongoing security situation,
chaikhana, kebab stalls, food stalls, and street vendors are still doing a thriving
trade. The food is always prepared and sold by men.

Chaikhana (teahouses), located throughout the country, are establishments
where weary travelers can be refreshed after long and dusty journeys. *Chaikhana*
are also meeting places where local men meet to exchange gossip and news
over tea from a constantly boiling samovar. Some serve such simple food as the

traditional teapot soup (*sherwa-e-chainaki*), a preparation of lamb, onions, and cilantro simmered in a teapot.

Kebab stalls can be found in the major towns and cities. Charikar, a town north of Kabul, is famous for its *seekh kebab*, while Jalalabad in the east is known for its *chapli kebab*. Kebab stalls (*dukan-e-kebabi*) are very basic. Some have rickety chairs and tables and they sell soft drinks, and some are attached or next door to a *chaikhana*, while others are just a stall where customers eat the tasty, succulent kebabs while standing around the stall or walking along the street. The *kebabi* (stallholder) stands behind his *manqal* (charcoal brazier), wafting his *pakka* (kebab fan) over the coals to keep them glowing and turning the skewered kebabs over from time to time. He often has an assistant, usually a young boy learning the trade, who fans the charcoal from the front.

All the major cities (Kabul, Herat, Mazar-i-Sharif, Kunduz, Kandahar, Jalalabad) and some small towns have food stalls and street vendors. They position themselves outside schools, shopping centers, cinemas, government buildings (although not recently because of the potential of suicide bombers), and in parks and bazaars, such as Kabul's Mandawi food market. Street-food stalls can also be found at popular picnic spots and religious sites and shrines.

The old-style street vendors, called *tabang wala*, have very basic equipment. They carry their wares on a large, flat, round wooden tray (*tabang*) and stake their claim to a particular street corner or patch. In recent years, the old-style *tabang wala* have been disappearing. Today, most street vendors have a more elaborate and better equipped mobile kiosk on wheels with a canopy and usually facilities for frying food on the spot. The type of food sold often depends on the region and the time of the year. A traditional street food is *shour nakhod*, chickpeas doused with a mint and vinegar dressing and served with vibrantly colored chutneys. The same dressing and chutneys are also an accompaniment to cooked red kidney beans or boiled sliced potatoes.

A recent development is *chaat*, a combination of boiled potatoes, kidney beans, and chickpeas sprinkled with pomegranate seeds and *chaat* spice powder, introduced by refugees returning to Afghanistan from Pakistan and India. Other snacks are *sambosa*, stuffed pastries, similar to Indian samosas, with a minced meat and pea filling subtly spiced with cumin and cilantro and a little chopped green chile, and *pakora*, made from such vegetables as sliced par-boiled potatoes, cauliflower sprigs, onion rings, or sliced eggplants dipped into a chickpea flour batter and deep-fried. They are usually served with a mint or coriander chutney.

Corn on the cob is roasted over a charcoal brazier and sprinkled with salt. Noodle dishes such as *mantu* and *aush* are also popular.

Street vendors are particularly active on such religious or festive days as Eid or Nauroz (the Persian/Afghan New Year on the first day of spring) when children and grown-ups go out for picnics or fly their kites. In the crisp spring air, people enjoy a plateful of steaming hot and spicy *pilau-e-tolaki*, or "weighed" *pilau*, so called because the *tabang wala* weighs out the *pilau* on scales, using stones that weigh one-quarter or half a pound. *Pilau* is rice cooked in stock with meat or vegetables with spices added and, in Afghanistan, often garnished with carrots, nuts, and raisins. Children buy roasted chickpeas, pine nuts, raisins, or sugared almonds served in cone-shaped paper bags. *Khasta-e-shireen* is a kind of nut brittle made by pouring caramel over almond or apricot kernels and forming large, round, plate-like shapes. Other sweet treats include *halwa-e-swanak*, a nut brittle made with pistachios or walnuts, and *halwa-e-marghzi*, a rather odd-looking sweet made with a milk, sugar, and walnut syrup. It is very viscous and is stretched and shaken in the air from a wooden pole until it sets hard.

Another common sight in the bazaars in spring is *kishmish panir*—balls of white cheese, known as *panir-e-khom*, displayed on a bed of green vine leaves. The fresh cheese, brought to the market by people from the mountains or outlying districts, is sold with red raisins (*kishmish surkh*).

In summer and autumn, *kishmish ab*, made of raisins soaked in water and served in a small bowl or glass, makes a refreshing drink. *Khakshir* is an herbal drink made from the seeds of *Sisymbrium irio*, also known as London rocket. The seeds are soaked in water with sugar for a few hours and then drunk, preferably over ice. *Khakshir* has long been valued as a medicine, especially for asthma and detoxifying the liver, but today it is sold by street vendors as a refreshment. Juices and sherbets are made from such fruits or vegetables as carrots, pomegranates, and cherries. *Ab-e-kista* is a juice made from dried apricots with the stone removed reconstituted in water. *Gholeng* is a similar drink made with a smaller variety of apricot, but the stone is not removed. *Ab-e-zafaran* is made by adding water to saffron with a little sugar. Lemon juice is also popular and is sweetened with sugar or sometimes salt. A juice is also made from sugarcane.

Such fruits as mango and banana are made into a kind of milk shake or smoothie. The fruit is whizzed up in a processor with almonds and milk or yogurt. Other popular drinks are *dogh* (a yogurt drink flavored with mint and often with grated or small pieces of cucumber) similar to the *ayran* of the Middle East. Summer is also the time for *sheer yakh* (ice cream) or *faluda*.

During Jeshyn, an autumn festival celebrating Afghan independence, street vendors sell the snacks described earlier as well as such seasonal fruits as slices of melon and watermelon, grapes, peaches, and nectarines.

Specialty food shops or permanent stalls serve specific dishes. In winter, *haleem* (a cereal and meat porridge served with melted ghee or oil and sprinkled with ground cinnamon, cardamom, and sugar) is bought by men early in the morning, especially on Fridays after going to the *hamam* (public baths). They take it home to their families for breakfast. *Sherwa-e-cala pacha* is another takeaway breakfast dish, a hearty and warming soup made from sheep's head and feet. *Cala pilau*, a rice dish made with the head of a sheep, is another popular takeaway. Winter is also the time for deep-fried local and imported fish and *jalebi*, an unusual combination. *Jalebi* is a sweet composed of whorls of batter, deep-fried and soaked in syrup.

Food hygiene and safety are a major concern for anyone eating outside the home. Despite the existence of a Department of Hygiene in the Ministry of Health, food hygiene is fairly basic, and one eats street food at one's own risk. The cleanliness of some of the implements and serving plates is often doubtful. Food served on naan or on paper plates poses less risk. Stomach problems and illnesses are endemic in Afghanistan. However, any food that is fried at a high temperature and served immediately is less risky than food that has been prepared earlier.

MAJOR STREET FOODS

Kebabs

The term kebab can describe any type of meat (except pork, which is forbidden to Muslims) grilled, barbecued, cooked in the oven, or fried. It can range from a whole baby lamb baked in a tandoor to ground meat formed into patties or sausage shapes.

The most common kebabs sold at stalls are *tikka* or *seekh kebabs*. Small cubes of lamb interspersed with fat called *dumba* from the tail of the fat-tailed sheep are threaded on skewers (*seekh*) and grilled over charcoal. The cooked kebabs are served on top of bread: either naan, a leavened, baked wheat bread; *lawausha*, a larger, thinner type of naan; or chapati, an unleavened wheat bread cooked on a griddle. Crushed dried sour grapes (*ghora*), salt, and red pepper are sprinkled over the kebabs. For takeaway, the crushed grapes and pepper are placed in little cone-shaped paper bags and the kebabs wrapped in the *lawausha* bread. If the kebabs are eaten in at the stall, they may be served with a salad of sliced onions and tomatoes with cilantro and some lemon or *norinj* (Seville orange) wedges as a garnish.

Kofta or *keema kebabs* are made with minced meat formed into sausage shapes, threaded on skewers and cooked over charcoal. *Karahi kebab* can be made from either *kofta kebab* or *seekh kebab*. The kebabs are removed from the skewers and placed in a round metal pan called a *karahi* with a little oil and fried quickly for a few seconds. Eggs are broken over the top and fried until cooked, sprinkled with salt and pepper, and served straight from the pan.

S*hinwari*, lamb chop kebabs (named after the Shinwari, one of the large Pashtun tribes of the North West Frontier), were once a favorite in the old town of Kabul. (A similar kebab, called *qaburgha*, is sometimes made from ribs of veal and is called *pushti* kebab by Pashtuns especially in Kandahar and Herat, two cities renowned for this type of kebab.) The old town of Kabul was also famous for kebabs made with liver (*jigar*), kidney (*gourda*), and lambs' testicles (*kebab-e-kalpura*), believed to be an aphrodisiac. Some vendors make *chopan kebab*, named after shepherds (*chopan*) who rub chunks of lamb on the bone with plenty of salt, skewer the meat on twigs or small branches, and roast them over fire while watching their flocks. A specialty of Jalalabad is fried *chapli kebab*, which can be very hot and consists of minced meat, lots of *gandana* (a type of Chinese chive), scallions, cilantro, and plenty of green chilies. *Chapli* means "sandal" in Dari, which this kebab resembles. Chicken kebab, previously an expensive commodity, has become popular. The legs, thighs, wings, or breasts are marinated and then fried in a pan over charcoal or gas burners.

Noodle Dishes

Noodle dishes come from northern Afghanistan and reflect the influence of Central Asia. *Aush* is a wheat-flour noodle soup to which chickpeas, red kidney beans, or other vegetables are added. Strained yogurt (*chaka*) or reconstituted dried yogurt (*quroot*) is stirred in, and the entire mixture is flavored with garlic, mint, and chile pepper. A dollop of minced meat cooked in an onion and tomato sauce is often added on top. *Aush-e-asli* are boiled wheat noodles to which are added meatballs cooked in a tomato sauce.

Mantu is a traditional Uzbek dish. Noodle-type wheat dough is stuffed with finely chopped lamb and onion and subtly spiced with finely chopped green chile, black pepper, and cumin, and steamed. These dumplings are served with strained yogurt and sprinkled with chopped fresh cilantro. Some are served with a carrot korma.

Boulanee

Boulanee is a stuffed fried pastry. Fillings may include squash, spinach, and mung beans, but the most popular ones are filled with chopped *gandana* or mashed potato and scallions. They are usually made in a half-moon shape and served with chutney.

Shour Nakhod

Shour means "salty" and *nakhod* are chickpeas. Chickpeas are simmered slowly in plenty of water over several hours, then mounded and patted together to resemble a cake on a large platter. The vendor takes a small plate and expertly cuts a portion of the chickpeas, without collapsing the mound, places it in a small bowl, and sprinkles generous amounts of mint and vinegar dressing on top. Chutney is served as an accompaniment.

OTHER STREET FOODS

Ice Cream

Sheer yakh means "frozen milk" in Dari (the Persian dialect spoken in Afghanistan). Traditionally, ice cream is a springtime or summer treat sold by the *sheer yakh ferosh* (ice cream seller) who makes it in a large tub-like metal cylinder with a smaller cylinder or bucket inside. The outer cylinder, which is stationary, is filled with salt and snow. The inner cylinder is filled with milk, sugar, and flavorings such as rosewater and cardamom. Sometimes *sahlab* (salep), a fine white powder obtained from the dried root tubers of orchids, is added to give a more elastic and smooth texture. The ice cream is rotated by hand; from time to time, the ice-cream maker inserts a long spoon-like pole to mix the ice cream from bottom to top. The rotation continues until the ice cream is frozen and has a creamy texture. Chopped pistachios or almonds are often sprinkled on top.

ICE AND SNOW

In his book *An Account of the Kingdom of Caubul* (1842), Mountstuart Elphinstone wrote of *faluda:*

> Ice, or rather snow, is to be had in Caubul, during the summer, for a mere trifle. . . . A favourite food at that season is fulodeh, a jelly strained from boiled wheat, and eaten with the expressed juice of fruits and ice, to which cream also is sometimes added.

Variations are found in Iran, India, Pakistan, and throughout West Asia. In Afghanistan, *faluda* is made by soaking whole wheat grains and grinding them with water to yield a milky liquid called *nishaste.* It is cooked to make a paste that is forced through a kind of colander or pasta machine into iced water where tiny rice-like grains or small vermicelli are formed. They are called *jhala,* which means hailstones. The *jhala* may be served with crushed ice and topped with a fruit sherbet or syrup, or are used as a topping for ice cream, *qymaq* (clotted cream), or *firni,* a milk pudding flavored and thickened with salep. All are topped with sprinkling of rosewater and chopped pistachio nuts.

Huge blocks of packed snow are "mined" from the slopes of the Hindu Kush and taken in large blocks in trucks to Kabul, where they are used for making ice cream and iced sherbets and for cooling drinks. A traditional drink called *shireen barf* (sweet snow) is made by pouring multicolored syrups, often flavored with rosewater, over shaved snow. S*heer barf* (milk snow) is milk mixed with shavings of snow and topped with a similar syrup.

Sheer yakh qalebi is another traditional ice cream made in cone-shaped metal molds. The same ice-cream mixture is placed into these molds that are sealed with dough before freezing. Today two innovative companies are producing factory-made ice creams that are sold from modern wheeled carts with covers. Some are served in cone-shaped wafers (*sheer yakh qalebi*). Ice cream is sold on a flat wooden stick and in a plastic container with a wooden spoon. This has led to the demise of "old-style" ice creams and *faluda*, although it is still served in the Old City and some upmarket ice-cream parlors.

HELEN SABERI

BANGLADESH

T HE PEOPLE'S REPUBLIC OF BANGLADESH, located between Burma and India on the Bay of Bengal, has an area of 144,000 square kilometers and a population of 142 million, making it the world's eighth largest country in population and one of the world's most densly populated. The climate is tropical. Around 80 percent of the landmass is on the fertile alluvial lowland called the Bangladesh Plain, which receives heavy rainfalls during the monsoon season.

The territory that now constitutes Bangladesh was under the rule of various Islamic rulers, including the Mughals, from 1201 to 1757, when it passed under British rule. From then until 1947, the year in which India gained its independence from Britain, the territory was part of the Indian province of Bengal. In 1947, the region became East Pakistan, a part of the Islamic Republic of Pakistan. East Pakistan gained its independence from Pakistan in 1971 and became an independent country. The capital of Bangladesh, Dhaka, has a population of more than 12 million people and is by far the largest city.

Culturally, linguistically, and gastronomically, Bangladesh has much in common with the Indian state of West Bengal. The main difference is religion. Whereas West Bengal is a predominantly Hindu region, around 85 percent of the population of Bangladesh are Muslim, 15 percent are Hindu, and 1 percent practice Buddhism or a tribal religion. Thus, most Bangladeshis follow Islamic food practices, which forbid the consumption of pork and alcohol.

The main crop of Bangladesh is rice, and it is the staple of the Bengali diet. Rice is heated in a sand-filled oven and popped to make *muri*, a popular component of many street snacks. The second dietary staple is wheat, which is grown in the western parts of the country.

The rich soil of Bangladesh produces a multitude of edible plants. Vegetables include eggplants, cabbage, cauliflower, beans, many kinds of gourds and squash, chilies, okra, amaranth, sweet potatoes, spinach, carrots, plantains, onions, radish, and water lilies. All parts of many plants are eaten, including the leaves, roots, stems, flowers, and stalks. Potatoes, grown in the winter, are widely eaten as a vegetable rather than a staple. Bangladesh abounds with more than 60 varieties of tropical and subtropical fruits. The most widely cultivated are mango, amra (a sour green fruit), pineapple, banana, lychee, citrus fruits, guava, papaya, custard apple, jambura (a large citrus fruit), sapodilla, coconut, tamarind, melon, watermelon, pomegranate, palmyra, plum, rose apple, and jackfruit (the national fruit of Bangladesh).

A major source of protein is fish, which is abundant in rivers, canals, floodplains, ponds, and lakes and in the Bay of Bengal. Because meat is expensive, consumption is low and is eaten by many Bangladeshis only on special occasions. The most common meats are beef, water buffalo, goat, and chicken. Bangladesh is a major producer and exporter of chilies.

While Bangladesh has a rich culinary tradition, with elaborate multicourse meals characterizing the tables of the country's richest citizens, the food served up on the streets is much simpler. Bangladesh has one of the world's highest poverty rates, and its street food is primarily made of ingredients that are cheaply available and affordable to all classes. Meat is a rarity, as is fish. While street vendors are found presiding over pots of spicy *haleem* (a wheat and meat porridge), beef kebabs, and *shutki* (dried fish), these dishes are the exception rather than the rule. Most Bengali street food is made from lentils, vegetables, nuts, fruits, and cheaply available staples like rice and atta (whole wheat) flour. Chilies, spices, sugar, and distinctive cooking oils give street-side foods the full flavor that Bengalis enjoy. Many popular street foods are similar to those sold in India and Pakistan.

Bangladesh has one of the world's highest population densities, and as a result, street-food vendors are found almost everywhere. Wandering hawkers and pushcart vendors are called *feriwala*, while vendors who sell at the same location, even with a single basket, are known as *dokandar*. Street-food sellers sell their wares in markets and residential areas, along roadsides, near bus and train stations, and near schools and hospitals. Most of the vendors are men assisted by small boys, although women are involved in preparing ready-made foods and in selling certain items.

Because of a lack of reliable clean water sources and the absence of sanitary conditions on Bangladeshi streets, food bought from vendors is a risky proposition that can lead to illness. Still, Bangladeshis consistently buy and eat food from vendors, even though they are aware of the risks, which is a testament to the appeal of some of the traditional street foods.

MAJOR STREET FOODS

Fuchka

The two most common Bangladeshi street foods are *fuchka* and *chatpati*. *Fuchka* are similar to the *pani puris*, or *golgappas*, sold elsewhere on the subcontinent. They are small, bite-size hollow *puris* (round wheat breads) fried until they are crisp. The hollow part is then filled with a spoonful of chickpeas, onions, potatoes, *chaat masala* (a spice mixture), and tamarind. *Fuchka* stands also often serve *chatpati*, a hot and sour mixture of boiled diced potatoes, boiled chickpeas, sliced onions, and chilies with grated boiled eggs and sour tamarind sauce on top.

Samosas and *Singharas*

Spiced meat, potatoes, or vegetables are stuffed into dough wraps that are deep-fried and served with chutney. These are staple snack foods all across the Indian subcontinent.

Jhal Muri

This spicy (*jhal* means "spicy hot") mixture of puffed rice (*muri*), crushed rice, *chana dal*, *chanachur* (a mixture of spicy pulses and nuts), green chilies, roasted peanuts, lime juice, and a dash of mustard oil is an emblematic Bangladeshi dish. Made fresh for the equivalent of a few cents, *jhal muri* is mixed according to the customers' wishes and handed over in cones made from scraps of old newspaper. *Murir moa* is a sweet version made with puffed rice and jaggery (unrefined brown sugar).

Pithas

These rice flour cakes are a favorite street-side teatime snack in Bangladesh. Countless varieties of *pithas* can be found throughout Bangladesh and eastern

India. Some are fried in oil, others are baked or steamed, and there are an infinite variety of fillings. Sweet *pithas* are made with *gur* (jaggery) and are filled with dates, nuts, coconut, sweetened fruit pieces, milk, or other stuffings. Savory *pithas* may be filled with small morsels of spiced vegetables or potatoes.

Vapa pitha, small round steamed dumplings, are very popular in the winter in Dhaka and are usually sold by women.

Bhortas

Bhortas are mashed foods composed of any number of base ingredients—potatoes, vegetables (such as eggplant, squash, or cauliflower), fish, chicken, beef, or offal, or some combination of these items. The ingredients are cooked (usually boiled) and then laced with spices and onions and mashed into a tasty paste that serves as an accompaniment to rice and breads.

Breads (Roti)

Roti shops are popular breakfast vendors in Bangladesh, serving up freshly heated flatbreads often accompanied with bananas or seasonal fruits. *Mughlai paratha* is a popular Bangladeshi street food consisting of a *paratha* (a large lightly fried wheat-flour bread) topped with ground spiced meat (*keema*) and egg (or sometimes egg alone), folded into square packets and deep-fried. *Bakarakhani* is a thick-layered bread made by repeatedly stretching a sheet of dough and spreading it with ghee and then baking or sautéing it. Stacks of *bakarkhani* lined up at bakeries are a common sight in the old part of Dhaka. It is often eaten with kebab. In Chittagong, it is dipped in sugar syrup.

Sweet Dishes

No brief overview of Bangladeshi street foods is complete without discussing the preponderance of sweets, which are usually sold in small sweet shops. Grouped under the collective name *mishti*, Bangladeshi sweets include deep-fried syrupy *jalebi* (spirals of chickpea batter deep-fried and soaked in sugar syrup), sweetened yogurt (*mishti doi*), and *rasagulla* and *sandesh* made from sugar and farmer's cheese. Different parts of the country are famous for different sweets. The city Comilla, for instance, in the southeastern part of Bangladesh, is famous for producing the country's finest *ras malai*, another sweet dish made of milk, eggs, and sugar and drenched in rich cream.

Dried Snacks

Peanuts toasted in the shell are sold plain or with small packets of salt and chile powder or shelled and fried with chile powder and salt. *Canacur* is a fried, highly spiced mixture of peanuts, puffed rice, and pieces of dough made from wheat and various types of lentils. It can also be mixed with green chilies, onions, boiled chickpeas, and mustard oil. *Nimki* are deep-fried strips of white flour dough that is salted and spiced.

Tea

Small tea stands often consisting of little more than a kettle, teacups, small plates, jugs and a tea strainer, and a small wood or charcoal burning stove made of columns of bricks are ubiquitous in Bangladesh. The tea is mixed with sugar and warm milk and must be drunk piping hot. Some customers bring their own biscuits, fried snacks, or sweets purchased from other stands to munch with the tea. A round cookie called bela biscuit is sometimes dunked into the tea.

Fruit and Vegetables

Freshly cut fresh fruit, often sprinkled with salt and red chile powder, or *kasundi*, a liquid condiment made from mustard seeds, spices, and water, is sold everywhere, as are fresh vegetables, such as cucumber. Pieces of the flesh of green coconut are sold as fruit. Freshly squeezed fruit juices are popular, while the vitamin-rich liquid in green coconuts is drunk directly from the shell. Vendors of sugarcane juice are a common sight. The juice is freshly squeezed from sugarcane and sometimes flavored with citrus juice or ginger.

Iftari (Fasting Foods)

During the month of Ramadan, Muslims fast from dawn to dusk. They break their fast with a meal called *iftar*, which is often obtained by street vendors. Typical *iftar* dishes, called *iftari*, are deep-fried eggplant; *chola bhona*, a fried mixture of boiled chickpeas, onion, green chilies, and spices; *piyaju*, spicy lentil and onion fritters; and *ghugni*, boiled chickpeas served with spices and green chilies. These snacks are sold other times of the years as well. *Piyaju* is a popular snack on Patenga Beach near Bangladesh's second largest city Chittagong on the Bay of Bengal. *Haleem*, a thick lentil and beef stew, is also popular during Ramadan.

FUAD AHMAD

INDIA

S OUTH ASIANS LOVE TO SNACK. Every city, town, and village in this vast country of more than 1 billion people has its roadside stands and hawkers. Indians eat street food at breakfast, lunch, and dinner, as an afternoon snack (often taken home for tea), and during festivals when special dishes are prepared. Vendors set up shop near office buildings, schools, railway stations, beaches (such as Mumbai's Chaupati Beach or Chennai's Marine Drive), Hindu temples, Sikh gurdwaras, mosques, and in crowded markets, such as Delhi's ancient Chandni Chowk or Mumbai's Khau Gali (food lane). There are an estimated 300,000 street-food vendors in Delhi and 130,000 vendors in Kolkata alone.

The Hindi word for vendor is *wallah*, which is attached to the name of the item being sold; for example, *kebabwallah* and *paanwallah*. Most *wallahs* are men. Their cooking equipment includes grills, *tawas* (a flat heavy griddle), *karahis* (a wok-like pot used for deep frying), or sometimes little more than a burner and a kettle to make tea. Street food can be savory or sweet, and often is vegetarian. This vastly expands the potential audience, since many Hindus do not eat meat or items that come in contact with it. Also, meat is expensive.

Many street foods are seasonal: roasted corn and sweet potato are favorites in the winter, and certain fruits in the summer. But everywhere you go, any time of the day or night, you'll find vendors selling chai—hot, milky, sweet tea served in disposable clay cups. Chai can be either plain or masala—boiled with various spices, such as ginger, cardamom, cloves, and even red chilies. In western India, it is sometimes served in saucers to cool the liquid quickly.

Street food is made to order and eaten on the spot, since in a hot climate, it is not safe to eat dishes that have rested a while. Some stalls have a few rickety chairs and tables, but usually the dishes are eaten standing or on the move. Food safety is a major problem because many vendors have no access to clean water or disposal facilities, and often cook and handle food with dirty hands. In 2007, the Delhi city government tried to ban the preparation of food at street stands, in a move supported by India's High Court, but the order proved unenforceable and has not been implemented. In theory, hawkers are licensed but in practice, only a small minority are, with the result that they are subject to harassment and demands for bribes by officials. Also, the residents of more upscale areas sometimes object to the presence of street vendors.

As a result, to a certain degree, street food is moving off the street, especially in urban areas. Chains like Jumbo King in Mumbai and The Great Kabab Factory offer sanitized versions of traditional dishes. Street-food courts are being added to modern urban shopping malls. Western fast foods are making inroads into India, and hot dogs, made from meat, vegetables, or paneer (a hard milk cheese) are especially popular. India has at least one food truck, Nick's Mom in Hyderabad, run by an Indian living in the United States.

For many Indians, street food evokes Proustian memories from childhood. As the journalist Santosh Desai writes, "Home food was wholesome, nutritious and predictable. It came accompanied by its own set of rules," whereas on the street, "food was wickedly delicious and fiendishly compelling." He continues:

> Street food exists for the tongue. Having avoided being classified as serious food with its attendant responsibilities, it is free to explore the nuances of our palate without worrying about wholesomeness. It is often greasy, spicy and unhygienic, and we love it.

Perhaps because of this nostalgia—and the sheer experience of eating on the street in the midst of humanity—street-food stalls continue to thrive, despite sporadic attempts at their suppression.

India is a vast country of 16 official languages, eight religions, and countless ethnic groups, each with their own customs. Thus, every city and region in India has its own special street foods. However, as transportation and communication improve and people move elsewhere in search of jobs, many foods have become universal and are enjoyed throughout not only India but also Pakistan, Nepal, and Bangladesh.

CHUTNEYS

A chutney (from a Hindi word meaning "to lick") is a spicy sauce that accompanies many Indian, Pakistani, and Afghan street foods. In India, the three most popular are red, green, and brown. Red chutneys are tomato based and slightly sweet. Brown chutneys are sweet and sour because of tamarind, dates, and jaggery. Green chutneys are made from coriander, mint, and green chilies and can be quite hot. Ketchup (introduced by the British in the 19th century) is another popular accompaniment and is perfectly authentic.

MAJOR STREET FOODS

Chaat (which derives from the same Hindi word as "chutney") is a generic term for the savory fried spicy snacks that are the archetypal Indian street food and in recent years have appeared on the menus of many top restaurants (at many times the original price). *Chaat* is also the name of a specific dish: a mixture of crumbled fried dough and potatoes, sometimes lentils or chickpeas, a spice blend called *chaat masala*, jaggery (a gritty brown sugar with a distinctive flavor), coriander leaves, yogurt, and two or three chutneys. The most common chutneys are a sweet-and-sour brown sauce made with tamarind and jaggery and a green sauce of coriander leaves, mint, and green chilies. A dollop of yogurt is added to aid digestion. The result is an appetizing combination of flavors—sweet, sour, hot, and cool. Each serving is made to order, served in a paper cone, and eaten on the spot.

Although Mumbai is famous for its *chaat*, the dish is most likely North Indian in origin. One of the most popular *chaats* in North India and Pakistan is *channa chaat* (also called *channa masala* or *chole masala*). The vendor starts with a layer of boiled chickpeas to which he adds (in order) boiled potatoes, finely sliced green chilies, chopped onions, and tomatoes. He tops this with a sour tamarind and a sweet mango chutney, yogurt, and *chaat masala*. According to legend, this dish became the rage in the 14th century at the court of a Delhi ruler whose physician recommended it to keep stomach problems and germs at bay. A common accompaniment is *bhatura*—a large slightly puffy wheat bread.

Papri chaat starts with *papris*—crisp fried round wafers made from white flour and oil—to which are added boiled potatoes and chickpeas, tamarind and chile sauces, yogurt, *chaat masala*, and a sprinkling of *sev* (thin crispy noodles made from wheat flour).

One of the most popular *chaats* is called *golgappa* in Delhi, *pani puri* in Mumbai, and *phhuchka* in Kolkata. It consists of a serving of *puris*—tiny rounds of a flour or semolina dough that are deep-fried until they puff up into hard hollow balls. The balls are punctured and filled with mashed potatoes or boiled chickpeas and then dipped in a sour or savory liquid that may contain tamarind, cumin seed, lemon juice, mint, or dates. The customer must pop the whole thing into his or her mouth to prevent it spilling all over.

A variation is *dahi puri*, in which beaten yogurt is poured over the stuffing. Typically five or six puris are served on a disposable plate made from leaves or paper.

Originally a popular snack associated with the city of Mumbai, *bhelpuri* became so popular that it has turned up on the menu of upscale Indian restaurants. Recipes start with a base of puffed rice and boiled potatoes, topped with *sev,* onion, coriander leaves, *chaat masala,* and brown and green sauces. At the request of the customer, the vendor can add tomato, peanuts, more chilies, diced mango, and other ingredients. Another popular *chaat* consists of seasonal fruits sprinkled with *chaat masala.*

Kebabs are grilled or roasted meat dishes that probably originated in Central Asia, where nomads roasted chunks of meat over a fire. Their relative ease of preparation makes them ideal candidates for street food, since all that is needed is a grill and wood or charcoal. They are usually served with bread, such as naan or *paratha,* and dipping sauces. The vendors are often Muslim, and in cities like Delhi and Hyderabad, kebabs are sold outside mosques. The common meats are goat, chicken, and beef (although the latter is avoided by most Hindus). Spicing can be intense and includes garlic, ginger, and such aromatic spices as cardamom and cloves.

Boti kebabs are chunks of meat marinated in yogurt, spices, and herbs, threaded on a metal or wooden skewer and roasted over charcoal. *Kathi kebabs* are *boti kebabs* wrapped in a roti and mixed with onions, chilies, and sauces. This dish, which originated in a restaurant called Nizam in Kolkata, is typically served wrapped in paper and is a favorite of students.

Seekh kebabs are sausage-shaped kebabs made from ground spiced lamb or goat threaded on long skewers and grilled. *Kakori kebab* and *galouti kebab* are light, delicate kebabs made with meat that is ground extremely fine and whipped.

A kebab that is also popular in Iran and Afghanistan is *shami kebab*—a diskshaped patty resembling a hamburger made of spiced ground meat and chickpeas that have been beaten until they are light and airy and lightly sautéed in a pan. *Chapli kebab* (from the Persian word for "sandal" because of its shape) is a large flat round kebab made of ground meat that is popular in Pakistan, Afghanistan, and North India.

Kofta is a generic term for a dish of well-kneaded ground meat mixed with vegetables, grains, and other ingredients and formed into balls, patties, or sausages. *Koftas* may be grilled, fried, steamed, or sautéed. *Pasanda kebabs* are long strips of meat marinated in yogurt and spices, threaded on skewers, and baked or grilled.

Indian workers returning from the Middle East have introduced shawarma.

MASALA

The word "masala" means "mixture of spices" and has many variations. While each vendor has his own special version, *chaat masala* often contains ground coriander and cumin seeds, dried red chilies, black pepper, black salt, and sour mango powder. *Garam masala* ("warm mixture") is often sprinkled on top of a dish, such as kebabs or biryani, to intensify the flavor. Its components vary depending on the region and the vendor, but a typical North Indian *garam masala* is likely to contain ground coriander, cumin, chilies, cloves, and nutmeg.

Shaved lamb, goat, or chicken is compressed on a rotating spit, grilled, and sliced off as needed. The meat is placed on a flatbread and topped with chutney or ketchup.

Jalebis are pretzel-shaped orange-colored coils of chickpea batter drizzled through holes in a spoon into boiling oil and soaked in sugar syrup that may be flavored with lime juice or rosewater. *Jalebis* are served either hot or cold. The sweet is of Arab origin and came to India in the 14th or 15th century. The most famous vendor is Delhi's Old Famous Jalebiwala in Chandni Chowk, which has been there since 1884 and sells only *jalebis* and samosas—a mouth-watering combination.

Pakoras are fried fritters, a universal favorite and a popular teatime snack. Chopped potatoes, onions, cauliflower, eggplants, spinach, egg, or paneer are coated in a spiced chickpea flour batter, deep-fried, and served with a spicy green chutney or ketchup.

Now a staple of Indian restaurants and cocktail parties, samosas remain a popular street food that people often take home to enjoy at afternoon tea. In the vegetarian version, mashed potatoes, peas, red chile powder, turmeric, and other spices are wrapped in a white wheat flour dough that is formed into little triangles, deep-fried, and served with coriander or mint chutney. A nonvegetarian version is filled with ground spiced meat, usually lamb.

Throughout India, hawkers sell fresh fruit and vegetable in season. Radishes, cucumbers, and tomatoes are sliced on the spot and sprinkled with a mixture of *chaat masala*, salt, and fresh lemon juice. Seasonal fruits are finely sliced and layered with marmalade and paneer to make fruit sandwiches.

Slices of fruits in season—mangoes, pineapples, oranges, grapefruit, jack-fruit, and many fruits without Western equivalents—are a popular street food.

Frozen Sweets

Kulfi is an ancient and very delicious sweet that can be flavored with dozens of ingredients, the most popular being mango, pistachios, and cardamom. Cream is frozen in triangular molds around a little twig or stick.

Western-style ice cream served in a cone is very popular. *Golas* are a poor man's version—basically crushed ice balls bathed in a colored flavored syrup, sprinkled with lime juice, black salt, and pepper, and served on a stick. There are hundreds of flavors, including traditional ones like mango, mint, rose, and orange and modern flavors such as chocolate and cocktail. The customer slurps loudly while licking the *gola* to remove the syrup, which the vendor will replenish.

Paan (Betel Quid)

Chewing betel nuts (areca nuts, the fruit of the Areca palm) wrapped in betel leaves (the leaves of a climbing vine) is a practice throughout Asia, including the Indian subcontinent, where it is called *paan*. The technical term is "quid," a word related to the word "cud" that means something that is chewed for a long time.

Paan is eaten at the end of a meal to stimulate saliva and gastric flow and freshen the mouth. It is said to have a mild stimulant effect, so it is used by truck drivers to stay awake. While *paan* is not considered narcotic, it can be habit forming. In recent years, there have been movements to restrict its sale and consumption both on sanitary grounds (chewers spit out copious amounts of red saliva onto city streets) and for health reasons, since it is a cause of oral cancers. Sometimes tobacco is added.

Paan is prepared and sold by *paanwallahs* (always men) who station themselves outside offices, shops, and residences. They prepare the *paan* to order from a small stand on wheels with little compartments containing various ingredients. Watching the *paanwallah* at work is part of the fun. First he trims a fresh green betel leaf into a three- by five-inch rectangle and applies a white dab of slaked lime (*chuna*) onto the leaf. Then he smears the leaf with catechu, an astringent sticky brown substance made by boiling wood from the Areca palm. To this, he adds dried betel nuts cut into thin slices or little pieces.

If nothing more is added, it is called *sada paan*, which means "plain." The *paanwallah* can add tobacco and such spices as cloves and cardamom to create *tambaku paan.* Another option is *mitha paan,* which has a filling of coconut, dried fruit, rose petal jam, cloves, cardamom, and other spices. If the customer has special requests, the *paanwallah* will do his best to accommodate them. The *paanwallah* folds everything into a neat little triangle-shaped package, sticks in a clove to hold it together, and hands it to the customer who pops the entire bundle into the side of his mouth. He chews the *paan* until it disappears, which can take several hours. Some people swallow the juice, and others spit it out.

OTHER STREET FOODS

Spicy roasted corn on the cob (in Hindi *bhutta*) is a staple of street food in India, as it is in many other developing countries since it is inexpensive and requires no special equipment to prepare. In India, it is associated with the monsoon season. After roasting over hot coals until the kernels start to blacken, the corn is generously sprinkled with a spice mixture that is unique to each vendor, but always includes red chile powder, salt, and lemon juice. Sometimes the corn is boiled and served with a tamarind chutney.

Momos are steamed dumplings filled with meat or vegetables. They originated in Tibet and became popular among hippies and trekkers in Nepal in the 1960s and 1970s. Today, they are one of India's most popular street foods, especially among students who enjoy them with a spicy chile sauce.

Cold Drinks
India can be searingly hot, especially in summer when temperatures in North India can reach 115°F, so there are many cooling, refreshing drinks sold on the street. Fresh limes or lemons are squeezed and mixed with sugar and salt to make *nimbu pani.*

Lassi is a cold yogurt drink that may be either salty or sweet. In the salty version, the yogurt is beaten with cumin seed, water, and salt until it is frothy. The sweet version is made of yogurt, sugar, and sometimes crushed banana or mango pulp.

Jaljeera is a mixture of ice water, lemon juice, cumin powder, salt, and sometimes mint. Many vendors sell sugarcane juice, made by pressing the stalks on the spot, and coconut water.

Sugarcane juice is popular throughout India, especially in the summer months. It is squeezed by roadside vendors using special equipment and served fresh in glasses with or without ice. Sometimes lemon, ginger, and mint are added.

REGIONAL SPECIALTIES

Northern India

A popular street food associated with the state of Punjab is *chole bhature* (also called *channa masala*): boiled chickpeas, sometimes mixed with boiled potatoes, fried with turmeric powder, ginger, sour mango powder, and other spices and garnished with green chilies and lemon wedges. They are served with a puffy deep-fried bread, such as *bhatura* or *puri*.

"Tikka," a word that means "bits" or "pieces," takes several forms. Chicken tikka consists of pieces of chicken brushed with clarified butter and grilled over coals. Paneer tikka are cubes of hard cheese marinated in spices and lemon juice, threaded on skewers and grilled. *Aloo tikka* are small patties made of mashed potatoes, pas, ginger, garlic, and other spices sautéed in oil. Sometimes paneer or chickpeas are added.

The Indian subcontinent is a paradise for bread lovers, with hundreds of varieties. In North India, a popular bread is *paratha*, a flaky unleavened wheat bread lightly sautéed in oil. It can be served plain or filled with many ingredients, including meat, potatoes, peas, cauliflower, and paneer. The country's most famous *paratha* vendors are found in Paranthe Wali Gali, a lane in Old Delhi's Chandni Chowk market. Patrons enjoy their freshly made *parathas* sitting on little stools and tables in rather grubby surroundings. On the final day of Ramadan, the Muslim fast, vendors outside mosques prepare giant *parathas* several feet in diameter that they cut into pieces and serve with sweet *halwa*.

Puris are small disk-shaped breads deep-fried until they puff up into spheres. Potato curry is a common accompaniment, and the combination is a best seller in all railway stations. Chapatis (also called rotis) are flat round wheat breads roasted on a griddle.

Dahi vada are savory balls made of black lentils (*urad dal*) that are soaked in water overnight, ground with ginger and other spices, deep-fried, smothered with fresh yogurt, and sprinkled with cumin powder, *chaat masala,* and a sweet-and-sour tamarind chutney.

The old city of Lucknow in Uttar Pradesh is famous for its delicate meat-based cuisine that developed at the court of the local Muslim rulers. A famous street food is *galouti kebab,* a patty made of finely minced leg of lamb that is smoked; flavored with onions, ginger, garlic, saffron, and a secret spice mixture; and sautéed on a griddle.

In Northern India, especially on the outskirts of cities, highways are lined with *dhabas*—small wayside stands with a few tables for the convenience of truck drivers and other travelers. In traditional *dhabas,* the customers sit or semi-recline on handwoven rope and bamboo cots. Some sell only vegetarian food; others also sell meat. The typical menu features five or six dishes served from large brass pots, such as *palak paneer,* spinach with cheese; *malai kofta,* vegetable balls in a creamy gravy; omelets; and *makhani dal,* a rich black bean stew, accompanied by chapatis or naan. The standard drink is chai.

Today *dhaba* food is becoming fashionable, especially among young urban professionals who drive out of town on a weekend to visit a favorite *dhaba.* Customers can sit at tables and chairs in an air-conditioned room and enjoy soft drinks and bottled water with their meal.

COLLEEN TAYLOR SEN

Western India
Mumbai (formerly Bombay) is the Indian city most famous for its street food, especially along the Chaupati and Juhu beaches, where colorful seaside stalls sell delicious snacks, especially *bhelpuri.* In their book *Street Foods of India,* Vimla and Deb Mukerji describe the scene this way:

> Each vendor is an expert and has a special style of serving his fare—some juggling the assorted ingredients in a leaf bowl, some continuously making a tac-a-tac sound hitting and scraping the griddle with a metal spatula, and others pouring and mixing a bright red fruit drink with crushed ice. None of these vendors are smartly dressed or wear gloves. They touch the food, nonalcoholic drinks, fruit juice and money with their unwashed fingers, but that neither deters the milling crowd surrounding them nor does it detract from the delicious taste of their wares. It is the same story all over the length and breadth of India.

PAV BHAJI

During the American Civil War, the North's blockade of the South ended cotton exports to Britain. The British turned to India as a source of cotton for their mills, and the cotton traders of Mumbai, then known as Bombay, became extremely busy (and rich) as a result. They had to work all night when orders and prices were wired in from America and Europe, and their need for food was met by street vendors who invented a late-night special: *pav bhaji:* leftover mashed vegetables fried quickly on a griddle with tomatoes and other spices.

A local version of hamburger, *vada pav* or *vada pao*, may be Mumbai's most popular and distinctive street food. (TV chef Anthony Bourdain called it the best thing he ate during his 2007 culinary tour of India.) Mashed, boiled, spiced potatoes coated with a chickpea batter are deep-fried and wrapped in two slices of *pao*—a western-style white bread of Portuguese origin (the Portuguese occupied nearby Goa until 1955). It's served with dry peanuts and a sweet-and-sour chutney. *Pav bhaji* is one of the fastest street foods to prepare and a favorite among workers in Mumbai. Leftover potatoes and other vegetables are mashed on a griddle with tomatoes and spices, simmered for a few minutes to form a gravy, and then served with butter western-style rolls, onions, and sliced lemon. Variations are made with cheese, mushrooms, bananas, buttermilk, and dried fruits.

A cousin of *vada pav* that is a specialty of the city of Pune is *daabeli:* two buttered toasted buns filled with potato, grated coconut, and onions, seasoned with green and brown chutneys and topped with roasted peanuts and *sev* (nicknamed called India's Sloppy Joe), a thick gravy of potatoes, tomatoes, peas, and onions flavored with coriander and spices and served with Western-style bread. Another hybrid that is a great favorite with students is grilled vegetable sandwiches. Slices of cooked beet, cucumber, and tomatoes topped with green chutney are served between two slices of toasted western-style bread with tomato ketchup to taste.

Ragada pattice is a mixture of mashed potato sautéed on a griddle, then served on a bed of spiced chickpeas garnished with minced onions, chilies, coriander, chutneys, and *sev.*

The former Portuguese colony of Goa, famous for its hybrid haute cuisine, has a lively evening street-food scene as well. A favorite is the ras omelet: a plain omelet dipped in a spicy coconut-based gravy, garnished with lime and onions, and served with *pao*. Chicken legs or local fish are fried and served with a cabbage salad. A *xacuti* burger is shredded chicken in a thick sauce served between slices of whole wheat bread (a concession to health concerns).

COLLEEN TAYLOR SEN

Southern India

India's southern states do not share the *chaat* experience to the same degree as the rest of the country, but they have their own specialties, many of them vegetarian and based on rice and lentils. *Idlis* are disk-shaped breads made from a batter of fermented rice and *urad dal* that is steamed and served with spicy *sambar*—a thin, spicy lentil soup, sometimes containing vegetables, and coconut chutney. *Dosas* are large, round, thin pancakes made of a batter of ground rice and *urad dal* that is mixed with water, lightly fermented, and poured onto a griddle where it is lightly fried. It, too, is served with a coconut chutney and *sambar*. Two other popular varieties are *masala dosa*, which is filled with boiled potatoes, onions, and spices, and *rava dosa*, which is made of semolina and white flour. *Idlis* and *dosas* have become universally popular in India and the West: one street stall in Mumbai offers 27 varieties, including a Chinese *dosa* and a noodle *dosa*.

In Chennai (formerly Madras), *idli* and *dosa* stalls, called *thattukadai*, are usually run by women. The king of street food is *parotta*, a flaky, layered slightly sweet bread made from white flour that is served with a vegetable korma, a stew of mixed vegetables in a coconut-based gravy, chicken curry, or mutton salna, a thin stew. *Parotta* shops are open in the evening, and business picks up after 10 p.m. A unique Chennai dish is *kothu parotta*, in which the bread is cut into bite-size pieces and sautéed with scrambled egg or minced chicken.

Bhaji, bondas, deep-fried lentil balls, and *vada* (a deep-fried doughnut-shaped bread made from lentils) are popular snacks, especially in the evenings when they are eaten with coffee or tea. Every neighborhood has its own humble *bhaji* stalls that are mainly vegetarian. But some parts of the city have stalls selling fried fish, including Chennai's famous Marina Beach, a favorite spot for promenades. Vendors also sell chicken or mutton biryani from huge pots at street corners and near bus stands. A unique feature of Chennai street-food life is the Burmese vendors selling *athouk*, a noodle salad, and *mohinga*, a soup made with plantain stem, onion, ginger, garlic, chile, turmeric, and rice flour.

Around closing time, many vendors sell hot soups, including healthy ones made from plantain stems and herbs, and sandwiches to people leaving their offices. A unique Chennai specialty is the *murukku* sandwich: slices of tomato, cucumber, and mint chutney are enclosed by two tiny, crunchy *murukkus*—coiled crispy rounds made of rice flour that are a popular snack.

So popular is street food in Chennai that a game has developed based on the TV show *The Amazing Race* in which participants have to follow clues that take them to street-food hot spots in the city. Once there, they don't just sample the food; they have to figure out how to make it.

In the southwestern state of Kerala, such large cities as Kochi and Thiruvananthapuram have large street-food courts called *thattukada* that are open from dusk to dawn each night. They began as a cheaper alternative for the state's migrant workers but now are popular among rich and poor alike, especially students and families on weekend outings. Some serve snacks, others meals, including local specialties and dishes from other parts of India. A typical local dish is *paratha*, a flaky bread, that is served either with onions and a vegetable curry at vegetarian stalls or a chicken, lamb, or beef curry at nonvegetarian stalls. Another specialty is *appam*, a disk-shaped rice flour pancake with lacy edges often served with a coconut-based vegetable stew.

Hyderabad is one of the great culinary centers of the subcontinent, celebrated for both its haute cuisine and its roadside food stands, called bandis. A famous street-food area is the market near the Charminar, an ornate 16th-century building. Hyderabadi cuisine combines elements of North Indian Muslim and South Indian vegetarian dishes and can be extremely hot thanks to the generous use of chilies. A famous Hyderabadi specialty is *kacchi biryani*, a fragrant mixture of rice and pieces of beef or goat meat served with yogurt chutney, *mirchi ka salan*, green chilies in a spicy peanut-based gravy, and perhaps *bagare baingan*, small, round, roasted eggplants in a sesame seed and yogurt sauce.

During the month of Ramadan, when Muslims fast from sunrise to sunset, many people break their fast with biryani and *haleem*, a thick paste-like stew made of pounded wheat and meat and served sprinkled with crispy fried onions. Other vendors sell such traditional South Indian dishes as *idlis*, *dosas*, and *sambar* as well as the ubiquitous *chaat* and *jalebis*.

CHITRADEEPA ANATHARAM AND COLLEEN TAYLOR SEN

Eastern India

Kolkata, the sprawling capital of the state of West Bengal, has long attracted people from all over India, and its street-food scene incorporates dishes from every region. Famous street-food areas include Lord Sinha Road, the AC Market, and Carnac Street. The city's once large Chinese population, dating back to the early 1800s, has declined with emigration, but Kolkata still has India's only Chinatown, Tangra, where street vendors sell a local version of Chinese food. The immigrants spiced the bland Cantonese sauces with sliced chilies and hot, red sauces, creating such unique dishes as chicken sweet corn soup, chow mein, chile chicken, and Manchurian cauliflower and chicken. In the process, they created a very popular hybrid cuisine that is today served in Indian–Chinese restaurants all over the subcontinent and in North American cities with large Indian populations.

A local Kolkata specialty that is popular all over India is the kati roll, invented in the 1930s at a restaurant called Nizam's. The original version was made by roasting pieces of meat on skewers, sautéing them with onions and red chilies, and wrapping the meat in a *paratha* with various chutneys and spices. Today kati rolls can contain vegetables, egg, chicken, or potatoes. They are wrapped in wax paper and eaten on the go. Another local specialty is *masala muri* or *jhal muri*, puffed rice mixed with mustard oil, boiled potatoes, minced onion, green chilies, and chickpeas and garnished with sliced coconut.

A uniquely Bengali dish is *kabiraji*, fillets of chicken, mutton, or fish coated with egg and fried to form a delicate lacy coating. (The word *kabiraji* is probably an Indianization of the word "coverage"). *Mughlai paratha*, a *paratha* sautéed with a spicy egg (or sometimes ground meat) filling, is popular at festivals.

Ghugni is a very popular evening snack in eastern India and is made by simmering chickpeas or yellow peas and potatoes with spice and tomatoes in water until a fairly thick gravy forms. It is served with puffed rice or bread.

COLLEEN TAYLOR SEN

NEPAL

THE FEDERAL DEMOCRATIC REPUBLIC OF NEPAL is a landlocked mountainous country bordered to the north by Tibet, and to the south, east, and west by India. It has an area of 57,000 square miles and a population of approximately 30 million. Nepal was virtually isolated from the rest of the world until the 1950s. The country then became a magnet for tourists, including trekkers, mountain climbers, and young people from Western countries.

Nepal is a predominantly rural country. The largest crop and the dietary staple is rice, which is grown mainly in the central region. At higher, drier altitudes, people cultivate wheat, corn, oats, barley, millet, buckwheat, amaranth, and root vegetables. The climate varies by altitude, and in the winter, temperatures in the capital Kathmandu can drop to below freezing. Perhaps because of this, street food plays a smaller role in Nepal than it does in India. In fact, many of the most popular street-food items are Indian and sold by both Nepali and Indian vendors, including *jalebi* (spirals of deep-fried chickpea batter), samosas (deep-fried triangular pastries filled with vegetables or meat), and *pakoras* (vegetables fried in a chickpea batter).

In Kathmandu, street-food vendors can be found near schools and businesses and in markets such as Indra Chowk. As in India, most vendors are men. Tea shops called *chiya pasal* are popular spots in the morning and evening. Customers stop by for a cup of milky sweet tea and a chat with their friends. Tea is also sold by street vendors and served in glasses.

In rural areas, roadside cafes that are set up to accommodate bus riders and trekkers serve the standard Nepali meal *dal bhat tarkari*: rice, black or yellow dal, mustard greens or other seasonal vegetables, a chicken or goat stew, and hot and sour pickles. A specialty sold near rivers in rural areas is *tareko machha*, a whole fish or eel deep-fried in spicy chickpea flour batter. Traditionally food was served on the leaf of a sal tree, but today a plastic or paper plate is more common.

MAJOR STREET FOODS

Momos

The most famous Nepali street food, *momos,* is of Tibetan origin. They are small steamed or fried dumplings made from wheat flour filled with spicy ground meat (generally pork or buffalo) and served with a hot and sour sauce usually made of tomatoes and cilantro. They were exported to India, where they are one of the most popular street foods.

Sekuwa (Nepali Barbecue)

Pieces of meat (usually goat, pork, or chicken) are marinated in spices and garlic, threaded on skewers, and cooked over charcoal. *Sekuwa* is sold in dedicated stalls and in restaurants. Another version, called *tas,* is made by sautéing sliced meat with onions, tomato, garlic, and other spices. Both are often served with *chiura*: dehusked rice that is beaten into flat light dry flakes. A standard accompaniment to Nepali foods, it is sold by many street vendors.

Sukuti (Meat Jerky)

Thin strips of meat, often buffalo, are dried slowly over charcoal until they are crisp. These strips are shredded and mixed with salt, ginger, garlic, spices, and mustard oil. Chopped onions and tomatoes may be served on the side.

Roasted Soybeans and Popcorn

Soybeans are roasted in an earthenware pot, mixed with popped corn, and sometimes served with a hot and sour chutney. Another version is made with roasted fava beans.

OTHER STREET FOODS

Corn is roasted over hot coals and served with ground-up green chilies. Peanuts are baked in their shells and eaten on the spot. They are especially popular in winter when people enjoy them while basking in the warmth of the sun.

Tilauri

To make this popular sweet, sugarcane juice is boiled down to produce a thick dark syrup, which hardens as it cools. It is mixed with sesame seeds and shaped into sticks or balls.

Seasonal Fruits

Nepal is a paradise for fruits, including tangerines, oranges, persimmon, custard apples, papayas, guavas, Indian gooseberries, bananas, watermelons, lychee, and many more. Distinctive Nepali fruits are lapsi, a small round fruit with a soft, white, sticky, sour flesh and green skin that is available between October and January, and kaphal, a tree fruit that looks like a red raspberry with a pit available between March and April. Fruit is sold fresh or squeezed into a juice by vendors at little kiosks with mounds of peeled fruit behind a glass counter.

LYCHEE

COLLEEN TAYLOR SEN

PAKISTAN

T
HE ISLAMIC REPUBLIC OF PAKISTAN WAS created in 1947 when British India was divided into two countries: India, a secular state with a Hindu majority, and Pakistan, an Islamic state with a Muslim majority. It originally consisted
of West and East Pakistan, but in 1971, East Pakistan declared its independence
and became the People's Republic of Bangladesh.

Like India, Pakistan consists of different ethnic groups and languages, each
with their own culinary traditions. The major ethnic groups are Sindhis, Punja-
bis, Pushtuns, Baluchis, Mohajirs (descendants of Urdu-speaking Indians), and
smaller tribal groups. The largest city, Karachi, with a population of 18 million
attracts people from all over the country and has the remnants of a once thriving
Chinese community.

For thousands of years, the subcontinent shared a common history, so it is not
surprising that there are a great many gastronomical similarities between Pakistan and its neighbors, especially North India and Afghanistan. The cuisine of
Pakistan's Mohajirs, with its rich, aromatic biryanis, pilafs, and kormas, is virtually identical to the food in such Indian cities as Lucknow or New Delhi, which
have large Muslim populations. Thus, there are very few dishes that are exclusive
to Pakistan, and this is true when it comes to street food. A major difference is ingredients. Pork is forbidden to Muslims, while many Hindus and Sikhs, only small
numbers of whom live in Pakistan, do not eat beef or are vegetarian. Moreover,
food in Pakistan tends to be much more meat based than that in India, at least for
those who can afford it. The spicing also tends to be stronger and more aromatic.

Most street-food vendors in Pakistan are male (often with very young boys as assistants). They sell their wares from pushcarts called *thailas,* some of which are elaborately decorated, or at roadside stands, which may have tables and chairs outside. The food is cooked over coals or propane-fueled burners on enormous *tawas* or *karahis,* concave pans that may be several feet in diameter. Some street-food stands are actually an extension of existing shops that move onto the pavement or road to attract more customers. As in India, these establishments are called *dhabas.*

In the winter, breakfast is a popular street food meal in Pakistan, especially steaming hot *nihari*—a stew made by slowly cooking pieces of beef, beef tongue, brain, or shanks overnight with ginger and chilies. Another breakfast dish is *haleem,* which probably originated in Central Asia or Iran. It has many variations but generally includes cracked wheat, lentils, spices, and pieces of beef or mutton. It is cooked for seven or eight hours over coals or a low heat, stirring constantly until a smooth paste is formed and then garnished with crispy fried onions, ginger, and green chilies. Because of their high nutritional content, both dishes are eaten when breaking the Ramadan fast, the ninth month of the Islamic calendar when people fast from dawn to dusk.

In the summer, when the temperature can reach 110°F or higher, cold fruit juice and frozen sweet dishes are universal favorites. Roasted or boiled corn sprinkled with lime juice and chile powder is served year-round, as are fresh seasonal fruits.

As in India, small stands selling *paan* (chopped betel nut, spices, and mineral lime rolled in a betel leaf) are found in every street and market. In Lahore's Anarkali Bazaar, there is even a separate street called *paan gali* dedicated to this popular snack and after-meal digestif.

MAJOR STREET FOODS

Chaat is the general term for a wide variety of fried spicy vegetarian snacks. One of the most popular is *channa chaat*—a mixture of boiled chickpeas, potatoes, green chilies, onions, and tomatoes, topped with tamarind chutney, sweet chutney, spicy yogurt, and *chaat masala*—a spice mixture that is unique to each vendor but may contain ground coriander and cumin seeds, dried red chilies, black pepper, black salt, and sour mango powder. A variation is *papri chaat,* crispy fried

---

STREET FOOD MARKETS

Pakistan's most famous street food area is Gawalmandi (Food Street) in the ancient city of Lahore, which is open 24/7 except during Ramadan, the Muslim fasting month, when all food establishments are closed from sunrise to sunset. At night, this and other districts are thronged with people who order their dishes at one of many stalls while sitting at a chair and table. Although it is Pakistan's largest city, Karachi had no equivalent market until mid-2011 when the Port Grand street food complex opened on the seashore. This upscale complex has dozens of vendors selling street food, arts and crafts, and fashion.

---

wafers served with boiled potatoes, boiled chickpeas, chilies, yogurt, and tamarind chutney, and topped with *chaat masala*.

Dahi vada (also called *dahi bhalle*) are sweet-and-sour balls made of black lentils (*urad dal*) soaked in water overnight, ground with ginger and other spices, deep-fried, then covered with yogurt and sprinkled with cumin powder, *chaat masala*, and a sweet-and-sour tamarind chutney. Fruit *chaat* is a medley of such fruits as tangerines, bananas, pomegranate, and guavas, seasoned with sugar and spices. When composed only of guava and bananas, it is called *kutchaloo*. *Pani puri* or *golgappa* is made by filling hollow *puris* (crispy round wafers fried until they are crisp) with chickpeas and a watery mixture of tamarind and chilies.

Of Gujarati origin, *bhelpuri* is a universal favorite throughout South Asia and abroad. Each vendor adds his own special twist, but most recipes include puffed rice, *sev*, onions, and diced, boiled potatoes, topped with a brown sweet-and-sour chutney made of dates and tamarind and a green spicy one with coriander leaves and chilies.

Samosas

Samosas, which may have originated in the Middle East, have been a popular snack in the subcontinent for many centuries. A samosa is a fried, triangular-shaped dough pastry with a savory filling, which may be ground meat (mutton or chicken) or potatoes and peas and served with assorted chutneys. The most common are made of coriander, mint, and chilies; tomato and sugar; and tamarind.

Pakoras

Pakoras are especially popular during Ramadan and in the rainy season. Bite-size pieces of vegetables—eggplants, potatoes, okra, onion, spinach, or pretty much anything—are deep-fried in a batter of spiced chickpea flour and served with a runny ketchup.

Kebabs

Meat kebabs are a universally popular dish, and the *kebabwallah* grilling pieces of meat on long skewers over a grill or in a portable tandoor is a familiar sight on Pakistani streets. They are always served with bread and various chutneys. Breads can be leavened or unleavened and are made from whole wheat or white flour. The most common cooking techniques are baking in a tandoor (naan, tandoori roti), sautéing in oil or ghee on a *tawa* (*paratha*), or cooking on a hot pan without oil (chapati). The customer breaks off a little piece of bread with his or her right hand, wraps it around the meat, dips it in a chutney, and pops it in his or her mouth.

Each region has its own varieties, but some are universally popular, including the following:

- *Seekh kebab*, spiced minced meat threaded on long flat skewers and grilled
- *Shami kebab*, a small patty of minced beef or chicken and ground chickpeas and sautéed
- Tikka kebab, cubes of meat (often chicken) marinated in yogurt and spices
- *Bihari kebab*, strips of spiced beef threaded on skewers
- *Boti kebab*, chunks of meat, often chicken, marinated in lemon juice and spices and grilled on skewers

Bun kebabs, a local version of burgers, are sold at roadside kiosks and pushcarts. Minced meat, either mutton or beef, is spiced with cumin and chilies and formed into a patty, fried, topped with a fried egg, onions, and an assortment of chutneys, and served between charred buns. A vegetarian version is made from mashed potato.

A popular roadside dish imported by Pakistanis who worked in the Persian Gulf is shawarma, made of shaved meat surrounding a spit that rotates around a burner and is sliced off as needed. It is usually served with naan.

Kata-Kat

Originally called *tawa gurda kapoora*, which means "kidneys and testicles in a *tawa*," the name was changed to the more respectable *kata-kat*, which refers to the sound made by the cook as he chops the organs with sharp knives in a regular rhythm while cooking them. He keeps slicing, dicing, and frying until the mixture becomes a thick curry. The customer can choose which organs he or she wants to include in his or her dish. It is served with mint chutney.

Chicken *Karahi/Karahi Gosht*

A specialty of Lahore's Food Street, this dish is made by stir-frying pieces of chicken with tomatoes, green chilies, ginger, and garlic in a *karahi*, the wok-like pan that gives the dish its name. The diner mops up the juice with pieces of naan. A variation is *karahi gosht*, made with mutton. This dish may have been the precursor of the popular British dish balti.

Sugarcane Juice

Sometimes called the national drink of Pakistan, sugarcane juice, or *roh*, is pressed from sticks of cane by roadside vendors. It is always sold fresh, since it quickly blackens from oxidation. It is served in glasses with or without ice.

REGIONAL STREET FOODS

A famous street food of the northwestern state of Balochistan and its capital Quetta is *sajji*, a leg of lamb that is salted and mildly spiced and roasted over an open fire until it is tender. It has become very popular throughout Pakistan. It is served with *kaak*, a rock-hard bread, and a yogurt salad.

Pakistan's Khyber Pakhtunkhwa is the home of chicken chargah, whole chicken marinated with yogurt, ghee, and spices, placed on a skewer and roasted over coals or in a tandoor, and served with bread. Another dish that originated in this region is *chapli kebabs*, which have become popular all over Pakistan and India. Minced beef or water buffalo is flavored with coriander seeds, onions, cumin seeds, and chilies, held together with chickpea flour or cornmeal, formed into flat patties, and fried in animal fat (sometimes the fat rendered from the tail of a fat-tailed sheep). Traditionally, they are eaten with naan, but in modern times they are often put between slices of toast or a roll.

In the seaport city of Karachi, *machli ke kebab,* or fish kebabs, are popular. Fish fillets are marinated in yogurt, ginger-and-garlic paste, and spices, shaped into kebabs, skewered, and grilled or baked.

Nimco

This word is actually a brand name dating back to the early 1950s that has entered into the language to describe a wide range of crunchy snacks sold by many vendors. They include *chevda,* puffed rice mixed with peanuts, curry leaves, and other spices; fried spiced lentils; spicy salted peanut and potato chips; *ghatia,* fried strips of chickpea dough; and many other varieties.

Sweets

A universal favorite are *jalebis,* spirals of spiced chickpea batter drizzled through holes in a spoon into boiling oil, deep-fried until they are golden, then dipped in a sugar syrup and sometimes flavored with saffron, rosewater, or cardamom.

A popular frozen summertime sweet is *kulfi* made of thickened sweetened milk that is frozen in small cone-shaped molds. Traditional flavorings are saffron, cardamom, almond, pistachio, mango, and rosewater; modern variations include apple, avocado, and strawberry. Unlike Western ice creams, *kulfi* is not whipped so that it is hard and dense. In Pakistan, it is served with *faluda,* thin noodles that are boiled, simmered in milk, and cooled over ice. Western ice cream is also available.

Gola ganda is a local version of a snow cone, a paper cone filled with crushed or shaved ice and topped with flavored sugar water and sometimes condensed milk.

COLLEEN TAYLOR SEN

SRI LANKA

THE DEMOCRATIC SOCIALIST REPUBLIC OF SRI LANKA, called Ceylon until 1972, is an island nation off the southeast coast of India. There is strong evidence for human settlement since 34,000 BCE. The descendants of these early people are the Wanniya-laeto ("people of the forest"). Aryan and Dravidian migrations from the Indian subcontinent established the Singhalese and Tamil populations, respectively. Situated at the junction of the southwest and northwest monsoons across the Indian Ocean and the source of prized spices—cinnamon and pepper—Sri Lanka became a major center for the exchange of goods between Arab and Chinese traders. As the spice wars and colonial enterprises of Europe entered the Indian Ocean, Sri Lanka was colonized by the Portuguese in 1505 and the Dutch East India Company in 1602; the descendants of their marriages with Singhalese and Tamils formed the Burgher community. The British were the final colonizing power, ruling from 1815 until Sri Lanka was declared independent in 1948.

This multiethnic demography is reflected in modern Sri Lankan foodways with two main strands—foodways in common with its South Asian neighbors and foodways shared with European cultures.

Rice is the staple whole grain, and rice flour is the basis for the Southern Indian shared "breads"—*thosai* (*dosa* in Southern India, a flat pancake from a batter of fermented rice and *urad dal*), hoppers (*appam* in Southern India, a bowl-shaped pancake from fermented rice flour), and stringhoppers (*idi-appam* in Southern India, thin rice noodles steamed on a bamboo mat). The generic term "curry" is commonly used to cover the range of dishes eaten with rice, both meat and vegetable, though some preparations retain such unique Sinhala names as *mallungs* (leafy greens, shredded, spiced, and steamed) or *baduns* (a meat preparation). Spicing is complex with several used in a single dish; the mix is flavor and for ascribed ayurvedic (medicinal) qualities. Coconut milk is the standard cooking liquid. Sambals and chutneys are eaten with the meal.

Wheat flour is used for European breads—loaves, rolls, buns—and sometimes in hoppers. Roasts, steaks, stews, chops, and baked and boiled vegetables make up the meals. The Portuguese and Dutch influences have been reduced to a handful of specialist meat dishes like *frikadells* (spiced meatballs), *smoore* (a pot-roast with a curry gravy sharpened with lime pickle), and cakes. More recently, Western fast food has taken its place within the daily diet.

Arab traders established the Muslim community in Sri Lanka who have a distinctive sub-cuisine similar to that of the Muslim communities of Kerala, Southern India.

The other significant influence on Sri Lankan foodways is the dietary laws of Buddhism (the religion of the majority Singhalese population and generally vegetarian) and Hinduism (the religion of the Tamil population with a proscription against eating beef or strict vegetarianism for the more religiously committed).

Street vendors draw on food from across this spectrum. They are usually single-person operations, both male and female, and are unlicensed.

MAJOR STREET FOODS

Vadai

At major transport hubs, in local shopping areas, at the beachside, *vadai* (also *vada* in Southern India) sellers station their glass-fronted wooden four-wheeled carts. There are two distinct types. *Masala vadai* are patties made of *toor dal* (yellow lentils) that are soaked and then ground into a paste. It is spiced with curry leaves, onions, turmeric, salt, and Maldive fish (smoked dried tuna), shaped in the palm and deep-fried. *Ulundu* vadai are made from a paste of parboiled rice and *urud dal* (black lentils) fermented for several hours, spiced as for *masala vadai*, then shaped into a doughnut and deep-fried. Both are eaten on their own or with curd. *Issu vadai* is a very popular variation on *masala vadai*: one or several small prawns are pressed into one side of the *vadai* before it's fried. Galle Face Green (the large seaside park where Colombo's families and courting couples go in the late evening on weekends to promenade, fly kites, and watch circus troupes) is famous for its *vadai* sellers, though now they compete with vans selling burgers, fried chicken, and pizza. But as night comes in, it is the *vadai* sellers' carts with their kerosene lanterns that make for magic.

Roti

Godamba roti (similar to Malaysian *roti canai*) is made from wheat flour, salt, water, and oil, mixed to a soft dough, rested, cut into balls, then rolled out flat and flung like pizza dough until it is stretched and becomes almost translucent. At this point, it is dropped onto a hot griddle and cooked rapidly until firm but slightly elastic. Pieces of roti are broken off to scoop up accompanying curries and sambals. Egg *godamba* is made by breaking an egg onto the surface of the roti as it cooks and is folded. A relatively recent variation on *godamba* is *kothu roti*. A cooked *godamba* is chopped (*kothu* means chopped) into bite-size pieces using two flat dough cutters or sharp knives. Spiced chopped vegetables or thinly sliced chicken or beef is quickly fried on the griddle, the *kothu* is added, and the whole is well mixed and served.

Mutton or Fish Rolls

Dry mutton or fish curry is spread onto small thin pancakes. They are then rolled, dipped in egg and breadcrumbs, and fried. They are sold by *vadai* sellers or in small bakeries and cafés.

Achcharu

At every bus terminus, outside every school or large office building sits the *achcharu amme*. Before her is a large *chatty* (earthenware cooking pot) that contains pieces of fresh fruit mixed with green chilies, onion, vinegar, salt, chile powder, and a little sugar, making a fresh pickle. The fruit may be one or a combination of firm ripe mango, veralu (fat green Sri Lankan olives, another remnant of the Portuguese years), ambaralla (golden apple or hog fruit), or pineapple. Once served in paper, it is now more usually served in a small plastic bag.

As a dry alternative, the fruit will be sliced and dipped into a mix of chile, salt, and sugar.

Curd

Homemade pot-set buffalo curd is sold from roadside stalls throughout the country; that of the southeastern coastal plains is particularly prized. Paired with kittul (commonly called fishtail palm) syrup, it is a perfect blend of sweet and sour.

OTHER STREET FOODS

Kadala and *Gram*

Vadai sellers will also often sell *kadala*, chickpeas that have been boiled, mixed with chopped Bombay onions, chile powder, salt, and a squeeze of lime. *Gram* (yellow lentils) is deep-fried and flavored the same way. Both are traditionally served in paper cones, but plastic bags and Styrofoam trays are often used now.

Murukku, a paste of rice flour and *urud dal* flavored with asafetida, salt, and sometimes cumin or sesame seeds, will also be on sale. Lengths are extruded from a barrel through a range of metal disks perforated to produce a range of shapes. The lengths fall into hot oil and are rapidly deep-fried.

Sarawath

Sarawath is a mixture of shredded betel nut (areca nut), brightly colored candied grated coconut, cumin, and fennel seeds wrapped in a betel leaf cone. It's less potent than the usual way of eating betel nut where the nut is sprinkled on a betel leaf spread with lime paste. *Sarawath* sellers ply their trade from a wooden tray slung from their neck in which the cones stand upright to show the color of the coconut.

DRINKS

Sugarcane

Sugarcane sold in arm-length pieces is chewed in one's mouth or crushed in a portable metal mill to release the sweet juice. It is a feature of the Hindu Vel festival held in July in honor of Lord Murugan during which carts in the form of towering temples are paraded through the streets, often decorated with bunches of sugarcane.

Thambili

Thambili—young coconuts—are a common refreshing drink. The top is sliced off expertly with a machete, and the coconut water is drunk directly out of the shell, or through a straw to prevent the water spilling. The fruit is then halved with a swift blow, a scoop is fashioned out of the sliced off top, and the soft white flesh is eaten.

Saruwath

Saruwath is a popular drink of swollen gelatinous basil seeds, a sugar-based syrup (rose, orange, and lime flavors are popular), and water.

SWEETS

Kalu Dodol

Kalu dodol is a popular sweet that is made by boiling down and cooling a mix of rice flour, coconut milk, and jaggery until it becomes a thick batter, at which point cashew nuts and cardamom are added. The mixture is reduced further and stirred until it comes away from the sides of the pan. It is then left to cool in a pan that is angled to let the coconut oil drain out. It is cut into firm jelly blocks and served.

Bombai Mutai

Children are always entranced by the *bombai mutai* (cotton candy) maker, as he spins the thin threads of luridly colored sugar round and round a stick.

PAUL VAN REYK

SOUTHEASTERN ASIA

INDONESIA

T HE REPUBLIC OF INDONESIA, an archipelago comprising more than 17,500 islands, is the world's fourth most populous country with more than 238 million people who belong to hundreds of linguistic and religious groups. Around 60 percent of the population live on the island of Java, including more than 10 million in the capital Jakarta alone. While the majority of the population (86 percent) are Sunni Muslim, there are large communities of Christians (9 percent of the population) and Hindus (3 percent) concentrated on the island of Bali. Indonesia has been a center of trade for thousands of years. The Indians, Chinese, Arabs (who brought Islam), Portuguese, Spanish, British, and Dutch all had outposts in the region, which was known as the Spice Islands. Indonesia was a Dutch colony for three and a half centuries until it won its independence in 1945.

Indonesia stands on both sides of the equator with south Asia to the north and Australia to the south. The nation's flora and fauna reflect both neighboring continents, and the country is the world's second greatest region for biodiversity. Much of the country is covered in forests, home to numbers of species that range from orangutans to tigers. The climate is warm year-round with only one rainy and one dry season. The climate and landscape are conducive to Indonesia's staple crops, the foods of everyday life: rice, cassava, and sweet potato. Rice is so important that the dish known best around the world is *rijsttafel*, literally "rice table." Actually, this is a Dutch colonial dish, but it does have Indonesian ingredients, especially rice.

International influences are reflected in the country's street food, which is one of the most vibrant and varied in the world. Each region has its own distinct dishes, and there are dozens of versions of major street foods that reflect local and regional ingredients, techniques, and customs. In such large cities as Jakarta, Surabaya, Bandung, and Semarang, vendors offer dishes from all over the country, but in smaller cities, vendors usually specialize in the local cuisine. This entry focuses mainly on the street food of Jakarta. Many of the dishes (e.g., satay, samba) are popular in other countries in Southeast Asia, which gives rise to international disputes over their true origins!

A typical Indonesian street-food cart is called a *pedagang kaki lima,* which means "five feet"—perhaps from the five-foot-wide footpaths between urban buildings. Many vendors have their own typical call or song that announces their presence as they drive through residential neighborhoods or station themselves on a busy street. A *pikulan* is a walking restaurant in which the cook carries his cooking equipment on a bamboo pole slung over his shoulders, but these are disappearing with modernization.

Warungs are small semipermanent stalls made of wood and bamboo with a roof, a bench for customers, and a counter where the proprietors sell soft drinks, snacks, and simple dishes, such as fried rice (*nasi goreng*) or noodles (*mie goreng*). They often stay open until the early hours of the morning. Customers eat at a single warung or move from warung to warung, sampling different wares. Food stalls often give their patrons a bowl of tap water with a slice of lime with which they wash their hands before and after eating.

MAJOR STREET FOODS

Soups

One of the most ubiquitous Indonesian street foods is *soto*, a soup made of broth, meat, and vegetables. Every region has its own version that includes different meats, spices, noodles or rice, broths, and so on. Typical spices used in this and other Indonesian dishes are shallots, garlic, galangal, ginger, coriander, salt, candlenut, and pepper. The most common meats are chicken, beef, and water buffalo. Because of Islamic prohibitions against pork, it is rarely used in Indonesia except in Bali with its Hindu population. The *soto* broth can be clear, yellow, or white depending on whether it is based on milk or coconut milk. Standard accompaniments include compressed squares of sticky rice, stewed quail or chicken eggs, grilled giblets or tripe, *krupuk* (shrimp crackers), fried tofu or tempeh, sambal (several kinds of spicy sauce, made with chilies), fried shallot, fried coconut, and lime juice.

Another popular soup is *mie bakso*, noodle soup with meatballs (*bakso*), vegetables, and tofu. The meatballs are usually made from beef mixed with a little tapioca flour, although chicken, fish, or shrimp can also be used. Other ingredients that can be added to the spicy broth are shredded chicken, chicken feet, *siomay* (dumplings), and fried wontons. Fried shallots and celery are sprinkled on top. Customers add sambal or sweet soy sauce to taste.

Typical Jakarta soups are *soto betawi*, beef and beef offal in a coconut milk broth, and *sup buntut*, an oxtail soup served with steamed rice.

Dumplings

A Chinese contribution to Indonesian cuisine, a *siomay* (derived from *shaomai*) is a steamed fish dumpling traditionally made with *tenggiri*, ground horse mackerel mixed with vegetables and steamed in a wonton skin. It is served with steamed cabbage or potatoes, eggs, and tofu. The *siomay* are cut into small pieces and served with peanut sauce or a sweet-and-sour spicy sauce. Horse mackerel is also used in *batagor*, dumplings that are fried until they are crispy. The two items are generally sold by the same vendor.

Fritters

A specialty of Pelambang, the capital of South Sumatra, *pempek* are popular throughout Indonesia as well as Malaysia and Australia. These deep-fried fritters are made from ground fish and tapioca with a boiled egg in the middle and served with yellow noodles and a dark rich sweet-and-sour sauce. *Gorgengan* are made by deep-frying battered vegetables, fruits, tofu, and tempeh. They are served with fresh green chilies on the side. Plantains deep-fried in a batter (*pisang goreng*) are sold throughout Indonesia.

Satay

Although Thailand and Malaysia lay claim to the invention of satay, it most likely originated in Java as a variation of Indian and Middle Eastern kebabs. From there, it spread throughout Southeast Asia and, in the 19th century, was taken by Malay immigrants to South Africa, where it was called *sosatie*. Pieces of chicken, goat, mutton, beef, fish, or tofu are marinated in a mixture of soy sauce and various spices, threaded onto skewers made from the ribs of coconut palm leaves or bamboo, and grilled over a wood or charcoal fire. Satay is generally served with *lontong*, compressed rice cakes cooked in banana leaves and a spicy peanut sauce.

Fruits

Indonesian markets are teeming with fruits, including such native tropical fruits as mangosteen, jackfruit, durian, banana, breadfruit, and rambutan as well as nonnative fruits, such as strawberry, melons, apple, and dragonfruit. Fruits are sold and eaten fresh, squeezed into juices, made into desserts or savory snacks, fried, or preserved. *Pisang goreng* is a popular snack made by deep-frying banana slices in a rice flour batter. *Pisang goreng* is one of several names for the dish depending on the region, and it served in varieties of ways, sometimes sprinkled with sugar and cinnamon or cheese.

Nasi Goreng (Fried Rice)

The Indonesian version of Chinese fried rice can be eaten any time of the day and is a favorite breakfast dish, made with leftovers from the previous night's dinner. It is a mixture of precooked rice fried in oil and various vegetables that is flavored with garlic, pepper, tomato ketchup, sambal, sweet soy sauce, and sometimes shrimp paste, fish sauce, or wine. The most popular version, *nasi goreng ayam*, is made with chicken and sweet soy sauce. Other ingredients are chicken gizzard and liver, beef, goat, prawns and other seafood, salted fish, sausage, vegetables, and pineapple. *Nasi goreng* is garnished with fried shallots, crispy *krupuk*, sour vegetable pickles (*acar*), sambal, fried eggs, or shredded omelet. It is often sold together with *bakmi goreng*, noodles with meatballs.

Noodles (*Mi* or *Mie*)

Bakmi are wheat-based noodles that are boiled, topped with chopped chicken meat, seasoned with soy sauce, and served with Chinese cabbage, wonton, and *bakso*. The soup is served in a separate bowl. Sometimes *bakmi* are served with a thick sauce or stir-fried with vegetables, sweet soy sauce, meat, egg, or other ingredients. In another version, *ifumie*, the noodles are first deep-fried. In Aceh province, goat meat or seafood is topped with a spicy curry-like soup to make a popular street food called *mie aceh*. In a South Sumatran version called *mie celor*, the noodles are boiled in a broth made from dried shrimp simmered with coconut milk and topped with bean sprouts, boiled eggs, and fried shallots.

Gado Gado (Cooked Vegetable Salad)

A very popular lunch dish, *gado gado*, is a cooked vegetable salad served in a sweet, hot peanut sauce and garnished with eggs, cucumbers, and onions. The vegetables can include cabbage, cauliflower, carrots, beans, and bean sprouts.

OTHER STREET FOODS

Krupuk

These crispy deep-fried crackers that look like potato chips are eaten as a snack or an accompaniment to a meal. They are made by mixing a starch, usually tapioca flour but sometimes leftover rice, with water and other ingredients that add flavor, especially prawns. The mixture is rolled out, steamed, sliced, and sundried; once dry, the crackers are deep-fried in oil. A popular variation is *emping* made from the slightly bitter seeds of the belinjo tree.

Sambal

This chile-based sauce is a standard condiment throughout Southeast Asia, the Philippines, Sri Lanka, and the Netherlands. Its main ingredient are chilies, which range from mild to extremely hot. Traditionally, the chilies are crushed in a mortar and pestle with other ingredients, including fresh shallots, garlic, onions, and basil, to make a paste called *bumbu*. Indonesia has as many as 300 varieties of sambal, which include such ingredients as sour tamarind, garlic, sweet soy sauce, lime, fermented durian, anchovies, palm sugar, and tomatoes.

Bubur Ayam

Bubur ayam is a popular breakfast dish, sold by vendors strolling through residential areas in the morning. The dish descends from Chinese chicken congee and is composed of rice placed in a bowl, topped with shredded chicken and various condiments, such as fried shallot, celery, preserved vegetables, fried soybeans, salty and sweet soy sauce, and *krupuk*. Sambal may be served on the side. It is also served at major international fast-food outlets, such as McDonald's.

PRESIDENTIAL FEAST

Former U.S. President Barack Obama, who lived in Indonesia for four years as a child, was deeply moved when his favorite boyhood foods were served at a state dinner hosted by the Indonesian president in November 2010. He especially enjoyed several common street foods that were served at the dinner: *bakso, nasi goreng, emping,* and *krupuk.* One of his teachers said that as a child, Obama's nickname was "krupuk" because he loved the crackers so much. "Semuanya enak," the president said at the end of the banquet. "Everything is delicious!"

Murtabak

Possibly originating in the Middle East or India, this stuffed, pan-fried pastry is universally popular in Indonesia and Malaysia. There are two versions: sweet and savory. In the savory version, the dough is folded over cooked minced meat (often lamb or beef) and mixed with onions, eggs, and herbs to form a six-inch-square pastry that is sautéed on an iron griddle and handed to the customer. It is often served with pickled cucumber and a sweet-and-sour sauce. The sweet *murtabak* is brushed with butter while cooking and sprinkled with sugar and sometimes crushed peanuts. There is also a delicious chocolate *murtabak.*

Beverages and Desserts

The most popular Indonesian beverages are coffee and tea, especially jasmine and green tea. Sweet beverages made from coconut milk or coconut sugar are popular in Java. Many drinks that are made with ice also serve as desserts. For example, *cendol,* a mixture of coconut milk, jelly-like noodles made from rice flour (the green color comes from pandan leaves), shaved ice, and palm sugar, is sold everywhere in Indonesian cities.

GREEN TEA

JASMINE

TEA

Tempeh

An important dietary source of protein in Indonesia is such soy-based products as *tahu* (tofu), kecap (a sauce made from fermented soy beans), and tempeh. Tempeh, which was likely invented on Java in the 18th century, is uniquely

Indonesian. It is made by boiling soybeans, dehulling them, boiling them again, adding a fermentation starter, and incubating the mixture for 24 to 36 hours at 88°F. This process binds the soybeans into a firm spongy rectangular cake. Tempeh may also be made from other kinds of beans, wheat, or a mixture of beans and whole grains. It is sold in the market wrapped in banana leaves.

Tempeh can be prepared by cutting it into small pieces, soaking it in a salty sauce, and then frying it to a golden brown to make *tempeh goreng*, an ubiquitous street-food dish. It can be eaten by itself as a snack with a peanut sauce, added to a stew, sautéed with vegetables, wrapped in banana leaves, and steamed or grilled. Deep-fried tempeh, with or without a batter, is a popular street snack.

Another fermented product is *oncom*, a specialty of West Java, made from the by-products from the production of tofu, peanut or coconut presscake, or cassava tailings.

COLLEEN TAYLOR SEN

THE PHILIPPINES

T HE PHILIPPINES is an archipelago nation of 7,107 islands. The islands' 22,549 miles of coastline, mountain ranges, five volcanoes, river basins, and lakes sit astride the Pacific Rim's southwestern edge. Scientists disagree on the geological genesis of the Philippines: volcanic activity, tectonic shifts, or Ice Age melts submerging land bridges to the west or from present-day Taiwan are some of the theories. Though historians disagree on who they were, the first humans settled there at least 67,000 years ago.

One of the 180 indigenous ethnic groups of the Philippines, the Ifugaos built the Banaue Rice Terraces 2,000 years ago, steppes carved out of the Cordillera Central, a mountain range on the island of Luzon that maximized and irrigated flat, arable land for rice. Like many other Asian cultures, the major food staple of Philippines was and is rice.

Since the 3rd century CE, a number of independent cooperative societies, similar to city-states, developed in the present-day Philippine islands and traded with their counterparts in Indonesia, Malaysia, China, and others. The Philippines shares many culinary touch points with these ancient trading partners, the traces of which can be seen in today's street food.

In pursuit of trade routes, Spain first made contact with the inhabitants when Ferdinand Magellan discovered the islands in 1521. Naming the nation after their king, Spain colonized the Philippines for 400 years. The Viceroyalty of New Spain, present-day Mexico, administered the Philippines until the former gained independence from Spain in 1821. The 250-year galleon trade between Acapulco and Manila—17,000 miles apart—brought the Philippines new agricultural products from Latin America: corn, tomatoes, potatoes, cotton, and tobacco.

The Filipinos rebelled against their Spanish overlords in 1898, but after the Spanish American War, they became a Commonwealth of the United States. In 1946, the Philippines gained its independence from the United States. English became one of the official languages, and many Filipinos are fluent in it. Ties between the United States and the Philippines have remained very strong, partly because some nine million Filipinos, or 10 percent of the population, emigrated to seek employment in other countries, especially the United States. As a result, American foods have influenced Filipino street food.

Filipino culture is much like its own beloved dessert, halo-halo, a multi-layered combination of crushed or shaved ice, condensed milk, chopped local fruits like jackfruit or macapuno (young coconut strips), and sweet beans, topped with a sumptuous helping of *ube* (purple yam) ice cream, or slices of leche flan, a Spanish-derived milk custard. "Halo-halo" translates literally in English to "mix-mix," describing how this dessert is enjoyed. The result is a unique, satisfying concoction whose sum is greater than the value of its individual components. The Philippines's culinary heritage is a mix of spices, sauces, preparation and preservation technology, and local and borrowed ingredients.

Everyone is a street-food patron in the Philippines. For most of Filipino society, street food is subsistence: convenient and inexpensive food that will get one through the day. Street food can be an energy boost or a refreshing snack on the long, hot, and arduous commute. The Philippines's tropical climate, paralyzing urban traffic, and varying comfort levels of public transportation make travel difficult. Located near public transport hubs and busy intersections, vendors offer food and drink to commuters, drivers, and conductors.

During workday lunches, office workers can get street food delivered to their desks by their favorite vendors, which is more convenient than bringing lunch from home and less expensive than eating at a restaurant. As the largest English-speaking country in Asia, many multinationals have based their outsourced business process operations and call centers in Manila. Guess where workers can get a hot meal while on break from answering customers' calls in the middle of the night? Organized by local municipalities and tourism boards, temporary, tented street-food centers in adjacent parking lots cater to these third-shift workers.

Street food can be enjoyed from home. In some residential areas, vendors ply their wares during mealtimes or at *merienda*, the afternoon snack time, from 3 to 5 p.m. The vendors might ring a bell, toot a horn, or yell to residents the name of the food they're selling as they walk by.

Outside the home, Filipinos eat street food outside the church in the plaza after Sunday Mass, near the open-air wet and dry marketplaces, in and around the malls, or while strolling around parks. Street foods are also a fixture during fiesta time, seasonal celebrations, or on saints' feast days. Street food also nourishes those who can't cook for themselves because they do not have kitchens: university students living away from home in dormitories, travelers on long bus rides to the provinces, and families visiting loved ones in the hospital. For the poorest of the poor, street food like *pagpag*, resold food scraps culled from trash bags thrown out by restaurants, is the only food affordable and available for squatters and the destitute living in makeshift refuges like Payatas Dumpsite, the capital's garbage dump.

An estimated 50,000 hawkers cook and sell street food in Manila alone. Street-food vendors are entrepreneurs, finding a living with a trade that will support them and their families. Few are professionally trained at culinary schools or have work experience at restaurants. More often, vendors cultivate their skill for food preparation at home. Street-food ingredients are inexpensive and readily accessible at open-air dry or wet markets called *palengke*. Merchants prepare and par-cook fresh ingredients at home, then finish cooking at the point of sale. A common question customers ask vendors is, "Bagong luto ho ba ito?" or, "Is this newly cooked?" Some vendors also offer frozen or packaged food that can be quickly prepared—like *pancit ramen* (ramen noodles).

Trade secrets, largely, do not exist when it comes to Filipino street food. Though specific provinces are known for particular foods, the basic recipes and preparation methods for street food are commonly known. What distinguishes one vendor from another are the proportions, combinations, cleanliness, and the quality of the ingredients. Over time, vendors develop trusting relationships with their regular customers, or *suki*.

Since no national policy exists on the regulation of street foods, regulation and enforcement fall on the local municipalities, resulting in uneven quality of street food. On the lesser-regulated side of street-food vending, vendors build their own stalls, carts, retrofitted public utility jeepneys or carrying implements. They set up where other vendors have already established a presence in order to avoid trouble with authorities. In other municipalities, vendors may be required to acquire security clearances and permits; to undergo ongoing training on food sanitation and regulations; and to submit to random visits and product testing. Some markets assign each vendor a stall that may include access to clean water and waste disposal. In these municipalities, local authorities have better control, enforcement capability, and working relationships with the vendors. Vendors may be organized into unions or cooperatives. Vendors may also have access to microcredit nongovernmental organizations. Street-food franchises are a popular entrepreneurial route. Consumers are very conscientious of brands, advertising, and perceived quality, safety, and consistency. Franchises dominate the food industry with professionally designed signs and consistent appearances.

MAJOR STREET FOODS

Chicken, Duck, and Other Fowl

BALUT
Of all the fowl-derived street food, the most famous—or, better *infamous*—is the *balut*. *Balut* is considered to be a native Filipino delicacy; for some, it's an aphrodisiac or a rite of passage given to newcomers to the Philippines. *Balut* are boiled duck embryos incubated for 17 to 22 days. Depending on one's taste for doneness, a consumer chooses a younger or older *balut*. The older the *balut*, the more mature the embryo: firmer formed bones, beak, and feathers. From the *balutan* (duck hatchery), vendors buy batches of embryos and cook them at home. What the vendors boil the *balut* in—clean water, vinegar, soy sauce, or any flavorings—is what distinguishes one's product. To avoid waste, hatcheries also sell *penoy* and *abnoy* at lower prices. A *penoy* is a *balut* egg that did not become fertilized and is without decomposition. An *abnoy* is a penoy that has some decomposition and, despite its foul smell, is still cooked into scrambled eggs.

KWEK-KWEK
Other fowl-related street foods include *kwek-kwek*, deep-fried quail eggs, hard-boiled and coated with a slightly piquant and distinctly orange batter. Its larger chicken or duck egg counterpart is called *tokneneng*. Day-old chick (which has no Tagalog name) is a duckling that is deep-fried and sometimes served whole,

skewered with a toothpick or snipped into pieces, and served with vinegar and chopped onions.

ISAW

Manila is approximately 1,006 miles north of the equator. For a nation with a temperate climate where the weather is usually warm enough to cook outside—and in fact, many times, it is too hot to cook inside comfortably—barbequing outdoors over hot coals or open flames is a common and inexpensive food preparation method.

The meats used for *isaw*, or barbeque, are not just skewered chicken cutlets or pork chops. Street vendors make use of every part of the animal for barbequing—often the most inexpensive parts. (People joke about supposed cuts of chicken or pork actually being stray dog or cat. So sometimes people prefer *isaw* that is easily distinguishable in form.) Vendors have commonly adopted amusingly descriptive names for each one. Chicken intestine accordioned around the skewer is called IUD (intrauterine device). Congealed chicken's blood formed into small, dark rectangles is called Betamax. Deep-fried chicken feet, talons and all, are Adidas. And finally, there's Helmet, or deep-fried whole chicken head.

Processed Meats

The Philippines has a long tradition of native butchery knowledge and of processed meat technology, such as the Spanish longganisa, Mexican chorizo, and the American hot dog. In a street-food context, processed meats usually take the form of meatballs. A major producer and exporter of seafood, the Philippines's food industry, along with those in other Asian seafood markets, developed processes to make use of the great volume of valuable yet initially undesirable seafood by-products. Meatballs—made of squid or fish meats—are a common street food, enjoyed after deep-fried skewers are dipped in any combination of soy-, vinegar-, or chile-based sauces, with garnishes that might include chopped onions, tomatoes, herbs, or peppers.

Siomai are a culinary export of the Chinese, long-time traders with the natives from pre-Hispanic times. The Chinese-Filipino community has a still-thriving enclave in the capital called Binondo. Descended straight out of a dim sum cart, *siomai* are steamed, wonton-wrapped, pork and shrimp meat dumplings. Vendors can purchase frozen bundles of *siomai* inexpensively at any market or grocery store. After steamed, *siomai* are served with soy sauce. Mass transit stations across Manila are not complete without a *siomai* stands. These stands also sometimes sell steamed *siopao*, commonly known in China as *baozi*, or rice flour buns stuffed with cooked meats and sauces.

Rice-Based Foods

There is a litany of street-food desserts based on rice, rice flour, or *kakanin*, ground glutinous rice. Some of these can be enjoyed only during the lead-up to and including the Christmas celebration on December 25. (Though in some communities, these Christmastime desserts are available during the entire Christmas season—September through December—or even all year-round.) The Filipino Catholic church observes Misa de Gallo, or Rooster's Mass, a 4 a.m. mass held daily for nine days leading up to Christmas. To warm up mass-goers during the cooler early morning hours, vendors peddle *bibingka* and *puto bumbong* in the plaza in front of or around the church.

Bibingka is a rice cake cooked in banana leaves, made of *galapong* (milled glutinous sweet rice dough), coconut milk, margarine, and sugar. The cakes are baked in special ovens, which cook both top and bottom, and are served with grated coconut meat. Special versions of *bibingka* feature strips of savory cheese or hard-boiled salted eggs baked into the cakes. Like *bibingka, puto bumbong* is based on *galapong*. *Puto bumbong*'s distinct violet appearance comes from a purple glutinous rice (*pirurutong*) or food coloring. The rice is steamed inside bamboo casings (*bumbong*).

Pandesal

Pandesal means "salt bread," but they are actually slightly sweet, wheat flour–based bread rolls, peddled far afield from the bakeries by street vendors. The beauty of *pandesal* is in its versatility; it can be eaten on its own or buttered, taken with morning coffee, served in homemade sandwiches with savory leftovers, or eaten with ice cream.

Taho

In the morning, vendors can be heard calling out, "Taho!" to tempt residents with the soft tofu with tapioca pearls in syrup. Merchants sell *taho* from two large aluminum cylinders tied to either end of a thick wooden plank or stick balanced on their shoulders. One bucket contains the tofu, and the other contains the tapioca pearls and syrup.

Saba

Saba (banana) is set on a long skewer and deep-fried. The coating caramelizes and is finished with a sprinkling of brown sugar. It is eaten hot from the frying pan.

Fruit on a Stick

Competing with meat on sticks: fruits on sticks. The Philippines grows 91 varieties of bananas, varied in sweetness and consistency. Banana cue are skewered, peeled bananas, which when barbequed forms a crunchy, caramelized crust.

Corn on the Cob

While not nearly as elaborate as Mexican *elotes*, corn is simply prepared, either boiled on the cob or barbequed in the husk.

Buko

Buko (coconut) juice is served right out of the shell. Vendors wielding large knives skillfully chop off excess husk weight, leaving just a centimeter or two surrounding the coconut flesh and its juices intact within.

Ice Cream

Sold by vendors from brightly painted wooden pushcarts, dirty ice cream, another misnomer, is locally produced ice cream. It comes in flavors like *ube*, macapuno, cheese, or corn.

SARAHLYNN PABLO

SINGAPORE

T HE REPUBLIC OF SINGAPORE is a city-state located off the southern tip of the Malay Peninsula, separated from Malaysia by the Straits of Johor. It united with other former British territories to form Malaysia in 1963 and became a fully independent state two years later. It consists of 63 islands and has a land area of just 272 square miles. It has a population of 5.1 million, of whom around 75 percent are of Chinese descent, 13 percent of Malay origin, 9 percent of Indian descent, and the rest from other groups. A financial center, it is one of the world's richest countries with a per capita GDP of nearly $60,000.

Singapore has developed a highly food-centric culture. A case in point is that in the National Museum of Singapore, the very first gallery in the museum is devoted to the street food of the country. The people of Singapore have also developed a term for food enthusiasm: *makan*. In Malay, *makan* simply means "to eat," but its connotation suggests a kind of feeding frenzy, an unquenchable enthusiasm for food.

Though vendors are still referred to as "hawkers" (people who call out to passersby to hawk their wares), the Singaporean government outlawed actual street food several years ago, and many of the street-food vendors in Singapore are now collected under roof-covered areas—food courts—with convenient tables where people can sit while they eat. Hawking itself has become rare. Still, Singapore understands good business, and now the government actively supports hawker markets, though it is encouraging lighter and healthier food options. In support of hawker markets, the government has even established a website, myhawkers.sg, for those seeking information about these marvelous Singaporean food resources.

Permanent buildings are much easier to monitor than transient street stands, and the level of sanitation in Singaporean markets is quite high. Napkins are abundant (which is not always the case in Southeast Asian markets), and many food courts have water and soap for cleaning up before or after dining.

Singaporean markets attract male and female customers from all social strata. Because markets are enclosed and feature tables, it's not uncommon to see families, mothers with children, and groups of friends and others gathered throughout the day to enjoy food. The vendors themselves are both male and female, unlike some other Southeast Asian markets that are managed mainly by women.

The food reflects the influences of all Singapore's ethnic groups, so that side by side, you may see Malaysian *nasi lemak* (rice cooked in coconut milk, served with vegetables and fish or eggs), Chinese Hainanese chicken (chicken cooked in its own broth, served with the broth and rice), and *roti prata* (a North Indian bread that is a staple on the Singaporean streets).

Singaporeans love to eat and love to talk about food. As English is the official language of Singapore, it's quite easy for Westerners not only to order food but to get into valuable food conversations with fellow buyers as well. It is not at all uncommon for tourists to sidle up to locals to inquire as to the appropriate use of condiments with a specific dish. Singaporeans seem to love to hear how much foreigners appreciate the food of their country.

MAIN MARKETS

The numerous hawker centers in Singapore are government owned and are spread all over the city-state. The major markets include the following:

- Lau Pa Sat in Chinatown uses a 19th-century building that houses hundreds of vendor stalls.
- Old Airport Road Food Centre occupies a perhaps unappealing location, but is a rich source for Singaporean chow.
- Jurong West 505 Market & Food Centre is not as large as Old Airport Road Food Centre, but was named the Favorite Hawker Centre in the 2010 City Hawker Food Hunt.

- Newton Food Centre was built in the early 1970s and is heavily promoted by the Singapore Tourism Board.
- Bugis Street Flea Market offers a range of street foods in addition to fashions and hard merchandise.
- Tiong Bahru is a popular market located near a large mall as well as a train station, making it a convenient spot to stop and grab a snack.

Because many Singaporean markets are housed in permanent structures, vendors are able to use a wide range of preparation techniques, including ovens, fry stations, and grills. The stability of their locations within food courts enables the vendors to offer sometimes more elaborate foods than that would be possible on the street.

MAJOR STREET FOODS

Given the range of cultural influences, Singaporean street food offers an incredible range of options.

Satay
This skewered meat is the Singaporean street food most likely to be immediately recognized by Westerners. Marinated and then grilled, satay in Singapore is usually made of chicken, but it's also possible to find satay of beef, mutton, and pork.

Hainanese Chicken
Chicken with rice cooked together in chicken broth is the epitome of Southeast Asian comfort food: simply flavored, rich and warm, nonthreatening. Tradition demands that it be served with sambal, a spicy sauce based on chile and sometimes ginger, as well as a small cup of the chicken broth. Though it apparently originated on Hainan, an island off the coast of mainland China, this dish is an enduring favorite in Singapore and throughout the region.

Black Pepper Crab
Cooked in oil or butter and coated with black pepper, this large crab is a delicious mess, with the sharpness of the pepper nicely balancing the richness of the oil. This is the kind of dish that will convince even the more abstemious that licking

fingers, though perhaps uncouth, is entirely justified under some circumstances. A variation is the somewhat sweeter chile crab.

Laksa

A spicy noodle soup, *laksa* is usually presented in two different forms: curry and asam. Curry *laksa* is made with coconut milk, shrimp, noodles, tofu, and spicy curry paste; asam *laksa* has no coconut milk and features a somewhat sour fish broth. There are many, many variations on these two basic themes. *Katong laksa* is a relatively new variety, named after a Singaporean neighborhood, and featuring thick noodles usually cut up into bite-size pieces.

Roti Prata

Though it has roots in the Indian subcontinent, *roti prata* is now considered a homegrown Singaporean dish. This flatbread is flipped in the air and manipulated until it is very thin, and then it's folded and fried. Though it can be eaten alone, it's most often seen in combination with other foods, such as sauced meat and vegetables. *Roti prata* proves an excellent sponge for sauce.

Murtabak

This is a local equivalent of an Indian stuffed roti. A dough made from white flour is wrapped around spiced minced meat and beaten eggs and folded into packets that are sautéed, cut into pieces, and served with a curry sauce. The word *murtabak* is derived from the Arabic word for "folded."

OTHER STREET FOODS

Fried Carrot Cake

This snack has nothing in common with what we in the West know as carrot cake. It contains no carrot, and it's not sweet. Rather, this street eat is basically a mixture of egg and radish with perhaps shrimp and fish sauce. In Singapore, this relatively simple carrot cake is called "white." Further north up the Malay Peninsula, soy is added, making for a "black" carrot cake.

Rojak

A somewhat conceptually challenging dish of fruit and vegetables with shrimp paste, *rojak* may include mango, pineapple, cucumbers, peanuts, and even small Chinese fritters. In Malay, the word *rojak* means "mixture," and in practice, this dish brings together an unusual blend of flavors.

Otak-Otak

A spicy paste made from fish, onions, eggs, sago, herbs, and spices is steamed or grilled in a banana leaf. *Otak* means "brains" in Malaysian; the ridges on the cooked fish paste are reminiscent of the wrinkles on a brain. Though it may be eaten alone, it is often served over *bee hoon*, vermicelli noodles wok-fried with condiments such as strips of egg, vegetables like onion and green beans, and sometimes shrimp.

Popiah

Although they are now considered indigenous to Singapore, the Peranakan were originally Chinese who immigrated to the island and developed their own culture, traditions, and foodways. These Straits Chinese, as they were called, have developed a number of characteristic foods, but the one most likely to be found in hawker markets is the *popiah*, a spring roll filled with vegetables and perhaps hoisin sauce, though fillings vary from vendor to vendor. The one constant is the thin wrapper that encloses the ingredients.

Beverages

In addition to water and soda, hawkers' markets offer several somewhat unusual beverages.

- Barley tea is basically water in which roasted barley has been boiled. This noncaffeinated herbal tea may be sweetened with honey. Barley tea is believed to be a natural diuretic, and a number of benefits have been attributed to it, including the ability to cleanse the body and even resist certain cancers.
- Cane juice, made of crushed sugarcane, yields a light-green nectar with very mild flavor and slight sweetness. Cane juice is created when whole stalks of sugarcane are run through a machine consisting of two rapidly

rotating steel wheels that completely crush the cane so that the juice runs into waiting receptacles.

Though Singapore seems not to have developed the extensive dessert menu of countries like Thailand, for sheer weirdness, consider the Singaporean ice-cream sandwich, which is basically blocks of ice cream between slices of white bread.

DAVID HAMMOND

THAILAND

HE KINGDOM OF THAILAND is located in the center of the Indochina peninsula in Southeast Asia. Unlike other countries in Southeast Asia, it was never subject to foreign rule. It has an area of 198,000 square miles and a population of 64 million people. About 75 percent of the population is ethnically Thai, 14 percent is of Chinese origin, 3 percent is ethnically Malay, and the rest belong to minority groups including Mons, Khmers, and various hill tribes. Around 95 percent of the population are Buddhists.

Thailand has one of the most exciting street-food cultures in Asia. Whereas people in West tend to eat three relatively large meals every day, people in Thailand and other Asian countries generally eat a number of relatively smaller meals throughout the day. This habit is conducive to the development of a strong culture of street food, which is portioned out in small quantities that can be munched on the run.

However, street food is a relatively recent phenomenon that really came to the fore in the 1960s as Thais left their family homes and farms and moved to cities in search of employment. Women especially played a large role in the markets as men pursued other careers, and today most Thai street-food vendors are women, in contrast with Singapore and other countries in Southeast Asia. Another influence on Thai street food has been the wave of Chinese migration in the 19th and early 20th centuries. Housed in communal accommodations, they ate on the streets. Their lasting legacy is the many noodle shops and vendors in Thai cities.

Although the Theravada Buddhism practiced by most Thais does not prohibit the eating of meat except as a voluntary practice, many Thai food vendors sell vegetarian preparations that can be very easily modified to be exclusively vegetable (for instance, the classic papaya salad, which can be prepared without fish sauce or crabs). In deference to the dietary concerns of the Muslim minority, pork does not have a strong presence in Thai street markets as it does in Singapore and Hong Kong.

Street-food vendors are ubiquitous in Thailand. Some have mobile carts ranging from old-fashioned baskets on their shoulders (now disappearing) to motorbikes attached to portable kitchens. Mobile vendors follow the same route every day. Others have semipermanent setups in markets, on busy thoroughfares, or in front of shops. Many have tables and chairs for their customers. Often vendors selling different items cluster together.

Everyone in Thailand stops at street-food vendors: kids in T-shirts, men in business suits, and women getting a quick bite while out shopping. Because a traditional Thai meal consists of many small dishes, working women short of time often buy some items on the street to take home and include in the family meal. The availability of plastic bags makes it possible to carry such foods as soup and curries home.

From an efficiency standpoint, it makes sense to have somewhat labor-intensive Thai food prepared by a person devoted to making one thing all day long. To make a papaya salad at home, for example, would require at least one hour of chopping and pounding and probably a lot of leftover ingredients. Moreover, a papaya salad can be purchased on a Bangkok street for less than one U.S. dollar.

STREET FOOD AS RELIGIOUS DONATION

Most Thais are Buddhists, and at some stage, they are supposed to spend time as monks, who must beg for their food. Giving food or alms to a monk gives the faithful an opportunity to acquire merit. Around dawn, monks leave their temples and make their morning rounds of the street markets. Some stallholders give their wares to the monks, others purchase it for them. Vegetable curries, rice, noodles, and sweet dishes are the most popular.

With a population of 8.4 million (and nearly 15 million in the greater metropolitan region), Bangkok accounts for nearly a quarter of Thailand's population, and many of the residents live in relatively modest apartments. They do not always have stoves and other cooking appliances, and even if they do, it is very hot to cook at home in Thailand's climate. This is why there is such an active night market: once the sun goes down, people come out and eat food prepared in the cool night air by others.

MAIN MARKETS

While there are small pockets of street vendors everywhere in Bangkok, several larger markets are noteworthy:

- MBK Center is a mammoth galleria-style shopping center with an indoor food court offering many traditional street foods with prices and safety standards that are higher than on the street. It's also air-conditioned, so while some of the gritty charm of street eating is lost, the customers gain comfort and security.
- Chatuchak Weekend Market is a weekend market that covers almost 40 acres and has more than 15,000 vendors.
- Floating markets are found in several Thai cities, and although they attract many tourists, you can get some good tastes if you make the effort to eat the food locals are eating.

The preferred method of preparation is grilling. Although some dishes, like salads and fruit snacks, can be prepared by simply cutting and seasoning and perhaps vigorously pounding raw materials, the grill is a common sight in Thai markets. Preparing food over an open fire has the added advantage of attracting buyers by spreading delicious smells throughout the air.

Aside from vendors established in food courts or brick-and-mortar structures, the vast majority of Thai street vendors seem to be folks who set up shop on the street, using tables, cooking appliances, and ingredients that can be reasonably mounted on a motor scooter (and we've seen Thai motorists carrying gravity-defying quantities of material on a single scooter).

Some characteristics of Thai food could help allay sanitation concerns. Much food has been subjected to open fire and contains chile heat and acidity that may reduce potentially dangerous food-borne bacteria. Although some vendors pull on gloves before serving, it requires a small leap of faith-in-sanitation practices to order street food in Bangkok. Running water at on-the-street vendors is rare. An exception is the food court in MBK, where it's easier for health inspectors to keep an eye on things.

MAJOR STREET FOODS

With the vast range of street foods available in Thailand in general and Bangkok specifically, it's difficult to narrow the major foods to just a handful, but some trends are evident.

Salads
Though it may be wise to avoid raw fruit and vegetables served on the street, many wonderful salads are sold.

- Papaya salad (*som tum*) is an iconic Thai dish that features on the menus of most North American Thai restaurants. Into the mortar and pestle go green papaya threads and other ingredients, such as chile peppers, small limes (so delicate that they can be eaten whole), tomatoes, green beans, bean sprouts, herbs, and salt. The street chef pounds these foods until the juices run together into a beautiful, aromatic, crunchy, and tastefully cohesive mess. In North American restaurants, the ingredients are sometimes not properly blended to ensure the flavors flow and merge.
- Smoked catfish salad (*larb pla duk*) leverages a fish that in North America is frequently ignored but which in Thailand and other parts of Southeast Asia is honored as a delicious addition to the table.
- In addition to the grilled meat, grilled beef salad contains lime, chile, and sugar, as well as shallots, mint, and onion.
- Long bean noodle salad includes papaya, chilies, and the very long namesake beans (also called "snake beans"). The beans are cut and pounded together with the papaya and chilies to release and marry the flavors. Palm sugar, lime juice, freshwater crabs, and tomatoes may be added at the end.

Grilled Fish and Meat

Grilled foods include plump fish, dusted with salt and stuffed with herbs; chicken, beef, and pork on skewers; spicy Thai sausages (sometime stuffed with meat, sometimes with rice only); and vegetables. The protocol for ordering is to select several skewers by placing them in a basket and handing it to the vendor to cook. After the items are grilled, the vendor places them in a box or bag. Most Thais like to accompany the grilled meat with glutinous rice and chile sauce, which is served in small plastic bags to take home or can be added directly to the food.

Seafood

Thailand has an extensive coastline, so that in addition to fish, there is a vast collection of crustacean products available that are eaten both raw and cooked.

- Oyster omelets are a cooked egg or pancake dough with oysters either mixed in or sprinkled on top. Hot sauce can be added to taste.
- Cockles are displayed in large flat trays and served in plastic bags with a shot of salt and hot sauce.
- Crabs, some quite large, are available both raw and cooked. Some work is required to extract the meat, so some people like to share them with a friend and take turns picking away at them.

Noodles

Noodles have been called the hamburger of Thai street food: simple, satisfying, cheap, and available everywhere. Noodle vendors generally specialize in this one food item. Rice is the predominant raw material for Thai noodles known as *kanom chin*, though some vendors prepare egg and mung bean noodles. Noodle shops open early and are closed by mid-afternoon. Most stalls sell several varieties of sauce to accompany the noodles. Diners are supposed to specify what kind of noodles they want and the ingredients. The most popular delivery system for many of Thailand's noodles is soup, though there are some dry noodle dishes.

- Wonton noodles are served along with meat and vegetable and a large array of condiments.
- Spicy noodles are served from carts that present buyers with a range of condiments they can add even without chilies, and the noodles can be pretty spicy.

The most famous Thai noodle dish served in all Thai restaurants as well as street carts is pad thai: thin rice noodles fried with pieces of tofu, dried shrimp, shallots, and eggs; flavored with fish sauce, tamarind, and sugar; and topped with ground peanuts and bean sprouts, with a slice of lime and crisp vegetables on the side. Some vendors sell mussel omelets as an accompaniment.

PAD THAI

THAI SAUCES

Thais like to mix and match, especially when eating noodles. The most traditional accompaniment to rice noodles is *nahm ya*, a thick spicy sauce made from fish, dried chilies, shallots, garlic, lemongrass, and wild ginger. Another popular sauce is *nahm prik*, a smoky sauce made from grilled chilies, shallots, garlic, and mung beans that is eaten with vegetables.

Curry

CURRY

Curry is one of the most iconic Thai dishes. The Thai word for curry, *gaeng*, means "any wet savory dish enriched and thickened by a paste." The starting point is an aromatic curry paste that contains shrimp paste (*kapi*) chilies, ginger, coriander root, basil, and other spices. The ideal is to achieve a balance of hot, sour, salty, and sweet flavors in both an individual dish and a meal. As Thai food expert David Thompson writes:

In a good Thai curry, each flavor should be tasted to its desired degree and no one flavor should overshadow another. The striving for a complex balance of ingredients is nowhere more apparent than in curries: robustly flavoured ingredients are melded and blended together into a harmonious, yet paradoxically subtle and cohesive whole.

Coconut milk–based curries are prevalent in Bangkok and central Thailand, and water-based curries are more common in northern Thailand. Thai curries are categorized by the color of the paste used in their preparation: red, made with red chilies and Indian spices; yellow, made with turmeric and curry powder; green, containing fresh green chilies, basil leaves, lime leaves, and often round green eggplants; panang, with dried red chilies, white pepper, and sometimes peanuts; and massaman curry, containing dried red chilies and aromatic spices. Depending on the kind, curries can be accompanied by rice, rice noodles, or roti, a flat, round bread made with white flour that is of South Asian origin.

Soups
A remarkable feature of Thai soups is the range of flavors and textures contained within a single bowl. It is not uncommon to have a soup that holds slivers of meat, a fried wonton skin, noodles, bean sprouts, fish balls, and vegetables. Unlike in the West where a meal starts with soup, in Asia, it is more traditional to have soup at some point near the end of the meal. Soups served on Thai streets include the following:

- Though pork in the form of belly or other meats seems less common than chicken or beef, Thai pork noodle soup is a Thai street classic. It is made by adding rice noodles to pork with pork broth, bok choy, dried shrimps, sugar, chilies, and other ingredients.
- Noodle soup may be the most popular street food in Thailand. It is a kind of comfort food and quite simple, as the meat-based broth is perked up with simple condiments.
- Hot and sour chicken soup may be presented in a clear broth or in a broth made creamy by the addition of coconut milk. Redolent of lemon grass, this soup is perked up with cherry tomatoes and chilies.

OTHER STREET FOODS

Thai street foods are so vast in their range that almost anything that grows in this country will, at one time or another, be represented on the streets of this country. A number of lesser known foods are worthy of attention.

Sticky Rice

Though not as visually arresting as green papaya salad or grilled fish, sticky rice is a staple in many Thai markets, and it's an easy grab-n-go item by itself or as an add-on with a larger dish. Though it contains no dietary gluten, sticky rice is highly glutinous (thus, sticky) and is usually sold wrapped in banana leaves, which imparts flavor and keeps the small balls of rice from sticking together. Sticky rice is frequently sold unadorned, though it may also be stuffed with meat or vegetables and sprinkled with herbs and spices.

Another popular rice dish, often served as a breakfast food, is *johk*, a savory congee or rice porridge. The porridge may contain meat, perhaps some ginger, and even an egg.

Chicken Butt

Wandering around Bangkok one afternoon, one can spot a vendor selling a number of grilled items, including small skewers of what seem clearly to be the triangular tail sections of a chicken. Each little piece of tail is a small package of unctuous fat, with a thin thread of meat inside. It may be brined before it is lightly caramelized on an outdoor grill over hardwood charcoal. With an added dollop of lime-laced hot pepper sauce, it proves a brilliant combination of the four classic flavors that make Thai food distinctive: sweet, sour, salty, and hot.

Fried Chicken

Perhaps because it requires a large quantity of hot oil (and consequently a number of safety precautions and perhaps extra steps), fried chicken is less common on Thai streets than grilled chicken, but the fried version is equally fabulous. In Thailand, fried chicken tends to have a lighter coating than American fried chicken, and this sheath is made of rice flour rather than wheat flour, so it clings more tightly to each chicken piece.

Fresh Fruit

Thailand has a great abundance of fruit and vegetables, and although such produce is readily available, freshly cut fruits and vegetables take a backseat to more savory dishes at Thai street markets. Still, it is difficult to ignore the brightly colored stacks of incredible tropical food items, some of which are transported around the city on motor bikes. Fruits are sometimes sprinkled with salt and a little hot pepper powder to accentuate the sweetness. Some of the more common fruits include the easily recognizable watermelon, papaya, and mango. If you prefer your street food cooked (and there's good reason why you might), consider fried bananas, creamy, sweet, and easy to eat while walking. At many fruit vendors, one can purchase a young green coconut, which is trimmed to fit in the hand and punctured to allow a straw to be inserted; the liquid of this fruit is only slightly sweet and is a good accompaniment for spicier foods.

Thai Desserts

Though many Asian countries seem relatively unconcerned with sweet desserts, the Thais have taken desserts to a whole new level with hundreds of brightly colored creations in jelly, marzipan, and rice. Some of the more popular deserts include the following:

- Thai sticky rice with mango.
- *Khanom*, a confection of rice flour, sugar, and coconut milk, may be served uncolored in relatively shapeless blobs or it may be brightly colored and cut into distinctive shapes (stars, flowers, etc.)
- Fried bananas, which may be eaten unadorned or with a chocolate or other sauce.

Chiang Mai

Chiang Mai, the largest city in northern Thailand and a popular tourist destination, also has a bustling street-food scene. On Sundays, a famous night market is open on Ratchadamnoen Avenue from 4 p.m. to midnight. Every evening, vendors set up their carts at the southern gate of the old city selling such delicacies as *pad naam*, a local sweet-and-sour sausage with noodles; morning glory with vegetables or crispy pork; stewed pork shank; and *khao soi*, a creamy curry-based noodle dish made with chicken, beef, and sometimes pork, coconut milk, and sprinkled with deep-fried noodles. Lime and picked cabbage add to the flavor. The quintessential Chiang Mai dessert is sticky rice with mango and condensed milk, which is also enjoyed for breakfast.

DAVID HAMMOND AND COLLEEN TAYLOR SEN

VIETNAM, LAOS, CAMBODIA, AND BURMA

T HOUGH THE PEOPLES OF SOUTHEAST ASIA have wide varieties of languages, ethncities, and cultures the cuisine of the region has many overlapping flavors and ingredients. The influence of colonization and the climate are the largest contributing factors to the cohesive cuisine in the countries discussed here. Located just south of China, Vietnam, Cambodia, and Burma are all partially bordered by coasts. Laos is not, and its street food has much less seafood as a result. A large Buddhist and Hindu presence is strong throughout the area. The moist land of Southeast Asia makes it ideal for cultivating rice. The grain is a staple ingredient for much of the food produced in the area, including street-side dining.

The population of Cambodia is largely Khmer or descendants of the Khmer Empire. At its peak from the 10th to 13th centuries, the Khmer Empire ruled much of Southeast Asia, including the countries discussed in this section. Cambodia was also attacked by the Thai and Vietnamese before it was placed under French rule in 1887. After gaining independence from France in 1953, Cambodia was occupied by Japan and Vietnam, and suffered a terrible genocidal government in the 1970s before it achieved its current relative stability in the 1990s. Burma was occupied by Britain from the 1820s to the 1880s and designated as part of India until 1937. Its street food shows a strong influence from Indian cuisine, including samosas and flavor combinations.

In the 18th and 19th centuries, Laos was controlled by Thailand until becoming part of French Indochina and then gained independence in 1953 following World War II Japanese occupation. Vietnam was under French rule from the 1880s. Though declared independent in the early 1900s, French control did not end until 1954. Indian, Chinese, American, and French cooking techniques are seen consistently in several foods throughout Southeast Asia. France had a major influence especially in the baguettes and crêpes popularly sold at street side to locals and tourists in Vietnam and Laos.

VIETNAM

Vietnam's street food culture is integral to the larger cultural identity of Vietnamese life. The country's cuisine has been shaped by a wide variety of influences, including the tropical Southeast Asian climate and relations with other countries. French and Chinese occupation shaped a cuisine that is both bright and satisfying. The country's more than 91.5 million residents eat at least one meal every day on the street. The communal culture of Vietnam is seen in the morning when thousands of scooters fill the streets, creating a commotion similar to that in a beehive. As the sun rises, shop doors open and plastic tables and chairs are set out for street-side dining.

Commuters and tourists are likely to be seen enjoying morning coffee at Internet cafés. Rich, dark coffee is brewed into a glass through a small filter, called a *phin* perched at the top. The coffee streams over ice into a waiting pool of sweetened condensed milk. Classic Vietnamese coffee is available from street vendors throughout the day. Internet cafés invite commuters to grab a quick cup of coffee and catch up with others in the community or work on computers. "Drive-through" culture does not exist as it is known in the United States.

Aside from the morning commute, other meals in Vietnam are also commonly consumed street side. Dinner is eaten late in the evening and often the whole family is together. Street-side cafés court passersby to grab a quick bite or stay and enjoy the company of friends and family. Glossy, tourist-filled areas like parts of Ho Chi Minh City have slightly less available street food than other areas. Vietnamese love to snack, so stalls selling snack food do brisk business sll day long and people will travel across the city for their favorite dish.

Food vending is a large industry in Vietnam. In street-side stands, an entire family can often be seen working. Parents cook and wait on customers while children assist with cleanup. Because street food is so mobile and diverse in Vietnam, a wide variety of people take part in the vocation. In a smaller city, like Hoi An, there are many different street vendors in a given area. A single block may contain a corner stand with a boiling pot of phô, a cart with fresh baguettes, rice milk ice cream, and even a small grill carried over one shoulder to prepare crisp, grilled corn on the street.

Major Street Foods

PHÔ

Many people interrupt their morning commute with a steaming bowl of phô, a rich, beef-based noodle soup. The national dish of Vietnam, and the most popular choice for breakfast, phô has several variations, including *phô bo* (beef), *phô ga* (chicken), and *phô chay* (vegetable). Phô is prepared by slowly simmering bones and scraps to create a clear broth. The broth is layered with rice noodles and topped with onion, ginger, and thinly sliced meat. The dish contains onions and the occasional bean sprout as well as the warm aromas of anise, cinnamon, and ginger. Street-side phô operations with tables generally give the diner a plate of mint, garlic, basil, lime, coriander, chile, and *nuoc mam* (fermented fish sauce) to customize their dish.

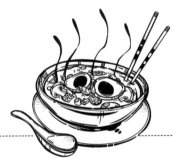

Phô, the national dish of Vietnam, is a popular choice for breakfast on the go.

BÁNH MI KEP

Crisp, fresh baguettes, called *bánh mi*, are ubiquitous in Vietnam. *Bánh mi kep* is one of the more popular street foods. A single loaf, approximately six- to eight-inches long, is cut down the side and generally stuffed with pork, though beef and chicken are used as well. In addition to the meat, *bánh mi keps* are filled with fragrant coriander leaves, pickled carrots, onion, chilies, and other vegetables.

BÁNH XÈO

The heavy French influence on Vietnamese cuisine is especially apparent in Hue and the rest of central Vietnam. Crêpes, or *bánh xèo*, are a savory example of French cuisine served on the streets of Hue and throughout the country. A salty, classic crêpe is made on a griddle with eggs and rice flour and then rolled around a filling comprising shredded pork, bean sprouts, and mushrooms. Seasonings vary by region and include *nuoc cham*, which is made with fish sauce (*nuoc mam*), water, sugar, vinegar, lime juice, garlic, and fresh chilies.

BÚN (NOODLE SOUP)

A popular street food served all day long are soups with noodles (*bún*). The noodles come in many shapes and sizes from thin to round and each are used in a different soup or cold dish. They are typically made by soaking rice overnight, then grinding and kneading the mixture. In the morning, they are served fresh but in the evening they are dried. Popular hot *bún* soups Include *bún thang* (mixed topped noodles) and *bún riêu* (paddy crab noodle soup) while cold soups man be made with grilled pork, fried tofu or beef.

Bún chả, made with cold noodles and freshly grilled pork, entered the culinary spotlight in 2016 when Anthony Bourdain and former U.S. President Barack Obama wandered into an unassuming family restaurant in Hanoi and ordered the dish. This dish is native to Hanoi's old quarter and uses *bún* and *chả* (Vietnamese-style pork roll, similar to a sausage). To enjoy this dish, the grilled pork *chả* is steeped in the vinegary goodness of the accompanying bowl of sauce. The pork is placed on top of your waiting bowl of vermicelli noodles. Fresh herbs are added for even more flavor. This meal is usually a lunchtime option in large cities because of the lightness of the dish that comes from using vermicelli rice noodles.

CÓM TẤM

This dish represents the virtues of street food, which means it is prepared quickly, uses local ingredients, and satisfies immensely. The uniqueness of the dish is inherent in its name, which translates literally as "broken rice." Rice grains are pounded down in to smaller bits that provide a textural vehicle for the other elements of the dish. Depending on the variation of *cóm tấm*, it may include grilled lemongrass pork chops, shredded pork skin, and pickled vegetables (mainly carrot and daikon). The spirit of this dish is similar to *nasi lemak* in Malaysia in that quintessential Vietnamese ingredients come together for a complete and humble meal.

Other Street Foods

GRILLED CORN

In Southeast Asia, it is common to see an individual, often a woman, cooking food and carrying her wares over her shoulder with two baskets, one balanced on each end of a bamboo pole. One basket is typically full of ingredients and supplies, and the other holds a steaming pot or small, sizzling grill. The operation can be set up anywhere hungry customers roam. The most common basket kitchens in Vietnam sell grilled corn. The charred husk is peeled back to reveal steaming kernels flavored with smoke.

DESSERT

Eating in Vietnam typically consists of several small snacks throughout the day rather than larger meals. Though dessert is not a central facet of street food, it has a constant presence. Stalls and stands selling cut pineapple, vibrant dragon fruit, and leathery jackfruit in plastic bags are available for snacking, along with baskets of spiky, dark red rambutans and other fruit. Baked goods are also sold street side, including elaborately decorated cakes and pastries. Rolling carts of glossy pastry appear most commonly in tourist-heavy areas of Ho Chi Minh City.

WHITNEY LINGLE

LAOS

Laotian street cuisine becomes much more active at night. Alleys begin to bustle in the evening as hundreds of tourists and locals descend on the markets. The night market in the city of Luang Prabang features pickles, dumplings, spring rolls, and various meats wrapped in banana leaves for grilling. In Vang Vieng, near the Kang temple, an endless line of buffets, staffed mostly by women, displays numerous stainless steel and plastic bowls awaiting customers. The Little Mekong Night Market features tables covered with a mélange of fresh produce, spices, fermented fish, shrimp, and bean paste waiting to be cooked to order.

Major Street Foods

LAAP

Laap is the national dish of Laos, a rich blend of toasted rice powder, or *khao khua*, and chopped meat, often pork or beef, mixed with lime and fish sauce. It is served with sticky rice, called *khao neow*. It can be served raw or cooked and features beef or fish and lime, *padaek* (Laotian fish sauce), chilies, coriander, and mint. It resembles a thick stir-fry and is sometimes also paired with a complimentary soup to complete the meal. On the street, one can find pop-up restaurants where flavor and ingredients can be customized on the table or taken to go.

KHAO SOI

This common street-food dish has a pork-based sauce with fermented bean paste, salt, garlic, chilies, and flat rice noodles. *Khao soi* noodles are usually fairly wide (approximately a quarter of an inch) and are paired with such vegetables as watercress, green beans, cabbage, pea shoots, and mixed greens. The rich pork sauce is slowly simmered with bean paste, spices, and tomatoes and is used to thicken the cooking liquid around the vegetables. The finished mixture is spooned atop boiled rice noodles and fresh greens and finished with crispy pieces of pig skin or rice.

Other Street Foods

PANCAKES

Throughout Laos, but especially in the town of Vang Vieng, pancakes are served alone or as a substitute for bread in a sandwich. The thick dough is stretched and handled until it resembles a translucent membrane. Slightly more substantial than Vietnamese crêpes, the pancakes of Laos still echo French influence. Made on a large outdoor griddle and drizzled with sweetened condensed milk or chocolate syrup, the pancakes are cut into bite-size pieces and placed in small cellophane bags for easy travel. In some cases, slices of fruit, most commonly bananas, are folded into the pastry during the cooking process.

TAM MAK HOONG

Variations of papaya salad abound throughout Southeast Asia, but in Laos, sweet papayas are mixed with chilies and tomatoes. The mixture is seasoned with lemon juice, sugar, salt, and paste made from prawns and ground with a mortar and pestle.

WHITNEY LINGLE

CAMBODIA

Cambodian cuisine is influenced by that of neighboring countries as well as the Chinese, French, and Vietnamese, who occupied the country at various times. The tropical climate and rich natural resources of the area lend themselves to diverse food production, much of which is available on the street. Women are the main attendants of stands and also walk the streets with baskets of snacks. Snacking aside, the staple of many larger meals in Cambodia is rice. Street vendors serve it with soup and stir-fries as well as in steamed cakes or sticky, sweet spheres for dessert.

Major Street Foods

FRIED INSECTS (*A-PING*)
One of the more distinctive facets of Cambodian cuisine is the consumption of fried insects, grubs, and arachnids, called *a-ping*. Bowls lining street vendors' tables showcase the deep-fried crickets, water bugs, and tarantulas available for sale. They are tossed in salt, sugar, and oil before deep frying until crisp. The insect trade is part of the local economy, as people prepare the specimens for market vendors (removing tarantula fangs, for example) or collect and sell the small creatures themselves.

COCKLES
In the street, cockles are sold for snacking. The freshwater clams are pushed down the streets in large carts ready for hungry passersby. They are either boiled or fried and then tossed with salt, chile, and garlic. The small pearly shells are then pulled apart by hand and the firm pinkish-gray flesh peeled from the inside.

KUY TEAV
Kuy teav is a rice noodle soup thickened with wheat gluten and flavored with beef or pork. Mushrooms, onions, lettuce, carrot, and green onion float throughout the dish, seasoned with garlic, dried squid, and cilantro. Balls of pork or other meat are added to the mixture, which may also include crab or shrimp. The rich breakfast is often an opportunity to use ingredients, especially meat, which might otherwise be wasted.

Other Street Foods

PONG TEA KHON

Fertilized duck or chicken eggs are one of the more sensationalized aspects of Cambodian cuisine. *Pong tea khon* is prepared by boiling a fertilized egg. They are held street side in large bowls or baskets and sold individually, or packed in a small bag with salt, pepper, and occasionally, other seasonings including lime juice.

SUGARCANE JUICE

Dteuk am bpoh, or sugarcane juice, is popular throughout Southeast Asia. The thick, fibrous stalks are squeezed through a heavy-duty appliance designed specifically for the task. Each piece of sugarcane is repeatedly fed through the machine until dry. The juice is shaken with ice and served very cold. It is sometimes flavored with citrus to cut the sweetness.

WHITNEY LINGLE

BURMA (ALSO KNOWN AS MYANMAR)

Burmese street cuisine is similar to that of other countries in Southeast Asia, but the largely Buddhist population, coupled with the presence of Chinese and Indian cultures, shapes a cuisine unique to Burma. Like other countries of Southeast Asia, Burmese cuisine is regional—the eastern regions are heavily influenced by Indian and Bangladeshi food. The country was formed by several dynasties and invasions by the British and Chinese. Burma gained independence from Britain during the mid-1900s.

During the country's formative years, the Burmese economy was largely agricultural. Larger cities have an especially wide variety of Burmese street food, including Yangon and Mandalay, where the local economies, especially economic power driven by women, heavily features street food.

Major Street Foods

MOHINGA

One of the country's most popular dishes, *mohinga*, is sold at both street-side stands and restaurants. *Mohinga* is a rich, fish-based broth with rice noodles flavored with typical Southeast Asian and Indian flavors, including lemongrass, garlic, and ginger topped with boiled eggs, banana blossoms, or fritters (*akyaw*). This soup is served throughout the day, but mainly for breakfast.

SAMUSAS

The Indian influence on Burmese cuisine is showcased in the *samusas* (known as samosas in India) sold in street stalls throughout the country. *Samusas* are fried pastries filled with meat or vegetables, similar to a savory handheld pie. In Burma, *samusas* are stuffed with pork or other meat, vegetables, especially potatoes and peas, and even spices including anise and cinnamon. Burmese *samusas* may also be served in soup: the pastry is cut into sections and covered in broth and herbs.

Other Street Foods

SKEWERS

Throughout Burma, but especially in Yangon, grilling and barbecuing is a street-food standby. Popular grilled items include bat, poultry, pork, tofu, fish, and quail eggs, and such vegetables as okra, mushrooms, zucchini, lotus root, garlic, and potatoes. The grilled dishes are seared street side on thin bamboo sticks convenient for consuming on the run. Little meat is wasted during the barbecue process. For bat skewers, the lean meat, including the bones, is wrapped around the skewers and roasted over a grill. All manner of meat is available and can be eaten plain, flavored by smoke, or dipped in a rich, oily broth.

MOHNT LAYMYAH

A small, puffy disk of dough, *mohnt laymyah* is a type of fried pastry filled with chickpeas, sliced scallions, and quail eggs. They are cooked in a large pan formed with circular dents throughout the surface, lending the appearance of a honeycomb. An initial dollop of batter is added to each hole, followed by a few pieces of the chosen stuffing. They are then covered in dough and flipped for even browning.

WHITNEY LINGLE

WESTERN AND CENTRAL ASIA

ARABIAN PENINSULA

HE GULF STATES OCCUPY THE SAUDI ARABIAN PENINSULA, which is bordered by the Red Sea on the west, the Indian Ocean on the south, and the Persian Gulf (also called the Arabian Gulf) on the east. They comprise Saudi Arabia, Kuwait, Bahrain, the United Arab Emirates, Qatar, Oman, and Yemen.

Until the latter part of the 20th century, the Gulf States had small populations concentrated in trading ports and villages with nomadic tribes making use of the arid inland areas. The social structure was built on family and tribal lines, and the religion was Islam. Charismatic tribal leaders headed small independent nation states. The principal occupations were trade within the Gulf and across the Indian Ocean; pearl diving and fishing; cultivation of oasis date orchards; and animal husbandry. The national food culture is derived from a frugal but rich heritage. It is complex and based on locally resourced ingredients with some significant imports such as rice.

As the century advanced, exploitation of oil resources dramatically changed the states' economies, defined political boundaries, and brought large influxes of workers from around the world. They in turn brought their food cultures.

The Arabian Gulf countries do not embrace the street-food format of on-street vendors with barrows or food stands seen elsewhere in the world. These concepts do not have a place in their modern planned cities, which are focused on car transport, not walking. Even in the traditional souks (markets), the foods on sale are predominantly ingredients with a few prepared foods.

In the past, the concept of selling prepared food would have been unthinkable to a nation. Their society was close knit with strong social bonds through the family and tribal affiliations. Their hospitality tradition required food to be freely provided to any guest. Homes ranged from coral stone palaces in the ports to goat hair tents in the interior. All had a hospitality area, the *majlis*, where guests could be entertained with conversation, some dates or small snacks, and coffee or tea.

The concept of selling food came with the commercialization of the countries, the change to modern city living, and a burgeoning population with wealth to enjoy.

Traditional foods and cookery are being challenged by the diverse cultures of the immigrant population combined with modern food sourcing, processing, and marketing. The incoming cultures have brought some of their street food with them, but it does not have the opportunity to be sold on the street and has instead been assimilated into the café and restaurant environment. Local government maintains strict controls on the streetscape, and within the cities, the itinerant vendor is not tolerated.

Traditional and imported foods do have a place in the cultural and shopping festivals that have become a Gulf leisure industry. At these events, a pastiche of street food from many traditions is made available, including national foods. Traditional local breads, *khamir, jabeeb,* and *logaimat,* are prepared to sample alongside such incoming food as *murtabak* in a context that mimics street food.

MAJOR STREET FOODS

Shawarma

The need for street sustenance on the move is provided by the sale of prepared food in a snack form on the street front, analogous to the modern Western culture of takeaway food. Shawarma was adopted as the principal street-food snack and is the mainstay of the snack food trade in the Gulf States. It is an import from a pan-Middle East tradition that now spans from Turkey to the Gulf States. It is a meat sandwich made on demand from freshly prepared ingredients. Despite competition from hamburgers and fried chicken takeaways, shawarma is maintaining its position as the preeminent street snack in the Gulf not only because of its excellent flavor derived from quality ingredients but also because it is a quick, convenient, and cheap food on the move.

Shawarma stalls are often small establishments, the core being the vertical roasting spits loaded with prepared lamb and chicken (*laham* and *djaj,* respectively), which are rotated by hand in front of a bank of gas burners. These are on the edge of the pavement and may be backed up with a small restaurant with just a few seats and cold cabinets for drinks. This is little more than a waiting and paying zone as all the action happens out on the footpath. Local ordinances may require that the food preparation is contained within a glazed frontage.

The meat is invariably identifiable cuts of meat. It is not the homogeneous processed mass of meat that is used in some countries that have adopted shawarma. The clientele is discerning and usually have a regular shawarma stall that they frequent.

The shawarma stall advertises itself with an enticing display of food to attract customers. Apart from the sight and aroma of roasting meat, there will be vocal calls to buy and the frequent rasp of carving knife on steel to attract customers. The scene is theatrical as meat is briskly sliced from the vertical spit, scooped onto opened flatbread, spiked with pickles and chopped herbs, doused with tahini sauce, and rolled tightly into a screw of paper to be proffered to the customer ready to eat. If chicken is chosen, the tahini is replaced with a garlic sauce, and perhaps a cold chip or two will be added. A vegetarian version will comprise several balls of falafel squashed into the bread pocket with pickles and tahini sauce. The bread used may vary: in Kuwait, long bread rolls called *samoor* were used in the 1980s, the inner crumb being hollowed out to make way for the meat.

This is all produced with a flowing sequence of well-practiced moves. There will usually be a cluster of customers being served and a posse of 4WD vehicles at the curb also waiting for orders. These are universally popular venues in the evening; whole families will be fed within the privacy of their vehicle, with food ordered by the driver and handed in through partially opened windows.

Beverages

These snacks are now accompanied by the international fizzy drinks in cans and bottles. Some shawarma stalls will offer a fruit cocktail. This is usually a drink in three layers of blended fruit, banana, strawberry, and mango, to be drunk through a straw so that layers may be sampled individually. An upmarket stall will have a selection of other fruits as substitutes.

Sweets

Occasionally, sweet confections, such as *ataif*, will be available. These are small pancakes that are folded over a filling of cream cheese or sweetened ground walnuts. They may be served in this plain form or deep-fried and soaked in sugar syrup.

In Yemen, on the southern coast of the Arabian Peninsula, a distinctive street snack is *mutabbagiyya*. It is made from two sheets of thin paste, one about 6 × 8 inches laid on another 12 × 18 inches square. Chopped green onions and a raw egg are placed on the small sheet, and the sides are folded over to make a 6 × 8-inch packet that is fried on a griddle. It is then cut into four neat pieces. Yemen also has many small truck stop cafés or stands that serve breakfasts of *ful* (soupy boiled fava beans with onions, tomato, and cumin), accompanied by narrow, squarish, hot-dog bun-like loaves of European-style leavened bread that are oddly referred to by the Indian name *roti*.

PHIL IDDISON

THE CAUCASUS

(Armenia and Georgia)

T HE CAUCASUS MOUNTAINS cover the isthmus between Europe (Russia) on its northwest, Central Asia on the northwest, and southwest Asia (Turkey and Iran) on the south. To the east is the Caspian Sea, and on the west, the Black Sea. Lands and climates are highly diverse, ranging from alpine and continental (warm summers and cold winters) in its mountains (the highest in Europe) to subtropical on the flat coastal areas of the Black Sea. The Caucasus has considerable biodiversity with plants, animals, and fungi that remain from the last Ice Age in the pristine mountains that have not been economically developed. Elsewhere, agriculture and mining are ancient industries that date to the early Neolithic and Bronze Age periods. What people eat today goes back to the natural environment and their history.

The peoples and languages of the Caucasus are as multilayered as the lands in which they live. Some 50 ethnic groups live there speaking as many languages and dialects. Some speak Turkic languages, others Indo-European, while still others belong to a unique group called Kartvelian. Georgian is the best known of these, Kartvelebi being what Georgians call themselves. The Caucasus is divided into almost 20 political entities, the largest in area being the Republics of Georgia, Armenia, Azerbaijan, and Dagestan. They differ in language, culture, and religion: Dagestan, one of the republics of the Russian Federation, alone has 33 different language groups. Religion also plays an important role in culture, with several branches of Christianity and several Muslim groups having adherents. Naturally religious practices affect what foods people eat and the kinds of holidays and festivals they observe.

The food history of the Caucasus countries is as complex as the peoples and landscapes. Empires, kingdoms, and states rose and fell, peoples migrated in from central and southwest Asia and Europe, but all the cuisines were based on indigenous foodstuffs. Agriculture and herding have been practiced in the region for more than 8,000 years. Sheep and goats pastured in the highlands have long provided meat and milk, while wheat has been there from the beginning. Eggplants, chickpeas, lentils, beans, many kinds of greens, nuts, and mushrooms are important ingredients. Viticulture is almost as old. Georgia, for instance, has had a grape wine industry for the past 6,000 years and grows some 500 different grape varieties. In ancient times, grape juice was placed in large ceramic containers set in the ground. The same technique is used to this day for much of the wine production. Georgian wine is famous and by far the most popular in Russia, as is Georgian cuisine. When New World foods appeared, farmers of the Caucasus took to them. Tomatoes, potatoes, corn, and peppers are all important elements of local cuisines.

Early Christians converted the northern Caucasus, so that today Eastern Orthodox and Oriental Orthodox churches hold sway. Their festivals, many of which resemble Greek and Russian Orthodox practices, feature red-dyed Easter eggs and sweetened *paska*. The mountains were home to wild boar, which were hunted, and today pork is eaten in the Christian nations. The southern part of the Caucasus is mainly Muslim, dating to the early days of Islam and later to the time when Turkish empires extended into the area. Naturally, Muslim festivals such as Ramadan and Eid are important, and dishes similar to Middle Eastern ones, such as ground chickpeas, are widely consumed. Since Muslims do not eat pork, characteristic meats are lamb, mutton, beef, and chicken.

Since the Caucasus was under the control of the Soviet Union from the 1920s to the 1990s (some of the northern regions are still part of the Russian Federation), many traditional foodways disappeared due to modernization introduced in that period. However, much of the home cooking tradition remained intact, and local industries such as cheese and wine making survived. These and local ingredients remain the base for today's street-food traditions. But another kind of modernization has taken root: fast food. McDonald's, for instance, has opened outlets in Georgia, Azerbaijan, and Armenia, and international soft drink companies sell products in the region.

MAJOR STREET FOODS

Whatever the divisions among peoples, some dishes are universal. By far, the most famous is *shashlik*, followed by flatbreads and cheese dishes.

Shashlik

Shashlik is a shish kebab made in much the same way as it is in the Middle East and around the world. Chunks of meat are marinated overnight in lemon juice with salt and onions, threaded onto skewers with onions, peppers, and tomatoes, and grilled over open grills. *Shashlik* can be made with lamb, beef, or pork, depending on the region; in Georgia, pork is popular, while in mainly Muslim Dagestan, it is made with lamb. Almost any meat or vegetable can be skewered. In Azerbaijan, on the Caspian Sea coast, sturgeon appears, served with a pomegranate sauce, while in Georgia, *tkemali*, a popular plum sauce, is an accompaniment. There is hardly a public event in the Caucasus that does not have *shashlik*, and it is a standard street food.

Khachapuri

Khachapuri is perhaps the signature dish of Georgia's cuisine. It is a raised bread filled with shredded cheeses, mixed with eggs and seasonings, and baked. It is served in slices in the same way as pizza. *Khachapuri* has a number of regional variations, each closely identified with its native region. Because it is so savory and filling, it is spread across the Caucasus nations and is sold as street food and takeout in many areas.

Kinkali, Hingal, Manti

Kinkali (in Georgian), *hingal* (in Dagestan), or *manti* (in Armenia) is a steamed dumpling that is thought to have originated in Georgia. In reality, *kinkali* is one of a range of filled dumplings that can be found across central Asia into east Asia and westward into Eastern Europe and perhaps even Italy. *Kinkali* is made by stretching out a thin sheet of dough, cutting it into circles and filling them with chopped meats, cheese, or vegetables. The dumpling is closed into a swirl shape and then steamed. There are many kinds of fillings depending on local tastes. Spicy lamb; strong goat cheese; chopped vegetables such as onion, garlic, and red peppers; and walnuts are common variations. Yogurt is often served as a topping and sumac as a herb flavoring.

Döner Kebabs

Döner kebabs have spread from Turkey across the globe. Various meats are packed into an upright spit and slowly roasted over an open fire. Thin slices of meat are cut from the spit, laid on flatbreads, and served with condiments. *Döner kebabs* are often accompanied by chopped cucumbers, tomatoes, onions, or potatoes and served with sauces, some yogurt based.

Stuffed Leaves

Cabbage or grape leaves are used as wrappers for portable foods. Called dolma in Greece, grape leaves are often stuffed with cold cooked rice mixed with nuts and raisins or finely chopped cooked meats. Cabbage leaves are also prepared this way. Armenian cookery is famous for such preparations that are served as street food and at festivals such as religious holidays.

Churchkhelas, Chuchkhel

Walnuts are important in the cuisines of the Caucasus. *Churchkhelas* (Georgian) or *chuchkhel* (Armenian) are long strings of walnuts or other nuts, such as hazelnuts, dipped into a thick grape juice for a long time and then hung up to dry. The sweet nuts become sweet and chewy and are a favorite treat.

Fruits and Corn

Countries such as Georgia and Armenia grow many kinds of fruits that are sold from stands and in markets. Quinces, apples, peaches (dried peaches are a Georgian specialty), plums (also featured in many preparations and as brandy), apricots, pears, pomegranates, and grapes are popular. Grilled corn on the cob is also a feature of roadside stands.

BRUCE KRAIG

IRAN

IRAN IS SITUATED BETWEEN the Caspian Sea and the Persian Gulf and covers 636,000 square miles. Largely mountainous and hilly in the north, the country gradually gives way to arid lowlands, a large desert in its center, and finally more lush, tropical climes at its southern border in the Persian Gulf. In the north, the area around the inland Caspian Sea is verdant and cooler.

Iran shares borders with Turkey, Iraq, Afghanistan, Pakistan, and the former Soviet bloc countries of Azerbaijan, Armenia, and Turkmenistan. At its largest, early Iran, or the Persian Empire, encompassed all of those nations within its environs. As a result, the cooking styles throughout the nation have been influenced by those who lived in the larger empire. Later, the Greek conquest of Iran brought foodstuffs including stuffed items such as grape leaves, while skewered marinated meats like *souvlaki* are thought to represent Persian influence on the Greeks.

Throughout this period and earlier, the Silk Road brought spices and goods from India and China into Iran. Through both trade and conquest, Iran influenced the cuisine of northern India. At its height in the Mughal dynasty, which lasted from the mid-1500s to the early 1700s, northern India demonstrated an artistry of food in the Persian style including prodigious use of lamb, elaborately layered rice dishes, and savory preparations that featured fruits, the use of saffron, and warm aromatic spices such as cinnamon. Today, Iranian food can best be described as most similar to northern Indian cuisine without the use of spicy peppers.

The political regime in Iran was a constitutional monarchy from the beginning of the 20th century until 1979 when, following a revolution, the Islamic Republic of Iran was declared. Under the previous regime, a significant effort was made to move the country toward the West and Western values and standards. After the revolution, a strict adherence to Islamic traditions resulted in laws requiring complete observance of codes of conduct covering all aspects of life, including private and public gatherings. Consequently, in the absence of many innocent pleasures taken for granted elsewhere in the world, the attention of Iranians has turned to food: all manner of restaurant, takeaway or fast food, including street food.

In the case of such a vast country with such diversity of climate, the variety of food offered on the streets differs from the north to the south, east, and west. Not unlike other countries and perhaps because of the usual migration from the four corners to the capital, a rich selection from all around the country is available and very much cherished in the capital city, Tehran.

Street food in Iran used to be mainly fresh seasonal fruit, herbs, and vegetables. In the past, small quantities were brought in from the countryside on donkeys or handcarts and sold on the street. Tasting the newly ripened fruit is still considered to promote health and bring good luck, quite apart from its nutritional value. People's appetite in early spring for sour under-ripe fruit countered the effects of the heavy, hearty, and usually greasy food of the winter. With the onset of autumn, the taste for richer food returns.

Today this is true of the cooked snacks and meals prepared and offered for sale on the street. In the cold months of winter, a craving for hot food is prevalent. Steaming sweet beetroot, cooked broad beans, and char-grilled corn on the cob are among the favorites. More recently, sweet corn, beef sausages, baked potatoes, and hard-boiled eggs have been added to the winter fare.

Starting in the 1950s, an increased awareness of food hygiene led to a certain suspicion of traditional street-food peddlers. The government under Mohammad Reza Shah (king from 1941 to 1979) tried to impose licensing and some basic standards of food safety on vendors' operations but with little effect.

The undeclared and unregulated nature of selling food on the streets in Iran is and has always had a particular attraction for the unemployed or those seeking to augment their salary. As economic circumstances continue to deteriorate, more and more people resort to ways of earning cash, including setting up a stall in the street to sell edible tidbits.

A conservative estimate based on firsthand interviews with street sellers puts the return on their money at 20 to 25 percent. Given that there is no tax, very little overhead, and no duties or license fees to be paid, it is quite an attractive business proposition. Very little skill is required, and the hours of business are such that it can be easily combined with another full-time job if necessary. Most of the cleaning and preparation of the food is done at home by female members of the family, and the ingredients are cheap and plentiful.

Nowadays, there seems to be a revival of the appetite for street food, and a profusion of new products are on offer. The main worry readily expressed by street vendors in Iran is the fear of police or municipality inspectors who stage regular raids in the areas where they operate to confiscate their equipment and chase them away. The sellers, however, are always one step ahead. Following are examples of some of their tactics:

- Some operate from the back of converted vans. These are equipped with storage boxes, work surfaces, and cooking facilities. The van is normally backed up against the pavement and obscured from the road by other parked cars. They normally cover out-of-town parks, popular mountain paths, and industrial zones.
- Working late at night or very early in the morning to catch late revelers or workers at the start of their day is another way to escape the long arm of the law. For the former, they target amusement parks or tourist attractions. They take their positions around 9 or 10 p.m. and work until midnight or just after. Car parks or streets around factories and car assembly plants are among the favorite locations for those catering to workers. They start between 3 and 4 a.m. to coincide with the start of the early shifts and finish around 7 a.m.
- Choosing equipment that allows a quick and easy getaway is another solution. Street vendors operating in and around the bazaar either carry their wares or operate from a clandestine central point from which they deliver plates of food to customers. Some cook on small charcoal braziers.
- Shop front stalls preparing and selling snacks and takeaway food as well as businesses located indoors are also plentiful. As part of a shop, they are minimally regulated and are not likely to be chased away by the authorities. If not cooked snacks, their wares usually consist of small prepacked bags of seasonal fruit, nuts, or dried fruit.

Special emphasis is placed on the preparation of the produce. That is, fruit and herbs are washed, peeled, seasoned where appropriate, and presented ready to eat. Where cooking is required, the ingredients are prepared beforehand as much as possible. For example, meat is cleaned, washed, and marinated, offal trimmed and cut to size, and beetroot washed and parboiled, so that they are ready to be cooked on portable stoves mounted on wheels to allow last-minute preparation. The setup is usually lit by a source of light, a primus stove, a battery-driven electrical device, or an electric bulb fed from a car battery. More often than not, an attempt is made to decorate the stall with colorful ribbons or artificial flowers.

Such an operation is generally a one-man show with the vendor singing the merits of his fare at the top of his voice to attract buyers. Since there is no scope for publicity or any kind of formal marketing activity to boost sales, a good reputation for fresh well-prepared food spread by word of mouth is essential for guaranteeing new and returning customers.

STREET FOOD IN RELIGIOUS RITUALS

At specific times of the year, coinciding with religious festivals or days of mourning, food is distributed to passersby in the streets. This is free, subsidized by donations and organized through the local mosque. Initially intended for the poor families in the district, nowadays food is handed out to anyone who accepts it. Traditionally, the most popular dish served is *aash*, a thick vegetable-based broth cooked in beef stock with rice and pulses to thicken it. Another favorite for these occasions, *qeymeh polo*, is rice cooked with diced lamb or beef, split peas, and spices, especially turmeric. The meaty sauce is cooked separately and then mixed with parboiled rice steamed gently over low heat.

Food is prepared in the mosque or in private houses, but the final stages of cooking are usually done on the street corner near the mosque. It is brought out in large pots and placed on gas rings to finish off cooking and keep warm, and it's handed out in plastic containers, on paper plates, or wrapped in large pieces of flatbread. On such occasions, families also offer food or dessert—mainly saffron rice pudding (*sholeh zard*) or a sweet *halva*—to ensure good health for their children and loved ones. This kind of offering is also prepared in the house and taken to poor districts of the town to be distributed.

MAJOR STREET FOODS

There is a tradition of treating yourself to an early (4 or 5 a.m.) breakfast after a night out or in anticipation of a day of hard work in cold weather. Typically, the meal consists of either of a hearty broth made from the feet, head, and tripe of lamb cooked slowly overnight with onions and garlic (*kaleh pacheh*), or a slightly sweet porridge made out of wheat and lamb cooked together, pounded well then simmered over a low heat, and stirred continuously for several hours (*haleem*). Both are cooked in a specialist shop—*kaleh pazi* for the former and *haleem pazi* for the latter. *Kaleh pazi*s usually have a few tables and chairs for those who would like to eat in, but most patrons prefer to take the food home. It is eaten with freshly baked flatbread (*sangak*) and pickles. *Haleem pazi*s do not offer seating, and *haleem* is bought and taken home to eat with fresh bread, a generous sprinkling of cinnamon, and a knob of butter.

Kebabs are an established favorite all over the country. A great variety of meat and offal is used for this purpose. *Kebab-e-jigar* and *del va qolveh* are prepared by washing and trimming calves' liver, heart, and kidneys, cutting them into strips, and stringing them separately on short, flat skewers. A daily visit to the local abattoir in the early hours of the morning ensures the freshness of supplies. The skewers are lined up on the side ready to be grilled as orders come in. The appetizing smell of liver over a charcoal fire is enough to lure people from several streets away.

Kebab koobideh are made by kneading minced lamb with ground onions to obtain a pale color and sticky consistency that allows the meat to stick to the skewers and withstand grilling without separating from the metal. Although a simple dish, there is skill and patience involved in preparing the meat.

Joojeh kebab consists of pieces of chicken marinated in lemon juice and/or saffron and then skewered in advance to be grilled on demand. *Joojeh kebab* is offered on or off the bone and in a choice of flavors.

Mahi kebab used to be a regional fish variation found in the towns and villages along the Caspian Sea. However, it is no longer fashionable and not as readily available. Small sardine-like fish were gutted, cleaned, and skewered whole to be grilled on charcoal braziers.

Kebab gonjeshk is another largely forgotten regional specialty from the southern cities of Iran. Sparrows were plucked, gutted, and cleaned before being loaded 10 at a time on a skewer made from sturdy twigs of a local tree. The two ends of the twig were bound together to make a ring. They were sold either raw to be cooked at home, or grilled on the street to be eaten on the go.

Bahtiyeh and *fereni*, both types of rice pudding, are specialties of southern Iran, especially Khuzestan Province, that are also seldom seen now. *Fereni* is rice pudding made with rice powder. The ingredient that sets these dishes apart from others is buffalo milk. The result is far creamier with a strong and distinctive taste. Both of these dishes were cooked at home by women the night before and sold from the pot on the street corners the next day.

Cooked or grilled vegetables are generally sold during the cold weather. *Laboo* (steamed beetroot) is widely sold all over the country during the winter months. Beets are partly boiled at home beforehand. A handcart is converted to house a heat source (gas or paraffin) underneath. On top, a large deep tray is placed on which the beets are piled high. To ensure that the *laboo* is sweet enough, extra syrup is added to the juice to baste the beets while they continue to cook.

Freshly picked cobs of corn are peeled and grilled on a bed of red hot coals to make a dish called *balal*. Once they are cooked to the taste of the buyer, they are doused in a bucket of salted water, shaken to get rid of the excess water, and handed to the eager customers.

Baghala pokhteh (cooked broad beans/fava beans) are sold in the spring and autumn. In late spring, they are cooked in their pods in a little salted water and sold to the passersby. Extra salt and powdered Persian hogweed (*golpar*) can be added to taste. In the autumn, dried broad beans are soaked overnight, boiled in water, and cooked to perfection.

SHAHRZAD GHORASHIAN

ISRAEL

HE MODERN STATE OF ISRAEL was founded in 1948 along the eastern coast of
the Mediterranean Sea. Parts of it are identified with the biblical and rabbinic
Land of Israel, Eretz Yisrael. Under Roman, Byzantine, and then Arab rule from
late antiquity, the area became part of the Ottoman Empire in the 16th century,
and small Jewish communities were found in Jerusalem and other cities among
the local Arabs. Modern Jewish immigration to Palestine from Europe began after pogroms in Europe in the late 19th century, with the creation of the Zionist
movement. After the foundation of the State of Israel as the Jewish homeland
in 1948, immigration increased to include Jews from many Arab countries and
more recently from the countries of the former Soviet Union and Ethiopia. The
local food culture has been influenced by this complex historical picture.

Israel today has about 7.7 million inhabitants, of whom about 75 percent are
Jews and about 20 percent are Arabs. The rest comprise a number of small communities, such as Circassians and Samaritans. Jews from Eastern and Northern
Europe are mostly known as Ashkenazim, while those from Spain and the southern and eastern Mediterranean are generally called Sephardim or Mizrahim
(Oriental Jews). Ashkenazim and Sephardim are about equally divided in the
present population, and there has been considerable intermarriage between the
communities. The Israeli Palestinian Arabs are mostly Muslims, but there is a
sizable minority of Druze and a number of Christian communities.

Many of the Zionist Jews who arrived in Palestine at the end of the 19th century, including the founders of the kibbutz (collective settlement) movement,

329

rejected the traditional culture of European Jews, including the heavy Ashkenazi foods, and embraced the local Arab Mediterranean ingredients and some of the cuisine. The small local Jewish communities who had lived for a long time under Turkish rule, especially those in the Yishuv haYashan, the old Sephardi settlement in Jerusalem, were already using local ingredients in their *borekas* and *sambousek*. The ultrareligious part of the Ashkenazi Jewish community tended to disapprove of eating food in the street, quoting the Talmudic maxim, "he who eats in the street is like a dog." The combination of all these factors has meant that street food in Israel today is almost always Sephardi or Arab, rather than Ashkenazi, and the iconic street food of Israel is the falafel.

Street food is eaten more by the young, the poor, and workers in industrial areas who cannot get home for lunch. It is eaten at kiosks, trailers, open-fronted shops especially bakeries, and market stalls; on the beach; and from supermarket trolleys and polystyrene boxes. Traditional groups such as elderly Europeans, old and middle-aged Arabs, and ultraorthodox Jews rarely eat on the street. This is now changing. Many young Arabs and Jews eat on the street at kiosks, and there are now stalls selling food for immediate consumption even in local village markets.

Types of foods derive from a number of sources, perhaps the strongest influence being the indigenous Palestinian Arab food. Each wave of immigrants have added their own favorites or adapted what they found: Israeli falafel, unlike Egyptian falafel, is made of chickpeas rather than fava beans. There is a two-way exchange of foods: just as Jewish Israelis have taken on Arab falafel, so the local Arabs have taken on *me'orav Yerushalmi* (Jerusalem mix), mixed grilled meats that they call simply "mix." Both Jews and Arabs eat shawarma and *borekas*. Bedouin and Druze women can be seen in many markets or in ad hoc tents making large *pitot* (pita bread) for immediate consumption, swirling the dough on their hands and baking it on a curved metal saj, sprinkling it with *za'atar/dukkah* (dried hyssop, soumac, and sesame seeds). The same Druze vendor makes and sells her *pitot* in the market of the Jewish town of Rosh Haayin on Fridays and in the market of the neighboring Arab village of Kfar Kassem on Saturdays. She also sells *sambousek, labaneh* (yogurt cheese), hummus (chickpea salad), cooked beans, olives, and stuffed vine leaves. These foods are popular with Jewish Israeli buyers as they are perceived as authentic and natural.

INFLUENCE OF RELIGIOUS REGULATIONS ON STREET FOOD IN ISRAEL

A considerable part of Ashkenazi rejection of European Jewish culture included ideological secularization and rejection of the religious regulations about kosher food, especially on the kibbutzim. Sephardic immigrants tended to be more traditional, and since they influenced street food more, this tends to be kosher, even if not supervised by a rabbi. Muslim Arabs also do not eat pig, so that *basar lavan*, white meat, is almost never sold on the street. Cooking methods tend to be in accord with the kosher rules, too, so that meats are usually sold grilled rather than stewed, obviating the need for soaking and salting. Meat and milk products are usually separated, also in accordance with the kosher rules. Some ingredients have been adapted to kosher rules—the pareve (neutral, neither milk nor meat) tahini made of ground sesame seeds is used as a sauce for kebabs, instead of the milk yogurt more common in countries of the former Ottoman Empire. Until a court ruling overturned this, local bylaws all over the country prohibited the open sale of leavened products during the eight days of the Passover festival, so that, for example, pizzas are baked on a matzo (unleavened bread) base for the duration.

MAJOR STREET FOODS

Breads and Stuffed Pockets

Almost all local dough is made with wheat flour. Perhaps the most common local bread is the indigenous pita, a small round soft pocket of leavened bread that can be conveniently filled. There is also a larger pita, made by sticking rounds of thin dough to the side of the tabun, oven, which when crispy (Iraqi) or thick (Yemenite) can be torn up and eaten and dipped into hummus; or a softer, thinner version, known as a laffa, which can be wrapped around a filling. Tunisian Jews brought French baguettes for their "Tunisian sandwiches," and Moroccans brought frena, elongated flatbreads, sometimes dimpled, that are flavored with olive oil and nigella seeds and baked on hot pebbles. Ordinary pita, often sold from the open front of the bakery, are also sometimes spread with olive oil and *za'atar*, powdered hyssop; with tomato sauce with or without yellow cheese; and with chopped onions. Yemenite Jews brought a number of their own dough foods and breads: *saluf*, an elongated flatbread similar to Moroccan frena but made on a grill; *jahnoun*, a yeast and oil dough cooked as a roll and eaten chopped up with pulverized fresh tomato sauce; *kubaneh*, yeast dough with *samneh* (clarified butter), or margarine, baked slowly in special covered pans (originally a Sabbath food baked overnight in the oven); *malaweh*, fried flaky pastry; *lahoh*, fried batter with lots of yeast added, which leads to a sponge-like bread looking like a flat English muffin. *Lahoh* is eaten (especially in the market at Rosh Haayin, an originally Yemenite town) with a sauce made of fresh tomatoes with cilantro and *zhug*, a sharp relish, or *hilbeh*, spicy fenugreek relish beaten to a froth.

The kosher rules forbid eating milk foods together with meat. Street vendors usually keep to this division and do not sell meat together with milk products. Cheese fillings are used for the wheat-flour baked version of the *sambousek*. *Sambousek* are found all over the Middle East, but the filling of the fried version, onions and chickpeas, is typically Israeli.

Sephardi, empanadas, and *pastellim*, dough pockets with meat fillings, are also popular. In effect, there is often little difference between *borekas, sambousek,* empanadas, and *pastellim* as they are sold on the street, although home and gourmet versions can differ considerably.

Qubeh, called "torpedoes" after their shape, are made of meat, preferably lamb, with a casing of either bulgur or semolina. The most sophisticated Baghdadi versions have mashed potatoes or rice. They can be fried and eaten as finger food or cooked in soup like huge dumplings. There is now a *qubeh* bar in the Mahaneh Yehudah market in Jerusalem, which serves both *qubeh* soup as well as different versions of the fried kind: Iraqi, Kurdish, Syrian, and so on.

Meats

Some of the meat foods sold on the street in Israel appear to date back to Turkish times to judge by their names: the local term for a charcoal barbeque is the Turkish *mangal*. Shawarma refers to slivers of meat cut off with a long knife from larger pieces on a revolving vertical skewer, cooked by electric plates. This was originally lamb or mutton, which was substituted by turkey meat. When street vendors in the 1980s reverted to lamb, or at least lamb fat, its popularity soared. It is now sold all over the country, served wrapped in a laffa spread with hummus or tahini with a choice of salads, pickles, and spicy hot or hotter sauces—*zhug* (Yemenite), *harissa* (Maghrebi), or *amba* (Iraqi)—and fried potato chips. Kebabs, minced meat with onions and parsley cooked on skewers, are likely be spiced with *baharat*, a mixture of cardamom, black pepper, allspice, cinnamon, ginger, and nutmeg. *Shishlik*, cubed and spiced chicken, is also barbecued on skewers over hot coals. Another local favorite is *me'orav Yerushalmi*, a mixed grill. The kibbutz communal dining room was probably the origin of the local conversion of the Austrian wiener schnitzel made of expensive veal beaten thin and fried in batter to the Israeli schnitzel made of much cheaper turkey or chicken breast. The batter is sometimes still eggs and flour, but more often the meat is dipped in flour and breadcrumbs, the latter usually a commercial blend with orange coloring laced with monosodium glutamate. Schnitzel is a favorite children's food, sold on the street like other meats in a pita or baguette with salad, pickles, chips, and plenty of tomato ketchup.

Me'orav Yerushalmi

Me'orav Yerushalmi is a mixed grill made of diced chicken together with kidneys, livers, hearts, and other offal, cooked straight on a heated metal plate. This is a kosher way to cook such meats without presalting and soaking. The meats are flavored with salt, pepper, and spices such as cumin, paprika, and *baharat*, and served with fried onions from a paper plate or in a pita or laffa. The best *me'orav* is found along Agrippas Street in Jerusalem, near the Mahaneh Yehudah market.

Falafel

It is symbolic of the tensions in this area of the Middle East that this popular food is claimed as *ours* by both Arabs and Jews. It is now sold everywhere and eaten by everyone, Arabs and Jews, old and young, religious and secular. The version of falafel popularized by the Yemenites uses chickpeas, coarsely ground and flavored with lemon, garlic, and cumin. The chickpea mix is deep-fried in little balls, which are then served in a pita (or half pita) with a choice of addition, but always with a *salat katzutz* of diced tomatoes, cucumbers, and so on, diluted with fresh cabbage when tomatoes are expensive. To top off a falafel, there are sauces in large squeeze bottles, more or less refrigerated: pale cream-colored tahini, yellow *amba* (sour mango sauce), hot red *harissa*, or hot green *zhug*. Each city has its own favorite falafel stand—there are numerous "falafel kings," and once Tel Aviv boasted a pair of "falafel queens." In times of galloping inflation, parents have even been known to peg their children's pocket money to the price of half a falafel.

Borekas

Borekas are made with phyllo dough or puff pastry and often filled with cheese, usually a salty feta, slightly more acidic Bulgarian cheese, or the pareve potato, spinach, or mushrooms. There are also versions filled with minced meat. Traditionally, each *borekas* has a different shape—triangular, square, horseshoe—to prevent people taking the cheese by mistake for a meat *borekas* or a pareve one, which is allowed to be eaten together with meat. This custom dates back at least to 18th-century Istanbul. *Borekas* are often sold together with brown long-cooked haminados eggs, in which case they are sliced in half horizontally, and the roughly chopped eggs are inserted between the two halves of this sandwich, sometimes with sliced pickled cucumber.

Sambousek

Sambousek is usually made from a yeast dough cut into circles and folded over the filling. It can then be baked or fried. Baked *sambousek*, with pinched edges forming a semicircular frill, have a variety of fillings, similar to *borekas*: cheese, spinach, and potatoes, and there is even a sweet cheese and raisin version. Fried *sambousek* are typically filled with a bright yellow filling of onions and chopped chickpeas with turmeric, and the edges are pressed together with a fork. *Sambousek* can also be made with *warka,* the thin flour and oil pastry used for the Moroccan cigar, a roll of pastry stuffed with chopped meat and onions.

Salat Katzutz (Israeli-Palestinian Salad)

Salat katzutz, finely diced tomatoes, cucumbers, and onions (and sometimes sweet peppers and chopped parsley), flavored with olive oil (hopefully), salt, pepper, and perhaps lemon juice, is the standard salad for filling pita. Street-food stalls are judged on the freshness of this salad and the size of the dice—the smaller the better, they say, just short of splitting the atom.

Sufganiyot

In the autumn and winter, and especially on the eight-day festival of Hanukkah, sufganiyot, jelly doughnuts made of yeast dough, are deep-fried, sprinkled with confectioners sugar, and sold hot for immediate consumption on the street and in supermarkets. Every year there are new fashions for fillings: chocolate, halva (sweet sesame paste), and dulce de leche, but the simple red jam of uncertain origin remains the favorite. There is even a popular song: "Are you on a diet? No, I'm not on a diet, I'm on sufganiyot."

OTHER STREET FOODS

Roasted Seeds and Nuts

Many Israelis love to nibble nuts and roasted seeds, and sometimes hot chestnuts can be found roasted on braziers in the colder Jerusalem winter. Salted and roasted black-and-white striped sunflower seeds, cream-colored pumpkin seeds, and watermelon seeds are eaten everywhere: on the street, at football matches, and outside synagogues. One synagogue in Petah Tiqvah is even known locally as Heikhal Ha-Garinim, the Shrine of the Sunflower Seeds, as its courtyard is always full of husks. The progress of groups of youth through the streets of the cities on a Saturday afternoon can be traced by the trails of husks. At least they are biodegradable. Eating sunflower seeds takes a certain degree of skill—you have to learn how to crack the seed into two between the front teeth without reducing it to splinters, so you can extract the seed from inside cleanly with the tongue. Sunflower seeds are part of the class of pitzuhim, things needing cracking, which includes peanuts, pistachios, cashews, and cracked and salted pecan nuts. They are sold in little bags from a grid of metal boxes, which also include different varieties of dried fruit: raisins, dates, figs, and so on.

335

Sweets

Innumerable types of sweet buns, cakes, and patisserie are sold from kiosks, caravans, and open-fronted bakeries and, together with coffee or bottled drinks, make a popular snack at any time of day or a quick breakfast eaten on the way to work or school.

Some of the dough-based foods already mentioned come in sweet versions as well: there is a sweet cheese-and-nut filling for the baked *sambousek*, for example. The famous Mediterranean pastry baklava, dripping with honey or syrup, is usually sold from open-fronted bakeries or market stalls in large quantities to take home, for parties, and especially to break the fast at Ramadan. But they are so good that some people cannot resist the temptation to eat them on the spot, wrapped in a napkin to hopefully stop them from dripping. In the autumn and winter and especially on the eight-day festival of Hanukkah, *sufganiyot* are sold hot on the street. Another Turkish-influenced food sold in little disposable cups especially in markets is *mallabi,* a very sweet pudding of corn flour or rice flour and maybe milk that is flavored with rosewater and topped by bright pink raspberry syrup, chopped green pistachios, and brown roasted coconut.

Drinks

The hot climate has always meant that drink is a prime need, particularly for travelers. Today there are many vendors of drinks everywhere: on the street, at bus, train, and petrol stations, at crossroads, in the markets, on the beach, and at every mass gathering. Everyone drinks on the street, even ultraorthodox Jews, except during the monthlong Muslim Ramadan fast and the occasional Jewish fasts. The markets still sell *limonada,* purportedly natural lemon juice horribly sweetened, but more probably adulterated with artificial lemon flavoring, with some grated lemon peel to make it taste more real. Once the small stands and market stalls all got electricity, *barad,* half-frozen slush in neon colors, became common. The colors—purple for grape drink, orange and yellow for orange and lemon flavors, are aimed at children. More recently, the yuppyizing trend has led to ubiquitous sales of *eiskaffee,* sweet milky coffee slush for adults. Some street juice stalls squeeze fresh orange and pomegranate juice. Some of the more old-fashioned markets, such as Ramle, still sell Turkish *leben,* a yogurt drink.

SUSAN WEINGARTEN

JORDAN

The Hashemite Kingdom of Jordan, a young country in the Middle East, is bordered by Israel, Saudi Arabia, and Syria. At 34,277 square miles, Jordan is slightly smaller than Indiana. Its population of more than six million is 98 percent Arab. Jordanians are approximately 92 percent Sunni Muslim, 6 percent Christian, and 2 percent other. About 75 percent of the population is urban. Bedouins who retain their traditionally nomadic lifestyle make up close to 10 percent of the population.

Most of Jordan is rocky desert, with a rainy season only in the west. Water is a rare and precious commodity. Only about 3 percent of the land is arable, and less than 3 percent of the population works in agriculture. The primary agricultural products are citrus, tomatoes, cucumbers, olives, sheep, poultry, stone fruits, strawberries, and dairy.

Jordanian cuisine, essentially Arabian, has much in common with food in other Middle Eastern countries. Olives and olive oil are consumed at every meal. Eggplant, bulgur (cracked wheat), tomatoes, yogurt, mint tea, garlic, and unleavened bread are staples. Among the country's Arab neighbors, Lebanon, Syria, and Palestine have had the strongest influence. However, the nomadic Bedouins have contributed to the cuisine of Jordan, and the influence of the Ottoman Empire can be seen in such foods as baklava and gyros-style meats (shawarma) that are often made with chicken or lamb.

Because Jordan is a Muslim country, there is no pork. Most main-course dishes include chicken or lamb. Fish is generally seen only in the south, nearer the port of

Aqaba. Goat is eaten on occasion, though most goats are kept for milk. Eggs, milk, yogurt, cheese, fava beans, and chickpeas are other important protein sources.

A common bread in Jordan, as throughout the Arab world, is the round, unleavened loaves called *khoubiz.* It is a little thicker than pita, but is similar, including having the pocket that makes it ideal for sandwiches. The second kind of bread, seen somewhat less often, is the soft, flexible Bedouin sheet bread called *shrak*, which is about 13 inches in diameter and a ¼-inch thick.

Tahini, a paste made from sesame seeds, appears at almost every meal, including breakfast. Yogurt is used plain and in sauces, or it is drained to create the soft, creamy yogurt-cheese called *labaneh.*

Rice may appear as a bed for roasted meats, in a pilaf, or as part of the stuffing for cabbage rolls. Bulgur is featured in many recipes, including the popular bulgur-and-parsley salad called tabouleh. It is also a key ingredient in kibbeh, which combines the bulgur with finely ground lamb.

Coriander, cumin, cinnamon, and black pepper are common spices, but the most distinctive regional spice is sumac (also spelled sumaq; this is *not* the poison sumac of North America). It has a deep, rusty-red color and a pleasantly sour taste. Sumac is a key ingredient in the spice mix *za'atar.* (The word *za'atar* can also refer simply to the herb thyme, but it more commonly refers to the spice blend, in which thyme is always a featured ingredient.)

Flat-leaf parsley is used so heavily that it actually constitutes a vegetable or salad green. It is a major ingredient in such salads as fattoush and often dominates the bulgur in tabouleh. Mint appears almost as commonly, in salads and other recipes, and is also almost always used in tea.

Lebanese influence is most responsible for Jordan's splendid pastries. Delicate, layered, honey-drenched sweets and rich cookies laden with pistachios, walnuts, and/or sesame seeds line the shelves of pastry shops.

MAJOR STREET FOODS

Wandering the streets of Jordan's cities and towns, one finds a wide range of food options: dates and apricots; lamb kebabs or shawarma stuffed into flatbread; baked goods, from savory bread rings to rich pastries and cookies.

Probably the two most common items amid the offerings found on the street are falafel and *manakeesh. Manakeesh*, sometimes referred to as Arab pizza, is a flatbread cooked with toppings. Olive oil and *za'atar* is the most popular topping, but toppings can include cheese, minced lamb, or chicken. *Manakeesh* is usually eaten folded in half and is often served with pickles and yogurt. More common still are the falafel makers, who sell from shops that open out onto the street. You can watch your falafel being made, so you know it's fresh. Falafel makers have a small, metal device into which they pack the uncooked falafel mixture and then eject it into the hot oil to fry. That makes it possible for every falafel to be just about identical in size and helps speed up the process for a busy vendor.

CYNTHIA CLAMPITT

LEBANON

THE REPUBLIC OF LEBANON is bordered by the Mediterranean on the west, Syria on the north and east, and Israel to the south. Its location at the crossroads of the Mediterranean basin and the Middle East has created a culture of enormous religious and ethnic diversity. Today around 60 percent of the population are Muslims and 40 percent are Christians of many different denominations.

The earliest inhabitants were the Phoenicians, maritime traders who flourished for nearly 2,500 years in the centuries BCE. Later conquerors included the Babylonians, the Persians, the Greeks, the Romans, and the Ottoman Empire. When the latter collapsed following World War I, France acquired a mandate over the area that today constitutes modern Lebanon. The country gained its independence in 1943 and became known as the "Switzerland of the East" because of its financial power and gorgeous scenery, which attracted tourists. Between 1975 and 1990, the country was rent by civil war.

The climate is Mediterranean: mild to cool wet winters and hot, dry summers. The country is famous for its cedar, pine, and olive trees and the abundance and variety of its agricultural produce.

People eat on the street in Lebanon for two reasons: for entertainment when they take a stroll by the sea or in the mountains or out of necessity. Street vendors cater to people working in the souks who cannot go home for their meal, to travelers, or to shoppers who need to stop for a meal, a drink, or simply a snack.

Today there is a strong established tradition that people can eat almost as well on the street as at home or in restaurants. The Lebanese do not regard street food as junk food as Westerners often do but as a fast alternative to restaurants or a convenient substitute for home cooking, albeit with less fine ingredients and sometimes questionable hygiene. Street food is also considered a treat, especially during religious feasts or festivals or in the case of particular specialties that are not easily replicated at home, such as shawarma.

Food is available on the street from breakfast onward, although not usually for dinner when people go home or to restaurants. The food changes as the day progresses. Very early in the morning is the time for *sahlab* (a hot milk drink thickened with dried powdered orchid tubers) if there is a need for something sweet and warming or hummus or *ful medames* (mushy fava beans) for something savory and filling. Another classic breakfast choice is *manakeesh*, a flatbread topped with a mixture of *za'atar* and olive oil that can be eaten plain or wrapped around olives, cucumbers, tomatoes, *labneh*, and fresh mint leaves.

For adventurous souls, there is *nifa* or lambs' heads roasted in the same ovens as *manakeesh*. For mid-morning snacks, the choice includes *fatayer* (savory pastries filled with greens or cheese), nuts and seeds, or *ka'k* (sesame galettes, or crusty cakes), which are available throughout the day. Lunch is normally sandwiches, the most common being shawarma and falafel. However, in Tripoli, north of Beirut, one can choose from a variety of fish sandwiches along the port or a *moghrabieh* (large couscous grains) sandwich in the souks. During the afternoon and early evening, vendors sell roasted nuts and seeds (pumpkin, watermelon, or sunflower), ears of corn cooked over a charcoal grill fitted onto the vendor's cart, or such sweets as *qatayef* (fried pancakes filled with cream or walnuts) or *nammourah* (syrupy sponge cake). Drinks range from seasonal freshly pressed juices to sugary sodas and syrups.

There are two ways to eat on the street. One is to buy something from a vendor's ambulant cart or a hole-in-the-wall stall and eat it on the go; the other is to sit at a communal or individual table to enjoy whatever specialty the café/restaurant serves, including grilled meats or *fatteh* (a composite dish made up of toasted bread, chickpeas, yogurt, and toasted pine nuts), which is another sustaining breakfast dish.

The government does not appear to have a policy on street food either by checking hygiene or by regulating the number and location of vendors. Despite this, most vendors' carts, stalls, or small cafes are fairly clean, and some are spotless. The vendors are fairly spaced out throughout cities, towns, or villages so that you always find something to eat without having too many street vendors in one place.

MAJOR STREET FOODS

Ka'k

Possibly the most iconic of Lebanon's street food, these sesame seed galettes look like handbags and are peddled everywhere, but they are particularly associated with the Corniche in Beirut. They are normally strung on wooden racks fitted onto the vendor's bicycle, which has a work surface on which the vendor lays the galette to slit open the fat part and sprinkle a little *za'atar* inside before handing it to the customer.

Shawarma

Shawarma is a very large, fat kebab, once made only with lamb but now with chicken as well. The meat is sliced into wide thin pieces, marinated overnight, and threaded onto a long skewer. Slices of fat are placed between every few layers; if chicken is used, the skin is included. The skewer is fixed in front of a vertical grill and left to rotate over a moderate heat for two to three hours, or until the meat is cooked through. During cooking, the fat melts down the whole length of the kebab, basting it and keeping it moist. Even before the meat is cooked all the way through, the shawarma seller starts slicing the outer cooked layer to order and piles the thin slivers of meat onto pita bread. He garnishes the meat with sliced tomatoes, onion, pickles, herbs, and tahini sauce if the meat is lamb or garlic sauce if it is chicken, then rolls the bread tightly over the filling. He half-wraps the sandwich in paper and hands it to the customer to eat standing by the stall or on the go.

Roasted Peanuts and Seeds

These are piled on wooden carts and scooped into paper cones usually made with used newspapers. Lupin seeds are an ancient pulse that has been part of the Mediterranean diet since the third century BCE. The seeds need to be soaked for a few days before they become edible. They are salted, and the thick opaque skin is slipped off before eating the seeds.

Seasonal Fruit and Juices

Depending on the season, you can buy a bag of green almonds in the spring, a small basket of mulberries in the summer, or prickly pears that the vendor peels for the customer. In the autumn, thirst can be quenched by freshly squeezed pomegranate juice served at the many fresh fruit juice stands.

Roasted Corn
Corn is another classic street food although it seems to be less in evidence these days than before the civil war. The vendor wedges the grilled ears along the side of his charcoal grill to keep them warm and sprinkles the ear of corn with salt and lays it on a piece of paper to hand to the customer.

Sweets
Sweets are very much part of the street-food scene, both on a daily basis and during religious occasions, especially Ramadan. During this month when Muslims fast, sweetmakers set up stalls outside their shops to make extra *qatayef* (pancakes) or *kellage*, a wafer-like pastry that is soaked in milk, wrapped around a thick semolina custard, and either served plain or fried and dipped in syrup. Another popular sweet is cotton candy, both the pink airy kind swirled around a stick and the more substantial *barbe à papa*, which you grab with your fingers to eat. Another messy sweet is *nammura*, a sticky sponge cake dripping in syrup that drips even if you hold it with the paper provided by the vendor.

Manakeesh
There are two types of the flatbread called *manakeesh bil za'atar*: one is baked in the oven and the other is cooked on the saj (a kind of inverted wok placed over charcoal or a gas fire), the latter being thinner and slightly more crisp. The topping, *za'atar*, is a savory mixture made with powdered dried thyme, sumac, and raw or toasted sesame seeds. Some bakeries also make *manakeesh* with *kishk* (a mixture of bulgur wheat and strained yogurt, which is fermented, dried, and rubbed to produce a very fine powder), halloumi cheese, sliced thinly and spread over the dough, or *qawarma* (lamb confit that Lebanese mountain people use in winter when fresh meat is scarce).

Fatayer
The *fatayer* sold on the street are much larger than the home-made ones. The shape remains the same, a closed triangle made with the same dough as pita bread, which is filled with spinach, Swiss chard, or curd cheese.

Thursday or Ramadan Bread

This is a stamped bread sold during Ramadan from wooden carts wheeled through the streets of Tripoli and other predominantly Muslim towns. They also sell other breads, including one filled with dates. Thursday bread is also sold in bakeries. It looks similar to the Holy communion bread of Greek Orthodox churches, *qorban*, though the stamped pattern is different. The Orthodox pattern is made of Greek letters within a cross, while the Muslim is made of round geometric designs. The breads are also different. The Muslim one is basically a thick pita bread flavored with *mahlab* (the kernel of a wild cherry that adds an intriguing fragrant taste to some breads and cookies), then brushed with water toward the end of baking and sprinkled with nigella seeds. The Christian bread is more like a Western-style spongy bread flavored with orange blossom water. It is reserved for church use while Muslims eat theirs throughout Ramadan, mainly for *sûhûr* (the last meal taken before the fast begins again at sunrise) with cheese or *labneh* (strained yogurt) and olives.

Sandwiches

An excellent place to buy fish on the street is the *mina* (fishing port) in Tripoli. A fleet of small fishing boats is moored just below the pavement, and set back from the road is a cluster of gorgeous old houses. Beyond these is a row of very modest looking cafés where two of the best sandwiches in Lebanon are found: *samkeh harrah* (spicy fish) and *akhtabût* (octopus). Both are prepared more or less the same way except that the sauce for the fish has tahini. At the entrance of the city is the clock square where there are buses and taxis to and from Beirut stop. Here there are many sandwich places and street-food vendors. A couple of stalls specialize in French fries sandwiches made with masses of crisp, hot fries that are sprinkled with lemon juice and rolled in pita bread spread with garlic sauce. An option is to add cabbage salad for a fresher taste.

Another interesting sandwich is made with *moghrabieh*, which means "North African" in Arabic and is the Lebanese version of couscous. The grains are bigger and more like *m'hamssa*, the large-grain couscous. The *moghrabieh* is sautéed with boiled onions and chickpeas, then rolled in a double layer of pita bread to serve as a sandwich.

Falafel

Falafel are originally from Egypt where they are known as *ta'miyah*. However,

HARISSA

Harissa is a spicy sauce made from red chilies, garlic, coriander, caraway seed, and olive oil. It originated in Tunisia but is in widespread use throughout North Africa and even Europe. In Tunisia, *harissa* is used as an ingredient in a meat stew, as a flavoring for *merguez,* or a marinade for meat and eggplants. In some European countries, it is used sometimes as a breakfast spread for tartines or rolls. *Harissa* is also the name of a porridge of pounded wheat and lamb that is popular in the Middle East.

Egyptian *ta'miyah* is softer and starchier than the Lebanese falafel. The sandwiches are also made differently. Egyptian pita is smaller and thicker, and the bread is cut across in half to produce a pocket that is filled with both *ta'miyah* and garnish. Lebanese pita, on the other hand, is large, round, and very thin. It is opened at the seam, and the two layers are placed one on top of one another with the rough side up. The filling is arranged down the middle and the bread rolled around it. As for the garnish, in Egypt, you can have potato chips or French fries, shredded lettuce, or tomatoes, radishes, or pickles, while in Lebanon, the choice is generally herbs, tomatoes, and pickles. Only the tahini sauce is constant in both countries although its name differs: *tahina* in Egypt and *tarator* in Lebanon.

Grilled Meats

A successful mini-chain in Lebanon called Kebabji (meaning kebab maker) specializes in kebab sandwiches with *kofta*, shish kebab, or *shish tawük* (chicken kebabs). The sandwich makers can make up to a dozen sandwiches at a time. They lay the opened pita breads in a row, slightly overlapping each other but leaving the middle free. Each bread is spread with a little hummus, then the kebabs ordered by the customer are pulled off the skewer and laid onto the hummus. Finally, a few slices of pickles are scattered alongside the meat. The breads are pulled apart, rolled, wrapped in paper, and stuffed inside a Kebabji-branded paper bag. Everything is done so quickly that it is quite mesmerizing to watch. The only snag to this superefficiency and speed is that you have to wait for your meat to cook on the charcoal barbecue, although it is reassuring to know that the meat is cooked to order.

ANISSA HELOU

SYRIA

T HE SYRIAN ARAB REPUBLIC is bordered by Turkey on the north, Iraq on the east, Jordan on the south, and Israel, Lebanon, and the Mediterranean Sea on the west. Traditionally the country's 18 million people are about equally divided between urban and rural, but in the 2000s there has been a heavy migration to cities due to prolonged droughts. Some 90 percent of Syrians are Muslim divided among several major sects. From the early 16th century to the end of World War I, Syria was part of the Ottoman Empire, and the Turkish influence is apparent in the cuisine.

Much of Syrians' protein comes from dairy products and pulses, particularly chickpeas and lentils. The main meats are lamb and chicken and, to a lesser degree, goat and beef. The largest city is Aleppo, which had a population of 2.3 million before a civil war that began in 2011 saw massive emigration, followed by the slightly smaller capital Damascus. Both cities had a rich and vibrant street-food life, which, like other aspects of life, has been disrupted by the current uprising. The main street foods are very similar to those found throughout the region: falafel, shawarma, fruit drinks, and various kinds of bread.

MAJOR STREET FOODS

Shawarma

One of the world's most popular street foods, in Syria, shawarma is made by threading thin pieces of lamb or chicken onto a long skewer that is placed in front of a vertical grill and rotated over heat for several hours. In Damascus, some shawarma makers wear spotless white outfits and make a great show of cutting the meat. They often use the bread to turn the tower of meat as revolves around the spit, then baste the bread in the meat juices, and cook the whole sandwich on the grill. It is served on a single piece of round, unleavened bread and topped off with a dollop of garlic mayonnaise and slices of sour pickle. The bread is rolled up and wrapped in wax paper.

SHAWARMA

"I ate the best shawarma I think I will ever have . . . It came from al-Mousali, a road-side emporium with a few plastic chairs, in the Jazmtiyeh district of Damascus. The meat was beef, unusually. It was as flavoursome as the roast at the Savoy Grill. It came in a delicate sauce of sour pomegranate. It was wrapped in evanescently thin laffa bread, and came with fresh vegetables and tankards of just-squeezed fruit juice."

Tim Franks, "Damascus Diary: Monday 10 December." *BBC News*, http://news.bbc.co.uk/2/hi/middle_east/7136057.stm.

Fuul

This soupy mix of chickpeas, lemon juice, and fava beans is a popular breakfast meal. It is served from small carts with a large colander in the middle containing the *fuul*, which is spooned into a pottery dish and eaten by the customer on the street.

Another common street food is *fuul nabit*. Fava beans are soaked for several days until they sprout, then boiled with crushed garlic, lemon juice, and cumin powder. The beans are served in a glass or china bowl rather than a paper plate, and the liquid is served separately in a glass with half a lemon as a side drink. The bean is squeezed from the skin, which is discarded.

Falafel, deep-fried chickpea balls with a crunchy outside and soft interior, is wrapped in flatbread and served with tomato and onion slices.

In the spring, vendors sell whole green almonds from carts, and in the summer prickly pears and whole fresh pistachios. Juices made from mulberry, licorice, pomegranate, and other seasonal fruits are sold by vendors with pots strapped to their backs or at corner stalls.

In the summer, ice cream is very popular. The most famous vendor in Damascus is Bakdash Ice Cream in the Souk Hamidiyah in the Old City, known for its homemade ice cream and freshly crushed pistachio toppings.

A specialty of Aleppo, Syria's second largest city, is *kebab bil-karayz*: lamb kebab served in a rich and tangy sauce made from local cherries. Aleppo is also famous for its pastries, including baklava, which is made with sugar syrup, not honey, and laced with rose or orange blossom on water.

COLLEEN TAYLOR SEN

TURKEY

T HE STREET FOOD OF TURKEY reflects its diverse culture and historical background as well as its unique geographical location. Turkey connects Southeastern Europe with Asia and the Middle East. The Black Sea lies to the north of the country, the Aegean and Mediterranean Seas are on the west, while the south borders the Anatolian peninsula. The European part of Turkey is called Thrace, and the Asian part Anatolia (Asia Minor). The capital of Turkey is Ankara, but the largest city is Istanbul, previously capital of the Byzantine and Ottoman empires. The country, founded in 1923, has nine neighbors: Georgia, Armenia, Azerbaijan, and Iran to the east; Iraq and Syria to the southeast; the island of Cyprus to the south; and Greece and Bulgaria to the west and northwest. The cuisines of all those neighboring countries have much in common with Turkish cuisine, and this is reflected in street food.

The Turks were a seminomadic people of Central Asia who made their way to Anatolia in the 11th century and continued to move westward, establishing the Seljuk and Ottoman empires. They settled in parts of the Balkan Peninsula and pushed their way deep into Europe, reaching as far as the outskirts of Vienna in the 16th century. Today's Turkish citizens are descendants of not only Turkic-speaking tribes but also an enormous ethnic mix that lived in former Ottoman territory. The Ottoman Empire also extended southward to the Middle East and Africa, and consequently, today's Turkish food culture has a very varied and complex historical legacy, enhanced by a diverse geography. Central Asian, Iranian,

THE WORLD'S FIRST STREET-FOOD STANDARDS

Turkey may have been the first country to have a written set of standards regulating food sold in the streets and at small eateries. The Bursa Edict of Standards, issued by Sultan Bayezıd II in 1502, is regarded as the world's first standard in the modern sense. This 500-year-old document covers products sold in Bursa (a city in northwestern Turkey), ranging from foodstuffs to market vendors' aprons, specifying everything from weights to origins of produce. It includes detailed listings of food prices and qualifications for bakers, butchers, chicken and egg sellers, fish mongers, grocers, staple suppliers, *helva*, and sweet makers. The edict also sets standards for cooked food served in eateries, giving ratios of the ingredients in blancmange, the meat content of fritters, the choice of meat in meals of prime cuts or pot stew with bones, kebabs on skewers, and listing fried meat dish prices, even mentioning details like the onions to be served as a side dish.

Middle Eastern, Mediterranean, and Balkan traditions echo in food and eating habits in the streets.

Istanbul and many Anatolian cities always had lively marketplaces and bazaars, which fostered the existence of varied street-food suppliers. Turkey also has a deep-rooted tradition of public kitchens called imaret established as institutions of charity. During the Ottoman times, imarets became an indispensable part of the urban landscape, offering free food for the needy. The recent phenomenon of setting up charity tents during the fasting month of Ramadan that distribute free full course meals to all to break the fast stems from this tradition.

Urban life, especially in bigger cities, inevitably develops a culture of street foods. Street food is readily available in every central shopping zone, squares, marketplaces, parks, strolling promenades, in front of schools, and so forth. Street food is quick and cheap but is not confined to the poor; on the contrary, it embraces all strata of the society and melts away class distinctions. As anywhere in the world, buyers of street food are people on the go, in a hurry, or on a tight budget.

Street food places in Turkey can be classified into two categories: mobile and fixed. Movable street-food vendors can be pedestrians carrying food in trays or boxes or displaying them in pushcarts or glass cases. The pushcarts are sometimes converted into a man-operated vehicle with the help of a makeshift bicycle mechanism. Many street vendors operate like movable little kiosks, stationing whenever and wherever there is an opportunity for good business. Sometimes a favorable spot becomes like a spontaneous marketplace with many vendors crowding into the same area. Fresh corn, roasted chestnuts, meatballs or little skewers of meat, pickles, ice cream, sweet wafer disks and candy, roasted nuts, and so forth, all are among such movable treats.

There might be favorite spots or even hours for some vendors, depending on the popularity of their food and their targeted customer. Everybody knows when and where to find a favorite snack. Late-night steam carts laden with buttery rice pilaf with chickpeas or mobile meatball grills are features of night life, while early morning birds can find *simit* vendors (sesame-sprinkled bread-rings) hawking in the street. Summer nights are enlivened with ice-cream vendors, sweet fritter (*lokma*) makers, pickle and pickle juice carts, and the quintessential assorted nut sellers.

Nibbling open sunflower, melon, or pumpkin seeds and spitting out the shells is a favorite Turkish pastime. Another summer favorite is corn on the cob, either boiled or grilled and simply sprinkled with salt. There are also sweet vendors with mobile street carts selling sticky semolina pudding *şam tatlısı* or big rings of fluted fried batter drenched in syrup. Amusement parks are never without pink clouds of cotton candy, bright red candy-covered apples, or wafer disks called *kağıt helva*, literally "paper" *halva*. Nougat-like sesame crackers and handmade lollipops are all sold by *helvacı*, the sweets man in mobile glass-sided pushcarts. One disappearing treat is *macun*, sugar paste, with an assorted selection of various flavorings tinted in bright colors, whirled around a stick.

For those who do not have the time to sit down for a full meal, a ubiquitous feature of modern Turkish cities is the *büfe*, or sandwich bar, which offers toasted sandwiches with cheese or *sujuk*, the spicy cured meat sausage. Cities have local specialties, such as the famous toast of Ayvalık, a seaside town on the Aegean coast. Some famous kiosks have signature dishes, such as the "wet hamburger," made by keeping the cooked meat patty in a spicy sauce, keeping the bun moist in a steam chamber, and eventually soaking the bun in the sauce. The *büfe* also serves as a juice bar offering freshly squeezed orange, grapefruit, pomegranate, carrot, and apple juices. *Büfes* always supply *ayran*, a diluted salted yogurt drink and *limonata* (lemonade).

Fresh fruit and vegetable vendors are usually markers of seasonal transitions. There is always an abundant variety of fruits sold by wandering sellers throughout the country, but only a few are sold as street snacks. Whole watermelons and other melons are sold in the streets but almost never in slices as a snack. Certain fruits make their first appearance of the season on street carts, as if to announce the coming of spring. *Çağla*, green unripe almonds, and *can eriği*, unripe green plums, are the first to appear. They are sold in little paper bags or cones with a tiny paper wrap of salt to dip into. In late spring and early summer, trays of fresh white mulberries and carts of apricots, cherries, and loquats enliven the streets. Unripe green chickpeas sold in bundles like brooms are the favorite of children. Cool cucumbers, peeled and salted on the spot, or juicy prickly pears, carefully stripped of their spines, are refreshers of hot summer days, the latter especially in southern cities. Toward the end of summer, fresh green or purple figs and shelled and peeled fresh walnuts appear. Fresh hazelnuts in shells are also among the end of summer treats. Fall is the time of wild gathered fruits; red and yellow azeroles (*alıç*) are stringed like necklaces; oleaster fruit (*iğde*), jujubes (*hünnap*), or tree strawberries (*koca yemiş*) are sold in paper cones. The quince vendor is a herald of winter.

Many eateries are formed around bazaars, another typical feature of Ottoman cities. Many shopping and business areas have little eateries called *esnaf lokantası* that mainly cater to shop owners, shoppers, and office workers, and often serve only lunch. The foods are mostly choices of soups, and a wide range of hot *tencere yemeği* (pot stews, vegetable and meat dishes) laid out warm for the customers to choose from. They also feature legume/vegetable and meat stews, eggplant dishes, stuffed vegetables with minced meat, chicken stew, or a slow-cooked meat dish, and rice pilaf. Simple desserts like fruit compotes, milk puddings, bread puddings, or quince and pumpkin desserts are available in these eateries.

Specialized eateries that offer one kind of food only are numerous. Foremost are places offering grilled meat dishes. A *köfteci* is a place to have meatballs, often accompanied by assorted pickles and *piyaz*, a bean and onion salad. *Ciğerci* specializes in liver skewers, while *ciğer tava* sells only thin slices of crispy fried liver. Wandering vendors sell cold fried liver cubes to be tucked into bread with onion slices. *Dönerci* sells the ubiquitous *döner*: meat slices roasted on a big vertical spit and shaved into slivers. Other grilled meat places sell *kanatçı* (chicken wings), *çöp-şiş* (tiny meat skewers), *tantuni* (meat stir fry), and *kokoreç* (grilled intestines). Many of these grilled meats are served in bread or wrapped in flatbread, to form a *dürüm*, literally meaning "a wrap."

Seaside choices include *balık-ekmek*, grilled fish in bread. The *pideci* serves *pide*, a thin, oblong flatbread topped with cheese, meat, spinach, or eggs, or a mixture. They usually also offer *lahmacun*, a flatbread with a minced meat topping. The *börekçi* has a variety of *börek* (layered savory pastries), often served chopped up on small plates to be eaten quickly on the spot. The beaneries serve only *kuru fasulye*, or bean casserole, served with buttery rice pilaf. *Mantıcı* serves only *mantı*, tiny Turkish dumplings filled with minced meat and served with yogurt sauce. The *işkembeci* sells *işkembe çorbası*, tripe soup, and is usually open overnight, as tripe soup is considered to be an ideal hangover remedy. The *çorbacı* is a soup restaurant, which again remains open until late at night from early hours in the morning.

Sweets are usually eaten in separate shops. The *muhallebici* specializes in *muhallebi*, milk pudding. Sweets soaked in syrup are also sold in specialist sweet shops, the favorite being baklava, a multilayered pastry filled with pistachios, walnuts, or cream. Others include *tel kadayıf* (pastry threads stuffed with nuts), *ekmek kadayıf* (rusks topped with clotted cream), *künefe* (pastry threads stuffed with cheese and served hot), *tulumba tatlısı* (fritters made of batter squeezed from a syringe), *lokma* (ball-shaped fritters), *revani* (cake made with semolina), and *şekerpare* (syrupy cookies).

Though prohibited by Islam, alcoholic drinks are widely enjoyed, especially in large cities and coastal regions. Drinking is considered a social occasion enjoyed at a table for long hours, and the most common location is a *meyhane*, typically offering a selection of small platters of *meze* to accompany the national drink, the anise-flavored spirit *rakı*. Street vendors are usually allowed to enter *meyhanes* or to wander between tables on the street to add a few specialties to the table. The usual ones include *çiğ köfte*, spicy raw meatballs; *midye dolma*, rice, pine nut, and raisin-stuffed mussels; *buzlu badem*, fresh almonds on a bed of ice. Another popular evening pastime is sipping beer at a stall, munching *midye tava*, batter fried mussels on a skewers with a garlicky dip.

Apart from all those traditional street foods, international fast-food chains and coffeehouses are common in many towns and cities. The Turkish response to this has been the recent phenomenon called *simit sarayı*, sesame ring palaces, offering varied ways to consume the *simit*, the sesame ring bread. Another recent development in the fast-food scene has been the phenomenon of *kumpir*, jacket potato, served with a wide choice of toppings.

Beverages constitute part of the street food. Places to pass the time between meals are mainly the *kahve*, the coffeehouse, where men traditionally congregate, or the more family-friendly *çay bahçesi*, or tea garden. *Çay*, black tea served in tulip-shaped glasses, is readily available everywhere, as there is a tea kiosk in every shopping area, neighborhood, or office block delivering tea to all. In every town, patisseries also serve tea and beverages along with their assorted sweet-and-savory baked goods. Nowadays, bakeries have started to serve their baked goods at small tables along with a glass of tea or home-made lemonade.

People's daily diet is based on home-cooked meals, but still street food plays a vital role in the routine of the urban population. Street food, however, is not usually junk food, but food freshly prepared from scratch, often quite healthy, usually not fried and free of additives and preservatives. Some street food constitutes a substantial part of urban food supply, while many others are only for fun.

Street-food vendors, in particular the wandering ones, are almost always male, with the exception of *gözleme* (flat pies cooked on a griddle) makers, who are always female, since the skills required for making the flat dough with various fillings seem to be confined to women. Small joints serving *mantı*, Turkish stuffed dumplings, are usually run by women, or at least the cook back in the kitchen is always a woman, and the same applies to the preparation of *sarma* and dolma, wrapped and stuffed food. Women are involved in the cooking process of much home-made ready food sold in street carts, like rice pilaf with chickpeas or fried liver cubes eaten cold. These are often family businesses, with the wife doing the home cooking and the husband doing the street selling. *Simit* vendors' ages can range from school-age kids helping the family to make ends meet to old men still struggling to earn a living.

MAJOR STREET FOODS

Simit

Simit is a sesame-sprinkled savory bread ring sold by vendors called *simitçi*. If there is one street food that can be considered as the national street food of

Turkey, it would be *simit*. It is often stacked on a tray balanced on the vendor's head cushioned with a cloth ring, the same tray serving as a makeshift stall supported on a folding leg wherever the vendor finds a good selling spot. In glass pushcarts, a few other types of baked goods are sold along with *simit*, like *açma*, a ring-shaped buttery bun or *poğaça*, a flaky savory plain or cheese-filled pastry. To make *simit*, the dough is shaped into thin rings, dipped in a grape molasses and water mix, coated with sesame seeds, and baked. In some regions, *simit* is called *gevrek*, meaning "crisp." Strangely, it is both crispy and chewy: crispy on the crust, chewy in the inside. It is usually consumed as is, sometimes paired with Turkish kasar cheese. A Turkish response to international fast-food chains has been the recent phenomenon called Simit Sarayi, literally meaning *simit palace*, a local chain in a bakery-café format.

Köfte

Köfte are meatballs, and they are sold by *köfteci*, which refers to the vendor or the shop that makes and sells grilled meatballs. If *köfte* are made on a street cart or kiosk, they are usually placed in a half or quarter loaf of white bread, with chopped onions, tomatoes, and a few slices of pickles or fresh green chilies. Nearly every town has its own specialty meatballs; the taste, texture, and consistency vary slightly. If the meatballs are made and sold in a small eatery, they are often accompanied by assorted pickles and *piyaz*, a bean and onion salad. Traditional pairing beverage is *ayran*, a diluted salty yogurt drink.

Döner Kebab

Döner kebab is a Turkish street food that has gained a worldwide reputation. It is popular in many countries under different names, gyros in Greece and shawarma (a word derived from Turkish *çevirme*, meaning "rotating") throughout the Middle East. The meat of choice was traditionally lamb, but nowadays it is a mixture of lamb and veal. The newly invented chicken variety is becoming popular. The essential secret is its rotating cooking technique. Slices of seasoned meat are stacked up like a huge inverted cone on a vertical spit, slowly sizzling against a vertically built grill. The rate of roasting is adjusted by turning the spit, and the sizzling crisp cooked part of the stack is shaved off by a huge knife that slices the best bits vertically down to the tray beneath the spit. The sliced shavings mixed with the drippings are either served on a bed of rice pilaf, *pilavüstü*, or wrapped in flatbread lavaş to make a wrap, *dürüm*; or put in a split loaf of bread, *ekmekarasi*. The famous *İskender kebap*, available only in an establishment specializing in this dish, is served on a bed of sliced flatbread and doused liberally with tomato sauce and melted butter.

Pide

The *pideci* serves *pide*, a thin, oblong flatbread topped with cheese, meat, spinach, eggs, or a mixture of these. Meat topping choices are minced meat mixed with chopped tomatoes and peppers; *sujuk*, spicy cured sausage; *pastırma*, spicy cured dried beef; *kavurma*, potted preserved meat chunks; and *kuşbaşı*, lamb meat chopped into little pieces. Almost every town in Turkey has its signature *pide* varieties, served piping hot from the wood-fired stone oven, consumed on the spot, or ordered as a takeout to houses or offices. A common practice is to prepare the topping at home and send it into the *pide* baker to be cooked and delivered back.

Börek

Börek is the generic name for a flaky, layered pastry filled with meat, cheese, potatoes, or spinach, and the *börekçi* is the maker and vendor of a variety of savory pastries; spiraled, coiled, layered, folded, wrapped, and so forth. It can be a hand-pushed cart or a small bakery-like shop, both offering takeaway or serve on the spot. *Su böreği*, literally meaning "water börek," is the stretched out dough that is first boiled in water, then layered with butter and baked. Samosa-like huge folded thin dough filled with juicy raw meat filling is called *çiğ börek* and is always fried upon demand.

OTHER STREET FOODS

Gözleme

Gözleme is thinly hand-rolled pastry filled with a variety of fillings, folded and cooked on a saj, a convex metal plate on fire, like an inverted wok. The filling can be cheese with fresh herbs, minced meat with onions, spicy mashed potatoes, cooked spinach, or wild greens. It is a vivid heritage from the nomadic past of Turks, still enjoyed in every city, and always accompanied by a cool glass of *ayran* or warm tea served in tulip-shaped glasses.

Manti

Manti is a dish of tiny pasta dumplings with seasoned minced meat and onion filling, boiled and topped with garlicky yogurt and drizzled with red pepper-infused melted butter. Sumac and dried mint are usually sprinkled on it for extra flavor.

Ice Cream

Traditional Turkish ice cream, *dondurma*, meaning frozen, does not contain any eggs or cream; it is made with sweetened milk thickened with *salep*, dried, powdered wild purple orchid root. As *salep* is very expensive and orchids are in danger of extinction, their current use is limited and other thickening agents like carob seeds are used. Sometimes flavored with *sakız*, mastic resin from a wild pistachio tree, milk ice cream has a chewy, stringy consistency. Fruit ices are traditionally not made with milk, but are like sorbets, the most popular flavors being *vişne*, sour cherry and lemon, melon, black mulberry, peach, strawberry, and apricot.

Muhallebi

Muhallebi is a milk pudding; the *muhallebici* specializes in all sorts of milk puddings and some sweets. They also sell chicken soup and rice pilaf with chicken as a by-product of the signature pudding of the place, *tavuk göğsü*, a milk pudding made of pounded cooked chicken breast, rice flour, milk, and sugar. The caramelized version called *kazandibi* is pan-roasted to obtain a caramelized bottom, cut into squares, and rolled up.

Boza and Salep

These are drinks only available on cold winter days. *Boza* is a thick fermented drink, loved by locals but an acquired taste for foreigners. Winter nights are pierced with the cries of *boza* sellers, who roam the streets carrying larges jug of a thick, almost pudding-like drink made from fermented millet. Pale yellow with a slightly sweet and tangy sour flavor, it is served in a glass with a spoon. *Salep* is frothy sweet milk thickened with the dried and powdered wild orchid root. It is good for the chest and warms you to the bones. Both are served with a sprinkle of cinnamon.

AYLIN ÖNEY TAN

UZBEKISTAN

INDO-EUROPEAN AND TURKO-MONGOLIAN PEOPLES have been living and warring in what is today Uzbekistan for more than 3,000 years. Mixing pastoral nomadic, agricultural, and urban settlement traditions, rulers and inhabitants of Uzbekistan have included Persians, Turks, Mongolians, Arabs, and Slavs. Great empires that have controlled the country's territory include those of Chingiz Khan, Tamerlane, and Tsarist Russia. Contemporary Uzbekistan became a re-public of the Soviet Union in 1924 and gained full sovereignty in 1991 after the Soviet collapse.

Street food—often sold in Central Asia's famous bazaars—has been a staple of the region since the reign of the Uzbek-born world conqueror Tamerlane (late 14th century). They reflect the cultures and peoples who have traveled along the Silk Road through this Central Asian nation and woven themselves into its culi-nary fabric. Persians, Turks, Arabs, Mongols, and Russians, to name a few, have left their gastronomic mark on this lively and delicious food culture that reflects pastoralist, nomadic, and farming culinary traditions.

Street foods here can come from vendors who've set up little grills on the sidewalk next to a bus station or strip mall, from women who've plopped down on street corner with huge fabric-draped baskets full of hot breads or savory turn-overs or a small merchant who's procured a pallet of ice-cream sandwiches. But most reliably, street-food vendors appear in Uzbekistan's colorful bazaars where they have more space and sometimes even makeshift tables and chairs to accom-modate diners.

Central Asian countries that border Uzbekistan—Kazakhstan, Kyrgyzstan, Tajikistan, and Turkmenistan—share similarities with Uzbek street food with *shashlik*, clay oven bread and dumplings being most ubiquitous. Every medium- to large-size town in Uzbekistan boasts at least one bazaar held on special bazaar days and in some cases every day.

In the Uzbek capital of Tashkent, the most popular is the Alaysky or Aloy Bazaar located near the governmental center. Here you will find whole halls and sections devoted to rice, vegetables, dairy, meat, spices, and even a special area where ethnic Korean women sell ready-to-eat kimchi along with garlicky salads made with strips of carrots, beets, and eggplant.

MAJOR STREET FOODS

Plov

Called *palov*, pilaf, or *pilau* in other countries, this flavored rice dish might seem like an unlikely street food, but is actually one of the most commonly offered food items on Uzbek streets and in its bazaars. In a country where disposable dishware is still a rarity, the rich rice dish is often served in ceramic bowls with aluminum spoons that patrons are expected to use and return. Patrons can also bring their own. The national dish of Uzbekistan, *plov* is often also called *osh*, which means "food" in Uzbek and can refer to simple stews in Persian.

Different regions and seasons call for different treatments of the dish, but the essential elements include rice, carrots, onions, cottonseed oil, spices (often paprika, cumin, turmeric), and usually a little meat—beef or mutton. Variations can include the inclusion of raisins, quince slices, sheep tail fat, pomegranate seeds, hot peppers, whole heads of garlic, hard-boiled eggs, black-eyed peas, and more. The resulting orange mounds of nutty, oily rice will almost always be prepared in a large, iron, demi-spherical pot called *qozon*.

In exchange for a modest price, customers can fill up on a large bowl of the savory rice topped with a few nuggets of meat (commonly beef). They can eat the dish standing up, squatting on the ground, or try to snag a little table and chair if the vendor has set one up.

Tourists to Uzbekistan are often surprised by the oiliness of the dish and the pool of orange oil that remains at the bottom of a pot. But chefs actually strive to produce a greasy *plov*, noting that it is full of calories and lipids for brain function. Many Uzbeks still eat *plov* with their hands, and for them, the mark of a good *plov* lies in the trail of oil that slides down to their elbows while lifting bites to their mouths. Cottonseed oil, a plentiful and cheap by-product of the nation's number one crop, gives the dish its distinctive orange hue and a vaguely nutty flavor. Some have expressed concern, however, about pesticide residue that may remain in the seeds of the historically heavily sprayed crop.

Shashlik

Known as kebabs or shish kebabs in other cultures, this (seasoned and often marinated) skewered meat cooked over hardwood coal is another favorite in Uzbekistan and all over Central Asia.

Diners typically order their meat of choice (chicken, mutton, beef, kofta/ground, liver, and, in some heavily Russian areas, pork) and eat it with a fresh, crusty, round loaf of clay oven bread called *non*. Skewers can be accompanied by raw onions, pickled onions, fresh cilantro, and hot pepper- and basil-infused vinegar. Seasonings often not only include salt and pepper but also dustings of cumin powder, crushed coriander seeds, and cayenne. Meat cubes are commonly interspersed with chunks of fat that are savored just as enthusiastically as the meat and serve to baste the meat as it sizzles over the coals.

Samsa

Much like the South Asian samosa, this savory turnover makes for an excellent handheld meal on the go. While some can be cooked in conventional ovens, most are baked while stuck to the inside walls of clay tandir ovens.

Doughs can vary from strong and chewy to flaky and shattery, taking the shape of gumdrops, triangles, and domes. Fillings can change seasonally and by regions with springtime bringing *samsas* full of chives, green garlic, and other young greens, while fall finds them stuffed with chopped onions and the flesh of hard-shelled gourds like pumpkin.

The most common filling, however, is chopped mutton and onions blended with nubbins of fat from the rump of the region's prized fat-tailed sheep. Although the Uzbeks rarely eat lamb (preferring the more economical mutton), lamb can be substituted in recipes.

Manti

Called *mantu, mantou,* and *mandu* in other cultures, these steamed, noodle-encased dumplings stuffed with savory fillings (almost identical to those in *sam-sas*) make for a slightly messy but delicious street food. Holding mutton, pump-kin, and green fillings, their delicate, wet, steamed noodle exteriors make them hard to eat by hand, especially since some vendors top them with a tangy, watery yogurt sauce and chopped green herbs or oil.

OTHER STREET FOODS

Lagman

If made properly, the delicious, pliant noodles for this noodle soup dish will be stretched from a single ball of dough by a strapping chef right before your eyes outdoors. If you're less fortunate, they'll come from dry packaged spaghetti.

Best eaten on the streets of the Uzbek–Kyrgyz border town of Osh, this dish bears distinct influences of Western Chinese Uyghur people who live over the border from Central Asia. In the best versions, fresh noodles are stretched and immediately tossed into a hot broth, rich with tomatoes, peppers, garlic, onion, and small amounts of meat. Condiments can include fresh cilantro, flavored vin-egar, and a bright, spicy chile paste. At his best, a lagman vendor can produce an amazing show followed by breathtaking chow.

Qurut

A nod to Uzbekistan's pastoralist population, these hard, little yogurt balls are fa-vorites among kids and as snacks with alcohol. The salty and sour balls taste a bit like a pungent cheese and are made by straining and drying yogurt, rolling it into balls and letting them dry in the sun. The resulting gumball-like snacks can be eaten with bread like a little concentrated cheese or sucked on like jawbreakers. An ideal way to preserve cultured dairy for long voyages, *qurut* can be an acquired taste and smell for visitors.

Non

While not exactly a street food, these warm, crusty, chewy frisbees are sold on Uzbek streets everywhere and can make for some of the tastiest snacking around.

Non loaves from professional bakers can rival baguettes for their combination of a chewy, crisp crust and a large, open, moist almost eggy crumb. Eat it with garlicky, Korean beet or carrot salads, or on their own and enjoy.

Just be sure to treat Uzbek bread with respect. Locals tear it (never cut it) to share, use all of it until its gone (rather than throwing it away), always place it right side up (never upside down), and often kiss it if it falls on the ground.

Humma

These deep-fried wheat-flour dough pucks are often stuffed with a smidgen of ground meat or potatoes and bear a very close resemblance to the common Russian street snack *ponchiki* or *piroshki*. An extremely cheap, calorific, often warm, savory snack, they are a huge favorite with the ambulatory dining crowd.

A holdover from the days of Russian rule, ice-cream sandwiches and soft serve ice-cream cones show up on the street sold from boxes or stands fairly often in Uzbekistan. They taste quite a lot like their Western counterparts.

MONICA ENG

CHAPTER 4

SHAWARMA
CRÊPES MARRONI
FRITES FOCACCIA
SAUSAGE
WHELKS

EUROPE

EUROPE

CENTRAL AND EASTERN EUROPE

AUSTRIA

A USTRIA IS A NATION OF eight million people, much of whose land is located in the mountainous Alpine region of Central Europe. Although small, it has an exceptionally rich cultural history and splendid cuisine, much of it centered in the capital city, Vienna. For hundreds of years, Austria was the center of the Habsburg or Austro-Hungarian Empire, a multiethnic state that stretched across middle Europe. Though a German-speaking country, Austria's food carries Czech, Hungarian, Croat, Italian, Polish, Ukrainian, French, Ottoman Turkish, and Jewish influences. Today's street food offers a vibrant food culture that combines the old and the new, local and global, domestic and immigrant. It offers a wide array of choices from the expected sausage to the not-so-expected Asian sushi and noodles, kebabs, and pizza.

MAJOR STREET FOODS

Sausage

Würstelstanden (sausage stands) are the most typical Austrian street food. These are mainly standing only and have a bar around the small structure, where people can set their paper plates and then eat. Sausage stands sell a wide variety of sausages. The most popular are *Käsekrainer* (literally "pus filled"), which is injected with melting cheese, *Debreziner* (thin spicy sausage), *Frankfurter* (often called

Wurstel mit Senf, meaning it's served with hot or sweet mustard on a roll), *Burenwurst* (thick chunky sausage), bratwurst (grayish-white sausage), *Weisswurst* (a fat bratwurst), and *Bosna* (bratwurst topped with curry powder and served with onions and mustard on a hot dog bun). Sausages can be served as a hot dog in a long bun or on a paper plate with a slice of bread or a roll, and a choice of spicy or sweet mustard, and pickles, onions, or hot peppers.

One Austrian specialty found at *Würstelstanden* and in many shops is *Leberkäse.* The word is directly translated as "liver cheese," though the actual liver content can vary from none to six percent. *Leberkäse* is made of ground meat, pork or beef, bacon, onions, bread crumbs, and spices, which is formed into a loaf and baked until it is spongy soft inside with a fine crust on the outside. It is usually served hot on a cut roll and with sliced pickles or mustard to taste. It can also be sold cold, in which case it is eaten thinly, cut as a cold cut. Aside from the regular *Leberkäse,* there are also *Käseleberkäse* (with melting cheese pockets), *Pikantleberkäse* (with pieces of paprika), and *Pferdeleberkäse* (made of horse meat), though the last one is available only in special delis that sell mainly horsemeat products.

International Influences

Sausage stands are popular among the older generation at lunchtime, but are patronized by younger people for a late-night snack after a night out. The same goes for the newly popular Asian noodle stands. With names like Happy Noodles or Crazy Noodles, meals are served in a box with the basic options being vegetables or chicken. Other versions contain duck breast, teriyaki chicken, salmon, sweet-and-sour shrimp, or spicy beef. Noodle stands are especially popular among younger people and often have long lines. They also sell prepacked sushi and maki boxes, as well as soups and mini spring rolls.

Because of immigration from Turkey and the Balkan countries, kebabs are sold all over Austria. There are several different kebab stands, ranging from those in green markets that are generally cheaper to those that double as Turkish restaurants and kebab-only places, usually on the main city streets. Kebabs can be made from chicken, lamb, or beef and are served on either a large white bun or wrapped in a tortilla-like pancake (called *Dörum*). They are topped with lettuce, tomatoes, onions, and yogurt sauce.

Pizza-by-the-slice is a classic street food in Austria. The slices are usually rather large, and the most popular ingredients are ham, mushrooms, salami (pepperoni), vegetarian (broccoli, sweet corn, paprika, tomatoes), spinach and feta cheese, and tuna and onions. Very often the same places that sell pizza also sell falafel, kebab, schnitzel, and lately even Asian noodle boxes.

Baked Goods

Much of what can be called "street food" is sold from shops as "takeout" to be eaten on the go. Baked goods are among them. Austria's bakery culture is probably only second to that of France. The country's numerous bakeries offer a wide range of rolls, breadsticks, pretzels, rye breads, sourdough and yeast breads, whole meal buns and loaves, filled puff pastries, doughnuts, cakes, and fruit loaves. Bakeries are located on main streets, in train stations, city squares, and shopping malls, and are the most popular breakfast choice of Austrians. Many also sell premade cold sandwiches in their own rolls, buns, and breads, as well as drinks. The most popular items are the *Salzstangerl* (kosher-salt bread stick), the *Semmel* (dinner roll), the *Laugenbretzel* (lye pretzel), the *Nuss-* or *Mohnbeugel* (sweet bread filled with sweet walnut or poppy seed), the croissant, and the *Kornspitz* (wholemeal bread with seeds inside or on top).

Deli Meats

Most supermarkets in Austria have a deli counter (*Feinkost*), where people can buy such takeout food as cold cuts, cheese, pickles, or spreads in a roll of choice prepared on the spot. These delis also sell prepacked sandwiches (triangles, baguettes, ham rolls), as well as packed salads, fruit salads, yogurt cereal, ready-made microwave meals, and even sushi boxes. Most have a hot box for *Leberkäse*, grilled chicken, schnitzel, *Stelze* (ham hock), roast pork belly, roast cumin pork, mince patties, and sausages. There are also special butcher/deli shops that specialize in cold cuts, which offer an endless variety of sandwiches, especially made of pork, and where one can usually get a warm meal as well.

Schnitzel

The schnitzel shop is another typically Austrian food shop, where, for a little money, diners get any of a huge variety of this classic Austrian dish—a thin cutlet of meat, often veal, coated in fine breadcrumbs and fried. The best known are *Schnitzelsemmel* (Viennese schnitzel, breaded and deep-fried, chicken, turkey, or pork served on a roll with salad, ketchup, mayonnaise, and/or sauce tartar); *Fischsemmel* (the same, but with breaded fish); cordon bleu (schnitzel with melting cheese inside); breaded fried cheese, mushrooms, zucchini, eggplant, and cauliflower; fried chicken wings, chicken drumsticks, and sometimes grilled chicken; and sides of French fries, wedges, potato salad, and cucumber salad. Some of these places offer limited seating for a quick bite, but mostly the food is taken and eaten on the go.

OTHER STREET FOODS

Other kinds of street food are sold at special events and during various seasons. Typically a lot of food is available in amusement parks and at festivals. These range from small snacks to more filling foods. Among them are caramelized nuts, seeds and nuts, popcorn, cotton candy, corn-on-the cob, ice cream, pancakes, cold drinks, hot dogs, burgers, kebabs, beer, and *Grillhendl* (grilled chicken). Some stands have *lángos* (a Hungarian type of flat dough, deep-fried till crispy, and topped with garlic oil to taste), *Pofesen* (French toast, filled with special plum jam called *Powidl*), *Krapfen* (doughnuts), and even pickles, sold by the piece straight from a huge jar. Kirtage, originally a village church festival celebrating the patron saint of the church, are nowadays more like traveling carnivals/amusement parks. They set up in town or village squares, featuring stalls with various handcrafted gifts, merry-go-rounds, and of course, food.

Once the summer season opens, *Eis* (ice cream) is extremely popular. Long lines forming in front of the main Italian ice-cream shops are a regular sight. Ice cream is sold by the scoop in cones or cups, and the variety of flavors is enormous. An option is to sit down, usually by the sidewalk, and enjoy it in a coup, served in a glass with fruits, nuts, sauces, and whipped cream.

From September to March, chestnuts and potatoes are sold on street corners and in main squares. Chestnuts are roasted on the spot, and sold in paper cones. The potatoes can be *Bratkartofeln* (roasted wedges, salted), wedges (American style), or *Rösti* (hash browns).

Christmas markets, which are held all over Austria for four weeks during the Advent season, also revolve around food. Since it is the cold season, people like to keep warm by eating and drinking. The main offerings are mulled wine and punch, *Lebkuchen* (honey ginger bread) and other traditional Christmas sweets, *Mohnnudeln* (potato dumplings with sweet butter poppy seed), *Kaiserschmarren* (sweet, scrambled pancakes with plum compote), roast chestnuts, potatoes, pancakes, *lángos*, and hot dogs.

Summertime green and farmers' markets also offer food on the spot. Not only can consumers get fresh fruit to eat immediately, but vendors also sell cold cut sandwiches, falafel, Turkish *börek* (a wrapped pastry), Asian noodle boxes, boxed sushi, Italian antipasti, kebabs, and all kinds of sweets.

Coffee

Austria has a long tradition of coffeehouses, but these are elegant sit-down establishments, where busy businessmen, students, and tourists have the option of having coffee on the go. They include American franchises, such as Starbucks, local ones such as The Coffeeshop Company, and smaller coffee shops. One can also buy cold drinks, smoothies, and shakes from some of these places. The most recent addition has been Tealicious, the bubble tea company, which opened in Vienna. There is an old saying in Central Europe that for the best and greatest varieties of food, there is no place like Vienna.

KATERINA NUSSDORFER

BELARUS

ELARUS, OR WHITE RUSSIA, is located in the heart of Eastern Europe. It is landlocked, surrounded by Poland, Lithuania, Latvia, Russia, and Ukraine. Most of the country is composed of lowlands, rolling hills, and marshes, and about 40 percent of it is covered by forests. The most famous of these is the ancient World Heritage Site, Belovezhskaya Pushcha National Park, which straddles the border between Poland and Belarus. Major rivers run through the country, the Pripyat, Dnieper, and Neman among them, and there are many tributary streams and lakes throughout the land. Because of its location, Belarus's climate tends to be cooler in summer than its neighbors and cold in winter. Climate and the nature of the land mean that wheat is not the main grain crop, but rye, barley, oats, and buckwheat are more important. Baked goods made from these grains are significant to Belarusian culinary culture.

The Belarusian language is closely related to Russian and Ukrainian and so are most of its people. Belarus was part of the Kievan state (centered on today's Ukraine) from the 9th to 13th centuries. When Mongols destroyed the kingdom, much of Belarus was controlled by a Polish–Lithuanian kingdom during which time foods and people moved across their mutual borders. In the late 18th century, Belarus became part of the Russian Empire, after that the Soviet Union, and in 1991, an independent country. Polish and Lithuanian-speaking people still live in Belarus, but Russian is far more important culturally. Partly this is because the Belarusian government still follows the Soviet model, and most Belarusians belong to the Russian Orthodox Church. Festivals and the foods that go with them are like those in Russia and the Ukraine. Jews were once an important group in Belarus.

In the late 19th and early 20th centuries, a great many left for United States taking their foodways with them and leaving their influence on Belarusian foods. Many chicken dishes and herring, for example, originated with Belarusian Jews.

Breads, potatoes, and mushrooms are at the center of Belarus food traditions. Upon entering someone's house, a guest is immediately offered a piece of bread with salt. The bread might be a sour dough rye or a mixed grain type. The Belarusian expression is "bread is lord in the home." Hearty soups are a core meal in Belarus and are made from various ingredients, including beets, potatoes, meats, sorrel, and mushrooms. They can be accompanied by the Belarusian dumpling called *kalduny*. These are close to Russian *pelmeni* but are made of dough wrappers filled with chopped meats, cabbage, cheese, or mushrooms and then boiled. Potatoes are everywhere—Belarusians are sometimes called *bulbashi* or "potato people." As Belarusians say, "potatoes are as good as bread." *Draniki* is the classic dish, fried pancakes made from grated potatoes mixed with onions, pork fat, sour milk, and salt. *Oladyi* (pancakes) made from grated, drained potatoes mixed with flour, eggs, and pork fat are often stuffed with mushrooms, chopped meats, shredded fish, or hard-boiled eggs.

MAJOR STREET FOODS

Pancakes and Dumplings

These dishes and similar ones are served as street food, near public markets, and at public events. The most popular are *blini*, originally a Russian dish (the Belarusian *nalesniki* is similar). These are thin pancakes, crêpes really, made from a batter, cooked on a hot griddle, and then stuffed with various fillings, from pickled cabbage, to jams and even caviar. True Belarusian *blini* are made with oat flour and are called *raschinnie*. There are even hot dogs wrapped in soft dough, like sausage rolls. But without pickled cabbage and sour cream, no dish is complete. Street foods also include soups, sausages, sandwiches (in cities), packaged candies—often sold by vendors from trays—and soft drinks. Products made by such international soft drink companies as Coca-Cola are widely available. The most traditional drink is *kvas*, which is made from old rye bread mixed with yeast, sugar, and water and allowed to ferment overnight. The result is a sparkling, refreshing drink, especially when served cold.

BRUCE KRAIG

CZECH REPUBLIC AND SLOVAKIA

F ROM 1918 UNTIL 1993, the Czech Republic and Slovakia were one country known as Czechoslovakia. Both had been part of Europe's greatest multi-ethnic state, the Austro-Hungarian or Hapsburg Empire, which was broken up into several smaller countries after the end of World War I. Czechs and Slovaks have much in common, including languages (Slavic) that are similar, a shared history, and many foods that are popular in both countries. But they also regard themselves as separate ethnic groups and, in 1993, peacefully separated into two independent states.

Both are landlocked nations located in Central Europe that share similar climates but different landscapes. Much of the Czech lands are rolling hills, and the valleys of major European rivers run through them: the Moldau, Elbe, and headwaters of the Oder. There has always been good farmland, although agriculture is not the major industry. Slovakia is more mountainous, especially in the south, and has large areas that are forested, but agriculture is very important here as well. Both countries produce wheat and barley, potatoes, food animals (especially pigs), and sugar beets, all of which are the basis of Czech and Slovak cuisine. Fish, poultry, wild mushrooms, and game are also popular. Grapes for winemaking are grown in the southern regions of both countries.

The Czech Republic encompasses two ancient regions of Europe, Bohemia (in the west), and Moravia (in the southeast), as well as part of Silesia in the northeast. Slovaks and Czechs migrated to their respective regions in Europe beginning in the 5th century CE and, over the next millennium and a half, interacted with neighboring Germans, Austrians, Poles, and Hungarians, so it is not surprising that many of the foods of these countries appear in the Czech and Slovak states, too. The Czech capital, Prague, was a major cultural center in the Hapsburg Empire, and the influence of Viennese cuisine can still be seen (and tasted) there. Sausages and schnitzels, sweet pastries and other flour-based foods (such as pancakes and dumplings), cream sauces and whipped cream, are all glories of traditional Czech cooking.

Beer is also deeply rooted in the foodways of the Czech Republic and Slovakia. Czech beers are world famous, the city of Plzeň lending its name to a style of beer made the world over: pilsner. The city of České Budějovice also gave its name to a renowned name in beer, Budvar, known as Budweiser in German and English. These beers are made with hops grown in both countries, which are considered some of the best quality in the world. Beer is a necessity at all public festivals and other events where food is enjoyed. Czechs are the world's biggest consumers of beer, downing 132 liters per person annually.

Czech wine is produced primarily in the southern part of Moravia, where the vast majority of vineyards are located. Slovak wine comes from the southern and southwestern parts of the country. Good-quality white wines are produced in both countries, as well as some reds and special types, such as sparkling wines and Tokajs. Czech and Slovak wines are popular in Central Europe but less well known outside that area.

MAJOR STREET FOODS

Like other developed European countries, the Czech and Slovak republics have a full complement of international fast-food chains. Wenceslas Square, in the center of Prague, is filled with them. But more traditional street foods are also available, and true to local food culture, many are fatty, whether sausages, cheeses, or sweets.

Sausages (*Klobásy*)

Called *klobásy* in general, sausages come in many types that have their own specific names. Street stands on Wenceslas Square display sausages hanging from hooks, ready for cooking on griddles or open grills. Sausage styles include several German types, spicy-red Prague sausages, and Polish, Hungarian, and Moravian sausages, served in different ways. One, called *párek v rohlíku* (usually translated as "hot dog in a bun"), is a long, thin sausage inserted into in a hollowed-out bun with mustard. Other sausages are thick, well-grilled, and oozing fat, served on plates with thick slices of chewy bread and garnished with mustard, onions, and other toppings. Sausages sold on the streets of Slovak cities such as Bratislava, the capital, are similar to those served in the Czech Republic. All are eaten with the fingers, not with a fork, even if the sausages are hot to the touch.

Smažený Sýr

One of the most popular street foods is fried cheese, *smažený sýr* or *smažák* (in Czech) and *vyprážaný sýr* (in Slovak). A thick slice of cheese is dredged in flour, beaten egg, and breadcrumbs and then deep-fried. The cheese might be a semi-soft cheese like Edam or Muenster, or a native Czech cheese called Hermelín, a soft cheese similar to French Brie or Camembert, which is runnier than the other cheeses when fried. *Smažený sýr* can be eaten with the fingers, the cheese first dipped in mayonnaise or tartar sauce, or it can be placed in a bun and served with fried potatoes and salad.

Langoš

An import from Hungary (where it is called *lángos)* now popular in both the Czech Republic and Slovakia, *langoš* is a leavened wheat bread formed into flat rounds and deep-fried, then garnished with a variety of toppings. Savory *langoš* are rubbed with garlic or covered with a choice of chopped garlic, sliced sausages or ham, sauerkraut, sour cream, grated yellow cheese, or soft fresh white cheese. Sweet versions are topped with fruit preserves or sprinkled with cinnamon and sugar.

Trdelník

Trdelník is very popular in the Czech Republic and Slovakia. *Skalický trdelník* (*trdelník* from the city of Skalica) is a name protected by the European Union as unique to that place. *Trdelník* is made from a sweet dough of eggs, flour, and sugar that is rolled by hand into long ropes, then tightly wrapped around thick wooden or metal rods and baked by slowly rotating the rods next to an open heat source. The final result is a crispy, hollow, barrel-shaped pastry that is dredged in a mixture of sugar, cinnamon, and chopped nuts before serving. Eaten by hand, this treat is sold from street stands year-round.

OTHER STREET FOODS

Potato Pancakes

Known as *bramboráky*, these are pancakes made from grated potatoes mixed with a small amount of flour and beaten egg, then panfried or baked on a griddle. Sometimes grated onions or sauerkraut are added to the batter. Popular garnishes include applesauce or sour cream.

Palačinky

Palačinky are very thin crêpes made from egg batter cooked on a griddle, then rolled around a filling. Savory *palačinky* are filled with meat or cheese, whereas sweet ones are filled with fruit preserves, sweetened fresh white cheese, or nuts (including chestnut purée), and sprinkled with sugar. *Palačinky* stands are often found around marketplaces and at festivals.

Carnival and Easter Treats

Street stands during Carnival (before Lent) sell deep-fried pastries rolled in sugar, pretzels sprinkled with salt, and caraway seeds or poppy seeds and sugar. Food stands at Easter markets feature yeast-raised buns made of braided dough often formed into the shape of rabbits, lambs, or birds, with a whole, red-dyed egg baked into them as part of the decoration.

Christmas Market Foods

In addition to many of the street foods described earlier, food stands at Christmas markets also sell gingerbread cookies (*perníčky*), cut into holiday shapes and often intricately decorated with white icing. (Many people buy them to take home and hang on their Christmas trees.) The favorite drink for keeping warm in the winter weather is *svařené víno*, hot mulled wine made of red wine, sugar, orange and lemon peel, cinnamon, and cloves. This drink is so popular that some street stands now sell it year-round.

Election Goulash

During the period between the two world wars, Czechoslovak political parties often set up stands that served free bowls of the famous Hungarian meat and potato stew called *guláš*, or goulash, near polling places on Election Day to influence the voters' choices. This culinary tradition was revived in 1990, shortly after the fall of the communist government, when the first free elections in 41 years were held in Prague. Political parties set up "goulash cannons" (big, black-iron, portable field kitchens often used by the military in the field) and dished out free bowls of steaming hot *guláš* to people lined up to vote. *Guláš* is still a popular dish sold at some street stands and at festivals.

Drinks

Beer (*pivo*) is the perennial favorite, and canned soft drinks are ubiquitous, as is hot spiced wine. But in autumn (especially in winemaking areas), street stands also serve "new wine" (*burčák* in Czech, *burčiak* in Slovak), grape juice that is still in the process of fermenting into wine. This cloudy, somewhat sweet liquid, which is lower in alcohol than real wine, combines the taste of yeast and freshly crushed grapes with the sparkle of champagne and the foam of beer. In Slovakia, it is often accompanied by *pagáče*, small, round, savory scones much like American biscuits.

Open-Face Sandwiches

Obložené chlebíčky (garnished breads) are not only popular appetizers for a meal but they are also sold as snacks at some street stands, especially during festivals. Thick slices of chewy white bread are spread with butter and topped with sliced ham, sausage, hard-boiled egg, cheese, tomato, fresh or pickled cucumber, or a variety of meat, cheese, or vegetable spreads.

Chestnuts

As in other European countries, roasted chestnuts are eaten as soon as the fresh nuts become available in the autumn. Slovakia has particularly good chestnuts from its mountainous regions, and vendors set up roasting tubs over open flames in cities and towns throughout the country. Customers eat the hot chestnuts from paper cones, often with *pivo* or hot spiced wine as an accompaniment.

Corn

Roasted ears of corn (*kukurica*) are a popular street food, more common in Slovakia than in the Czech Republic. These are roasted in their husks, and then peeled and eaten with salt, butter, and often mayonnaise or a type of tartar sauce.

BRUCE KRAIG

HUNGARY

T HE REPUBLIC OF HUNGARY is a landlocked Central European country that shares borders with Romania, Ukraine, Austria, Croatia, Serbia, Slovenia, and Slovakia. It has a population of 10 million, about one-fifth of whom live in the capital Budapest, and an area of 36,000 square miles. Much of the country consists of flat to rolling plains and low mountains. Though Hungary is blessed with fertile soil and is a major agricultural producer, the cuisine is dominated by meat, especially pork.

Hungarian is a language unrelated to its neighbors, but its culture is fully integrated with Central Europe. For centuries, it was part of the Hapsburg dominions, later called the Austro-Hungarian Empire, not becoming an independent country until after World War I. Hungarian chefs and bakers influenced the imperial capital, Vienna, and in turn the Hungarian capital, Budapest, mirrored the culture of the Empire. Hungarian cuisine remains one of the most influential in Central–Eastern Europe. Hungarian wines are world famous, and *gulyás* (goulash) and paprika are the country's best-known contributions to world cuisine. However, Hungarian street food is much more diverse.

Street food is sold at tourist places such as squares, fortresses, bridges and parks, and also at seasonal fairs and festivals, where vendors sell dried fruits, seeds and nuts, popcorn, *vattacukor* (cotton candy), roasted chestnuts and potatoes, *forró bor* (mulled wine), and traditional pickled vegetables (gherkins, onions, peppers, etc.) sold by the piece from large vats and barrels filled with salty and sour brine. A remnant from the Communist era are the mini-markets/

groceries with street entrances that sell fruits, vegetables, drinks, nuts and seeds, dry sausages, cheese, and breads.

MAJOR STREET FOODS

Gulyás

Although served and eaten in homes and restaurants, *gulyás* is an inseparable moment of the Hungarian street-food experience. It is a stew of potatoes and veal/beef chunks, cooked and served in an aromatic, thick, and rich paprika-infused broth.

Lángos

The best-known Hungarian street food is the ubiquitous *lángos* (which means "flamed"), a savory, yeast flatbread that is deep-fried on the spot and served plain or with different toppings, including garlic oil, cheese, sour cream, or jam.

Kolbász (Sausage) and *Szendvics* (Sandwiches)

Kolbász is sold in stands and kiosks and served in a *szendvics,* or grilled sandwich, and as a hot dog or *wimpi* (the sausage is served on an open-faced bun) accompanied by bread, pickles of choice, and mustards or other condiments. Especially interesting is the *mangalica kolbász* made of the meat of the special, particularly flavorful and fatty, velvety-and-gamey-in-taste Mangalica Hungarian pig.

Meleg Szendvics (Warm Sandwich)

A thick slice of toasted bread with *sonkás* (ham) or *sajtos* (cheese) or *tejfölös* (sour cream) is another street-food classic. Hamburgers are common, made of a pork–beef mix, and served on large buns with salad and/or fries and sauces. Fries, especially twisted or curly fries and wedges, can be purchased separately, accompanied with ketchup and other condiments.

Sweets

For those with a sweet tooth, a classic is *palacsinta,* a thick crêpe, rolled and filled with sweet or savory filling. A uniquely Hungarian street-food delicacy is the *kürtőskalács* (chimney or tunnel cake)—sweet milk loaf cake dough that is grilled around a thick vertical spit to make a cylindrical hollow cake that is topped with crushed nuts, ground walnuts, cinnamon, vanilla, cocoa powder, caster sugar, or coconut flakes, all of which stick nicely to the warm dough. Another dish popular with Hungarians is *fagylalt* (ice cream); usually several scoops are served in a small cone on top of each other. In summer, one can also buy *hókristály* (literally meaning snow crystal, and similar to an ice slush)—ground/crushed ice with a shot of brightly colored fruit syrup.

OTHER STREET FOODS

Pizza

Small shops or makeshift kiosks sell some or all of the following dishes: pizza (by the slice), and pizza variations such as *töki pompos* (small deep-dish pizza squares), and the recently popular *kenyérlángos* (bread *lángos*), also known as *langalló* (a newly coined word). The latter is a pizza-like dough baked in the oven and topped with butter, sour cream, cheese, ham, salami, onion, or yellow paprika, among other ingredients.

Soup

Small establishments sell various kinds of *leves* (soup) in small takeout cups. Flavors change daily and include chicken, beef, vegetable, dumplings, cream of potato, and cream of mushroom. These places typically also sell *kávé* (coffee to go), as well as cold beverages such as mineral water, soft drinks, and beer.

Bakeries

Bakeries on every street corner sell an array of breads, pastries and doughs such as *kifli* (yeast-and-milk dough triangles), *zsemle* (rolls), *perec* (pretzel), *pogácsa* (round savory filled dough), pita (sheet pastry filled with ground meat, spinach, cheese, etc.), and various cakes, including *bejgli* (sweet poppy seed or walnut yeast roll) and *rétes* (strudel). Many of these delicacies are sold in cake shops, which are more elegant establishments with tables and chairs that also serve more intricate layered cakes, the most famous of which is *Dobos torta*. They also offer coffee and tea.

KATERINA NUSSDORFER

POLAND

T HE REPUBLIC OF POLAND is bordered by Germany to the west; the Czech Republic and Slovakia to the south; Ukraine, Belarus, and Lithuania to the east; and the Baltic Sea and Russia to the north. Over the centuries, the country has been divided and occupied by its more powerful neighbors, so that large sections were at various times part of Austria, Germany, and Russia. Poland gained its independence in 1919. After World War II, the country became Communist, but the Communist regime fell in 1989. Today Poland is a member of the European Union and enjoying an economic boom. With more than two million private farms, it is Europe's leading producer of potatoes and rye and a major producer of sugar beets.

Poland's position on the crossroads between East and West has influenced its cuisine, which shares features with those of Russia, Germany, Austria, and even France thanks to intermarriage between Polish and French aristocrats in the 17th and 18th centuries. Although some people equate Polish food with sausages (and indeed, the Poles have developed sausage-making to a fine art), vegetables, especially salads, play an important role. Common ingredients include cabbage, carrots, beets, parsnips, potatoes, horseradish, grains such as groats (*kasza*) and barley, mushrooms, and berries. Flavoring may come from wild mushrooms, juniper berries, marjoram, and dill.

Traditionally, there has not been much street food in Poland. The Communist regime discouraged private enterprise, many ingredients were in short supply, and eating on the street was frowned on by middle-class people. However, this has changed, and in recent years, local and regional governments have even been promoting food as a tourist attraction by holding festivals for pierogi, cheese, sausage, and other regional items. At the Pierogi Festival in Cracow, for example, tens of thousands of pierogies are consumed each day.

Pierogies—small dumplings filled with meat, potatoes, mushrooms, cheese, vegetables, and fruits—are ubiquitous in Eastern Europe and considered Poland's national dish. However, they are not usually sold as a street food but are rather eaten in restaurants or at home. In the United States, on the other hand, pierogies are a staple of street-food trucks in several cities.

MAJOR STREET FOODS

Pastries

One of the most popular categories of street foods are pastries, sold from carts, kiosks with glass fronts, and bakeries. Poland has a rich tradition of pastry making that dates back to the first half of the 18th century when King August III brought in pastry makers from France. Probably the most famous are *pączki* (pronounced "ponchki," sometimes translated as "doughnuts")—deep-fried balls of dough with a wide variety of fruit and cream fillings. They are traditionally eaten on the last Thursday before Ash Wednesday.

Rurki z kremem are long thin tubes of wafer-thin pastry filled with cream. *Gofry* (from the French *gaufre*) are Belgian-style waffles cooked on a griddle and topped with fruit and cream. *Kolaczki* are small, square- or diamond-shaped pieces of dough-filled cream cheese, fruit, or even poppy seeds.

Kremolki, a derivative of the French pastry napoleon, are a specialty of the town of Wadowice, birthplace of Pope John Paul II. These cakes are made with a shortbread crust on the bottom, followed by a layer of golden custard cream, and topped with puff pastry. On a visit to Wadowice in 1999, the pope mentioned that as a boy he and his friends would put their money together to buy one of these cakes. Now it is sold everywhere in Wadowice under the name *kremowka papieska*, the papal cream cake.

Zapiekanka

A popular street food throughout Poland is *zapiekanka,* a baked open-faced sandwich that always contains sautéed mushrooms, melted cheese, and generous amounts of ketchup (and sometimes mayonnaise) in a sliced roll. It became popular under Communism when these ingredients were more readily available during a period of shortages. Today there are many varieties: Hawaiian (pineapple and barbecue sauce), gypsy (ham, sweet-and-sour sauce), diablo (bacon, pickled cucumber, spicy sauce), Greek (olives, feta cheese, mixed vegetables), and with fish, a popular home-made version is called "student's *zapiekanka*," which is made from bread, cheese, and whatever else is in the kitchen cupboard at the moment!

Obwarzaneki

Sometimes termed the Polish pretzel or bagel (although this is a source of contention), this snack is particularly associated with the city of Cracow, where it is sold at nearly 200 street carts. *Obwarzanki* are wreath-shaped circles made from flour that are crispy on the outside and bready on the inside with a large hole in the middle. They can be sprinkled with salt, sesame or poppy seeds, spices, cheese, or onions. However, unlike their cousins, bagels, they are not toasted or cut in half to make sandwiches. They are popular among students because of their low price, their availability at stalls near bus stops, outside college buildings, and on many street corners, and their filling qualities. *Obwarzanki* were served at the royal Cracow court as early as the 15th century. The bread was baked originally during Lent.

Bagels are also sold in Poland and were apparently invented in medieval Germany's Jewish communities and migrated with them to Poland. The first known mention of the word *bajgiel* was in the community regulations of the city of Cracow in 1610, which stated that the item was given as a gift to women in childbirth. Jewish immigrants from Poland brought it to the United States, where it is a characteristic dish of New York City.

Döner kebabs, sold in small kiosks and outside restaurants, are a popular late-night snack in Polish cities. Originally Turkish, they probably came from Germany and are especially popular with British tourists. They consist of bread filled with grilled mutton, white cabbage, and a yogurt or spicy red sauce.

Regional Specialties

Oscypek is a smoked cheese made of salted sheep's milk and up to 40 percent cow's milk that has been a specialty of the Tatra mountain region since the 15th century. The cheese is poured into artistically decorated spindle-shaped molds.

Oscypek has been granted a regional designation by the European Union. It is sold directly by the farmers or by street vendors in Zakopane, a summer and winter resort town in the Tatras. It can be eaten cold or grilled and always accompanied by cranberries. A popular winter drink in Zakopane sold on the street is tea with rum.

Along the beaches of Poland's northern coast, holiday goers can enjoy freshly smoked fish, grilled sausages with sauerkraut, grilled pork shank, barbequed ribs, kebabs, and hot dogs sold by individual vendors or restaurants that prepare the dishes outside their stores.

COLLEEN TAYLOR SEN

ROMANIA

MODERN ROMANIA WAS ESTABLISHED IN 1918, after World War I, when a treaty added Transylvania to the provinces of Wallachia and Moldavia, but the country has a very long history. It straddles a huge plain that the Romans considered their breadbasket, and the Ottomans frequently crossed on their way west to attack the Vienna-based Hapsburgs and the Carpathians, a magnificent horseshoe-shaped mountain range that separates Western Europe from the East and the southeastern Mediterranean lands. This geography has dictated Romania's turbulent history and is the reason for its rich mixture of peoples—Romanians (who speak a Romance language descended from Latin), Hungarians, Saxons, Rroma (Romanian Roma), Jews, Armenians, Ukrainians—living in its villages, towns, and cities.

Romania is an agrarian country with communities proud of their traditions. Its short, hot summers are crammed full with festivals, and life is lived outside. Festival foods range from the modern and simple (corn on the cob, jacket potatoes) to the traditional (jam-filled pancakes, sweet and savory pies, meat grills)—all sold from stands that can be easily transported. Throughout the year, along busy city streets, vendors sell *covrigi* (bread rolls), *plăcinte* (pies), and grilled dishes—*şaorma* (gyros, or *döner kebab*) and *frigarui* (small kebabs). Both men and women sell street foods, but men usually work a grill. Some street foods are the preserve of a particular community—*kürtős kalács* ("chimney cake"), for instance, is sold by Hungarian-speaking Transylvanians.

During the long, often-harsh winter, hot pies, breads, chestnuts, and meat grills provide warmth and nourishment on city streets for working people, but there is little or no street food in villages or small towns, where it's easy to return home to eat. Excepting those who grill, and bakeries that have an outlet onto the street, vendors are mobile and go where the crowds are. Since 2007, when Romania joined the European Union, street foods have become increasingly regulated (often because of sanitation considerations), but with incomes remaining low, these inexpensive foods are a valuable source of sustenance to some and, at festivals, highly enjoyable for many, so are unlikely to disappear soon.

MAJOR STREET FOODS

Mici/Mititei

The name of these small spicy meat patties—*mici* or *mititei*—is said to derive from their origin. The story goes that sausages were a favorite dish at a popular mid-19th-century Bucharest inn. One night, with all the sausages eaten and the customers wanting more, the chef had to improvise. So he made little sausage-shaped patties out of his leftover meat and grilled them. The customers loved these wee ones without skins, and a national dish was born.

In fact, *mici* probably date from at least a hundred, if not many hundreds, of years earlier: the Ottomans had a centuries-long presence in Romania, and grilled ground meats were one of their popular, and common, street foods. *Mici*, seasoned with garlic, salt, pepper, summer savory or thyme, and paprika, are always grilled outside and served with mustard, pickles, and bread. Until two generations ago, *mici* grills were so ubiquitous in the streets of Bucharest that their grill smoke was said to be the city's defining symbol in much the same way as the Eiffel Tower represents Paris.

Covrigi

Covrigi are the ideal street food. Inexpensive, tasty, and easy to hold, these warm bread rolls, made from unsweetened dough and similarly shaped to pretzels, are topped with poppy seeds or sesame seeds and large salt grains. Toppings vary from region to region (plain salt is especially favored in central Romania), so *covrigi* are often given as holiday gifts by townspeople visiting their friends or family in rural areas.

It is said that *covrigi* were introduced to Romania by Greek merchants in the early 1800s, but their similarity to other Romanian pastries, and to the shape of German pretzels, suggests an earlier origin. The town of Buzău is known for its fine *covrigi*, and in 2007, the European Union accorded Buzău *covrigi* protected geographical status.

Kürtős Kalács

You will find *kürtős kalács* (*tulnic*, in Romanian)—"chimney cake" or "stove cake"—wherever there's a fair, a carnival, or any kind of street festivity in Transylvania, Romania's largest province.

This pretty and very popular pastry takes some skill to make. The cinnamon-spiced yeast dough is prepared hours earlier, rolled out into thin sheets, and cut into six-inch-wide strips. These are carefully wound around a long cylindrical spit, which the cook revolves over an open fire, all the time brushing the pastry with a sugar syrup to ensure it caramelizes evenly. With a sweet, crispy exterior and soft, smooth interior, and topped with chopped walnuts or almonds, *kürtős kalács* is a lovely sweet treat.

OTHER STREET FOODS

Plăcintă

Plăcintă (plural, *plăcinte*) means "cake," and its etymology suggests that it may have a Roman origin. *Plăcinte*—flat pies with sweet or savory fillings such as apple, cheese, jam, or sausage—are fried or baked and sold, wrapped in paper. Throughout Romania, they vary in size, shape, and fillings: along the Black Sea coast, *plăcintă dobrogeană* resembles *borek*, a small pie that's found throughout the old Ottoman-occupied lands.

Poale'n brâu

Poale'n brâu (sweet cheese and raisin rolls) are one of many kinds of sweet or savory pastries—stuffed with cabbage, cheese, ground meats—sold by street vendors. A specialty of the Moldova region, the colloquial translation of their name—"the bottom of the skirt raised to the waistband"—aptly describes the technique used to make them: the baker arranges a dollop of sweetened cheese and raisins in the center of a square of yeast dough, pulls up each side to enclose it, and bakes the pies until golden brown.

Clătită

Popular at festivals, these thin pancakes are sold with all sorts of sweet fillings— chocolate, jam, bananas, ice cream.

Şaorma

Şaorma, or gyros ("turned" in Greek, *döner* in Turkish), are as common and as popular in Romania as elsewhere throughout Europe. As the mixture of highly seasoned, finely ground beef, veal, chicken, or lamb slowly turns on an upright, revolving spit, the cook slices the meat onto a round of pita-like flatbread and smothers this in a warm, garlicky mayonnaise sauce. With side dishes of fried potatoes, sliced peppers, cabbage, onion, and tomatoes, they are an inexpensive, quick, and tasty snack.

Frigarui

Frigarui—kebabs of highly seasoned pork, beef, lamb, or chicken alternated with fatty bacon, sausages and onions, tomatoes, or bell peppers—are substantial, inexpensive, full-of-flavor street food, especially popular with students. The best are when the meat is marinated in a mixture of herbs, yogurt, garlic, lemon, sugar, ginger, and/or paprika.

ROSEMARY BARRON

RUSSIAN FEDERATION

F OR A COUNTRY LOCATED SO FAR NORTH ON THE GLOBE, Russia has a surprising number of street-food outlets, many of which do a thriving business even in winter. Vendors sell their wares on city streets that have heavy pedestrian traffic; at the entrances to subway, train, and bus stations; at ports for passenger ships; at open-air markets and around the perimeter of municipal covered markets; at city parks and amusement parks; and on beaches in summer. And for several centuries, street foods have been an integral part of many public festivals.

Many of the foods sold on the streets of Russia today reflect the long history of foreign influences on Russian cuisine. Trade with the Byzantine Empire from the 10th to 13th centuries added buckwheat, rice, cloves, and black pepper to the Russians' diet. From the mid-13th to late-16th centuries, Mongols originally from Central Asia ruled large areas of what is now Russia and introduced many foods previously unknown to the inhabitants of those regions: noodles and filled dumplings; sauerkraut and other pickled vegetables; citrus fruits, melons, figs, dried apricots, and raisins; sweet pastries and confections; spices such as cinnamon, cardamom, ginger, and saffron; *kumis* (fermented mare's milk) and, later, tea.

In the early 18th century, during the reign of Tsar Peter the Great, Russian cooking was influenced by ingredients and dishes introduced from Austria, Bavaria, Saxony, Holland, and Scandinavia, including coffee, brandy, chocolates, hard cheeses, little open-face sandwiches called *buterbrody* (buttered bread with various toppings), and potatoes (although potatoes did not become a staple of the Russian diet until the second half of the 19th century). In the 19th century, the expansion of the Russian Empire also brought new foods from the Caucasus and the Black Sea: olive oil, garlic, eggplants, tomatoes, bell peppers, skewered meat grilled over an open fire, a variety of meat- and cheese-filled pastries, and sweet wines. Some of these foreign culinary influences eventually found their way into the street foods of Russia. Street vendors in Russia sold small filled pies known as *pirozhki*; ring-shaped breads of various sizes (threaded on strings for portability); seasonal fruits such as apples and grapes; *sbiten'*, a hot drink made of honey and spices, dispensed from a big copper urn carried on the vendor's back; and steaming hot tea poured from large copper or brass kettles into reusable glasses provided by the vendors. Vendors also hawked their wares at open-air markets and seasonal trade fairs. Religious festivals were also the excuse to eat lots of rich street food, like *blini*.

After the establishment of the new Soviet Union in 1922, the economic and agricultural policies of the communist government resulted in many hardships for the people, including food shortages, which continued, to a greater or lesser degree, until the collapse of the Soviet Union in 1991. After World War II, the state gradually set up stands to sell ice cream, small savory pies, breads and pastries, *ponchiki* (the Russian version of doughnuts, puffy balls of deep-fried yeast dough sprinkled with sugar), and nonalcoholic drinks at train stations, parks, and a few street locations. Vending machines on the streets dispensed carbonated water, plain or mixed with berry syrup, into a communal cup that hung from a chain attached to each machine, with an apparatus for washing the cup before using it. Street vendors also sold *kvas*—a lightly alcoholic carbonated beverage brewed from rye bread, fruit, or berries—dispensed from little portable barrel-like containers that resembled miniature tanker trailers.

With the political collapse of the Soviet Union in 1991, its 15 constituent republics formed separate independent nations, one of which is the Russian Federation, geographically the largest country on earth. Although nearly 80 percent of the Russian Federation's 138 million people are ethnic Russians, street foods in today's Russia also reflect the culinary influences of other ethnic groups formerly living within the borders of the much larger Soviet Union, as well as contemporary Russians' desires for Western-style fast foods.

Russian-owned kiosks and small food trucks also sell their wares on the streets of many cities, and clusters of them can be found near subway, bus, and train station entrances. The largest chains include Kroshka Kartoshka (Little Potato), which sells baked potatoes topped with a variety of garnishes, and

Teremok (Fairytale Cottage), which advertises "Best *Blini* in Town," although its specialty is actually large thin *blinchiki*, the Russian version of French crêpes, offered with a choice of many toppings, from meat, cheese, fish, and caviar to berries, jam, and chocolate. Other street kiosks sell rotisserie chicken, small pizzas, boiled dumplings, smoked or grilled fish, or grilled meats. And even in winter, one of the most popular street foods in Russia is ice cream, sold at special ice-cream kiosks or by street-corner vendors.

MAJOR STREET FOODS

Pirozhki

Since at least the 17th century, *pirozhki* (singular *pirozhok*) have been the favorite street food in Russia. These little pies, small enough to be eaten by hand, consist of an outer layer of dough that completely encompasses a sweet or savory filling. Made with yeast-raised dough or flaky pastry dough containing butter or lard, *pirozhki* can be round, oval, square, rectangular, triangular, or semicircular in shape. They are either baked or fried. Savory fillings include seasoned ground meat, cheese, potatoes, onions, mushrooms, turnips, carrots, cabbage, sauerkraut, and rice. Sweet fillings are made of fresh or preserved fruits and berries, poppy seeds, nuts, and sweetened fresh curd cheese.

PIROZHKI

Chebureki are also popular little pies, which originated with the Crimean Tatars living near the Black Sea. Made of a thin layer of pasta dough filled with ground lamb or beef seasoned with onions, garlic, and parsley or cilantro, these half-moon or rectangular pies are always deep-fried. Both *pirozhki* and *chebureki* are sold by individual street vendors, who carry them in portable insulated metal boxes that keep the pies warm. These small pies are also commonly sold at farmers' markets, public festivals, and on railroad platforms.

Shashlyk

An ancient dish, well known to herders and nomads across a wide swath of the

Caucasus and Central Asia, *shashlyk* became popular in Russia in the mid-19th century after Georgia, Azerbaijan, and part of Armenia were absorbed into the Russian Empire. In those regions, *shashlyk* originally referred to cubes of grilled lamb cooked on skewers, whereas *basturma* was the grilled beef version of this dish. But Russians have broadened the term *shashlyk* to mean any kind of meat—pork, beef, lamb, venison—cut into cubes, marinated for several hours, threaded onto skewers, and cooked over hot coals. The marinade ingredients vary from region to region and from cook to cook—sunflower or olive oil, red or white wine, vinegar or pomegranate juice—seasoned with onions, garlic, and a variety of herbs and spices. *Shashlyk* is eaten across all of Russia, from the Baltic coast to Siberia and the Russian Far East. A popular food at public festivals and farmers' markets, *shashlyk* is also featured as a main course at many Russian restaurants and special *shashlyk* cafés and is a favorite food for picnics.

Morozhenoe

Ice cream (*morozhenoe*) is said to have been introduced into Russia from Western Europe in the 1700s, and by the mid-1800s, some Russian households even had their own hand-cranked ice-cream makers. In the 1930s, the Soviets started the large-scale production of commercial ice cream to be sold at kiosks in major cities. Ice cream became one of the most beloved of Russian street foods, almost as popular in winter as in summer. During the Soviet era, street vendors in winter sold unwrapped ice-cream cones, stacked in cardboard boxes, with no fear of their melting in the frigid air. Individually wrapped ice-cream bars imported from the West became fashionable in the early post-Soviet period, but many Russians still prefer traditional Russian-made products containing no artificial flavorings or other chemical additives. Chocolate, vanilla, and strawberry have traditionally been the flavors of choice, but customers now also flock to the Baskin-Robbins outlets in more than 80 Russian cities, which offer a total of 125 different flavors.

Blini

Blini (singular *blin*) are a type of Russian pancake traditionally made from a batter of buckwheat flour and yeast. From the 18th through 20th centuries, they were eaten primarily at the pre-Lenten festival of Maslenitsa, where people consumed huge quantities of *blini* freshly cooked by street vendors and topped with melted butter, sour cream, mushrooms, fish, caviar, fresh curd cheese, honey, or jam. Today *blini* are a year-round street food sold at many outlets, including the Teremok and *Russkoe blini* (Russian pancakes) chains of *blini* stands. Most contemporary street-food *blini* are actually *blinchiki*, the easier-to-make, nonleavened Russian version of French crêpes, made with wheat flour, which are wider, thinner, and lighter in color than traditional Russian buckwheat *blini*.

OTHER STREET FOODS

Shawarma

A more recent, very popular addition to the Russian street-food scene is shawarma, stacks of beef, lamb, chicken, or pork cooked on a rotating vertical spit (like Turkish *döner kebab* or Greek gyros). The meat is sliced off the spit and served inside a folded flatbread, garnished with sliced tomatoes, cucumbers, and onions, shredded cabbage, garlic-seasoned yogurt sauce, and sometimes dried hot red pepper flakes.

Pel'meni

Little boiled dumplings introduced to Russia by the Mongols, *pel'meni* not only are considered "the national dish of Siberia" but are also popular throughout Russia. Pockets of filled pasta dough formed into the shape of little ears, *pel'meni* are similar in shape and size to Italian cappelletti. The most common fillings are ground pork or beef combined with minced onions, but *pel'meni* can also be filled with fish, game, cheese, mushrooms, or fresh greens. *Pel'meni* are served hot, in bowls, garnished with butter, sour cream, Russian hot–spicy mustard, vinegar, or sometimes soy sauce. A street food traditionally served outdoors at winter festivals in Siberian villages, *pel'meni* can now be bought year-round at some kiosks and food trucks in Russian cities. *Vareniki* are the Ukrainian version, little half-moon-shaped boiled dumplings usually filled with cherries or fresh curd cheese.

Kartofel'

Potatoes (*kartofel'*) are a relative newcomer as a street food, although they have been a staple of the Russian diet since the second half of the 19th century. Vendors sold potato salad and boiled potatoes on railroad platforms in the 20th century, and French fries were popularized by the Western fast-food chains that have proliferated in Russia during the past 20 years. The Russian-owned

Kroshka Kartoshka (Little Potato) chain of kiosks specializes in selling baked potatoes served with a wide selection of toppings.

Chak-Chak

Some street foods in Russia are very regional, such as *chak-chak*, a favorite sweet sold at street stands in Tatarstan, a region bordering on the Volga and Kama rivers. *Chak-chak* consists of little cylinders or balls of egg flour dough deep-fried in butter or oil, drenched with honey or sugar syrup, and pressed into molds or formed by hand into fist-size cubes, balls, or pyramids.

Kvas

An ancient drink made in Russia for at least a thousand years, *kvas* is a slightly sweet, mildly alcoholic beverage brewed from rye (or other) bread, or from fruits or berries, combined with water, sugar, and yeast. Probably one of the earliest drinks sold by street vendors in Russia, *kvas* is still popular today. Since the mid-20th century, *kvas* has been dispensed on city streets from little blue or yellow portable metal barrels that resemble miniature tanker trailers with a spigot on one end. Vendors used to pour the *kvas* into small glasses (supposedly rinsed clean after each use), but now they use disposable plastic cups.

Western Fast Foods

During the past 20 years, Western fast-food chains have popularized many other foods that are now commonly eaten on the streets of Russia, including hamburgers, hot dogs and other sausages, French fries, and pizzas—all of which, in one form or another, originated in Europe before they became associated with giant American fast-food companies operating on a global scale. Many of these companies now have franchised outlets in Russia. Sausages were certainly sold as street foods in Russia long before the recent revival of a market economy there, but in the 21st century, a greater variety, and better quality, of sausages are now sold at Russian street stands, including sausage styles from Germany, Hungary, and Poland.

SHARON HUDGINS

UKRAINE

U KRAINE IS A LARGE COUNTRY IN EASTERN EUROPE bordered by seven other countries, the most important of which is Russia to the north and east. The country has coastlines to its south on the Black Sea and Sea of Azov. Major rivers run through it, the Dnieper and Dniester being the most important, both economically and historically. Ukraine has some varied landforms, but by far the most important are the vast fertile plains that are among the world's greatest wheat producers. Temperate climate with cold winters and warm summers allows for good agriculture, while the southern coast has a warmer Mediterranean climate that permits wine production and tourism.

Although most Ukrainians consider themselves as belonging to the same ethnic group, various people have passed through what has been called the "crossroads of Eastern Europe," and some have remained. Ukraine is significant in Russian history because the first Russian state began in Kiev in the 9th century. Scandinavian warriors and merchants who sailed up and down the Dnieper River were called "Ruotsi," thus giving their name to the future country to the north. The Kievan state later fell to Mongols in the 12th century and after that was ruled by Lithuanian and Polish monarchies. Through most of the 20th century, the country was in the Union of Soviet Socialist Republics, but with the collapse of that political body in 1991, Ukraine became an independent country. Today, there is a significant Russian minority, most of who live in the eastern parts of the country and urban areas such as Kiev and Odessa on the Black Sea. A smaller population of Tatars—remnants of the old Mongol Empire—now lives in the Crimean Peninsula, a region annexed to Russia in 2015. Although the Ukrainian language is close to Russian, it has many dialects within it and loanwords from Polish and Russian. Naturally, all the people who have been in and through Ukraine have left their marks on the country's cuisine.

Important as outside influences have been in Ukrainian food, there are two anchors to which it is moored: religion and bread with potatoes. Most Ukrainians belong to a branch of the Eastern Orthodox churches. Like Greeks, Russians, and many others of similar faith, Ukrainians have elaborate festivals at the major holidays, Easter and Christmas being the most important. Many characteristic dishes made at home appear for sale in public around churches and squares so no street-food scene is complete without this holiday fare.

As for bread and potatoes, these are the foundation of life in the Ukraine. Wheat has been grown in the Ukraine for almost 7,000 years, and today many kinds of breads and wheat-based pastries are made and sold. Traditionally, when someone enters a Ukrainian home, they are offered a *rushnyc*, a small round white bread and salt, to be eaten on the spot. White breads, rolls, rye breads (made with a wheat and rye mixture), brown breads, and rolls, some with herbs, in many shapes are readily available from shops and small restaurants. The greatest bread glory comes on the holidays when special fancy versions are made. *Kalach* is made from three long strands of dough, representing the Holy Trinity, braided together and baked. *Paska* is a round sweet bread, often with shapes made of dough on it in the forms of crosses, flowers, or eggs. *Babkai* is a tall cylindrical sweet bread often baked with raisins and dried fruits that is another Easter specialty.

MAJOR STREET FOODS

Dumplings

Wheat dough is used as wrappers for Ukraine's most popular street food, dumplings. These are commonly sold in such public places as train stations, squares, and parks, often by older women called *babtia* (grandmothers). The kerchiefs that they often wear on their heads are called *babushkas* in Russian, a term commonly used throughout Eastern Europe for women street vendors. *Perohy, varenyky,* and *pyrizhky* are all forms of savory pastries that are boiled or fried before serving. They can be filled with mashed potatoes, onions, ground meats, chopped cabbage, and mushrooms and are often served with sour cream and dill. Mushrooms are very important in Ukrainian cuisine and used in a great many dishes.

Holubtsi

Holubtsi are cabbage rolls—boiled cabbage leaves filled with rice or rice and chopped meat, then rolled up and steamed or cooked in a thin tomato sauce, and served with sour cream. *Holubtsi* and dumplings are always found at Eastertime, sold by women of each church, and eaten before and after services.

Perepichka

One really popular specialty is called *perepichka*. A specialty of Kiev that is now found across the country, this is a sausage wrapped in the kind of dough used in *varenyki* and then deep-fried.

Central Asia and the Crimea where Turkic-speaking Tatars live have influenced Ukrainian street food. One of their dishes is *shashlik*, skewers of beef or lamb often threaded with onions, tomatoes, and sweet peppers that are cooked on open grills, preferably charcoal-fired, on streets across the country. They are served either plain or with chewy white bread or rolls. Because the meat is already marinated with paprika as an ingredient, sauces are not usually served with the *shashlik*. But if the vendor prepares the dish in the popular Georgian style, then a plum sauce is sure to accompany it.

OTHER STREET FOODS

Potatoes

Though potatoes came into wide use only in the 18th and 19th centuries, they are served with almost every meal at home. Several fast-food chains and local restaurants in Kiev and other cities serve baked potatoes that are mashed and topped with fried mushrooms, herring, sour cream, cottage cheese, shredded vegetables, and more. Urban fast-food restaurants modeled on western hamburger chains always have French fries and other forms of potatoes.

Chebureki

Half-moon-shaped *chebureki*, Central Asian versions of dumplings filled with lamb, mushrooms, and other ingredients, are deep-fried and sold on the streets of Kiev, Odessa, and other cities.

Beverages

Popular drinks include international soft drinks and local versions. Two specialties are not much found outside of Eastern Europe: *kvas* and *uzvar*. *Kvas* is a mildly alcoholic drink made from dried rye bread, yeast, and water, which is allowed to ferment overnight. *Uzvar* is made from dried fruits such as apples and plums that are steeped in water with sugar. Both are very popular and almost always sold at festivals and fairs.

BRUCE KRAIG

NORTHERN EUROPE

DENMARK

ENMARK IS A SMALL COUNTRY located on a peninsula bounded by the Atlantic Ocean and the Baltic Sea. As a result, most of the year, it is cold, wet, or windy. Most people live near their workplace, and with short commute times, breakfast usually is eaten at home. Lunch is normally a cold meal, often a home-made lunch pack with open sandwiches or a meal in the canteen at work or at school. The famous Danish *smørrebrød*, an open-faced sandwich, is eaten at lunch in restaurants or brought home and eaten with a knife and fork. Cakes and Danish pastries are bought at the baker's and brought home for coffee or eaten at a café where it is warmer than outside. For most people, supper is the hot meal of the day.

Until a few decades ago, eating out was only for special occasions. In the last 30 years, increasing wealth has opened up new possibilities for eating out, especially in the cities. Street food is not very widespread, and most of it is international food sold via fast-food chains. Street food is limited to snacks and intermediate meals like hot dogs, an apple, candy, chocolate bars, ice cream, and cold drinks.

MAJOR STREET FOODS

The Wiener Cart

An exception to the relative absence of street food is the wiener cart, or *pølsevogn*, which has become a symbol of Danishness. It offers a cheap, fast meal, and people from all layers of society occasionally buy a meal here. The carts roll out mostly during the daytime and sometimes at night, especially during weekends outside train and bus stations and other busy places.

The wiener cart came to Denmark from Germany in 1921, when six mobile carts were set up in Copenhagen, and in the beginning, only wieners and buns were sold. Wiener carts quickly spread to smaller towns, where they became places of rendezvous for young people. A wiener cart is mobile and completely self-sufficient. It does not need mains and water supplies, and has gas and batteries that run 24 hours on a single charge. It is motorized and can be packed up in 15 minutes. Vendors in Copenhagen and in some other municipalities are given priority in getting licenses if they have disabilities. In the second largest city, Aarhus, most wiener carts are run by the Children's Office, a charity for troubled children. This rule is fading, however, as hot dogs have become ever more popular—something like 4,500 carts in the country, many owned by the Steff Houlberg/Tulip corporation.

The first wiener carts sold a pork-based red-colored wiener, served with mustard and wrapped in greaseproof paper for 25 øre (about 5 U.S. cents). Those who wanted bread with it bought a 5-øre roll. Because the red coloring agent can cause allergies, it was banned in Denmark in 1981. Since the red color is important to Danes, today's hot dog sausages are allowed to be colored because they are dyed with nonallergenic cochineal. The types of sausages offered on carts have expanded greatly over the years. Sausages with a roll typically consist of roast sausages, red sausages, larger frankfurters, sausages wrapped in bacon, Danish pork sausage, and spicy sausages with garlic and chilies. They are served with tomato ketchup, sweet and strong mustard, and raw or fried onions.

Because of the immigration from Muslim countries, the halal sausage was introduced in 2002 to adhere to Islamic food rules. It is sold with the same kind of accompaniments as the ordinary Danish sausage. Some frankfurter carts are organic and a few sell vegan sausages.

Hot Dogs and French Hot Dogs

Hot dogs are considered to be one of several sausage types, unlike in the United States. Typically, it is a pork and beef frankfurter placed inside a roll of bread. Back in 1921, the sausage was put inside a day-old roll that was kept warm by the same heated containers used for sausages. In 1951, master baker Julius Paaskesen began baking oblong hot dog rolls for Copenhagen vendors, and the hot dog got its present look. Traditionally, a hot dog is a half-sectioned roll, a frankfurter, raw or fried onions, ketchup, mustard and sometimes rémoulade (a cold, yellow sauce made from mayonnaise and pickles), and pickled cucumbers or cucumber salad. There are regional differences, and in the provinces, it is not uncommon to offer red cabbage instead of cucumber salad. In Denmark, people prefer the sausage to be longer than the roll, although in other countries, the roll and the sausage have the same length.

Some carts also sell sandwiches with roast pork loin, burgers or meatballs, *frikadeller*, and "hand-deller"—a handheld *frikadelle*. Such nonalcoholic beverages as cold cocoa milk are sold from the cart.

A French hot dog is a frankfurter in a hollowed-out bread, an instant success from the moment it was introduced in 1983. The sauce is a mayonnaise-based dressing or ketchup. It is sold in a paper case and is easier to carry than an ordinary hot dog. The French hot dog is designed for people who do not want to be seen eating at a cart or who think ordinary hot dogs are too messy.

In later years, there has been more focus on gourmet hot dogs with homemade dressings and unique combinations. For some years, chefs have competed in making the best hot dog of the year.

Pork Loin Sandwich

Pork loin sandwiches are popular at Christmas markets, grill bars, select wiener carts, and festivals. They are made with thin slices of roasted pork laid on bread slices that have been spread with mayonnaise or rémoulade. Sandwiches are topped with crisp cracklings (fried pork skin), pickles, sour–sweet red cabbage, and sometimes pickles or raw apple. The quality varies greatly, depending on the bread, meat, and garnish used.

Handheld Bottled Beer

In Denmark, it is socially acceptable to drink a cold beer from the bottle on squares, in parks, or on the quays of the many small harbors. It is common to see people meeting in these public places to have a beer and a chat.

Ice-Cream Cones

Since they live in a large dairy-producing country, Danes know a lot about ice-cream creations. During summer, old-fashioned ice-cream cones with scoops of ice cream are very popular. They can be elaborate, topped with *guf* (Italian meringue) or whipped cream, jam, and maybe a cream puff. Many vendors have their own cone bakeries.

Smoked Herring

On the island of Bornholm, herring are traditionally smoked during summer in smoke houses along the coast and served with raw egg yolk, chives, sliced radish, rye bread, and often with a beer.

Æbleskiver (Apple Doughnuts)

Æbleskiver is one of the oldest festive foods in Denmark. They are baked in special frying pans with hollows and may be filled with apple, prunes, raisins, and so on. They are eaten with icing sugar and jam. Often they are industrially produced, but at many Christmas markets, they are cooked in the classical way. These days it is a seasonal food from November until January. *Æbleskiver* is often served with a warm drink, glogg, which is a variation of German *Glühwein*, hot red or white wine mixed with spices and served with raisins and almonds, and sometimes seasoned with port wine, rum, or brandy. Nonalcoholic variations are served too.

Festival Food

At the annual international music festival at Roskilde, local clubs sell a broad range of food: everything from Thai food to burgers and vegan food. The pork loin sandwich is a great hit here too.

Other Vendors and International Food

Street food is sold at market squares all over the country, usually during summer on specific days and around Christmas. Most snacks are sold from gas stations, pizza bars, kebab bars, convenience stores such as 7-Eleven, and supermarkets with ready-made meals. All these places are staffed by non-skilled employees.

International food has poured into Denmark for the last 30 years, and a number of fast-food chains have become part of the street scene. The first international burger bar, Burger King, came to Denmark in the 1970s, and the first shawarma bar in 1980. There are similar vendors in towns all over the country, selling burgers, sandwiches, pizza slices, falafels, durum, kebab, China boxes, and pancakes. Some street vendors sell roast chestnuts and burned almonds in the fall. During summertime, disposable or small portable barbecues are used for grilling sausages, grilled fresh corn and more appear in town parks everywhere.

KATRINE KLINKEN

ICELAND

I CELAND IS AN ISLAND IN THE NORTH ATLANTIC OCEAN, just touching the Arctic Circle. Because even the summers are fairly cold and often windy and wet, this is not a climate that will spark a rich street-food culture.

The country was settled in the 9th and 10th centuries AD, mostly by Norwegians and other Scandinavians, although recent gene research indicates that a large portion of the women they brought with them came from the British Isles. Despite this, there is very little Celtic influence to be found in traditional Icelandic cooking. It is Scandinavian in origin but heavily influenced by the harsh climate and conditions of this remote land that was for centuries at the very edge of the known world. Almost no grain was grown in Iceland, nor any vegetables or fruits. There was a lack of firewood, and even salt was scarce and expensive, so the Icelanders developed their own methods of preserving food, mostly by covering it with soured whey or *skyr*, a yogurt-like dairy product. The settlers brought pigs, but they gradually disappeared so Icelanders ate mainly lamb and mutton.

During the first thousand years of Iceland's history, not only was street food virtually unknown but so were taverns, inns, and even street markets. There were no villages, no places where food of any kind could be bought, except at the farms themselves. During the summer, a few ships braved the treacherous seas between Iceland and Europe to trade with the locals and markets sprung up at several harbor sites. There may have been food stalls, but no one knows for sure what they offered.

The modern culinary history of Iceland can be said to begin in the mid- or late

19th century, when villages and small towns began to appear along the coast. The upper class of these villages, merchants and craftsmen, were mostly Danish and Norwegian, and they brought with them their food culture. Upper-class Icelanders that returned after receiving their education in Copenhagen joined them in having a great influence on Icelandic food. Most of the dishes today considered old-fashioned home cooking are Danish in origin, sometimes with an Icelandic twist: they are made with lamb instead of pork, for instance.

MAJOR STREET FOODS

Hot Dogs

Hot dogs are the most popular street food in Denmark and in Iceland; Danish-style hot dogs are the only real street food. They are very popular and can be bought almost anywhere. There are a few stands in Reykjavík and some larger towns that sell only hot dogs and cold sodas, but they are also sold at many small shops, gas stations, and virtually every roadside shop around the country. In many cases, they will be the only hot food available to travelers.

An Icelandic hot dog (*pylsa*) is always a wiener. The most popular brand is made from a mixture of lamb, beef, and pork although other brands may be made from pork or a pork and beef mixture. Traditionally, it is simmered in water although some vendors now cook it on a flat grill. The only equipment needed is a hot dog cooker with two compartments, one for simmering the wieners and the other for steaming the buns.

The *pylsa* is served in an elongated bun or small bread that is split almost into two, along with a choice of toppings. The most popular are tomato ketchup, mild gravy-like mustard, rémoulade, crunchy fried onions, and raw chopped onions, and that is exactly what customers who ask for "one with everything" will get, even if the stall offers other types of toppings as well. They may include pickled gherkins, chile sauce, cocktail sauce, Dijon mustard, potato salad, or even a creamy mayo-based shrimp salad. Grilled hot dogs may also be bacon-wrapped.

The best-known hot dog stall in Iceland is without doubt Bæjarins Beztu, a small shack in downtown Reykjavík that has been run by the same family since 1937. There is always a line, even in pouring rain, but the clientele changes through the day: first businessmen or laborers grabbing a late breakfast or quick lunch, then tourists or hungry locals on their way home from work, youths on their way to a movie or people going to a bar. On weekends, the stall stays open until 4.30 a.m. to serve people enjoying Reykjavík's boisterous night life. There are no fancy extras here, just the basic toppings. The stall has had some famous clients, and those who ask for a "Clinton" will get a hot dog with mustard, which is what former U.S. president Bill Clinton had when he stopped by.

Sandwiches

Many shops and stalls sell various types of prepacked sandwiches and sometimes have a microwave oven or grill so hungry customers can warm the sandwiches they buy. Although there are also hamburger stalls, none of the international chains are represented. (McDonald's left Iceland after the economic crash of 2008.) Downtown Reykjavík has two very popular submarine and sandwich shops: Hlöllabátar at Ingólfstorg (and now at various other locations around the country) and Nonnabiti in Hafnarstræti. Both serve juicy submarine sandwiches with meat, seafood, cheese, and various other fillings. Each has its own secret sauce, and both are extremely popular with late-night revelers. But no truly local street food has emerged, despite various attempts to create versions of popular traditional dishes, like *plokkfiskur* (mashed fish).

There is one exception, although it is more a takeaway than actual street food. BSÍ, the bus terminal near downtown Reykjavík, has a cafeteria, Fljótt Og Gott, that operates an all-night drive-through counter selling snacks, beverages, hot dogs, hamburgers, and more and was for many years the only place in the capital where you could get anything to eat after midnight. Their specialty is *kjammi og kók*, a halved lamb's head, singed and boiled, served cold with a bottle of Coke. The popularity of the dish is said to have soared after the movie *Jar City* was released in 2006, as its main character, world-weary policeman named Erlendur, often stopped by BSÍ to buy himself a *kjammi* to munch on.

NANNA RÖGNVALDARDÓTTIR

NORWAY

N ORWAY IS A MOUNTAINOUS COUNTRY with only small areas of arable land along the coast and in the valleys. The coastline is long, with fjords cutting deep into the land. The Gulf Stream provides a better climate than could otherwise be expected in a northern country. Still, the growing season is short, and the soil is unproductive during much of the year.

Transport along the coast and to inland areas used to be difficult for much of the year. This made it necessary to rely on conserving food for later use. Farm animals were usually slaughtered in the autumn: the meat would keep better during the cold season. The harvesting of foods from the ocean, lakes, forests, and mountains was also seasonal. Fish, game, and wild berries had to be conserved for use during the rest of the year.

The concept of street food is little known in Norway. The term *gatemat*, a literal translation, is in use on the Internet, but it is almost exclusively used to describe street food in foreign countries. No foods are exclusively street foods. More often, these foods will be classified as either *hurtigmat* (fast food) or *gatekjøkkenmat* (street kitchen food), but both terms include foods eaten in a simple restaurant and takeaway food.

Eating meals at home is the rule. When going to work or to school, everyone, from schoolchildren to managing directors, used to bring a packed lunch, a *matpakke*, consisting of paper-wrapped slices of buttered bread with spreads like cheese, ham, or pork liver paste. The packed lunch is still common, but is gradually replaced by canteen food. Both the abundance of packed lunches and a rather cold climate may be reasons why street food does not have a long tradition in Norway.

The first hot dog carts and vendors arrived from Germany early in the 20th century. Other foods and ways of selling them were imported in the 1950s and 1960s, mostly from the United States, including street kitchens, snack bars, and grills. Pizza restaurants followed in the 1970s and hamburger restaurants in the 1980s.

Fish and chips were an early import from the United Kingdom, but never caught on to the same extent. However, Fishanbua in Kristiansund, whose most popular food is *fishan* (fish and chips), may well be the oldest still existing street-food venue in Norway. It was established in 1950 and still goes on, though with new owners and in a new location.

Baked goods are generally not considered street food or fast food with a few exceptions. *Skoleboller* or *skolebrød* (literally school buns or bread) are large sweet buns with icing, grated coconut, and a custard eye. These are sometimes known locally under different names like *12-øres* (named after the original price) in Kristiansand or *purker* (literally "sows") in Arendal. A healthier and very popular choice is to buy a basket of fresh strawberries or sweet cherries when they are in season.

Young people eat street food and other fast food more frequently than adults. Thirty percent of young Norwegians say that they eat in such places at least once a month. Only a few percent do so more than once a week. However, young people are gradually becoming more health conscious and avoid this kind of food. Healthier choices also appear more frequently on the menus of fast-food outlets.

Both production and sales of street foods tend to be moving away from the streets. More and more products come ready-made from an industrial producer and are simply heated up by the retailer. Small independent vendors are disappearing and being replaced by chain outlets with a wider range of products, where street foods are just a small portion of their sales. The international chain 7-Eleven has more than 100 outlets in Norway. Deli de Luca is a more upmarket Norwegian chain with 28 shops so far. Gas stations today are small stores with a large selection of groceries and a wide variety of hot dogs, hamburgers, pizza, and other fast-food items.

The Norwegian Food Safety Authority, Mattilsynet, is the governmental body responsible for the safety of food and drinking water. Norway is not a member of the European Union (EU), but is required to adopt much of the EU legislation due to our participation in the European Economic Area. There are three main regulations founded on the Norwegian food act, Matloven. These are the regulations on internal control (*internkontrollforskriften*), the regulation on the production of and trade in foodstuffs (*forskrift for produksjon og omsetning av næringsmidler*), and the regulation on food hygiene (*næringsmiddelhygieneforskriften*).

MAJOR STREET FOODS

Hot Dogs

Hot dogs, *varme pølser*, are most often served on a bun, *pølse i brød*. Or you may have it rolled up in a thin soft bread instead, *pølse i lompe*. A local variation in Moss, a coastal city, is to serve the hot dogs in a sweet waffle, *pølse i vaffel*. Various kinds of sausages are on offer, the most popular being wiener and grilled sausages. A variety of toppings and condiments are available. Some people like ketchup and/or mustard only, others ask for raw onions, fried (soft or crispy) onions, or cucumber relish. More unusual is *rekesalat*, a salad of shrimp and chopped vegetables in mayonnaise.

Kebab

Kebab has become very popular in recent years. Kebab in Norway most often means *döner kebab* or shawarma. Usually ground meat or even mechanically separated meat rather than slices of whole meat is put on the spit. Lamb, beef, or chicken is the preferred meat. In eastern Norway, the kebab is served in a pita bread; in western Norway, it is wrapped in a thin soft bread, called *rullekebab*. The main salad ingredients are Chinese cabbage, cucumber, onion, and sweet corn, dunked in tomato and chile dressing, sour cream and garlic, or both.

Ice Cream

Despite the cool climate, ices are popular as street food—perhaps because Norwegians like to celebrate the arrival of warmer spring days with something cold. Soft serve, *softis*, is particularly popular on the street. You can have it in a cone or in a cup, with a choice of different toppings. Any number of other ices are also available: ice creams and fruit ices; on a stick, in a cone, or in a paper cup; plain, with strawberry, chocolate, or lots of other flavors.

OTHER STREET FOODS

Fish Cakes

Fiskekaker are panfried cakes made from fish forcemeat. Most often they are made with saithe (*Pollachius virens*) or haddock (*Melanogrammus aeglefinus*), but many other kinds of fish can be used. *Fiskemat* is the generic term for fish forcemeat and the products made from it. The city of Bergen has had a number of shops specializing in *fiskemat*. Søstrene Hagelin is one of these, where people still pop in to buy a few fish cakes to eat on the go.

Shrimp

Shrimp trawlers are a common sight in some coastal towns, and whenever possible, people take the opportunity to buy freshly cooked shrimp, *reker*, directly from the boat. There is no street food fresher and healthier than that.

FRESH SHRIMP

Waffles

Norwegian waffles, *vafler*, are made in a round waffle iron where each waffle easily separates into five heart-shaped pieces, *vaffelhjerter*. Waffles are eaten with a topping of butter, sour cream, and/or jam.

OVE FOSSÅ

SWEDEN AND FINLAND

S WEDEN LIES ON THE EASTERN SIDE of the Scandinavian Peninsula. On the west and north it borders Norway and on its northeastern border it merges with Finland. Together the countries form what is known as the Fennoscandian region. Although Swedes and Finns speak different languages, the two countries were under Swedish royal rule for 650 years and share many featuers of culture and cuisine. Trade across the Gulf of Bothnia has always been strong, there is a long-standing population of Swedes in Finland, and Swedish is one of Finland's official languages.

The countries are the northernmost in Europe and have similar climates. Due to the Gulf Stream the southern parts of Fennoscandia have surprisingly mild climates. They are pleasantly warm in summer and places like Gotland do not average much below freezing in winter; Helsinki is colder in winter. The northern areas, however, move up to the Arctic Circle where long, cold winters prevail. Sweden has much more agricultural land than Finland and before the later 19th century was a mainly agricultural country. Recurring famines led to heavy migration to North America in the decades around 1900. Around 1.5 million Swedish and Finnish immigrants settled in the Midwest, especially Minnesota, and their descendants still eat characteristic dishes at every holiday and festival, such as preserved fish—*lutefisk* in Swedish, *livekala* or *lipeäkala* in Finnish—and flatbread—Swedish *lefse, rieska* in Finnish.

The historical regional cultures of Sweden and Finland are reflected in their foods. Sweden's main population centers, including Stockholm, Malmö, and

Gothenburg, are along the coast. Naturally fish is a major part of the Swedish diet as it is in Finland. Both countries have major commercial fishing industries that produce salt water fish. They also have many freshwater lakes and streams that provide fish for home and public cooking. The crops in both countries (mainly wheat, barley, rye, and oats) were unpredictable, so when potatoes were introduced in the 18th century. they became a core of peoples' diets and populations greatly increased. Northern berries, such as cloudberries and lingonberries, as well as mushrooms are also important parts of northern cuisine.

One group in the northern parts of the Scandinavian peninsula called Lapps in Finland and Sami in Sweden, followed a nomadic way of life. Around 1500 they domesticated reindeer and lived as herders following their flocks seasonally. Today few Sami are reindeer herders, and reindeer meat is a specialty on Finnish and Swedish tables.

Both Sweden and Finland are highly developed industrial countries. Their average incomes and quality of life quotients are among the highest in the world. As a result, street food is not an essential part of peoples' nutrition as it is in lesser developed nations. It is usually a quick snack on the run or enjoyed while shopping or strolling on streets and in parks; it is also an important element of fairs and festivals. Street foods are sold mainly from kiosks and occasionally from food trucks. In Finland wood box-like kiosks called *grilli,* located in city urban spaces such as railway stations and parks, sell everything from hot dogs to newspapers. They are especially popular at night for theater and movie goers and after drinking parties. In the last few years food trucks with more diverse food options have been arriving on the streets of major cities. Sometimes they are owned by enterprising Finns bringing in new ideas, or immigrants supplying Middle Eastern and Southern U.S. foods (such as falafel and pulled pork, respectively) as well as traditional Finnish favorites.

MAJOR STREET FOODS

Fish

Fish sandwiches of various kinds are among the most popular street foods in Sweden and Finland. *Strömming*, or herring, is the very symbol of Swedish fish because it comes from the Baltic Sea. Boned and filleted herring is fried or pickled and served on hard or soft bread from kiosks. Mashed potatoes are often an accompaniment. Herring is often sold from a *strommingsvagnen*, or "herring wagon." Food service trailers are stationed in many squares and subway stations in Stockholm. Customers can buy herring burgers or fried herring, usually with hard rye bread and covered with onions, mustard, and dill.

In Finland, herring is also popular, but salmon even more so. Stalls in the marketplaces scattered throughout Helsinki sell *graavilohi* (pickled salmon) sliced and served on hard rye bread topped with mustard and onions. Sometimes *loimulohi* (blazing salmon) appears. It is prepared by placing long filets of salmon on boards and roasting them in front of an open fire. This ancient way of cooking makes for a distinctive flavor. *Muikku* ("vendace" in England and Scotland) is a small fish that lives in fresh or brackish-water lakes and marsh areas. It is a specialty at the great weekly Senaatintori market in Helsinki where big batches are fried in a huge four-foot wok. The tent-stands where it is sold are usually jammed with customers, who eat the fish whole, like sardines.

Hot Dogs and Sausages

Called *korv* or *korv med bröd* in Sweden and *makkara* in Finland, sausages served as hot dogs from kiosks in every city are probably the most popular street food. The basic hot dog is a longish sausage, mildly seasoned, grilled, put on a bun, and served with toppings. Mustard and ketchup are common, but Swedish *korv* often comes with mashed potatoes and sometime a shrimp salad on top. Other kinds of sausage, either grilled or boiled, are also sold at kiosks. Some are mixtures of processed meats and potatoes or grains. *Makkarat* often have so many more fillings than meat that Finns jokingly call them a "vegetable." Potato sausages are a famous Swedish holiday dish, often served with a dilled cream sauce. In the 1970s, meat-and-barley sausages called *ryynimakkara* (much like Polish *kiszka*) were very popular.

Döner kebabs

Meats packed into a vertical spit and roasted while it revolves is a Middle Eastern specialty that has arrived in Scandinavia mainly through Turkey and Greece. Popular across the world, this dish is now found in food stands throughout Sweden and Finland.

Seasonal Pop-Up Kiosks

Locally sourced and sustainable foods have become passions of Swedes and

Finns. When the growing season starts, pop-up stands appear in cities and countryside in both countries. The new potato crop followed by strawberries, sugar peas, blueberries, arctic cloud berries, and other fruits and vegetables are bought enthusiastically and eaten on the spot like street food.

Coffee

Finland has the highest per capita coffee consumption rate in the world and Sweden is not far behind. Swedes joke that they prefer it to water. Coffee is sold at every food kiosk, at coffee stands and from vending machines at all times of the day or night. *Fika* is a somewhat formal coffee institution in both countries. It is a break during the day when people socialize, always accompanied by coffee and usually pastries or cookies. *Fika* is an important social event in people's everyday lives, and it is fueled by coffee.

Wraps and Other Street Foods

Tunnbrödsrulle is a very common Swedish street food. It is thin soft bread with small holes that is filled, rolled up, and eaten out of hand. Various fillings include the inevitable mashed potatoes, meats, including sausage (called *tunnbröd*) or various fish such as herring, salmon, or shrimp salad. One of the most famous versions consists of two small sausages, mashed potatoes, onions, pickles, lettuce, tomatoes, mustard, ketchup, and shrimp salad. This is a meal in itself and popular in cold weather. Finnish equivalents include several kinds of sandwiches and wrapped dishes. *Grilli* are famous for greasy sandwiches, especially made with ground meats. Among others are *porilainen* (flatbread filled with a thick slab of sausage layered with pickled cucumber, mustard, ketchup, and *karjalanpiirakka*, a popular snack consisting of rice, potato, or carrot filling partially wrapped in a very thin rye bread. It is topped with an egg butter mixture, butter, or nothing at all. A regional dish from the east of Finland sold in the Helsinki market is *sultsina*, a crêpe-like flatbread made of barley that is rolled up with wheat porridge. *Muurinpohjalettu* is very similar to *sultsina* and can be filled with jelly, whipped cream, or salty porridge.

Other dishes include *pyttipannu* (a kind of hash made with all sorts of ingredients from potatoes, vegetables, beef or sausage with a fried egg on top), *lihapiirakka* (meat pie), *lihapulla* Finnish meatballs with French fries and condiments are sold at kiosks in that country while in Sweden, the world-famous Swedish meatballs are also to be found.

BRUCE KRAIG AND ROB ROUNDS

SOUTHERN EUROPE

THE BALKANS

T HE BALKANS (sometimes called the Balkan Peninsula) is an area in South-eastern Europe surrounded by the Adriatic Sea on the west, the Mediter-ranean Sea on the south, and the Black Sea on the east, with the Danube, Sava, and Kupa rivers as the country's northern boundary. It is a mountainous region, which affects the ethnic/national makeup, as well as the kinds of foods eaten by people there. Within the Balkans are the nations of Albania, Bosnia and Herze-govina, Bulgaria, Greece, Kosovo, Macedonia, Montenegro, Croatia, Serbia, Slo-venia, and in the past, Romania. Except for Albania, Greece, and Romania, the Balkan nations speak Slavic languages

Because of centuries of shared history, much of it under the rule of the Ot-toman Empire (1299–1923 CE), food throughout the region has many similar-ities. The subtle differences are sometimes detectable only by a connoisseur of the food of the region. Street food is most prominent in those countries/regions where the traditions of the Ottoman Empire are most apparent: Bosnia and Herzegovina, Bulgaria, Kosovo, Macedonia, Montenegro, and Serbia. Croatia and Slovenia were under Ottoman rule for a short period and then part of the Austrian–Hungarian Empire, and this is reflected in their culinary traditions.

Although the street-food culture of the Balkans is not as important as in some other European countries, it is gaining in popularity with the advent of Western fast food. This combination of old traditions and new trends offers a unique picture of food consumption in urban spaces. Thus, *burek* (traditional Ottoman filled pastries) can be found throughout the region alongside such global foods as pizza and hamburgers. While *burek* is a typical Balkan food, there are countless ways of preparing it, some of which became the standard in each country.

Western-style fast food is very popular among the younger generation, but street food is liked by everyone. Many street foods are part of the national diets and are enjoyed by people of all ages and walks of life. Street food is consumed throughout the day: as a late breakfast/early lunch for working people, high school and university students; as a late-night snack before or after going out; or as a cheaper option to a restaurant meal.

Unemployment is fairly widespread in the region, and selling food is sometimes a means of self-employment, although it yields a relatively low income, especially for mobile or fixed carts that sell such foods as *gevrek*, sesame ring, *perek*, or pretzel, seeds and nuts, cold drinks, popcorn, pancakes, mini-doughnuts, cotton candy, corn on the cob, and roasted chestnuts. However, much of what is considered street food in the Balkans is sold in such registered business establishments as bakeries, mini markets, grocery stores, fast-food restaurants, and green market stalls. Vending machines are almost nonexistent in the Balkans with some exceptions (in Slovenia, some office spaces, airports). Generally, street food is considered safe and sanitary, especially when it is sold in semi-closed or closed eateries or shops.

Some foods are sold throughout the region with no or minor differences among them. They include such seasonal foods as boiled corn on the cob, which is usually sold during the summertime, but increasingly in other seasons. Corn is cooked and sold in special mobile carts, wrapped in paper and eaten with salt. Another seasonal food is roasted chestnuts, which are cooked and sold directly in the street in paper cones from October through late December. Crêpes are thin pancakes, usually sweet and filled with jam, honey, sugar, nuts, or chocolate spread. They can also be savory and/or coated in bread crumbs and deep-fried. Crêpes are sold in special shops or on street corners, where they are cooked on the spot on special hot plates.

Popcorn and cotton candy are popular in all Balkan countries and typically sold in amusement parks, fairs, on city squares and promenades. In Macedonia, mini-doughnuts are a common outdoor food.

A relatively new food gaining in popularity throughout the region are *fornetti*, small puff pastries, with sweet (jam, chocolate) or savory (cheese, mince, spinach, mushrooms) fillings. Fornetti is also the name of the bakery chain that sells them. Standard accompaniments are *boza*, a thick sweet, slightly acidic

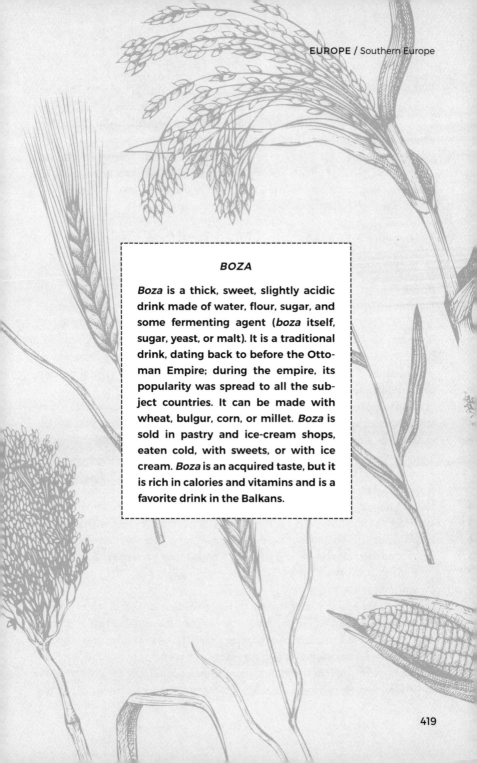

BOZA

Boza is a thick, sweet, slightly acidic drink made of water, flour, sugar, and some fermenting agent (*boza* itself, sugar, yeast, or malt). It is a traditional drink, dating back to before the Ottoman Empire; during the empire, its popularity was spread to all the subject countries. It can be made with wheat, bulgur, corn, or millet. *Boza* is sold in pastry and ice-cream shops, eaten cold, with sweets, or with ice cream. *Boza* is an acquired taste, but it is rich in calories and vitamins and is a favorite drink in the Balkans.

fermented drink; *ayran*, a frothy salty yogurt drink popular in many Middle Eastern countries; yogurt; or Western-style soda.

Ice cream is a favorite street food in the summer, with slight differences from country to country. In Bulgaria, it is sold from mobile carts, soft-serve machines, or in ice-cream parlors. In Macedonia and Bosnia, it is sold in traditional sweet shops offering Turkish-style delicacies, sweet, drinks, and home-made ice cream, while in Croatia and Slovenia, it is sold in Italian-style gelato shops.

MAJOR STREET FOODS

Burek

Burek is the most popular street food in the Balkans. The word is applied to a family of baked or fried pastries made of a thin flaky dough similar to phyllo and filled with cheese, minced meat, vegetables, or fruits. It was probably invented in the Anatolian provinces of the Ottoman Empire and spread through Europe and the Middle East as far as North Africa. It may be made in a large pan and cut into portions after baking or prepared as individual pastries.

In the Balkans, *burek* is sold in bakeries or special shops. Most have chairs and small bistro tables; many also have windows for buying takeout food. In Bulgaria, where it is called *banitsa* or *banichka*, it is sold as small individual pies or as one large pie cut in quarters. Popular fillings are spinach, cheese, and pumpkin. It is accompanied by *ayran* or *boza*. In Serbia, it is sometimes sold by weight, sometimes by the piece. In Macedonia, where *burek* is mainly eaten for breakfast, it can be filled with minced meat, white cheese, spinach, leeks, or mushrooms, ham, and ketchup (so-called pizza-*burek*) and cut into quarters or eighths. In Slovenia, *bureks* are usually snail-shaped and are eaten at night in *burek* stands. In Croatia, they are sold in bakeries, mainly with a cheese, spinach, or a sweet filling.

Ćevapi

After *burek*, the most popular street food in the Balkans are *ćevapi* (a variation of the word kebab) and its diminutive *ćevapčići*. They are usually made of ground pork, beef, or lamb formed into long sausage-shaped tubes and grilled over hot coals or an electric burner. In the former Yugoslavia, the vendors are Muslim Bosnians or Albanians. In Bulgaria, where they are called *kebapcheta*, they are slightly bigger and thicker than elsewhere in the region and eaten with white bread and a paprika spread. In Serbia, *ćevapcici* are served in a special white bread bun, with many such side dishes as cream salad, sour cream, ketchup, roast pepper, hot peppers, crushed red pepper, cabbage, mayonnaise, mustard, onions, and lettuce. In Bosnia and Herzegovina, they are sold in special restaurants in Baščaršija, the old part of Sarajevo. The Macedonian version, *kebapchinya* is sold in traditional restaurants in the Old Bazaar section of Skopje and in grill-by-the-kilo booths in other parts of the city. They are eaten with onions, crushed chilies, grilled hot green peppers, and white bread. In Croatia, *cevapčići* are not as popular as in the other countries, but are still easy to find. In Slovenia, they are mainly available in sit-down restaurants as part of a Serbian-style grill.

Pizza

Pizza is served in various ways throughout the Balkans. In Bulgaria, pizza is sold in street stands or special pizza booths, and in Serbia, cream salad can be added as a topping. Croatian pizzerias are ubiquitous, especially in Zagreb and the seaside towns, and in neighboring Bosnia and Herzegovina, there are fast-food pizzerias, whole or by the slice. In Slovenia, the Neapolitan-style margharita or Slovenian prosciutto are the best sellers, while in Macedonia, pizza slices are mainly sold in bakeries or smaller fast-food places.

Western-Style Hamburgers

Hamburgers, including those sold at chains like McDonald's and Burger King, which are different from local hamburgers, have become popular all over the Balkans since the early 1990s, with a larger presence in major cities and urban areas, and mostly among the younger generation.

BULGARIA

In addition to the street foods described earlier, another popular street food in Bulgaria is *gevrek*, a baked dough sesame ring, very much like its Turkish original sold in the street, from carts, or improvised stands. Sandwiches, which are usually soft baguettes filled with *kajma* (cream cheese), yellow cheese, and cold cuts, are sold in stands at bus stops and underground walkways. *Döner kebabs*, cooked on long spits, are served from small storefront restaurants and usually accompanied with French fries and *ayran*. Fried doughnuts are commonly sold on street stands, eaten with powdered sugar. Roasted pumpkin, cut into pieces with the shell on, is sold in the autumn by street vendors, though it is not too common.

KATERINA NUSSDORFER

SERBIA

In addition to *burek,* bakeries sell home-style pita (pie) and various pastries such as Bavarian Kipferl, ciabatta with olives, garlic bread sticks, mini pizzas, hot dog rolls, and puff pastries. One cannot avoid the *gevrek,* the sesame dough ring that can be baked or boiled like a bagel. Hamburgers are very popular and are served in special white bread bun called *lepinja* with many side dishes such as cream salads, vegetables, and sauces. Also widely eaten are breaded fried yellow cheese, fried or grilled chicken, or chicken/pork skewers, all served with bread. Sandwiches, usually made with cold cuts, cream cheese, and salads, are sold cold or hot. Gyros, the Greek version of *döner kebab,* is made with chicken or pork and served in a pita bread with French fries, as are grilled kebabs (chicken or beef). Hot dog stands are also present, and very popular street food is *pomfrit,* French fries, served in a paper cone with ketchup, sour cream, and/or mayonnaise.

KATERINA NUSSDORFER

CROATIA

In Croatia, bakeries offer various savory and sweet pastries, muffins, and traditional strudel-style pies. Surf'n'Fries (a Croatian chain specializing in fries, even chocolate-covered fries!) is a real hit, and so are Subway sandwiches. Kebabs are easily found, and so are sausage stands where *debrecinke* and *kranjske kobasice* (types of sausages) are best sellers. In Zagreb, small wooden huts with red checked table decor offer different puff pastry pies with various fillings, called "Grandma's pies." Cold sandwiches and even slices of bread with lard can be bought in sandwich booths. There are also health food alternatives, the most popular of which are salad bars. In Zagreb, and especially in seaside resorts and towns, there is always a hole-in-the-wall eatery only known to locals, which usually serves excellent fresh food, namely, small fried fish to go, or grilled meats, fish, and seafood.

KATERINA NUSSDORFER

BOSNIA AND HERZEGOVINA

In this predominantly Muslim region, a popular street food is *somun*, a hot bread sold in the streets in the morning and after sunset during Ramadan (the monthlong holiday when people fast during the day). Pretzels are sold by street vendors, while bakeries sell bread, *kipferl*, baguettes, and filled pies. Bosnian national dishes like *sogan-dolma* (onions stuffed with chopped beef, rice, paprika, and sour cream), bean soup, and stews can be bought ready-made in small shops called *ašćinice*. Sandwiches, French fries, burgers, hot dogs, and chicken are sold in fast-food places, while fruit juices and sodas are also sold in the street. Kebabs can be bought in towns and cities and in restaurants along major highways. As in the Middle East, many street- and fast-food outlets serve falafel, hummus, lentil soup, curries, and healthy cakes. Pastry shops offer traditional ice cream, all sorts of cakes, sweets, *boza* (fermented flour drink), and lemonade. Nuts and seeds are sold in street carts as everyday snacks to be eaten on the go.

KATERINA NUSSDORFER

SLOVENIA

Slovenian street food shows the influence of both Balkan and Austro-Hungarian cuisine. Bakeries sell *štručki*, flat pastries covered with cheese, seeds, and grains; *zavitki* pastries with a sweet filling, usually cheese curd; and another sweet cheese curd-filled puff pastry called *polžki*. Breads include *žemljici* or bread rolls and croissants. Packaged sandwiches are sold in supermarkets, gas stations, and vending machines. *Döner kebab* is popular, as are falafel and hummus, though they are sold mainly in the capital city, Ljubljana. Takeout salads with a packet of dressing are sold in supermarkets. One can buy traditional sweet pies in supermarkets and bakeries. These include *sirovi štruklji*, cooked dough layered and filled with cheese curd, raisins, or jam; *prekmurska gibanica*, layered cheese curd and walnuts pie; and *potica*, a famous sweet poppy seed, walnut, or raisin cake.

KATERINA NUSSDORFER

MACEDONIA

Macedonian street food is extremely varied. Bakeries and street carts sell *gevrek*, sesame rings, *perek*, pretzels, and *vareno gevrek*, a bagel-like boiled snack. Other popular street foods are *banichka*, a spiral-shaped pie filled with white cheese, and *simit pogacha*, an unfilled *burek* served on a bun. Bakeries sell a wide range of *proja* (cornbread), *krofni* (doughnuts), and pie. Very popular is *tost*—a large soft white roll filled with ham, cheese, and/or mushrooms that is pressed on a grill and eaten with ketchup and mayonnaise. Pork gyros are served in pita bread with fries, onions, ketchup, and mustard. A Macedonian specialty is *pastrmajlija*, pieces of pork or chicken (originally cured mutton, or *pastrma*) on an oval-shaped piece of pizza-like dough, sometimes with a baked egg on top.

Other favorites are *mekici*, deep-fried yeast dough that is hard on the outside and soft inside, and *pirozhki*, filled crêpes that are breaded and fried. There is a wide variety of sandwiches, including *francuski/kombiniran*, a hot or cold baguette or roll filled with cheese and ham with salad or French fries inside; whole wheat bread with veggie spreads from health-food stores; pizza-sandwiches, calzone-style baked dough filled with pizza-type filling; and *panzerotti*, fried dough pockets filled with cheese, ketchup, mince, or ham. *Skara na kilo*, grilled meat sold by the kilo, is found in small restaurants with improvised sit-down places.

Hamburgers and hot dogs are different from those in the United States, since they feature large patties or hot dog links and are served in a bun along with French fries, ketchup, and mayonnaise or mustard. In the city of Ohrid, the traditional regional specialty sold in street or green markets is *gjomleze*, multi-layered thin dough baked in a large pan and cut into small pieces. National foods like *tavče gravče*—baked beans, stews, casseroles, and soups—are also sold to-go from shops specializing in "home-made" meals. Pastry shops, especially in the Old Bazaar in Skopje, sell traditionally made baklava, phyllo-type pastries filled with honey, nuts, and dried fruits; *tulumba*, fried pieces of oval-shaped batter soaked in sugar syrup; éclairs; lemonade; *boza*; and ice cream. Street carts also sell takeout snacks such as seeds, nuts, candy apples, and candies.

KATERINA NUSSDORFER

ALBANIA

The Republic of Albania is bordered by Montenegro, Kosovo, Macedonia, and Greece, with coastlines on the Adriatic and Ionia Seas and just 45 miles from Italy. Albania was at various times occupied by Greeks, Serbians, and Italians and part of the Ottoman Empire from 1431 until 1912, when it gained its independence. All these cultures have left their mark on its cuisine. Many Albanians immigrated to Greece and Italy in the 1990s and brought back with them gyro, pizza, moussaka, and other dishes that have become a part of the daily food.

As in the other Balkan countries, a popular street food is *byrek*, flaky triangle puffs filled with cheese, spinach, and meat that are sold in tiny storefronts. Another favorite is *ćevapčići*, made with ground beef and topped with onions. Roasted chicken and sausages are also sold.

COLLEEN TAYLOR SEN

GREECE

S TREET FOOD IS NOT QUITE AS WIDESPREAD IN GREECE as it is in other countries in the region. One reason is the ubiquity of coffee shops that serve snacks (*meze*)—and tavernas—small informal eating establishments offering bread appetizers, salads, soups, mains dishes, wine, and ouzo for lunch and dinner. Most have outdoor areas with chairs and tables that spill onto gardens, courtyards, even the pavement. They are typically open from noon until late at night.

However, in urban areas, street food is an important source of breakfast for many Greeks, especially in the capital Athens in the south and Greece's second largest city Thessaloniki in the north. Morning commuters purchase freshly made *koulouri* (small ring-shaped bread covered with sesame seeds) and little pies from mobile vendors or local bakeries. They can be eaten in one's hands. *Koulouri* street vendors generally close down their stands at noon. Some even sell their wares at traffic lights to commuters in their cars. Later in the day, vendors offer the famous Greek dishes gyros and *souvlaki* from mobile cards as midday snacks or a light meal. Some operate throughout the night for late-night revelers.

Greek street food goes back to ancient times when the first cities emerged in the 6th century BCE. Two modern street foods that can be traced to antiquity are the *koulouri* and the cheese pie. Many of these foods were rediscovered during the Byzantine period (330–1453 CE) and continued to be made under Ottoman rule over parts of Greece, which lasted from the 15th century until Greece won its independence in 1821. In the Ottoman capital, Istanbul (formerly Constantinople), there were many mobile street vendors, many of them Greeks and Armenians who specialized in a single item. Their wares included pilaf, fried liver, meatballs, roasted chickpeas, coffee, and *salepi*, a drink made by boiling orchid root that was sold in Athens as late as the 1930s.

In the 19th and 20th centuries, these street foods were brought by immigrants to Athens and the Greek mainland. The tradition of grilling meat on a stick over coals is one of the most ancient cooking techniques; Greek *souvlaki* are a version of kebabs (*souvla* means the stick on which meat was cooked). The climate and terrain favors breeding of goats and sheep over cattle, so beef dishes are uncommon. Normally fish and seafood are not sold as street food.

The street-food business in Greece is dominated by men. Women play a minor role, largely because regulations forbid the distribution of home-prepared food by street vendors. The only cooking technique allowed on the street is barbecuing (a traditional male occupation). The ingredients are supplied from commercial companies. Thus, all the *koulori* in Athens are supplied by three or four specialized bakeries, five factories supply pita bread to all parts of Greece, while special butcher shops prepare.

MAJOR STREET FOODS

Koulouri

This ancient bread has inspired others, such as the identical Turkish *simit*. It is a round ring-shaped bread with a hint of sweetness topped with sesame seeds. They are eaten for breakfast or as a snack, either as is or cut in the middle and filled with butter, honey, jam, turkey, tomatoes, olives, and other ingredients. They are sold both in bakeries and by street vendors in markets. On Sundays, there are sold outside churches.

Gyros

Probably the best-known Greek food worldwide is gyros. The name means "round" or "circle," referring to its method of preparation: slices of lamb or pork (increasingly popular because it is cheaper than lamb) are placed around a long vertical metal skewer that rotates slowly in front of an electric bar. The heat melts the fat, and the turning cone of meat becomes brown. The meat is sliced off, placed on a whole pita bread (a round unleavened bread made from white flour), and served with various accompaniments, such as tomatoes, onions, lettuce, or even French fries. In Athens, it is topped off with a dollop of *tzatziki*, a sauce made of strained yogurt (usually from sheep or goat's milk), cucumber, and garlic. In northern Greece, it is sometimes served with mustard or ketchup. The gyros is wrapped in a piece of paper and served in a cone to the customer who can eat it standing or sitting if a table and chairs are available. Gyros have become a standard fast food in North America.

A variation is *döner kebab*, which came from Turkey. It is made from ground beef and/or lamb shaped into a cone around the skewer. In the early 1970s, the use of ground meat was banned, but the prohibition was later lifted.

Souvlaki

This ancient dish was mentioned in the works of Aristophanes, Xenophon, and Aristotle. Meat, usually pork, is cut into one-inch cubes, marinated in lemon juice, olive oil, herbs, and spices (such as mint, oregano, thyme, basil, and garlic), strung on little wooden skewers, sometimes separated by vegetables, and broiled. Customers order it plain (*sketo*) or with pita bread garnished with sliced tomatoes, onions, and *tzatziki*. A variation is *kalamaki*, which means "little sticks." (However, in northern Greece, the word is not used since it means "drinking straw.") Sometimes the pita bread is sautéed in the meat drippings.

Pies

Small pies, called *pittes*, are the breakfast of choice for many Greeks and are sold in every neighborhood by mobile vendors, bakeries, and specialized little shops. Thin flaky sheets of phyllo dough or puff pastry are filled with custard, feta cheese made from sheep, or goat's milk cheese and honey, spinach, eggplant, artichoke, and other vegetables.

OTHER STREET FOODS

Sweets

Some vendors sell *loukoumades*, balls of fried dough. They are sold by the dozen or half dozen. Another popular sweet is *chalvas*, or honeycake, made of semolina baked in butter and scented with cinnamon and cloves. The *halva* of the Middle East and Balkans made of sesame paste is also sold in Greece.

Snacks

Many vendors sell roasted and salted peanuts, chickpeas, sunflower seeds, pumpkin seeds (called *passatempo*, meaning "to pass the time,"), and *pastelli*, sesame seeds covered with honey, especially during festivals and sporting events.

Corn on the Cob

Roasted corn on the cob has become a popular street food sold by street vendors on summer evenings and is especially loved by children. In the winter, the same vendors often sell roasted chestnuts.

Salepi

In the winter, vendors in central Athens traditionally sold this white, thick drink that goes back to ancient times. It is made by boiling the pulverized root of a species of orchid (*Orchis mascula*) that grew in the mountains with water. It is sweetened with honey or sugar and flavored with cinnamon or ginger. However, *salepi* vendors are becoming fewer as coffee becomes the drink of choice. Moreover, the plants are threatened with extinction because of overharvesting and are now protected by law, so most vendors sell *salepi* made from cornstarch, sugar, and artificial flavoring.

COLLEEN TAYLOR SEN

ITALY

TALY HAS A LONG AND RICH CULINARY TRADITION, characterized by strong regional differences. Each region, and even each town within the same region, has unique preparations and ingredients, determined by geography, topography, and Italy's turbulent history. One unique feature of Italian culinary traditions is their continuity. Many of the foods Italians consume on a daily basis date back several centuries. One of the longest-lived culinary traditions of Italy is the tradition of street food, food prepared by street vendors and consumed on the street, often using only one's hands to eat.

Italian street foods are deeply rooted in tradition, history, and geography, reflecting both regional gastronomic traditions and the numerous conquests and invasions that have left a mark on the territory. Since Roman times, the lower classes have lived out a portion on their lives in the streets and alleys, celebrating, mourning, and sharing their experiences with their neighbors. The dwellings in crowded ancient Rome did not have kitchens or stoves that could be used to cook food, so the population relied on street vendors and cookshops where meat or fish could be fried, bought, and enjoyed on the run. The attractions at the Roman Coliseum went hand in hand with the consumption of large quantities of foods cooked right there and consumed by the crowds who came to watch the spectacles. On the streets of imperial Rome, hawkers sold a variety of items, including *panis ac perna*, grape must sandwiches stuffed with ham cooked in the water of dried figs.

In the Middle Ages, a period of severe food shortages and widespread famine, the church helped establish central markets within the walls of cities partly as gathering places for the population. These markets housed food stalls with a variety of delicacies. The church also established feast days, which were both an attempt to keep the population's connection to their religion and an opportunity for occasional displays of excess. For much of the population plagued by famine, this was the only relief from hunger. Food was the center of the saint's day's celebrations. It was prepared by food vendors and enjoyed communally, most often outdoors. A whole animal might be roasted for such feasts, and each part of the animal was consumed, so nothing was wasted.

In some areas, street-food vendors provided an important service in poor neighborhoods well into the 20th century. Street vendors in Naples provided the poor residents of this crowded city with sustenance as most urban dwellings had no kitchen. Pizza, arancini, potato croquettes, fried fish, and vegetables and even spaghetti were consumed in the street, simply wrapped in a piece of paper. To this day, Naples has one of the liveliest street-food cultures of any Italian city.

The globalization of food and the proliferation of fast-food restaurants led to a change in eating habits around the world, including Italy. But Italy has managed to preserve many of its centuries-long culinary traditions, including those related to street food. There are dozens of Italian recipes for foods to be consumed rapidly in the street and most rely on centuries-old traditions. Pizza, panzerotti, focaccia, arancini, and lampredotto are still sold by street vendors and small kiosks around the country and consumed by locals and visitors alike.

A number of initiatives have been aimed at protecting traditional street foods and promoting the culinary traditions related to them. Streetfood, a nonprofit association, promotes awareness of traditional street foods and the people who sell them. It strives to provide a "healthful and sustainable alternative to globalization" and clearly communicate the importance of culinary traditions, many of which are on the verge of extinction. There are also events dedicated to the valorization of street food such as the International Street Food Festival, held in Cesena and the street-food area within Turin's Salone del Gusto, in association with Slow Food.

MAJOR STREET FOODS

Pizza

The most famous Italian street food, which has spread around the world, is pizza, which was first created in Naples and consumed folded over as a snack or sandwich. By the early 18th century, a custom had developed in Naples of dressing a disk of baked bread dough with tomato sauce and sometimes cheese. While it is not certain who created the first pizza, it was Raffaele Esposito who brought pizza to stardom. Esposito had inherited a pizzeria from his father-in-law, who in turn had bought it from Pietro Colicchio, who in 1780 opened the first pizzeria in Naples called "Pietro . . . e basta cosi" ("Peter . . . and that's enough"). In June 1889, Raffaele Esposito was called on to prepare the pizza for King Umberto I and his wife, the first Queen of Italy, Margherita of Savoy, during their visit to Naples.

Raffaele Esposito decided to offer three different pizzas. One was seasoned only with olive oil and cheese, one was garnished with small fish, and, finally, Esposito's own invention was topped with mozzarella, tomato, and a few leaves of fresh basil to resemble the colors of the Italian flag. The queen liked Esposito's tricolored pizza and complimented Raffaele who, in the queen's honor, called it pizza margherita. Pizza margherita became an immediate sensation in Naples and gradually spread to other parts of Italy and eventually to the United States when Neapolitan immigrants brought it with them to the East Coast.

Over time, Italian immigrants spread pizza around the world, and today this street food remains one of the most popular dishes around the globe and the standard bearer of Italian gastronomy.

Focaccia

The ancestor of pizza, focaccia, in essence a yeasted bread dough topped with oil, herbs, and other ingredients, has a much longer history. The Etruscans, Greeks, and Romans used to bake flatbread to be consumed both plain and flavored. This flatbread was made and cooked by street-food vendors as most households in ancient times did not have kitchens or ovens. Naples is the birthplace of pizza, but various types of focaccia have been prepared throughout the Italian peninsula since ancient times and show strong regional differences. To this day, they are made by bakeries, sometimes specialized focaccia bakeries or stands, and consumed at any time during the day as a snack or light meal.

FOCACCIA

Focaccia Genovese is from the port city of Genoa and is half an inch thick, seasoned with olive oil, sea salt, and occasionally onion—ingredients in which the region abounds. Focaccia di Reco is a unique Ligurian specialty that was traditionally produced in coastal villages. It is unique in that it consists of two thin layers of dough between which is an equally thin layer of hot, melted Crescenza cheese. Focaccia di Bari is from the port of Bari in Puglia, in the south of Italy, and ranges from a quarter inch to a half inch in thickness. This southern specialty is made with durum wheat flour and extra virgin olive oil, then garnished with fresh tomatoes, olives, and occasionally capers, all ingredients typical of Puglia.

Sfincione, typical of the city of Palermo, is flatbread that is topped with tomato sauce, Sicilian cheese, and onions. Focaccia Messinese, made a quarter inch to a half inch thick, is from the Sicilian port of Messina and is cooked in rectangular or square metal pans and topped with vegetables, tomato, cheese, and anchovies.

A variety of other flatbreads are consumed in various parts of Italy. The tigelle in Emilia-Romagna are thin, yeasted flatbread cooked between heated tiles. They can be opened and stuffed with meat and cheese. To the east in Romagna, the most famous traditional street food is *piadina*, a flat circular piece of dough cooked on boiling hot rings and stuffed with a variety of toppings including the cheeses and cured meats Romagna is famous for.

Arancini

A common street food of Sicily, arancini are balls made of rice (or risotto) and stuffed with meat sauce and sometimes mozzarella. They are coated in beaten eggs and breadcrumbs and deep-fried in olive oil. The soft filling contrasts in texture with the crisp shell.

Arancini probably date back to the 10th century. During the Arab domination of the island, it was customary to place a large plate of saffron rice with meat and vegetables in the center of a banquet table. Guests were encouraged to help themselves by taking a handful of rice. Therefore, originally, the Sicilian rice ball was simply a ball of rice with some seasonings and pieces of meat.

Later, the court of Frederick II came up with the idea of breading and frying the rice balls so the emperor could carry them on hunting trips. The balls were easy to transport, nonperishable, and tasty. Thus, arancini were likely created to meet the need of those looking to consume a meal in a hurry, which made them the perfect street food.

Supplì, a variation on arancini, are usually cylindrical in shape. The meat or tomato sauce is incorporated into the rice. The *supplì* are then stuffed with a piece of mozzarella, which melts when they are cooked.

Tripe (*Lampredotto*)

A traditional street food of Florence, *lampredotto* is boiled tripe sold from tripe kiosks throughout the city. The tripe is slowly cooked in a vegetable broth and seasoned with herbs. It is served in a bread roll and can be topped with a green or spicy sauce. Locals often ask for a *panino bagnato*, in which a portion of the bread roll is dipped in the flavorful cooking juices before being served. *Lampredotto* is a favorite with locals and has survived many changes in tastes and fashion over the centuries.

Seadas (or *Sebadas*)

This traditional Sardinian street food is now considered a snack, but in the past, it was often considered an entire meal. A square of thin dough prepared with flour and lard (but no yeast) is wrapped around a piece of pecorino cheese and deep-fried. The *seadas* are then drizzled with honey and enjoyed hot.

Fritto misto

Fried foods have been popular in Italy as street food for centuries and are one of the highlights of Italian gastronomy. A variety of ingredients are coated or dipped in various ways (in batter, egg wash and breadcrumbs, or simply flour) and then deep-fried in either olive oil or lard. Special food kiosks, called *friggitorie*, were used to fry and sell a variety of foods. What is fried and how it is fried depends on the region. The ingredients can vary from vegetables, fish, and offal to such sweet delicacies as *zeppole*.

Fritto misto is a combination of bits of meat, seafood, and vegetables dipped in batter and fried in olive oil. In Venice, *fritolin*, fried small fish served in a paper cone to be eaten in the street, was very popular in the 18th century, but it is on the brink of extinction today. This street food was also popular in Rome in the 18th and 19th centuries, but it is much less common today. In Naples, fried fish and vegetables remain a popular street food sold in paper cones and enjoyed as a snack any time of the day.

A variety of fried foods based on dough remain popular as street food in Italy. Some are prepared for specific feasts. Others are everyday foods created centuries ago and still consumed as snacks or light meals. One such street food is *gnocco fritto*, a specialty of Emilia. The yeasted dough is cut thin and deep-fried in lard. In the past, it was served to busy workers as a mid-morning snack with salami and Lambrusco to keep them going through the day. It was quick, hot, and filling.

Olive all'Ascolana

A street food from the town of Ascoli Piceno in Le Marche region of Italy, this delicacy is now also served as a popular bar food in the region. The large green olives are pitted and filled with a soft meat filling. After being dipped in batter, the olives are fried and sold by street vendors or in bars in paper cones. They are a delicacy specific to the region around Ascoli Piceno, but have recently spread throughout Italy.

VIKTORIJA TODOROVSKA

PORTUGAL

ORTUGAL IS A COUNTRY located along the eastern edge of Europe's Iberian Peninsula. It fronts on the Atlantic Ocean, and to the west and north is its only neighbor, Spain. Portugal is a country of 10 million people, small by world standards, but it has had an incalculable effect on world food because of its centuries-long world trade and its colonies, such as Brazil. Corn and chilies are just two of the food plants sent around the world by Portuguese merchants: both have changed world cuisines.

Portugal is a land of some geographical and climatic diversity. The coastal regions are temperate to even subtropical in low areas. The interior has mountains where skiing is a popular activity during wintertime. Some areas are hot and dry, but others have rolling plains and river valleys where agriculture is rich. One of these is the Douro River, where the climate is conducive to wine grapes, olives, and almonds. Portuguese wines from the valley Vinho do Porto are famous the world over and known as port. Portugal's farmers grow products for the rest of Europe and, as a maritime nation, export lots of fish. Fresh vegetables, meats, and fish of various kinds all form the base of Portuguese cuisine and street food.

Street food in Portugal has a long tradition. There is evidence of street food being sold in Portugal since the 15th century, continuing on throughout to the present day. Beginning with Portugal's admission as a full member of the European Union in 1986, stringent food safety requirements associated with tougher protocols for issuing permits to street hawkers put extra demands on these small businesses. Nevertheless, a relaxed outdoor lifestyle and increased demand, especially from the tourist industry, have led to an increasing and renewed interest in making street food's revival promising and more vibrant than ever.

The Portuguese are renowned for their sweet tooth. The earliest evidence of street food in Portugal refers to hawkers selling honey lollipops (*caramilo*) to children in the streets of Évora in the late 1400s. Likewise, in the 18th and 19th centuries, there is evidence of female street vendors walking the streets of Lisbon selling different types of sweet street food such as small dried cakes (*linguas de sogra*), lollipops (*chupa-chupa*), nougat (*torrão de Alicante*), and rice pudding (*arroz doce*). Professional confectionary makers also sold sweet couscous and candied fruits in street stalls.

The long tradition of street food in Portugal reached its peak in the 19th century. An increased migration of rural populations into the large urban conglomerates promoted the establishment of street foods as a means of income for many individuals. Ambulatory vendors became a vibrant feature of the urban environment, especially in Lisbon. In summer, the city streets were animated by women selling fresh vegetables and fruits, eggs, and sweet fresh figs. Likewise, the freshwater hawker and the *varina* (female fresh fish vendor) became iconic figures of the city ethos. Their street-cries and routines are still an integral part of popular culture.

The *varina* represents the peasant women who migrated from rural areas to the urban center hoping for a better life. The *varina* sold her fresh fish—mainly sardines—to other street vendors, who would then cook them in small barbeques by the side of the street. The cooked fish (*sardinha assada*) would be sold on top of a slice of bread for 10 réis (15 cents in today's value). Nowadays, the *varina* has mostly disappeared, but Lisbon's picturesque suburbs, where the narrow alleyways still mirror the pathways of many centuries ago, were as recently as the 1970s still walked by these female street vendors.

Although barbecued fresh sardines have always been a favorite street food, other morsels have also constituted the foodways of urban everyday life. *Pastel de bacalhau* (codfish cakes) and *iscas-no-pão* (pan-fried liver steaks in bread rolls) were popular snacks among the male population who, on their way home from work, would stop for a quick bite accompanied by a glass of wine. The hawkers were mainly located in such provisional sites as small side-street spaces, where the counter would be the separator between the street and the vending space. Under these rudimentary conditions, customers ate their food while standing up and leaning against the counter.

PEOPLE'S FAIRS

In June, Lisbon residents go to the streets to take part in the Festas Populares (The People's Feasts/Fairs). The fairs (*arraial*) take place in the old suburbs of Lisbon, where people dance and sing all night long as they eat *sardinhas assadas* and drink a glass of new red wine. They commemorate the city's patron—San Antonio. Over approximately one week, people enjoy the balmy nights, listen to popular and traditional music, and eat sardines. The smell of barbecued fresh sardines can be detected from a distance. Small portable barbecue grills attended by one individual are in constant service in the narrow streets of the old suburbs of Alfama near the Castel de San Jorge, where the fat sardines are cooked over hot coals, which will be sold on a slab of bread and perhaps accompanied with a small side salad of fresh ripe tomatoes, lettuce, and onion, well seasoned with olive oil and white wine vinegar.

More recently, other spaces were made available for snacking and street-food vending. Small business (cafés, *tascas*, *quiosques*, *esplanada*) constitute the backbone of an industry that populates large and small urban areas. A characteristic sight of Lisbon Harbour are the *quiosques* (kiosk) patronized by stevedores. Past and present maritime workers used them in their breaks for a quick snack, and a cold drink of wine (in the old days) and beer (more recently) as stay-dry policy during working hours has recently been implemented. Kiosks usually serve small savory foods such as *pastel de bacalhau* (codfish cake), *croquetes* (meat patties), *rissóis* (savory pastries), *bifanas* (steak sandwich), *cachorros* (hot dog), and *iscas* (pan-fried liver) on bread rolls. Mixed sandwiches are also popular.

CULTURAL HABITS AND WAYS OF LIFE

In general, Portuguese do not have the habit of rushing their meals. People like eating out, but they don't like eating on the run. Rarely will you see Portuguese eating as they walk. In Portugal, people prefer to sit down or at least stand-up against a counter while they eat, even if it is only a sandwich, a small cake, or savory morsel. Currently, and despite tight working schedules, most employees are still allocated one hour for lunch. It is a ritual in everyone's daily lives. After 1 p.m., small cafés are populated by hungry customers. Some have their simple meal either standing up against the counter or sitting down on high stools by the counter. Their meals can be as simple as a plate of soup with bread, small portions of rice and duck, small pastries, or sandwiches. People handle the food with their hands or the food is served in takeaway dishes. Other customers prefer the comfort of sitting down for a simple meal. One thing is for sure—everyone eats out at lunchtime. In fact, for some people, lunch is the only full meal they have, since busy working families have made the habit of having a complete meal at lunchtime and a lighter snack for dinner.

This lifestyle does not equate to high incomes or expensive meals. On the contrary, Portugal has one of the lowest per capita incomes in the European Union, and disposable income is also limited. The difference is that these everyday meals are inexpensive. A full meal with a drink and a *bica* (espresso coffee) can cost as much as 7 to 10 euros, which in some places would be the cost of a drink and a sandwich. It is an economy that generates employment and solves the problem of working families, some of whom live in dormitory suburbs with long working days and a lack of eagerness for nighttime meal preparation.

MAJOR STREET FOODS

Any reference to street food in Portugal needs to include the winter favorite: *castanhas assadas*—charcoal-roasted chestnuts sold by hawkers in the city streets. In summer, the preference is for ice creams and *farturas*, a traditional Portuguese doughnut formed in long spirals that are cut up into long pieces. *Farturas* are a favorite not just in the city but also in regional fairs where they are sold still piping-hot sprinkled with a mix of sugar and cinnamon. *Farturas* are a culinary trace of the Moorish presence in Portugal, and they can be considered as the twin sisters of the Spanish churros and the Madeira Island's (also part of Portugal) *malassadas*.

Everyone cherishes summertime and the street food associated with the beach—*bolas de Berlim* (a spherical custard-filled doughnut), potato chips, and ice creams. Soccer stadiums are also popular sites for street food. Before the game, long queues of hungry customers line up to the small carts selling *sandes de corato* (pork steaks in bread rolls). The rendered pork fat soaks through the bread giving it a specific taste (and calories). These are usually sold accompanied by a beer since in Portugal, the selling of alcoholic beverages does not require special licensing.

Malassadas are a deep-fried sweet pastry made from a thicker dough that are traditionally made just before the beginning of Lent on the Portuguese Island of Madeira. This tradition has been taken by Portuguese migrants to the United States, where it has become a popular street food.

PAULA ARVELA

SPAIN

S PANIARDS SPEND A GREAT DEAL OF TIME in the streets. It is an important part of their culture. It is in the streets of the towns and villages where some of the country's best food is to be discovered. Spanish street food is as original and diverse as Spanish regional food, carrying the same historical legacy. It may differ a great deal from what is found in New York, the Caribbean, or the torrid streets of Saigon or Shanghai, but remains a part of the great family of street food.

The influence of the cultural heritage of the Mediterranean region is seen everywhere as is that of the Atlantic Ocean, which from the 15th century onward made it possible to exchange food with the Americas. Spanish food is a cooking pot layered with original ingredients and different methods of cooking. It has been enriched since time immemorial by agricultural expertise and different culinary traditions brought to the country by foreign invaders: Phoenicians, Romans, Arabs, Moors (North Africans), and centuries later, the French. The Romans who controlled Spain from the 3rd century BCE to the 6th century CE gave the best gift of all: irrigation. They planted grain on a large scale as well as vegetables and fruit, cultivated olives, and made wine from the local grapes. The Moors— Arabic-speaking Islamic states in Spain until 1492—improved on the original Roman irrigation, converting barren land into rich orchards and rice paddies. They also introduced into the local diet saffron, fideo pasta, and couscous, which Spaniards still call *alcuzcuz*. It was from the Moors that local people learned to enjoy food in the streets and to share food in a convivial and unconventional manner. During the long centuries in which they ruled Al-Andalus, the Arabic name for Spain, Christian, Jewish, and Moorish food traditions were shared in streets and markets all over the country.

Starting at the end of the 15th century, new crops came from Central and South America, which improved the diet of the poor. The first arrivals were corn, capsicum peppers, and beans. Later, potatoes and tomatoes were planted. Despite these changes, food remained scarce for much of the population well into the middle of the 20th century. The well-to-do drank chocolate brought from Mexico by Spanish nuns made with sugar and dusted with cinnamon. Later, this custom moved into the realm of street food to accompany churros, or fritters, a food with a Middle Eastern origin. Throughout the 17th, 18th, and 19th centuries, regional food developed into the food eaten by Spaniards today, including street food. In the last 20 years, the influence of Spanish avant-garde chefs has also become evident in street food.

In Spain, geography and climate play a fundamental role in agriculture. The North is a world of mountains and pastureland, moody skies, and ever-changing seas. Galicia, Asturias, Cantabria, and the Basque Country look out over the Atlantic Ocean. In the hinterland over the mountains, chestnut forests and apple orchards share space with grassy pastures, where beef and dairy cattle feed. There are also thousands of small vegetable gardens planted with corn, runner beans, and tall cabbages. In local fairs and festivals, grilled sardines are as popular as the large beef cuts of rib, called *chuleton*, as well as *chuletillas*, little lamb cutlets grilled on metal *parrillas* over the hot embers of a fire. Moving east, Northern Navarre, Aragón, and Catalonia share borders and food culture with the Pyrenees and France. The food of East Catalonia, Levante, the Balearic Islands, and eastern Andalusia in the South belongs to Mediterranean Spain. Calçots, or large spring onions, are grilled in the streets of Tarragona in early April, while *cocas*, sweet or savory open pies, are bought in bread shops everywhere.

In Madrid, street sellers offer their customers the traditional *rosquillas del santo*, a doughnut that is eaten to celebrate the local Saint's day. In Extremadura, on the border with Portugal, dried smoked red peppers are made into pimentón, which is the most common spice in Spain. Pimentón is used in the making of chorizo and other traditional Spanish sausages. It is also used in an array of such traditional street food made with meat as the *pinchitos morunos*, or Moorish kebabs, usually made with pork instead of lamb. Some of the world's finest cured hams, which are always present on festive days, are made from the legs and shoulders of the Ibérico, an indigenous breed of pig that feeds on acorns in Extremadura and Andalusia. The first potatoes from the Americas were planted in Seville to embellish the gardens of hospitals and city buildings. Today the same potatoes are fried in the open air at fiesta time. In Spain, street food takes many shapes and is eaten on many different occasions.

MAJOR STREET FOODS

Churros

Churros are long, ridged fritters made of flour, water, and salt, fried in oil and served piping hot with sugar sprinkled on top. You can find them in the streets of North Africa as well as in Central and South America. In Spain, churros are sold in paper cones mainly in the *churrerias*, purpose-built shops often located close to local markets. Churros and a variation called *porras* are bought by the public in the morning to eat in the street or take home for breakfast. Churros are also fried on festive days and at local fairs in mobile *churrerias*. Today many of the humble *churrerias* have been upgraded. Built into large modern trucks with state-of-the-art equipment, the traditional churros and hot chocolate can be seen on sale everywhere in the streets of Spain.

Castañas Asadas

Chestnuts, roasted in the streets on glowing braziers, herald the arrival of autumn in Spanish towns and cities. The custom of roasting chestnuts in a perforated iron pan over an open fire originated in villages that were close to chestnut forests. In the past, this was part of the evening entertainment for the long winter nights. Traditionally, they were sold by *castañeras*, women who spent their evenings on street corners selling hot chestnuts by the dozen in small paper cones. In Catalonia, chestnut vendors also sell roasted sweet potatoes and sweet corn.

Pulpo a la Gallega and Empanada Pie

Local fiestas and patron saint celebrations are working days for street vendors. Galicia, in the northwest corner of the Iberian Peninsula, is where the best potatoes in Spain are grown. Here a national dish that is a popular treat on festive days is the *tortilla de patatas,* a thick egg omelet sold in large slices tucked inside a piece of local bread made from the same dough used to make empanadas.

Empanadas are pies made with a wheat or maize flour dough. Traditionally, they are filled with salt cod, saffron, and raisins, with cockles or even with mussels in a rich tomato and chile sauce. The classic empanada filled with tuna fish and a rich onion, parsley, and tomato sofrito is as popular as the *empanada de sardinillas,* tasty minute sardines. These pastries, cut into squares or triangles, are sold from any number of stalls during the local fiestas that take place at the end of every summer.

Another great Galician delicacy from the family of Spanish street food is *pulpo à feira* (market-style octopus). Large octopuses are boiled in copper cauldrons until tender. Then they are cut into little slices with scissors and served warm, dressed with hot pimentón, sea salt, and olive oil. The *pulpo a la gallega,* served on a bed of delicious boiled potatoes, is a variation of the same recipe.

Snails

In May, during the festival of the L'Aplec del Caragol (the Snail Festival), tons of snails are cooked in the streets of Lérida in Catalonia following traditional recipes. The snails are first boiled, then sautéed in large paella pans with olive oil, salt, and fresh herbs. Once they have been purchased, they are eaten hot at large communal tables, served with a pungent alioli sauce made with olive oil and garlic. Snails *a la llauna* (roasted in a tin with a sauce of pounded garlic, parsley, and olive oil) are equally delicious.

Paella and Other Rice Dishes

All over the Spanish Mediterranean coast, rice dishes cooked over wood fires in the open air have always been prepared by men on Sundays. Today, similar rice dishes cooked in a large metal paella pan with meat or seafood, vegetables, saffron, and pimentón have become a permanent feature in open markets and modern food courts in Spain and in many other countries. Street sellers tend to cook two different dishes at the same time: the traditional paella made with chicken flavored with rosemary and *arroz de pescado y marisco* prepared with a rich stock, prawns, and squid. Less authentic versions of the paella, cooked with meat and seafood at the same time, are demanded by the public.

Pescaíto Frito (Fried fish)

In Seville, fish fried at the local *freiduría* is taken away by customers to be eaten at home or in the street. Fifty or sixty years ago, these same shops fried fish only in the evenings, while in the mornings, they sold fresh fish to women to cook for the family at lunchtime. The menu has never changed: *soldaditos de pavía* (cod fritters), *merluza* (large hake), *pijotas* (small hake), *acedias* (small sole), *calamares* (squid), and *chocos* (cuttlefish).

Bocadillos de Calamares
One of the most popular foods sold in the streets of old Madrid around the Plaza Mayor is a bread roll filled with piping hot fried squid rings. The *bocadillos de calamares* are bought from bars that have hatches that open onto the street.

Modern Spanish Street Food
Today modern tapas as well as top-quality food products are sold from stalls in newly refurbished old markets and have become the face of modern Spanish street food. The Mercado de San Miguel in Madrid has recently been converted into a street food and market court. Inside, some stalls sell vegetables and fish, meat and sausages, coffee, and tea, and others cook modern or traditional recipes, which until very recently were sold only in the traditional tapas bars. Creative chefs are behind some of the best tapas and exquisite *pintxos* (a piece of bread with something delicious on top supported by a toothpick). Of Basque origin, *pintxos* bring the most original combinations of ingredients and food design into the realm of street food.

MARÍA JOSÉ SEVILLA

WESTERN EUROPE

BELGIUM

B ELGIUM IS A SMALL, prosperous country in northwestern Europe. Lying between France on the south, Germany on the east, and the Netherlands to the north, the country has a surprisingly diverse geography. The coastal lowlands provide rich pasture lands for the country's fine cheeses. A belt of higher lands in the middle are good for agriculture (about 27 percent of the country is farmland). The southeast hold the famous Ardennes Mountains, heavily wooded but home to religious abbeys that make famous beer and cheeses. Beer is one of Belgium's characteristic products, sold and enjoyed worldwide.

Belgium is composed of two distinct linguistic groups. In the south are French speakers, called Walloons by their neighbors who speak a form of Dutch called Flemish. The country is mainly bilingual, and, like the Dutch, large numbers speak English. The names of towns, cities, and foods can be either French or Flemish, but are usually the latter, such as *Frieten*.

MAJOR STREET FOODS

Frieten Met Mayonnaise
The most popular street food in Belgium is *frieten*, or what Americans call "French fries." The "French" refers to the cutting technique; these fries are potatoes cut in small wedges. It is not that Americans discovered fries in France;

Americans became familiar with fries in Belgium during the world wars. However, the French do claim to have first made and sold them at the Pont Neuf in Paris, although they are still searching for the inventor and the proof of this. The Belgian history of *frieten* starts with an oral legend (from Jo Gérard, 1781) that says fries came to existence in the late 17th century in the southern part of Belgium. Inhabitants from the cities surrounding the River Meuse had a tradition of frying little fish caught from the river. When weather conditions were not appropriate to fish, they cut potatoes into the shape of little fish and fried them. That is the story that Gérard's great-grandfather used to tell. Unfortunately, he never wrote it down, and no sources exist to confirm this beautiful legend. In fact, potatoes first came to Belgium in the 18th century, and many doubt if ordinary Belgians could afford what was, in the 17th century, very expensive cooking oil for frying potatoes.

But written proof and even pictures show fries being made in Belgium in the second half of the 19th century. And so were the *frietkoten* where they were sold. A *frietkot*, or fry shack, is a small stall on the street that sells fries with different kinds of sauces. Laws required that the first fry shacks had to disappear at night, and only after World War II were they allowed to have a fixed position on the streets. Today some of these traditional fry shacks remain, but they are no bigger than a little hut with no place to sit. Many modern fry places are housed in units that resemble fast-food chains. That is because in the last few decades, local governments have begun to enforce strict hygiene regulations. Some think the traditional stall can be dangerous (for fire or explosions); others believe they are too ugly, especially when standing next to historical buildings (which for the fry shacks are the best spots, of course). Still, simplicity is the charm of a true fry shack according to most Belgians. And even if it has become more difficult for the traditional stalls to continue to exist, no one believes that they will ever fully disappear.

Big or small, fry shacks today all sell fries with a range of sauces and other fried foods (mainly fried meat). However, no Belgian will leave a fry shack without a pack of traditional fries, and the traditional Belgian way to eat fries is with mayonnaise, a sauce made from egg yolks and oil.

In terms of healthy food, they are the nutritionist's worst enemy. Full of carbohydrates and fat, they are not the best choice. Still, most Belgians eat them about once a week. They are cheap and very filling, which makes them accessible for the rich and poor; they are tasty, and they are part of Belgium's history.

Brusselse Wafels (Belgian Waffles)

Belgians are also known for *Brusselse wafels* or waffles. The history of this sweet baked dough with a squared pattern goes back a very long time. Baking dough between plates was already common among the ancient Greeks. In the 13th century, a goldsmith refined this technique by making metal molds to bake patterned dough. And that is when the *wafla*, which is French for honeycomb—referring to the squared pattern of the waffles—came into existence. The first waffles were produced in France, followed by the Netherlands and Germany, which are all neighbors to Belgium. It is only in the late 19th century that recipes of *Brusselse wafels* started to appear in household cookbooks (e.g., Cauderlier's book on sweet pastries that appeared in the late 19th century) and in pamphlets sold at fairs. Because eating waffles was and is very popular during fairs, it is a street food for special occasions. One of the most famous vendors of waffles at fairs was (and still is) Max, named after Maximilaen Consael, who opened up his stall in 1856. It is then that the famous Brussels waffles were born.

Brusselse wafels should not be confused with their sweeter variant, *Luikse wafels*, or waffles from Liege, a town in the Southern part of Belgium. According to legend—though written proof is not existent—these emerged in the 18th century when the prince of Liege asked his chef to prepare him a sweet dish with sugar. Little pieces of sugar were added to the waffle dough, and the prince loved them.

Although still popular today, *Luikse wafels* are different. Not just because of the difference in the amount of sugar used, but also because of their shape: *Brusselse wafels* have 20 holes, and *Luikse wafels* have 24.

Oliebollen/Smoutebollen

Also popular at fairs in Belgium are *oliebollen* and *smoutebollen*, which consist of sweet dough fried in oil or lard (*smout*), respectively. Basically they are a mix of *frieten* and *wafels*. In terms of ingredients and preparation, they can be compared with doughnuts, but they have a different shape, small balls (the size of a golf ball). Similar to fries, the traditional way to serve them is in a paper cone. They are not served with mayonnaise, but with lots of powdered sugar.

Similar to waffles, *smoutebollen* are traditional street foods for special occasions. They are popular at New Year but can also be found at fairs throughout the year and are especially popular on Vette Dinsdag (Fat Tuesday, or Mardi Gras), the day before Lent when people fast.

Today *smoutebollen* are still most popular at fairs, and some stalls sell them together with waffles and fries. Because they have become popular with tourists, they are also outside the context of festivities, but they are not as common as waffles and fries, which can be easily found in every major city.

OTHER STREET FOODS

Gentse (Gestreken) Mastellen

A traditional, though less known, street food from Ghent, a lovely city in the north of Belgium, is *gentse mastellen*. *Mastellen* are sweet breads, comparable with a sandwich with a hint of cinnamon, and shaped like a bagel or doughnut. They emerged in Ghent about a century ago when Carmelites started to produce them for daily consumption. The tradition began in the 12th century when one of the bishops of Ghent installed a holy day (St. Hubert's Day on November 3) to protect his people using *mastellen*. People would bring them to morning church, and they would be blessed; bakers still do it. A blessed *mastel* supposedly protects people from diseases like rabies.

Mastellen became popular street foods at the Patersholfeesten, a three-day outdoor festival that takes place in the second weekend of August in a part of Ghent known as the Patershol. The *mastellen* are sold as *gestreken mastellen*, which literally means "ironed mastels" and that is exactly what they are, at least in their traditional fashion. Until a couple decades ago, they were made by ladies from a traditional bakery in that area. They filled the *mastel* with sugar and flattened them using a warm iron. Today the original bakery no longer exists, but the ironed *mastels* have remained popular. Perhaps a little too popular, because to cater the high demands, they are nowadays made using the big irons they also use for warm sandwiches.

Geutelingen

Another regional street food from Belgium that is quite well known is *geutelingen*. They are similar to pancakes, but baked on stone in a wood oven. Similar to other street foods in Belgium, *Geutelingen* are food for special occasions; they are traditionally made and eaten around Candlemas (February 2). On that day, people also tend to eat regular pancakes. Pancakes are easier to make than these *geutelingen,* which require people to take their dough to a place with a wood-fired oven or to the home of someone who owns one.

Until the first decades of the 20th century, these *geutelingen* were common across Belgium, but they started to disappear in the late 1930s except in Elst, a city in the north of Belgium, where the tradition was kept alive. In 1981, a special committee was even installed to guard this tradition. Ever since the tradition has become very popular, people travel to Elst especially for these *geutelingen* and other festivities.

Karakollen

Karakollen, or whelks (small sea snails), are another well-known street food. They are popular not only along the coastline, but also in the capital of Belgium, Brussels, where Mie Caracol has been selling these delicacies for more than 50 years. She is based in one of the old neighborhoods of Brussels called the Marollen. Born in a family that ran amusement attractions at fairs, she started selling *karakollen* at these fairs. Nowadays her stand is at the corner of the Hoogstraat and Vossenstraat, selling the best *karakollen* in town (and worldwide according to some). Her recipe remains top secret.

KARAKOLLEN

CHARLOTTE DE BACKER

FRANCE

S TREET FOOD (the French use the English term) has not been as popular in France as other countries for several reasons. A traditional lunch in France is long and comfortable; the custom is to eat slowly and to chat the same length of time after eating. France has a worldwide reputation of culinary refinement, so that a quickly cooked and easy-to-transport meal is the antithesis of French food. France, especially Paris, did have a vibrant street-food scene during the Middle Ages, but when indoor restaurants began to flourish in the 19th century, merchants stopped selling food on the street. However, picnics remained popular at every level of French society and have been shown in many paintings by such celebrated artists as Jean Renoir and Henri Toulouse-Lautrec.

However, today French culinary habits are evolving with the urban way of life. Working people do not have as much time for lunch as they did in the past. As in other countries, students want inexpensive food that can be eaten on the run. Moreover, today street food is being promoted as a healthier alternative to junk food. But France also does have some traditional street-food specialties. Bakeries, which are found everywhere, sell the long thin loaves of bread called baguettes as well as sandwiches, crêpes, and pastries. French fries are another typical dish. Hot wine and roasted chestnuts are sold on the street during winter.

Some dishes are regional specialties. For example, crêpes originated in Brittany and were popularized in Paris by Breton migrants in the mid-20th century. More recently, immigrants from North Africa and the Middle East have taken over a large share of the street-food market. In fact, anyone walking the streets of

Paris is more likely to find kebabs, falafel, and pita bread than traditional French products!

Usually street food is sold from stands and fixed stalls rather than trucks, except for the popular pizza trucks along the roads and French fry trucks in the north of France. However, a new trend from the United States is reaching France: food trucks.

Some renowned chefs have even entered the food-truck market, such as Thierry Marx, who opened a street-food workshop in Blanquefort near Bordeaux. Marx, who has extensive culinary experience in Asia, claims that street food provides an excellent alternative to *malbouffe* (unhealthy eating or junk food). In 2015, Marx launched a web series called Food Truck Party in which different chefs prepare their specialities at a food truck parked outside his restaurant.

One is more likely to find street food in walkable neighborhoods of the biggest cities, especially the central and historical districts. In Paris, street food is sold in the Marais, the Latin Quarter, and Ménilmontant. But the neighborhoods of Chateau Rouge and Belleville, which have large immigrant populations, have the largest concentrations of food stalls. In Chateau Rouge, there are African meat dishes and fruits, and in Belleville, street food from Asia. In the city of Lyon, the neighborhood called le Vieux Lyon and especially the Rue Saint Jean serve traditional French street food while La Guillotière offers more ethnic food. Around the Place des Terreaux, there are both.

The south of France has its own local street foods. The most famous specialty of Nice and nearby Monaco is *socca*, a pancake made from chickpea flour, water, and olive oil with a moist interior and crispy outside. It is first cooked on a griddle and then baked in a wood-fired oven. In Vieux Nice, the old part of that famous coastal city, *socca* is served with other such local specialties as *pissaladiere*, an onion pizza, and *pan bagnat*, a small bun brushed with olive oil and filled with green pepper, olives, onions, tomato, anchovies, and hard-boiled eggs.

The city of Marseilles on the Mediterranean is home to a large North African population and has a bustling street-food scene, especially in the Noailles, the Arab Quarter. Here tiny food stalls, kiosks, or stand-alone tents sell such delicacies as *mahjouba*, large crêpes filled with tomato, red pepper, onion, and *harissa*; flatbreads; kebabs; and *merguez*, a sausage made with lamb, beef, or a mixture stuffed into a lamb-intestine casing, heavily spiced with chile powder or *harissa* and other spices, and grilled. It can be eaten with couscous (a steamed porridge-like dish of tiny granules of dough) or in sandwiches, sometimes served

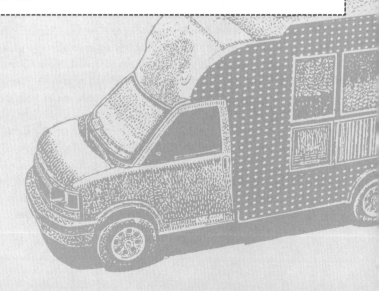

AMERICAN FOOD TRUCKS COME TO FRANCE

According to the *New York Times*, in the spring of 2012, two young American chefs opened Cantine California, which serves tacos, and Le Camion qui Fumer (The Smoking Truck), whch sells cupcakes and thick hamburgers with fries. Despite warnings that the French would never eat with their hands on the street, the trucks became enormously popular among both American expatriates and hip young Parisians who praise a dish by calling it "tres Brooklyn." Most French had never eaten a soft taco, much less one filled with pork carnita and chipotles in adobo, all imported from Mexico. Today there are over 40 food trucks in the Paris region. They serve two types of food: gourmet hamburgers that cost as much as 11 euros and international dishes, including Vietnamese sandwiches, bagel sandwiches, Argentinian empanadas, kebabs, and Chinese dim sum. Food trucks are not allowed to drive around but are assigned to certain markets and days. A website (only in French) tracks their location.

with French fries. Pastry shops sell such North African delicacies as beignets, deep-fried dough sometimes filled with meat or vegetables; makrouds, cookies made of ground almonds; and *cornes de gazelles,* crescent-shaped pastries made of ground almonds and orange water.

Street food is more widespread at certain times of the year, especially Christmas when there are special markets. In Lyon, La Fête des Lumières (Festival of Lights) is held in December. The city is illuminated, and streets vendors are selling French specialties, hot wine, and cider.

MAJOR STREET FOODS

The Sandwich

Born in the United Kingdom, the sandwich reached France in 1830 and was soon available in every café in Paris. The French sandwich is famous for using the traditional crusty baguette. It is split into two halves, then sliced open along its length, buttered, and filled with different ingredients. The most typical and popular, despite its simplicity, is the *jambon beurre* made with ham, butter, and pickles. Sometimes the bread is filled with crudités like tomatoes, lettuce, and cucumber, or with comté or Emmental cheese. The standard accompaniment is mayonnaise or Dijon mustard. The reasons for its popularity are understandable. The baguette is the staple of French food. Sandwiches are inexpensive, usually costing between 3 and 5 euros ($4–$6). There are, however, some expensive versions with ingredients like foie gras now on the market. They are wrapped in a piece of paper so are very convenient to eat and are among the few foods French people will eat on the street. Some cafés will let people bring in sandwiches bought from a vendor provided that they buy a drink. A related sandwich is the *croque monsieur.* It is a hot sandwich made from a square loaf of bread filled with ham and a cheesy béchamel sauce.

Crêpes

The crêpe appeared in Brittany around the 13th century. It was originally made with buckwheat, thought to have been brought by crusaders from the Middle East. Later, white flour was used. The topping can be either salted or sweet. During the 20th century, crêperies opened all over France, especially in the neighborhood of Montparnasse in Paris thanks to the immigration of a great number of Bretons. Like sandwiches, crêpes are conveniently wrapped in a piece of paper and can be found at every street-food stand. The usual toppings for salted crêpes are ham, eggs, and cheese. Ask for all three and it's a *crêpe complete*. Sweet crêpes are garnished with sugar, jam, whipped cream, chocolate, or strawberries. At a street-food truck or stand, the dough is usually already made when the customer orders the crêpe. The seller cooks the pastry in the oven and adds the garniture in front of you. Crêpes are typically sold during celebrations, fun fairs, and children's events.

French Fries

French fries (*frites*) have a contested and polemic origin and are a subject of dispute between the French and Belgians. The potato was first cultivated in South America and was brought in Europe in the 16th century, but not cut into strips and deep fried until the later 19th century. The classic version is served from trucks (*baraques à frite*) in the north of the country. They can either stay at the same place all year or move around. Their usual locations are at village or city centers or along national roads with heavy traffic.

French fries can be served in a cone or in a container. The first is usually preferred because the fries stay hot. They are generally served with mussels and ketchup, mustard, or mayonnaise.

French Pastries

French pastries are baked goods made from a yeast-leavened dough, eggs, butter, milk, cream, and sugar. They are typically eaten at breakfast or as snacks. Among the best known are the croissant, *pain au chocolat*, brioche, *chausson aux pommes*, and *pain au raisins*.

Croissants are the most popular. They are made from a flaky pastry and so called because they are crescent (croissant) shaped. Baked in the early morning, they are usually served in bakery stands and very convenient to eat in the street. The first croissant was sold in Paris at the beginning of the 19th century, but the current version became a French culinary symbol only in the 20th century. Since the 1950s, the croissant has been a traditional element of the French breakfast. *Pain au chocolat* is a croissant with a chocolate filling; brioche a soft, light-textured bread-shaped into a round bun; *chausson aux pommes* an apple turnover; and *pain au raisin* a spiral-shaped sweet pastry with raisins.

OTHER STREET FOODS

Kebab

Kebab is far more popular in France than hamburgers, especially among students. As in other countries of Western Europe, in France, "kebab" refers to a sandwich made of meat (usually lamb) that is put on a spit, grilled, then cut into thin slices, and served in pita bread with crudités, French fries, and sauce. It is a cousin of gyros, *döner kebab*, and shawarma. Many kebab stalls were opened by people from Turkey. Kebabs are so popular that they even inspired a rap song "Mange du Kebab" ("Eat Some Kebab").

Pizza Truck

Although pizza is from Italy, it is very popular in France and a key element of the street-food landscape. Pizza trucks are found not only in cities but in small villages, camp grounds, and along national highways.

Hot Wine and Cider

Wine is the most iconic French drink. During winter, wines turn into a street drink as vendors sell hot wine—usually red, but sometimes white—and hot cider during Christmas markets and celebrations. The merchant heats the wine and adds such spices as cinnamon, ginger, and clove. This has been done since the Middle Ages with spices received from Asia. Originally a specialty of Alsace, it has spread out all over the country. Cider, a product of the fermentation of apple juice, comes from Normandy. During the Fête des Lumières (Festival of Lights) in Lyon, it's the custom to drink hot wine or cider while walking through the illuminated streets.

CLOTHILDE FAÇON

GERMANY

G ERMANY HAS A RICH STREET-FOOD CULTURE. Until the 1990s, however, eating while walking in the street was considered rude behavior, while drinking from a beer bottle in public was a sure sign of homelessness. Today it is normal to see people walking around German streets eating or with a drink in their hands. Fast food carries with it notions of fun and social freedom, especially for young people who want to escape family restraints and meet friends for a quick inexpensive meal.

Fast-food stands, called *Imbiss*, sausage stalls (*Würstchenbude*), and kiosks are especially popular in busy city centers and open air markets, near large department stores and tourist attractions, and in or around train stations. The most popular street foods are freshly squeezed fruit juices and ready-cut fruit, ice cream, pretzels, salads, soup, wraps, *Chinapfanne* (a stir-fry of thinly sliced Chinese vegetables and bean sprouts), all kinds of bratwursts (grilled sausages), pizza, pickled, smoked or fried fish in rolls, baked *Leberkäse* (meat loaf), and *Schwenkbraten* (pork roast). In Germany, the modern era of fast food (which is difficult to distinguish from street food) began after World War II.

Kiosks and improvised shacks on bomb sites sprung up to sell whatever food was available. They were modeled on *Trinkhallen* (drink kiosks) that arose in industrial areas in the second half of the 19th century to sell workers carbonated mineral water and other nonalcoholic drinks. Many served regional specialties. In Cologne, for example, some kiosks sold potato fritters and fried meat patties, goulash, and hot sausages. Immigrants, many of them from Turkey, opened fast-food stalls, especially at the end of the economic boom of the 1970s when many lost their industrial jobs. Germany's two most popular street foods are *döner kebab*, a form of gyros, and *Currywurst*. American fast-food chains, including McDonald's and Burger King, also have a firm foothold in Germany.

MAJOR STREET FOODS

Bratwurst

Germany has many kinds of bratwurst, each of them considered to be the cultural heritage of the city or region in which they are made. Strictly speaking, bratwurst means "fried sausages," and in the past they were sold by a *Würstchenmann* (sausage man) who sold them from a metal hot water container hung around his neck. These hot water bathed sausages are also called *Wiener Würstchen*. Today, bratwurst is sold mainly by vendors who have round portable grills hanging from their shoulders and an umbrella attached to their backs in case of rain.

THURINGIAN BRATWURST

The most famous bratwurst, *Rostbratwurst*, comes from the central German region of Thuringia, where it has been made since the early 1400s. The cities of Weimar and Erfurt are well known for their sausage stands, or *Imbiss*. Thuringers are about nine inches long and made from finely chopped pork or mixtures of pork and beef. They are all natural casing sausages, meaning that the meat is stuffed into pork or sheep gut. Each region of Thuringia has its own flavors, which always include marjoram, caraway, garlic or even nutmeg, and ginger. By German law, fresh sausages must be cooked on the same day that they are made, so grilled bratwurst sold in German cities and towns are always completely fresh. Grilling is the preferred way of cooking. In Thuringia, grills are often doused with beer to cool them down to the proper temperature and to flavor the sausages. Thuringers are usually served in a small bun (*Brötchen*) that covers only the middle of the sausage. Mustard is usually the only condiment served. The greatness of Thuringian *Rostbratwurst* is memorialized by its own museum near Arnstadt.

NÜRNBERG BRATWURST

Perhaps Germany's most popular bratwurst comes from Nüremberg in the Franconia region. It is small, around three to four inches long, and made of pork, hence its white color. The main seasoning is marjoram. Nürnberg bratwursts are grilled, preferably over an open flame, and served several at a time. Often street vendors put three into a single small bun. When served on plates, Nüremberg bratwurst is usually accompanied by potato salad (made with vinegar, not mayonnaise) and sauerkraut. Dijon-style mustard is the standard condiment. Under European Union law, any sausage called Nürnberg Bratwurst must be produced only in the city of Nüremberg using local ingredients.

WEISSWURST (WHITE SAUSAGE)

In the southern state of Bavaria, *Weisswurst*, or white sausage, is so popular that it is virtually identified as the official state sausage. It is a finely ground pork and veal sausage of medium length seasoned with parsley, onions, and mace. Like other fresh German sausages, *Weisswurst* should be consumed as fresh as possible (before noon), but as they are scalded, there is no legal requirement on this. It is simmered in water and then eaten with large, soft Bavarian pretzels, sweet mustard, and with *Weizen* (wheat) beer.

Weisswurst is the sausage of choice at the Munich Oktoberfest and in many towns for Carnival (Mardi Gras), held on the Tuesday just preceding Lent. Each year, thousands of visitors attend Oktoberfest and gobble, especially in the morning and during the day in beer tents. At night, they consume heartier dishes such as grilled chicken and pork knuckles.

BERLIN *BOCKWURST*

Bockwurst is a thick sausage, a version of a wiener or frankfurter, made from veal and pork. It is usually smoked first and finished by cooking in simmering water. It can also be grilled, but heated until the case splits. It is served as street food, especially at fairs and festivals. It is accompanied by brown mustard, horseradish, and sometimes sauerkraut.

CURRYWURST

An unusual candidate for Germany's most popular street food is *currywurst*—a finely grained, grilled pork sausage cut into bite-size pieces, sprinkled with curry powder and paprika, and topped with tomato ketchup. It is prepared *mit* or *ohne*—with or without skin—and *scharf* or *extra scharf*—hot or extra hot, depending on the sauce. Options include a white roll and French fries (called *Pommes* or *Fritten*) topped with ketchup, mayonnaise, or both. Customers purchase it from sidewalk stalls, called *Imbissbuden*, and from food trucks and eat it standing up with a small plastic fork on a paper plate. A serving costs the equivalent of $3.00. Almost

---

BULETTEN

How individual foods got their names is often mysterious. One of these is the term *Bouletten* or *Buletten* used in the German city of Berlin as a synonym for *frikadellen*, or meat balls. *Frikadellen* are the most famous dish of Scandinavian Europe, especially Denmark, which borders on north Germany. This word descends from early terms for frying, maybe from the Latin word "frictura" or "frigere," or it could be a word for "steamed meat."

Because the word *Bouletten* seems to be French in origin, it was thought that the term came to Berlin and its region in the 1600s when French Protestants, called Huguenots, sought shelter from persecution in France. Another possibility is that the word came into use when the Napoleon Bonaparte, the emperor of France, conquered and occupied the area in 1806. The French word for meatballs is *boulettes de viande*. A third possibility is that French cuisine and culture was so much admired by other Europeans that chefs in Berlin picked up the term and used it to mean really good or fancy meatballs. Whatever the origin, *Bouletten* has stuck as a Berlin food term.

---

a billion *Currywursts* are consumed in Germany every year, and a study indicated that 80 percent of Germans consider it a central part of their diet. There is even the world's only Currywurst Museum near Checkpoint Charlie (marking the old dividing line between East and West Germany before the nation was reunified in 1989) in Berlin. The dish is so dear to the German heart that a fight has emerged over its origins. It is the quintessential Berlin street food, and Berliners claim that it was invented in 1949 by Herta Heuwer, owner of a snack bar the site of which is now marked with a plaque. One explanation for its invention is that when a British soldier in occupied Berlin asked for a curry, Frau Heuwer served him a sausage sprinkled with curry powder. However, residents of Hamburg claim that *Currywurst* was first made in their city in 1947 by Lena Brucker, the central character in a 1993 novel by Uwe Timm called *Die Entdeckung der Currywurst* (*The Discovery of Currywurst*) that has been made into a film.

Döner Kebab

Also called *döner*, it was introduced in Berlin in the early 1970s by Turkish

MUSTARD

Sausages are rarely served without mustard, a very old condiment. It seems that human beings have always liked piquant (or "hot") flavorings in their food, especially if the food is somewhat bland. Mustards belong to the same family of plants as cabbage and broccoli (*brassica*) and have some of the same sulfurous flavor compounds that makes cabbage smelly when cooked. Mustard seeds contain volatile oils whose hot flavors disappear quickly when the seeds are crushed. Vinegar is one way to preserve those tastes, which is why prepared mustards have that sour undertone. Mustard was a main food flavoring in Medieval Europe, where three main kinds were cultivated: white or yellow, brown, and the spicier black. German mustards are typically made from brown seeds and are usually milder than English versions. The mustards served in sausage stands in German-speaking countries come in several forms, ranging from the standard mild yellow products to hot Düsseldorf, Löwensenf, and sweeter Süssersenf versions in the south. Germans migrating to the United States brought brown mustard with them, and it is still used where German and East European traditions linger. In recent years, a mildly spicy French variety called Dijon has become popular in public dining places.

immigrants. However, it has little in common with its Turkish and Persian prototypes, which are mutton or lamb roasted on a spit and more closely resembles Greek gyros. Meat—originally mutton, but now often mixed with beef, chicken, or turkey— is marinated with salt, spices, onions, milk, or yogurt, and formed into long oval block, thicker at the upper end, and weighing 4 to 22 pounds. Most of the blocks are made by special producers. The block of meat is placed upright on a spit and slowly rotates around an electric grill. As the outer layer cooks, it is cut off in thin strips in with a long knife and falls into a metal scoop underneath the block. The meat is served in a quarter of a Turkish pita, a round flatbread, cut open to form a pocket. Alternatively, it can also be wrapped in a very thin bread called *yufka* to make a dish called *dürüm döner*. It is topped with sliced lettuce, tomatoes, onions, red cabbage, and yogurt sauce. Hot red pepper flakes are optional. The result is a fat pouch that takes some practice to eat without spilling it over one's clothes.

OTHER STREET FOODS

Frikadellen or *Bouletten*

Frikadellen is a German and Scandinavian word for "meatball." More literally, meatballs are called *Fleischkloesschen*, or "meat dumplings." In Berlin, they are called *Bouletten*, supposedly from a French word meaning "pellets." *Frikadellen* are made from ground meat, mixed with egg, water or milk, dried breadcrumbs, and seasonings such as salt, pepper, parsley, and marjoram. Made into small balls, they are fried in oil or until browned. They are sold from street stands, accompanied by mustard and ketchup.

Pizza

Pizza is so popular that it is virtually a naturalized dish. As street food, it is often sold under the name of Minipizza, similar to the Italian pizza al taglio. Recently, there has been a renewed interest in quality, replacing plastic cheese, canned mushrooms, and vinegar-brined peppers with fresh ingredients.

Falafel

Some *döner* stands serve Lebanese falafel as an alternative for vegetarians. These are deep-fried balls of pureed chickpeas served with tahini (sesame seed sauce) in a pita flatbread.

COLLEEN TAYLOR SEN AND BRUCE KRAIG

GREAT BRITAIN

IDEAS ABOUT STREET FOOD in Great Britain have changed in the past 40 years. In the mid-20th century, it was considered bad manners to eat and drink in the street. This social rule has vanished, and it is now commonplace to see people eating on the hoof. The change probably reflects a return to an earlier norm, when many, especially the poor, availed themselves of street food.

Street food as items made from cheap local ingredients sold from temporary stalls is a rarity, but many items relate to the idea. They are impossible to separate from takeaways (hot meals from specialist shops), snacks from bakers, supermarkets and chain stores, and fast food. The popularity of hot ready-to-eat foods has been affected by the imposition of tax, especially for poorer people who traditionally relied on them as treats or easy meals after work, and stringent hygiene regulations.

Types of food and the phrases used for it have social and regional nuances: for instance, a hot meal purchased from a shop is a takeaway in England, but a carry-out in Scotland.

MAJOR STREET FOODS

Fish and Chips
Fish and chips is the major British contribution to the world's repertoire of street food. It is filleted white fish, usually cod or haddock, but possibly other species

---

LONDON IN THE 1860S

The relative poverty of British street food is recent. In 1861, the social reformer Sir Henry Mayhew described the street sellers of eatables and drinkables in his work *London Labour and the London Poor*. They included sellers of pea soup, hot eels, pickled whelks, fried fish, sheep's trotters, baked potatoes, ham sandwiches, pastries, pies, boiled puddings, plum dough or duff (a type of pudding), curd and whey, cakes, ginger nuts, ice creams, and medicinal confectionery among other things. To wash them down, one could buy ginger beer, sherbet, lemonade, elder wine, rice milk, or peppermint water. Coffee stalls (apparently an innovation since the 1840s, when the common hot drink had been saloop, a version of Turkish *salep*) were popular and sold other hot drinks as well as sandwiches, boiled eggs, bread and butter, and watercress. Mayhew vividly described the vendors, their wares, and their customers and detailed the daily and seasonal rhythms associated with the different foods.

---

such as plaice or rock salmon (dogfish), dipped in batter and deep-fried, accompanied by coarsely cut chips (fries). Fried potatoes are sometimes mentioned as a 19th-century street food, and cold fried fish was hawked in north London streets by Jewish peddlers. Where and when the two got together is unknown (both London and northern England between Bradford and Manchester are suggested), but they were popular by 1900 and have remained so.

Fish and chips are usually prepared in special fish and chip shops whose opening hours (generally midday and from 5 p.m. until late) reflect peak times of demand. Until worries developed about printer's ink, portions were invariably served on newspaper, at which point the question "Open or wrapped?" indicated a choice. Buying open meant immediate consumption in the street, seasoned with malt vinegar and salt. The smell of hot fat, vinegar, and newsprint evokes memories of frosty evenings for many Brits. Wrapped indicated that they would be taken home and eaten in private, a treat to which even those with status to defend sometimes succumbed. There are regional preferences for certain fish (a wider variety in cities, especially London) and the frying medium (beef dripping in parts of northern England).

Scraps, fragments of batter detached during cooking, could be added. Mushy peas (dried green peas cooked to a purée) are often available. Curry sauce, a type of thick, heavily spiced gravy, evolved sometime in the 1960s or 1970s. Fish cakes, slices of fish between two slices of potato, were also available until recently. A chip butty is a sandwich, a white bread bun with chips and tomato ketchup or brown sauce.

Sausages dipped in batter and fried, roast chicken portions, and meat pies are also sometimes sold in fish and chip shops. Mediterranean travel led to a demand for squid rings dipped in batter and deep-fried. Late 20th-century developments associated with Glasgow included haggis, pizza, and infamously, Mars bars, each item coated with batter and deep-fried.

Meat Pies and Pasties

Pies, usually beef, with onions and sometimes potatoes are a common snack food. They are sold from hot cabinet bakeries, fish and chip shops, and other outlets. Pasties are similar, but the pastry is folded to enclose the filling, with a seam down one side. They are a traditional food of Cornwall, but the idea has spread well beyond the southwest of England and has recently become the basis for a chain of shops. Sausage rolls, sausages baked in pastry, are also popular.

Ice Cream

Perhaps the most ubiquitous street food is ice cream. In parks, at fairs, on seaside promenades, and around housing estates, roving ice-cream vans announce their presence by tunes played on chimes. Under the brand name Mr. Whippy, they dispense vanilla-flavored soft ice cream piped into wafer cones, with optional raspberry syrup. A 99 has a flake (a type of flaky chocolate bar) stuck into the ice cream. Other companies also sell ice cream made with varying degrees of authenticity and ranges of flavors. Although well known in England before the end of the 19th century, ice-cream selling as a trade was vastly expanded by an influx of Italian immigrants who sold hokeypokey from chill cabinets mounted on bicycles.

Shellfish and Seaside Foods

Seaside resorts have a strong tradition of street foods. As well as outlets for fish and chips, ice cream, and seaside rock (candy sticks with patterns or words running through them), shellfish stalls are a feature of these towns. Portions of shellfish, especially tiny brown shrimp (*Crangon crangon*), prawns, cockles, winkles, whelks, dressed crab, and latterly crabsticks (made from fish protein and crab flavor), are sold for immediate consumption. They are usually sprinkled with vinegar and eaten from disposable packs using wooden forks.

Fairs and Markets

Hot dogs made from frankfurter sausages heated in water served in a split roll with mustard and onions are sold at funfairs and other outdoor meetings. Toffee (candy) apples and candy floss (cotton candy) are also often sold at fairs, but fairings (usually sweet biscuits spiced with ginger) are now mostly extinct as fairground food.

The range of foods sold in fairgrounds, at agricultural shows, and in farmer's markets has expanded in the last 20 years to include hot sandwiches of grilled bacon or sausages, and hog roasts of pork, served in bread buns with sage and onion stuffing and apple sauce. Food trucks that have served these venues have spread out into cities, usually selling hot sandwiches and sausages. German sausages, macaroni and cheese, doughnuts, and even tacos are sold from vehicles on London streets.

A strong London tradition, sometimes found in other cities, is a winter one of hot roasted chestnuts, cooked over coals and sold with a little salt.

London and Lancashire

The Eel, Pie, and Mash shop used to be common in poorer areas of London, especially the East End. They sold eels boiled and cooled in a jellied mass, or hot with liquor, a thin green parsley sauce, and mashed potatoes. Small meat pies were an alternative as was bubble and squeak, a cabbage and mashed potatoes mixture named for the gastric results of eating the concoction. Such shops still exist but are fewer than in years past.

Black puddings and black peas are a tradition of urban markets of southwest Lancashire. Black puddings are heated in hot water and served with mustard. Black peas, small round dried peas cooked until soft and served hot dressed with vinegar (always malt), are sold in markets and at fairs. These have declined in popularity, as the industrial communities that demanded them have also declined.

Sandwiches

The sandwich, a favorite form of transportable snack from its origin sometime in the late 18th century, has developed a multiplicity of forms. Originally sliced ham or beef with mustard between two slices of bread, these have evolved into a vast range, from more traditional bread rolls filled with meat or cheese and salad to wraps of flatbread around Chinese- or Indian-style fillings, panini with cured meat and cheese, and filled croissants. They are available from many outlets, but are most obvious in supermarkets, chain stores, and chain cafés that have become a feature of the British high street, also selling coffee, soft drinks, and pastries to takeaway. Fashion and marketing both play a part in the choices presented.

Foreign Influences

Immigration has brought food from the Mediterranean, China, and India to Britain. Turkish *döner kebabs*, minced lamb cut in slices from a mass mounted on a spit, served in pita bread with salad are now sold from hot food shops and food trucks as a late-night snack. Pizzas are available from many independent and chain shops. Takeaways selling Indian or Chinese food can be found at any settlement above the size of a large village, although the food is often taken home for consumption. Other imported ideas include chains selling fast-food burger or fried chicken.

LAURA MASON

IRELAND

I RELAND HAS A LONG TRADITION of street food and markets, but nowadays, due to stringent adoption of European food safety laws, most food eaten out of one's hand in the open air is sold from permanent food stalls in shops or food courts. Itinerant street vendors selling snack foods such as burgers and hot dogs exist, but they ply their trade mostly at fairs, music festivals, sporting events, or at night near dance clubs and late night bars. In recent years, gourmet street food by Michelin-starred chefs has become a feature of some prestigious music festivals such as the Electric Picnic. Farmers' markets have become increasingly popular and numerous in the last decade. Despite a proliferation of multinational fast-food outlets, the most popular street foods are sandwiches and potato chips during the daytime and food from traditional chippers (fish and chip shops) later in the day and into the night. Turkish *döner kebabs* became a popular street food in Irish cities in the 1980s, particularly after closing time in the Irish pubs. The thin strips of spit-roasted meat is served in pita bread with shredded Dutch cabbage and topped with tomato-based chile sauce and garlic mayonnaise sauce.

The island of Ireland is the most westerly country in Europe. Called the Emerald Island, Ireland has a temperate climate that allows grass to grow nearly all year-round and is renowned particularly for its beef, sheep, and dairy industries. Bounded by ocean and sea, fish is critical to the Irish diet, and Ireland was the first European country to adopt the potato as a staple crop in the late 16th century. The population of the island is about five million (one million in Northern Ireland, a part of the United Kingdom). Catholicism is the dominant religion although religious influence on diet, such as eating fish on Friday, has significantly declined in recent decades. Over the last 15 years, Ireland has become a truly multicultural society with the influx of immigrants from the Baltic States, Eastern Europe, Africa, and Asia, many of whom work in the food business, particularly at hot-food sandwich counters and in the fast-food sector. Street food is eaten by all classes in Ireland but most frequently by the lower social classes.

The main sources of carbohydrates in Ireland are bread and potatoes although pasta, noodles, and rice have become increasingly popular. This dominance corresponds with the proliferation of sandwiches and chips within Irish street-food culture. Preprepared sandwiches are widely available, the most common being ham, chicken and stuffing, and the BLT (bacon, lettuce, and tomato). Hot food/sandwich counters have opened in most convenience stores and gas stations selling breakfast rolls in the morning (baguette filled with sausages, bacon, fried egg, and black pudding) and specializing in made-to-order rolls and sandwiches for the lunchtime business. One of the most popular lunchtime items is a chicken fillet baguette (a breaded chicken breast chopped and served in a baguette with mayonnaise and shredded iceberg lettuce). Potato wedges (plain or spicy) are another popular item from these hot food counters. Juice and smoothie bars also became popular sources of street food during the recent economic boom.

Street traders have been selling food in Irish cities for hundreds of years. Some of these from the 18th century have been captured in a series of drawings called *The Cries of Dublin* by artist Hugh Douglas Hamilton. Food sold included oysters, fresh milk, apples, fish, hot peas, and herbs. The quintessential Dublin anthem "Molly Malone" is about a fishmonger who sold "cockles and mussels alive, alive oh." Nowadays there are fewer street dealers, as they are known, and their continued existence is partly due to the late parliamentarian Tony Gregory, who went to jail to defend the trading rights of these predominantly female dealers. The tradition continues in locations such as Moore Street and Meath Street in Dublin and in the English Market in Cork. These dealers sell mostly fruit, vegetables, and fish, rather than food to be eaten on the spot. Some sell reduced-priced chocolate bars (often seconds), a practice popular outside sporting occasions and music events.

In the last 10 years particularly, there has been a sharp increase in farmers' markets. These come in a number of categories: markets where the farmer or family member sells their products directly; markets where there is a mix of farmers and other itinerant food sellers who often sell imported products at a higher price with the illusion of it being locally sourced; and specific markets specializing in organic food. The good farmers' markets provide a direct link between the producer and consumer and are particularly popular with the growing number of artisan cheese makers, pork butchers, jam makers, and bakers. A popular street food sold at such markets is crêpes, which can be sweet (sugar and lemon, or Nutella—a chocolate hazelnut spread) or savory (e.g., goat's cheese, rocket (arugula), and red pesto).

MAJOR STREET FOODS

Sandwiches

Sandwiches still remain the most popular lunchtime food for the working public. Historically, the majority of workers and schoolchildren made their sandwiches at home. There were always shops that would make sandwiches to order, but prepacked sandwiches were associated principally with railway catering. With growing economic success and increasing female participation in the workforce during the 1990s, prepacked sandwiches became the market leader in convenience street food. The value of the combined deli and prepacked sandwich market in Ireland is worth half a billion euros annually. Ireland's largest sandwiches company, Freshways, has a quarter of the prepacked market. The made-to-order sandwich business also increased dramatically with sandwich counters appearing in most convenience stores. A number of sandwich bar chains opened, the most famous being O'Briens Irish Sandwich Bars, which franchised its business globally. Sandwich bars also sell coffee, and specialist coffee shops also sell sandwiches. One of the leaders in specialty and gourmet sandwiches has been the Marks & Spencer supermarket chain, which has a number of outlets in Ireland. More than 900,000 sandwiches a week are purchased in Ireland today. Sandwiches are often eaten with a bag of Tayto crisps.

Traditional Irish Italian Chippers

Chips, or French fries, are by far the most popular hot street food in Ireland. This niche business was set up by the Italian immigrant community, which began to arrive in Ireland around the 1880s. These Irish-Italian families, who all came from the Val di Comino in southern Italy, began working in the food business

---

SPICE BURGERS

The spice burger is a unique Irish product made since the 1950s by Walsh Family Foods. The patented recipe is a blend of Irish beef, onions, cereals, herbs, and spices coated with a traditional outer crumb. The product has featured in the menus of Irish chippers for generations and is also sold in supermarkets. In June 2009, the company closed due to the financial crisis. There was public outcry for the loss of this unique part of Irish culinary heritage. A "save our spice burger" campaign was started on Facebook and other social media outlets. The publicity stoked the interest of catering distributors and retailers to have placed sufficient orders with the company to justify a resumption of production, saving valued jobs in the Dublin factory.

---

selling ice cream and fried sliced potatoes (known as chips). Their combination of fish and chips became known as a one and one in Dublin and among some denizens of Cork as "a bag of blocks and a swimmer." Giuseppe Cervi is credited with being the forerunner in these operations, opening his business in 1885 on Great Brunswick Street (now Pearse Street). In the early part of the 20th century, these Italian families ran ice-cream parlors, soda fountains, fried fish restaurants, and grills. A second wave of immigrants also from the Comino valley arrived after World War II, and chippers became more widespread particularly with the growth of suburban living. In recent years, the Irish Traditional Italian Chipper Association, which has around 200 participating members, have designated May 25 as the Irish National Fish and Chips Day. On this day, there are queues outside most chippers as fish and chips are sold at a special reduced price.

The most popular fish is cod (fresh and smoked), but ray is also very popular in Dublin. Both fish and chips are usually topped with salt and malt vinegar and served in paper bags. The combination of seasoning and steam from the closed bags produces a unique flavor and texture. Other classic chipper dishes include onion rings, batter burgers, battered sausage, and garlic mushrooms. Curry sauce and garlic mayonnaise have also become popular as condiments. Another peculiarly Irish takeaway food associated with chippers is the spice burger—a commercially produced blend of Irish beef, onions, cereals, herbs, and spices, coated in a traditional outer crumb, usually deep-fried (see box on page 472).

Many chippers such as those run by the Macari and Borza families have diversified over time and also sell burgers, southern fried chicken, and sometimes *döner kebabs* and pizza. Dublin's most famous chipper is Leo Burdock's in the historic center of the city and has a regular local and vibrant tourist trade.

TAYTO CRISPS

One of the most popular snack foods in Ireland are crisps, which are commonly known as Tayto's. Crisps are deep-fried wafer thin potato slices, known in the United States as potato chips. They are sold in sealed foil bags. The Tayto company began making their cheese- and onion-flavored crisps in 1954, and the word *Tayto* has been synonymous with crisps in Ireland ever since. Salt and vinegar is the second most popular flavor. In recent years, Tayto has lost market share to companies such as King and Walkers, but Irish immigrants still yearn for a packet of Tayto crisps when they are away from home.

Ice Cream

Ireland has one of the highest per capita ice-cream consumption rates in the world. There are two main varieties of street consumed ice cream: ice pops/ice-cream bars and Mr. Whippy's freshly whipped ice-cream cones, which, with the addition of a chocolate flake, are known as 99's. Ice cream is widely sold all year-round, but whenever a particularly hot day arrives, ice-cream cabinets are often emptied by early afternoon of products such as choc ice, brunch, iceberger, fat frogs, and wibbly wobbly wonders. One of the most famous locations for Mr. Whippy's is Teddy's in Dún Laoghaire, which has been operating since the 1950s. The sound of certain music has excited children for decades as it signals the arrival of an ice-cream van in their neighborhood. These Mr. Whippy vans are still a regular part of Irish life.

Specialized Street Food

Certain foods are associated with particular parts of Ireland. Blaa is a yeast bread roll that is found principally in Waterford. The selling of cooked periwinkles as a street food was widespread in the past but is now found only in Kilkee in County

Clare, sold alongside dillisk (edible seaweed). Drisheen is a type of sausage made from sheep's blood and sold nearly exclusively in Cork. Candy floss (cotton candy) is associated with traveling circuses, funfairs, and seaside resorts. Yellowman or yallaman is a type of Irish toffee, golden in color and brittle, sometimes known as honeycomb candy or sponge toffee. It is traditionally associated with the Auld Lammas Fair, which has run on the last Monday and Tuesday of August in Bally-castle Co. Antrim since 1600. The yellowman is broken into small chunks with a hammer and sold by street traders in small paper cones.

MÁIRTÍN MAC CON IOMAIRE

THE NETHERLANDS

SITUATED ON THE NORTHWESTERN RIM of the European mainland, the Netherlands has a rich history as a seafaring nation. The country's main seaports, Rotterdam and Amsterdam, have been receiving foodstuffs of all description for several centuries, both for local consumption and for reexportation. Always avid traders who grasped whatever means they could to gain and hold their position, the Dutch had replaced the Spanish as the most important cacao traders in the world by the middle of the 17th century. Much of the world's production continues to pass through these ports. Trade and subsequent colonization brought in spices from the Indonesian islands and cane sugar from its Caribbean possessions, among other things.

The country's reputation for tolerance encouraged ethnic minorities to seek shelter there. Large numbers of Sephardic Jews settled in Amsterdam when they fled the Spanish Inquisition at the end of the 15th century and French Huguenots received a warm welcome from their Calvinist brethren upon escaping persecution in France in the latter part of the 17th century. Following World War II, Indonesia claimed independence and many Indonesians, primarily those who had fought for the Dutch during the war, left the islands to settle in the Netherlands. In the 1960s, labor shortages forced companies to look further afield for willing workers and set in train an immigration wave of Turkish and Moroccan men, who later brought their families to join them. The Dutch colony of Surinam became independent in 1975 and led to mass migration to the Netherlands. As a result of the historical development of sugar cultivation and production, the Surinamese people had varied ethnic backgrounds: African, Indian, Indonesian (predominantly Javanese), and Chinese. Natural disasters and political currents continue to bring in refugees from all parts of the world, and in recent years, Dutch society has been enriched with Vietnamese, Somalis, and Afghans among others. This ethnic composition is reflected in street and snack food in the Netherlands.

Most towns have one or more market days a week, and local councils rent out space to vendors on a contract basis. Fairs and special celebrations also attract food vendors. All sellers of food are expected to comply with HACCP (Hazard Analysis and Critical Control Points) regulations, and inspectors carry out regular checks in the interest of public health.

MAJOR STREET FOODS

The Snack Wall

The snack wall or *automatiek* is a well-known feature at street corners and railway stations and is one of the quickest ways to get a snack on the run. It resembles a vending machine that is built into an expanse of wall and can contain several dozen warmed compartments that hold mainly popular deep-fried snacks such as *frikandellen* (a long minced meat sausage); *kroketten* (croquettes made from thickened meat stock and pieces of meat that are usually eaten with mustard); *kaassoufflés* (literally "cheese soufflé"), which are small envelopes of thin dough with a cheese filling; *nasischijven* (rissoles made from Indonesian-style fried rice); *bamischijven* (as before, but made with noodles); and many other similar snacks. When the correct payment is inserted into the slot, the door unlocks and the snack can be removed.

French Fries

Patates frites are known locally by either of the two component parts with a simplified Dutch spelling: *patat* or *friet*. It is often shortened to the diminutive *patatje* with the kind of French fry coming after the word, for example, *patatje oorlog*. The original name is an antiquated form of French and may have originated in Belgium, where both French and Dutch are official languages. They form a cheap and warming snack. Trucks equipped with deep-fat fryers stand at strategic points in towns and cities, and consumers can choose from the following variants that come in the form of single toppings or combinations:

- *Met* literally means "with"; with mayonnaise.
- *Speciaal*, "special," is a mixture of curry ketchup (which can best be described as a cross between tomato ketchup and brown sauce with spices), mayonnaise, and finely chopped onion.
- *Pinda*, "peanut," is a smooth spiced peanut sauce that is the usual accompaniment to the popular Indonesian dish of satay (grilled skewered pieces of chicken or meat).
- *Oorlog*, "war," is a mixture of mayonnaise, peanut sauce, and finely chopped onion.
- *Kapsalon* (literally "hairdressing salon") is the most recent addition to Dutch street food. Thinly sliced meat of the type cooked on rotating spits in Turkish and Middle Eastern eating establishments is arranged over the fries. Optional cheese can be added, and the whole is then grilled. It is finished off with a helping of salad and sauces such as garlic or hot pepper sauce.

Fish

As may be expected from a country with a generous coastline, fisheries form an important part of the economy. There are more than 1,200 mobile fish vendors in the Netherlands, which together account for about 19 percent of the country's total sales of fish. All open-air markets have at least one fish stall in the form of a fully equipped truck; many villages without a market are visited once a week by a licensed vendor. Raw fish is also sold, and any fish of choice can be fried on the spot. Most popular are chunks and fillets. *Kibbeling* consists of marinated chunks of thick white fish that are quickly pulled through a thin batter before being fried. Optional sauces are available on the side, including mayonnaise-based garlic and tartare sauces. *Kibbeling* used to be made from cod (*kabeljauw*) from which the name is derived. Nowadays cheaper and more ecological alternatives are used. The fillets are called *lekkerbekjes* and usually come from haddock or similar fish, dipped in a thin light batter before being fried and sprinkled with spiced salt.

Smoked fish, including salmon, eel, and mackerel, can be put into a soft white bread roll to be eaten on the spot. Lightly brined herring called *maatjesharing* is cleaned and skinned, but the last piece of the backbone is left intact so that the tail joins the two fillets. There is a purpose to this as the fish is eaten in one of two ways: on a soft bread roll sprinkled generously with freshly chopped onion or dipped in onion, held by tail, and lowered bit by bit into a waiting mouth. This herring is governed by strict regulations on many levels. Fishing takes place in May and June when the fish has the required fat content of between 16 and 25 percent. After the fish are caught, the gills and intestines are removed, but the pancreas is left in place because it contains enzymes that help with the curing process. The prepared herrings are soft in texture, and the brevity of the curing process prevents them from becoming too salty.

Sweet Snacks

The tradition of selling sweet snacks at street corners dates back several centuries, but in most cases, modern techniques have replaced the solitary vendor with a simple pan or griddle. Almost every open-air market has a *stroopwafel* vendor. These thin and crisp wafers are cooked on a portable griddle, then skillfully split and sandwiched with warm, buttery caramel. *Poffertjes* (puffy little pancakes like silver dollars) are cooked to order at many markets and fairs, using a special griddle with small indentations, which give the pancakes a puffy appearance. They are eaten with a knob of butter and a sprinkling of powdered sugar. *Oliebollen* (round doughnuts with or without dried fruit) are a seasonal treat. They are made and eaten in Dutch homes on New Year's Eve, but from the beginning of November to the end of December, fully equipped trucks decorated to look like old-fashioned kitchens take up positions all over the country. The doughnuts are fried and dusted generously with powdered sugar before being eaten on the spot or taken home to share. *Appelbeignets* are also sold by the same vendors. These are round slices of apple that are dipped into batter before being fried.

OTHER STREET FOODS

Many new foods introduced by immigrant communities are sold from small stalls and trucks that either have a fixed position or visit a different town every day. The Vietnamese refugees who settled in the Netherlands from the 1980s introduced the Vietnamese *loempia* to the Dutch public. This spring roll differs from the

Chinese and Indonesian versions in that it is slender and elegant, with a thin and crisp wrapper. Sweet or spicy chile sauce is added to taste by the customer.

Lahmacun, a paper-thin Turkish bread with a smear of spicy meat topping, is known locally as *Turkse pizza* ("Turkish pizza"). It is baked quickly in an oven or on a griddle, topped with the buyer's choice of salad items such as lettuce, cucumber, and onion, then drizzled with hot chile or garlic sauce before being rolled up into a cylinder.

Many Surinamese snacks are sold from stalls in larger cities with a more mixed population. These include *bara* (split pea fritters), bread rolls filled with curried chicken, and roti (Indian flatbread) stuffed with various kinds of curry.

GAITRI PAGRACH-CHANDRA

SWITZERLAND

S WITZERLAND IS A SMALL COUNTRY located on the borders of France, Germany, Austria, Italy, and Liechtenstein. It is most famous for the Alps, the mountains that dominate the southern part of the country, and the Jura chain in the northwest. In fact, Switzerland has a variety of landscapes and climate variations. Most of the country's cities are on a large plateau between the mountains, and here the climate is much like the rest of Central–Western Europe. Major European rivers begin in Switzerland's mountains, including the Rhine, Rhone, Ticino, and Inn. The valleys can be warm, and wine grapes are grown on hill slopes in the Valais. Switzerland also has famous lakes where climates are more temperate than the glacial mountains: Lake Geneva on the French border to the west and Lake Constance next to Germany to the north. Small farms have long been the mainstay of Swiss agriculture, the most famous product being dairy—as in cheeses such as Gruyère, Emmenthaler, and other varieties that are known internationally as "Swiss cheese."

Because the country has broad rivers, valleys, and passes over the Alps to the south, it has always been a crossroads for travelers and settlers. Switzerland is really a confederation of independent states, called cantons, each of which speaks one of the country's four official languages. Swiss German is the main language of the north and center, and most Swiss speak a dialect of a Swiss version called Schwyzerdütsch. Zurich, Bern, and Basel are cities in this linguistic zone. French is the language of the west, especially Geneva, Lausanne, and Lucerne. Italian is spoken in the south, and in the mountainous south, a Romance language called

Romansh. Although such traditional culture as folklore and religious practices differs from region to region, a good deal of food is eaten in common across the country. Some items are very German, such as pretzels and sausages; others are French such as crêpes and some cheeses.

Switzerland is one of the world's richest countries, so street food is not a basic necessity of life as it is in lesser developed nations. It is, however, enjoyed because of its high quality, and it is part of everyday Swiss culture. Public dining is also a feature of fairs and festivals. Much of it is hearty as befits a country that prizes outdoor activities and its ethic of hard work.

MAJOR STREET FOODS

Pretzels

Called *brezel* in German, these are raised wheat-flour dough, formed in the traditional "crossed arms" shape and baked until golden brown. Swiss pretzels are neither like the packaged hard ones sold in American stores nor exactly like the soft ones sold at American fairs or on streets of cities. Instead, the Swiss *brezel* is large, soft, and very chewy. Not only are there all kinds of toppings available but it can also be cut horizontally and filled with interesting ingredients. The most popular is cheese, but tuna and ham are also widely consumed. The most famous chain is Brezel Koenig (Pretzel King).

Sausages

Swiss sausage makers are world famous, and several versions are sold from stands in all parts of the country. The most beloved sausage comes from St. Gallen, called St. Galler Kalbsbratwurst. It is a thick, pale sausage made from veal, some bacon, and a little milk; it is normally grilled and served with slices of thick bread or inserted into a crusty pretzel-like bun in the style of hot dogs. A horseradish-laced mustard is the most common topping (in St. Gallen, it is eaten plain). *Cervelat* is almost equally popular. Made from beef, pork, and bacon, this large sausage (usually four ounces) can be boiled, fried, or grilled. One special sausage called *longeole* is served from stands at such festivals as the Escalade in Geneva during December. This is a huge pork sausage that is heavily spiced with fennel among others, cooked with potatoes and lentils, and served in thick slices with bread. The best time to sample sausages on the street is the national Wurst-fest held in November.

Crêpes

Crêpes are very popular in Switzerland. They are served from mobile trucks, and there are many kiosks in places like train stations that sell crêpes to commuters and other travelers. Crêpes are thin pancakes made on the spot and usually rolled up with fillings and sometimes toppings. Some are savory, meaning that they are filled with cheese or even chopped meats. The most popular are sweet crêpes, with fillings such as jams and the sauce that the Swiss love most—*apfelmus* (applesauce). Toppings usually include cinnamon and powdered sugar.

Marroni

When the cold season starts, *heissi marroni* (hot chestnuts) vendors appear on streets in every city and town. Large tubs heated with hot charcoal are set up, and the chestnuts are slowly roasted until they are cooked through and soft inside. To eat them, the soft shell must be opened to get at the nutmeat. The smell and taste of roasted chestnuts are sweet and perhaps not familiar to people who have not become accustomed to eating them. But they are the great indigenous Swiss street food because of the chestnut tree–forested mountains of the country's south.

Chestnuts are the great indigenous Swiss street food.

Magenbrot (Stomach Bread)

This is a thick, spicy, crispy cookie from northern Switzerland sold on streets during festival time when there is a lot of heavy food eaten on the street. Made with ginger, cinnamon, and cloves, it is called "stomach bread" because spices in it are thought to settle the stomach after overeating. Folklore is not wrong because ginger is widely used to treat nausea and digestive distress.

Panini and Flatbreads

A panini is an Italian sandwich that is sold from trailers and from fixed kiosks. One way to serve them is cold, as a sandwich filled with such Italian ingredients as prosciutto and cheese, but Swiss vendors often grill them in a special press and serve the sandwich warm. *Piadina* is a flatbread from central Italy that has made its way to such Swiss cities as Zurich. It is a flat disk of dough that is cooked on a flat griddle until it has blackened spots on it. The *piadina* is then filled with various ingredients, from ham to cheese, folded over, and served warm. Pizza slices are also quite popular, though made and sold from small open-fronted kiosks in urban locations.

Kebabs

Like many other places in Europe, Turkish/Middle Eastern kebabs have become popular street food everywhere. Kebabs can be made from chunks of lamb, beef, or chicken skewered on rods plain or with tomatoes, onions, and peppers. The most popular are *döner kebabs*, the Turkish version of gyros. Large skewers of compressed meat—often veal in Switzerland—is set on a horizontal grill and cooked. Thin slices of meat are cut from the skewered meat, set on a thin flatbread, and served with lettuce, tomatoes, and a choice of sauces ranging from spicy hot to mild and creamy. Probably the best known are on Zurich's Langstrasse (long street), an area that has become well known for ethnic foods and a go-to place when visiting the city.

BRUCE KRAIG

CHAPTER 5

MILKSHAKE PASTRY
CHIKO ROLL
KULAU HANGI
TAPIOCA
SANDWICHES
PEA, PIE, AND PUD

OCEANIA

OCEANIA

AUSTRALIA

T HE COMMONWEALTH OF AUSTRALIA consists of the Australian continent, the island state of Tasmania, and many small islands around the continental mass. Australia has been continuously inhabited by Aboriginal and Torres Strait Islander peoples for more than 50,000 years. Indigenous foodways—bush tucker—drawing on native plants and animals have remained marginalized. The indigenous peoples remained isolated from developing civilizations in South East Asia until trade in trepan (sea cucumber) with the Bugi fisherman of Macassar in the early 15th century followed by the colonization of the continent by Britain beginning in 1770, but there is little influence in the cuisine from this source either.

Over the next 200 years, six independent self-governing British Crown colonies were established, and these formed the Commonwealth of Australia in 1901. For most of its modern nationhood, Australian foodways have largely derived from British traditions.

Southern Chinese were the first large-scale migration heading for the Victorian goldfields from the mid-1850s. The local Chinese restaurant became a recognizable feature of every town in Australia and has remained so. Post–World War II migrations from Europe brought whole communities of Italians and Greeks together with Jewish survivors of the Holocaust. It was to this migration Australia owed the development of a European café culture, with its profusion of cakes and pastries at one end and the town milk bar at the other, selling milkshakes, fish and chips, and hamburgers. The 1973 dismantling of the White Australia

Policy, which had restricted migration of nonwhite peoples, and the end of the Vietnam War saw large migrations of South East Asians and a growth in tourism by Australians into Asia. This led to the development of the fusion of Western and Eastern food-ways that became known as Mod Oz and the transformation of Asian hawker stalls into indoor food halls in shopping centers. Refugees from the Middle East, Africa, and South Asia have further diversified the population and the cuisine.

Street food underwent parallel changes to the home and dining-out diet. Other factors also have shaped it in Australia. The first is a long-standing Anglo Australian attitude that considers it bad manners to eat in the street. The second factor, and one of more consequence, is the enactment of hygiene regulations at all three levels of government that made it increasingly hard to sell food from barrows, vans, stalls, and even more difficult to prepare food on the street. Other legislation that affected street food grew out of laws protective of the city markets and the small corner stores and cafés that removed vendors from roadways where they impeded traffic flow. Recent reverses to this trend include eat carts in the city selling gourmet and snacks and pavement restaurant dining.

MAJOR STREET FOODS

Pies and Pastries

Pies have been a staple of Australian street food since its earliest days as a colony, sold by the pie man on foot, from a pie cart, or increasingly from cafés and hotels as small businesses grew. Harry's Café de Wheels in Woolloomooloo is the last still operating. Pie fillings have varied with the cost of meats, health concerns, and most recently gourmandizing. They range from chunky meat in thick brown gravy, through low-grade mince (plain or curried), to meat and vegetable combinations (meat and potatoes, chicken, and mushroom), and to lamb shanks cooked in red wine. The South Australian pie floater is often cited as a uniquely Australian dish, a meat pie afloat in a soup of peas gravy. The pie has been accompanied throughout by the Cornish pasty, or also a meat- and vegetable-filled half moon–shaped pastry. Sausage rolls, mince wrapped in a log of puff pastry, have been the other constant. Tomato sauce remains the traditional condiment for all of these. Multiculturalism brought with it Greek spanakopita (phyllo pastry) and Turkish *gözleme* (a roti-style pancake) both enclosing spinach and feta or mince in the case of the latter, and both accompanied with a slice of lemon. Cosmopolitanism brought variations on quiche. Vegetarianism brought lentil pies.

Sandwiches, Rolls, and Wraps

Like encasing fillings in pastry, putting a range of ingredients between two slices of bread and variations of this form a large part of Australian street food. The bread or the roll (round or torpedo shaped) has changed from white bread through a range of wholemeal and multigrains to artisan breads and sourdoughs. Fillings have evolved from the simple, like egg and lettuce, tomato and cheese, or pressed meats (devon, salamis), to virtually anything from the multicultural menu that

SANDWICHES

can be spread or sliced. Focaccia is filled with chicken and avocado and served fresh or toasted. Pita and other flatbreads are opened into pockets that are filled with or wrapped around hummus, tabouleh, kebab meats, or shawarma. Vietnamese pork rolls pile together pate, roast pork slices, pressed pork, grated carrot, sliced cucumber, sprigs of coriander and fish, and chile sauces. The hamburger plays a central part, both in its earliest form of a homemade meat patty topped with beetroot, tomato, and lettuce (and occasionally pineapple), and in its fast-food forms.

Grills

The sausage sizzle—a range of sausages cooked outdoors on a grill or hot plate—began as a picnic and grew into a ubiquitous food at charity fund-raisers, outside public houses and at large sporting events. The sausage is eaten in a sandwich or a roll smothered in grilled onions and tomato sauce and now mustard and chile sauce also. Its cousin is the steak sandwich similarly prepared.

Fried Food

Seafood is battered and/or crumbed, sprinkled with vinegar, dusted with salt and a wedge of lemon, and is served wrapped in paper. Potato chips or scallops are enjoyed as accompaniment or as a meal themselves. The chiko roll is the only

Australian street food for which an identifiable inventor and moment of creation can be verified—Frank McEnroe, 1951, in Bendigo (rural Victoria). McEnroe took the Chinese fried spring roll, gave it a thicker pastry cover, stuffed it with minced mutton and sliced vegetables, and supersized it.

Salads

With increasing concern for healthier eating, prepackaged single services of salad have become a staple street food. Pasta salads (cold cooked pasta mixed with a variety of ingredients), Greek salads (olives, tomato, capsicum, feta, and lettuce with vinaigrette), and tropical fruit salads are particularly popular.

OTHER STREET FOODS

Drinks

Milkshakes (milk, flavoring, and ice cream blended) remain a favorite along with smoothies (yogurt, fruit, and milk blended with freshly blended fruits), vegetable juices or crushes (with ice), and commercial carbonated drinks.

Ice Creams

Choc tops (a scoop of ice cream covered with a hard coating of chocolate sauce served in a cone) are popular cinema fare. Suburban streets still ring to the tones of "Greensleeves" as the Mr. Whippy soft serve ice-cream van comes by. Gelato outlets create flavor combinations to reflect changing tastes.

Fruit and Nut Stalls

The fruit and nut barrows of the first half of the 20th century are gone. In their place are more permanent booths now also carrying salads, sandwiches, and wraps.

PAUL VAN REYK

NEW ZEALAND

L YING ABOUT 2,500 MILES to the southeast of Australia in the South Pacific Ocean, the nation of New Zealand is a modern country with strong international connections. Modern transportation systems bring about 3 million visitors a year to this nation of 4.7 million people. Many Kiwis, as New Zealanders are known, named for the native flightless bird, have travelled the world. Along with immigration from Asian, Polynesian, and Melanesian countries, the result is a nation with a diverse and vibrant food scene.

The New Zealand land mass is 10 percent larger than Great Britain but has only 6 percent of its population. It is mainly composed of two islands, called North and South Islands, with most people living on the more temperate northern land mass. Like neighboring Australia, New Zealand is one of the world's most urbanized countries with 86 percent of is people dwelling in and around cities. Auckland, with 1.5 million people, is the largest city; Wellington, the capital, holds close to 350,000. South Island is thinly populated but has the most diverse climate and landscapes. Both islands have mountainous spines, the southern one with spectacular snow-covered alpine slopes. The fiords, beaches, rolling plains and remaining forests that cover South Island are known worldwide because the popular *Lord of the Rings* and *The Hobbit* movies were filmed there. From the 19th century until recent decades, the sloping grasslands were home to huge flocks of sheep raised for wool and meat. In recent years, the country's dairy industry has become the lead exporter; its butter and cheese are sold across the globe. Rich farmland on both islands and a famous wine industry keep agricultural sector vital and provide the basis for New Zealand's thriving food culture.

In the 2013 census, 74 percent of New Zealand residents were of European origin, 11.8 percent Asian, 7.4 percent from the Pacific region and, 14.9 percent as Māori. Māoris migrated across thousands of miles of open ocean to New Zealand in their long canoes around 800 to 1000 CE. They settled in as small-scale farmers, hunters, and gatherers. Among the native foods gathered were seaweed, fern shoots, berries, grubs, shellfish, crayfish, thistles, fish, wild birds, and local herbs. They also brought new foods including the all-important sweet potato. When British settlers arrived, Māoris quickly adapted pigs, chickens, corn, wheat, and others, melding them into their own culinary traditions. Today, native foods have become popular among chefs, some finding their ways into street food.

An important catalyst in the creation of a dynamic food scene has been the growth of the New Zealand wine industry. Two hundred years ago, an early British settler said that "New Zealand promises to be very favorable to the vine," and the first vineyards were planted as early as 1819. The industry grew slowly in the 20th century but rapidly expanded in the 1980s following investments by overseas companies. Today, the country's sauvignon blancs and pinot noirs have a major presence in international markets. With the growth in domestic wine consumption, aided by a relaxation of restrictions on its sale, came high-end restaurants (Wellington is said to have more bars and restaurants per capita than New York). There are more than 100 food and wine festivals annually in New Zealand.

Today New Zealand has a diverse and exciting street food culture that incorporates local and foreign influences. Many restaurant owners and chefs, or aspiring owners, have opened food stalls in every city. However, street food in New Zealand has a long history.

As in Australia, roadside stands, called pie carts, were widespread during the depression in the early 1930s, providing hot meals at low prices. They were usually converted caravans (a caravan is a vehicle people can live in, towed by a car, similar to a camper in the U.S.) with a hinged side that served as an awning to shelter customers as they placed their orders. The typical fare consisted of mince (chopped meat) pies with mashed potato and peas covered with gravy, known as "pea, pie, and pud." They remained a source of fast food in small towns until the 1970s, when competition from fast-food outlets led to their virtual disappearance.

Today a few pie carts are still operating in New Zealand, though they no longer offer pies and instead sell burgers, toasted sandwiches, steaks, and chips (French fries). One of the most famous pie carts is the White Lady in Auckland, a converted caravan opened in 1948 and still run by the same family. Open in the evening, it is famous for its hamburgers and has become an iconic institution for locals and a must-visit destination for tourists. Another popular street food stand, started in the 1970s, is Nin's Bin on the coastal road from Christchurch to Kaikoura on the east coast of South Island. It is famous for its freshly harvested crayfish and mussels accompanied by white bread and butter and its spectacular views.

Today, night markets (sometimes called "noodle markets" when other goods are sold), street food festivals, and wandering caravans have become ubiquitous in urban areas. Their fare reflects a wide variety of influences, from Chinese and Korean to Mexican and modern American. For example, in Auckland popular trucks include the Lucky Taco Food truck, with an extensive menu of Mexican-inspired dishes; Brooklyn Dogs, which serves hot dogs; the Roaming Dive, which serves dishes from the American country fairs, including chicken and waffle sliders and po'boys; The Food Truck, known for its healthy burgers and tacos made with whole grains, fresh ingredients, and vegetables; Acho's, with its Japanese take on New York street food; the Tin Kitchen, whose signature dish is a Cajun-spiced crab burger with tamarind mayo and mango chili; Judge Bao, an artisan Chinese eatery run by two well-known chefs; and Coreano, which sells Mexican-Korean fusion dishes. Many of these mobile trucks can also be found at The Street Food Collective on Ponsonby Road, which is open seven days a week. Vendors also set up shop along the city's waterfront, at the Glenfield and Pakuranga night markets or at the Night Noodle Markets in North Hagley Park.

In Wellington, the annual Visa Wellington on a Plate festival features a food truck trailer park where vendors park for up to a month. A selection of the city's more than 40 street food trucks can be found along the waterfront year-round.

A traditional Māori dish, hangi, can be found at Māori festivals and the small storefront Kiwi Kai in Rotorua. Origially a mixture of meat and root vegetables wrapped in a leaf and cooked on hot stones, at Kiwi Kai the meat and vegetables are wrapped in a cabbage leaf and served in fried bread.

BRUCE KRAIG AND COLLEEN TAYLOR SEN

PAPUA NEW GUINEA

Papua New Guinea (PNG) was formed after World War II from the merger of the Territory of Papua (formerly a British colony transferred to Australian administration in 1905) and German New Guinea. Australia continued to administer the country till its independence in 1975. Taking up half of the island of New Guinea, it is located in the Melanesian region of the Pacific.

Most people are of Papuan or Melanesian descent, and there are small populations of Chinese, Fijian Indian, Australians, Europeans, and Americans. Just more than 80 percent live in rural and remote areas in villages.

Foodways in Papua New Guinea reflect this demography. The basic food profile is similar to that of Melanesia. The staples are starchy vegetables and fruits such as taro, cassava (manioc), yam, plantain, *kaukau* (sweet potato), and sago. Rice and breads are now also regularly eaten as part of the starch component. Accompanying the starch are *kumu* (green leafy indigenous and imported vegetables), Asian and European vegetables and fruits, indigenous meats such as cuscus possum or tree kangaroo, chicken, river and ocean fish, shellfish, and crustaceans. Pigs are reserved for bride price and for ceremonial feasts. Imported lamb flaps, a fatty offcut from the ribs, have become a major source of meat with unhealthy effects. Salt is the main seasoning, followed by stock cubes. Western fast food (roasted and fried chicken, burgers, deep-fried potato chips, pizza, highly sugared carbonated drinks) has made inroads into the diet, particularly in urban communities, also with unhealthy results.

In rural and remote areas, food is cooked over wood fires—on improvised metal grills, boiled or fried in saucepans—or in the ashes. Town dwellers use electric cooking ranges supplemented by outdoor wood fires.

Street food is an extension of these foodways. Most is sold in the informal economy, the substantial unregulated sector in Papua New Guinea in which individuals and families sell goods directly from the front of their house, in markets, or at roadside stalls.

MAJOR STREET FOODS

Market Food

This is the longest established style of street food and includes tapioca or sago wrapped and steamed in banana leaves (sometimes with a banana); grilled fish; bunches of peanuts on the stem; other nuts like *galip* (canarium); fruit; and *kulau* (young coconut from which to drink coconut water). Scones or buns have become popular in recent times.

Lunch Packets

Developed specifically for urban clerical, service, and industrial workers who cannot return home for midday meals, these are usually a prepackaged small Styrofoam tray of boiled rice with fish or chicken, a boiled starchy root, boiled leafy green vegetables, and slices of fresh carrot and onion or an *igir*—a mix of vegetables and fish or chicken cooked in coconut milk served on a banana leaf in an aluminum foil parcel.

Roadside Food

This is a relatively recent development to provide snacks for long-haul transport drivers and the constant stream of people traveling between villages on public motor vehicles. The main roadside foods are boiled corn on the cob, grilled starchy roots and fruit (taro, *kaukau*, plantain), grilled lamb flaps and saveloys (a spicy red-colored sausage), boiled eggs in their shell, peanuts, and Western fast food. Carbonated soft drinks have become the beverage of choice on the road.

PAUL VAN REYK

SELECTED BIBLIOGRAPHY

Barth, Gerald A. *Street Food: Informal Sector Food Preparation and Marketing, Equity Policy Center.* Iloilo City, The Philippines, 1983, http://pdf.usaid.gov/pdf_docs/PNAAP942.pdf

Bhat, R.V., and A.P. Simopoulous, eds. *Street Foods, World Review of Nutrition and Dietetics.* Volume 86. Basel, Switzerland: Karger Publishers, 2000.

Bowles, Tom Parker. *The World's Best Street Food: Where to Find It and How to Make It.* Melbourne, Australia: Lonely Planet, 2012.

Cross, John and Alfonso Morales. *Street Entrepreneurs: People, Place, & Politics in Local and Global Perspective.* New York: Routledge, 2007.

Davidson, Alan. *The Oxford Companion to Food.* Oxford: Oxford University Press, 1999.

Diamanti, Carla and Fabrizio Esposito. *Street Food: A Culinary Journey through the Streets of the World.* Nyack, New York: Ullmann, 2011.

Edge, John T. *The Truck Food Cookbook: 150 Recipes and Ramblings from America's Best Restaurants on Wheels.* New York: Workman Publishing Company, 2012.

Fellows, Peter and Martin Hilmi. *Selling Street and Snack Foods.* Diversification Booklet Number 18. FAO (Rome 2011).

Ferguson, Clare. *Street Food.* New York: Time Life Education, 1999.

Grant, Rose. *Street Food.* Freedom, Calif.: Crossing Press, 1988.

Kime, Tom. *Street Food: Exploring the World's Most Authentic Tastes.* London: Dorikng Kinderseley, 2007.

Kiple, Kenneth F. and Kriemhild Coneè Ornelas. *The Cambridge World History of Food*. Cambridge: Cambridge University Press, 2000.

Kraig, Bruce. *Hot Dog: A Global History*. London: Reaktion Press, 2009.

Luard, Elizabeth. *European Festival Food*. London: Grub Street, 2010.

Mallet, Jean-Francois. Take Away. San Francisco: Chronicle Books, 2012.

Rolek, Barbara. East European Street Food, http://easteuropeanfood.about.com/od/crossculturalmaincourses/tp/street-food.htm

Simopoulos, Artemis P. and Ramesh V. Bhat (Editors). *Street Foods* (World Review of Nutrition and Dietetics) (v. 86). Basel, Switzerland: Karger, 2000.

Smith, Andrew. *Hamburger: A Global History*. London: Reaktion Press, 2008.

Smith, Andrew Franklin. *Fast Food and Junk Food [2 volumes]: An Encyclopedia of What We Love to Eat*. Westport, CT: Greenwood, 2011.

Tinker, Irene. *Street Foods, Urban Food and Employment in Developing Countries*. New York and Oxford: Oxford University Press, 1997.

Walker, Harlan, ed. *Public Eating: Proceedings of the Oxford Symposium on Food and Cookery 1991*. Totnes: Prospect Books, 1992.

Wells, Troth. *The World of Street food: Easy Quick Meals to Cook at Home*. Oxford: New International Publishers, 2005.

www.streetfood.org

www.who.int/foodsafety/fs_management/No_03_StreetFood_Jun10_en.pdf

www.who.int/foodsafety/publications/consumer/travellers/en/index.html

Illustration credits

ABOUT THE EDITORS AND CONTRIBUTORS

EDITORS

Bruce Kraig is professor emeritus in history at Roosevelt University in Chicago. Kraig has taught courses in history, prehistory, popular culture, American social and cultural history, the history of food, world cultures, and film and television documentaries. He has lectured on these subjects, including baseball and food, in the United States, Europe, Latin America, and Australia, and he is the writer-host of a national public television series on world cultures as seen through food and foodways. Kraig has published widely in food history, including *Mexican-American Plain Cooking, The Cuisines of Hidden Mexico, Hot Dog: A Global History, Man Bites Dog: Hot Dog Culture in America* (with Patty Carroll), and *The Encyclopedia of Chicago Food* (with Colleen Taylor Sen and Carol Haddix). He is associate editor of the *Oxford Encyclopedia of Food and Drink in America*, editor of the Heartland Foodways series for the University of Illinois Press, founding president of the Culinary Historians of Chicago, and the Illinois Scholar for the Smithsonian Institution's Museum on Main Street project, "Key Ingredients."

Colleen Taylor Sen is a food historian and writer specializing in the cuisine of the Indian subcontinent. Sen's articles have appeared in the *Chicago Tribune, Chicago Sun-Times, Travel + Leisure, Food Arts,* and other publications. She is the author of three books—*Food Culture in India* (Greenwood 2006), *Curry: A Global History* (Reaktion 2009), and *Pakoras, Paneer, Pappadums: A Guide to Indian Restaurant Menus* (2010)—and is currently writing *A History of Indian Food and Drink* (Reaktion). Sen has contributed entries on South Asian food to *An Encyclopaedia of World Food, An Encyclopedia of Vegetarianism, Oxford Encyclopedia of Food and Drink in America, Meals in Science and Practice,* and *Food Cultures of the World.* She was awarded the Palmes Académiques by the French government for her contributions to French culture.

CONTRIBUTORS

Fuad Ahmad is a multimedia artist who works as a writer and creative specialist for Leo Burnett Worldwide. He is currently based in Chiang Mai, Thailand.

Chitradeepa Anatharam is a subeditor and reporter at *The Hindu,* one of India's leading English language newspapers, specializing in cuisine and travel. She lives in Chennai and studied journalism at the University of Madras.

Paula Arvela is a PhD candidate at the University of Wollongong–Australia. Her dissertation examines the role of food in the production of national identities, focusing on *bacalhau,* the Portuguese national dish. Arvela hopes to dedicate her future research to cultural aspects of food consumption.

Rosemary Barron is the author of *Flavors of Greece,* which won several international awards, and *Meze: Small Bites, Big Flavors from the Greek Table,* and is a regular participant in the Oxford Food Symposia. She has also served as an independent consultant to food companies and restaurants on Greek and British regional cuisines, and to NGOs on educational program planning.

Manya Brachear is a Chicago-based religion writer and adventure traveler.

Cynthia Clampitt is a culinary historian, world traveler, and award-winning author. In 2010, she was elected to the Society of Women Geographers.

Charlotte De Backer is assistant professor (docent) at the University of Antwerp, where she teaches courses on interpersonal communication, intercultural communication, and business communication. Since 2010, she has conducted research in food studies with a focus on media effects on eating habits.

Monica Eng is a Watchdog reporter with the *Chicago Tribune* who focuses on food and consumer issues. She has won various awards for her coverage of cultural and consumer issues and has been nominated for five James Beard awards. Before coming to the *Tribune*, Eng worked as a construction worker in Nicaragua, a researcher in Uzbekistan, and a journalist at the *Daily Southtown* and *Chicago Sun-Times*.

Clothilde Façon is a graduate student at the École Normal Supérieure in Lyon.

Rachel Finn is a freelance writer and the founder of Roots Cuisine (http://rootscuisine.org), a nonprofit created to promote the foodways of African Diaspora. Her work has appeared in *Gastronomica, Chicago Sun-Times, Seattle Weekly, The Root,* and other publications. She has also contributed articles to *Food Cultures of the World Encyclopedia* (2011) and the *Oxford Encyclopedia of American Food and Drink* (2012).

Ove Fosså is a Norwegian amateur food historian specializing in Nordic traditional foods. He has written for the *Oxford Symposium on Food and Cookery* and the *Oxford Companion to Food* and was awarded the Sophie Coe Prize in food history in 1995.

Olívia Fraga is a Brazilian food reporter. She writes about Brazilian food and chefs for magazines and is a contributor to *Paladar*, the eight-page weekly food section inside *O Estado de San Paulo*, one of Brazil's major newspapers.

Shahrzad Ghorashian worked for BBC World Service, monitoring for 23 years before taking early retirement from her position as the managing editor. She is the coauthor of *New Persian Cooking: A Fresh Approach to the Classic Cuisine of Iran.* She is working on her second book on the history of Persian cuisine. She divides her time between London, the UK, and Cannes, France.

David Hammond is a Chicago-based food journalist who writes a regular column for the food section of the *Chicago Sun-Times*. He also comoderates LTHForum.com, the 8,000 member Chicago-based culinary chat site, and contributes reviews and articles to the *Chicago Reader, Time Out Chicago,* and the *Chicago Tribune.*

Anissa Helou is a writer, journalist, broadcaster, and blogger. Born and raised in Beirut, Lebanon, she is the author of numerous award-winning cookbooks including *The Fifth Quarter: An Offal Cookbook*; *Modern Mezze*; *Savory Baking from the*

Mediterranean; Mediterranean Street Food; Café Morocco; and *Lebanese Cuisine,* which was a finalist for the prestigious André Simon awards and chosen as one of the *Los Angeles Times*'s favorite books in 1998.

Richard Hosking lives in London and is professor emeritus at Hiroshima Shudo University, where he taught for 25 years. He has published many papers on Japanese food, delivered at international conferences, and his book *A Dictionary of Japanese Food—Ingredients and Culture* received an André Simon Award in 1997. In 2010, he received the Japanese Minister of Agriculture Forestry and Fisheries' Award for Overseas Promotion of Japanese Food.

Sharon Hudgins is the author of four books and more than 700 articles on food, travel, and culture. Her memoir, *The Other Side of Russia: A Slice of Life in Siberia and the Russian Far East* (2003), won two national awards in the United States. In 1996, she received a Sophie Coe Subsidiary Prize in food history at the Oxford Symposium on Food and Cookery for her paper on the foodways of Siberian Buriat-Mongolians. She is also the author of an award-winning book about the regional cuisines of Spain.

Phil Iddison is a civil engineering consultant who has worked in the United Arab Emirates, Kuwait, and Iraq for a total of 15 years. He has published articles on the food culture of the Gulf countries and received the Sheikh Mubarak Bin Mohammed Award for these publications in 2002.

Katrine Klinken has written around 20 Danish cookbooks, including one in English: *Smørrebrød: Danish Open*. She also writes for the weekly magazine *Hjemmet* and the daily paper *Information*. She is a qualified chef and is the Slow Food Convivium leader in the Nordic countries.

Robert Launay is professor of anthropology at Northwestern University. He has undertaken fieldwork in Cote d'Ivoire among Muslim trading minorities, the subject of two books: *Traders without Trade: Responses to Change in Two Dyula Communities* and *Beyond the Stream: Islam and Society in a West African Town*. He also edited a volume on Islamic education in Africa.

Whitney Lingle is a graduate student in Ball State University's Department of Anthropology in Muncie, Indiana. She has studied in Southeast Asia and researches food, culture, and sustainability.

Máirtín Mac Con Iomaire is a chef, culinary educator, broadcaster, and food historian. He lectures in culinary arts in the Dublin Institute of Technology. In 2009, he became the first Irish chef to be awarded a PhD for his thesis *The Influence of French Haute Cuisine on the Emergence and Development of Public Dining in Dublin Restaurants 1900–2000: An Oral History.* He has written extensively on the history of Irish food and has presented numerous papers at the *Oxford Symposium on Food and Cookery.*

Ian Martin is professor of English and the coordinator of the Linguistics and Language Studies Programme at Glendon College, York University in Toronto, Canada. He has been a frequent visitor to Cuba since the early 1990s.

Laura Mason is an independent researcher and writer, fascinated by tradition and region in British food. Her books include *Sugar Plums and Sherbet* (1998), on sugar confectionery; *Taste of Britain* (2006); and three recipe books for the National Trust.

Marcela Mazzei lives in Buenos Aires and is an editor of the food website Cukmi. com, which appears in one of Argentina's leading dailies, *La Nación.* She is also a writer for the digital edition of *Ñ,* the culture supplement of the newspaper *Clarín.*

Adrian Miller is a culinary historian who specializes in African American foodways and U.S. presidential foodways. He is the author of *Soul Food: The Surprising Story of an American Cuisine, One Plate at a Time.*

Katerina Nussdorfer (nee Pejovska) was born in Skopje, Macedonia, and studied at the University of Skopje and Roosevelt University in Chicago. In 2010, she obtained an MA degree in International Economics from the Institute of Economics-Skopje. Since 2009, she has been enrolled at the University of Vienna as a PhD student of American Studies, where she works on her PhD thesis *Examining Food and Eating Practices in Select 20th- and 21st Century American Texts.*

Sarahlynn Pablo is a writer, and this is her first published work. She blogs about culture, food, and alcohol at sarahlynnpablo.com. The Chicago-area native studied at the University of Pittsburgh, the Ateneo de Manila University, and Northwestern University.

Gaitri Pagrach-Chandra is a food historian and author. She is the author of *Windmills in My Oven: A Book of Dutch Baking* and *Warm Bread and Honey Cake.* The latter was named Cookery Book of the Year 2010 by the UK Guild of Food Writers. She has also received a Sophie Coe award for food history. Her newest book, on sweets around the world, was published in the fall of 2012.

Jorge Pérez, interpreter by profession, has always been a student of communications and cultural exchange. Local food has been one of his interests in his many trips abroad from Chile, his native country.

Birgit Ricquier is pursuing a PhD in linguistics at the Université Libre de Bruxelles and the Royal Museum for Central Africa, Tervuren, Belgium, with a fellowship from the Fonds de la Recherche Scientifique—FNRS. Topic of her PhD project is "A Comparative Linguistic Approach to the History of Culinary Practice in Bantu-Speaking Africa." She has spent several months in Central Africa, of which one month in the DRC as a member of the Boyekoli Ebale Congo 2010 Expedition, and two months of research focused on food cultures in the south of Congo.

Nanna Rögnvaldardóttir is an Icelandic food writer and editor. She has written about food for several Icelandic publications and is the author of an Icelandic cooking encyclopedia, *Matarást*, and 10 cookbooks, including *Icelandic Food and Cookery*, *Cool Cuisine*, and *Cool Dishes*.

Rob Rounds is an engineer who explores international foodways in his travels with special attention to Finland.

Helen Saberi is a London-based food historian and writer who married an Afghan and lived in Afghanistan for nine years. Her first book was *Noshe Djan: Afghan Food and Cookery*. She was Alan Davidson's assistant in the completion of *The Oxford Companion to Food* and coauthor with Davidson of *Trifle*. She has also coauthored, with David Burnett, *The Road to Vindaloo: Curry Cooks and Curry Books*. Her latest book is *Tea: A Global History*. She has regularly attended the Oxford Symposium on Food and Cookery where she has presented several papers on the foodways of Afghanistan.

Heba Saleh is a Virginia-based writer, Internet enthusiast, and most importantly, a food lover dedicated to whole, sustainably sourced ingredients and traditional cooking. She has cofounded midEATS (http://mideats.com/), a hub for Middle Eastern cuisine and culture that has been steadily growing since August 2011.

María José Sevilla is a writer and broadcaster specializing in the food and wine of Spain. She is the author of many articles and two books and has been connected with television programs as a researcher, writer, and presenter. She is currently the director of Foods from Spain and director of Wines from Spain in the Spanish Embassy in London.

Mike Sula is a staff writer for the *Chicago Reader*, who writes primarily about food. He won a James Beard Award for food writing in 2013, and his work has appeared in *Best American Food Writing*, *Harper's*, the *Chicago Tribune*, the *New York Post*, and elsewhere.

Richard Tan is a sommelier based in Chicago. He is currently working on a book on early colonial Mexican cuisine.

Aylin Öney Tan is a food writer based in Turkey. She is the author of many articles on Turkish cuisine and the book *Taste of Sun & Fire: Gaziantep Cuisine*. Since 2003, she has written a weekly food column for *Cumhuriyet*, a national daily. She is the leader of the Ankara Convivium and was a jury member for Slow Food Award 2000–2003. In 2008, she won the Sophie Coe Award on food history in 2008 at the Oxford Symposium on Food and Cookery.

Viktorija Todorovska is a food and wine writer specializing in Italian food. She studied Italian cooking at Apicius, the International School of Hospitality in Florence, Italy, and is the author of *The Puglian Cookbook: Bringing the Flavors of Puglia Home* (Surrey Books, April 2011). She is an accredited sommelier (International Sommelier Guide), French wine scholar (French Wine Academy), and certified specialist of wine (Society of Wine Educators).

Karin Vaneker, who is based in the Netherlands, has written for numerous newspapers and magazines, specializing in cultural and other histories of gastronomy, cuisines, and ingredients. She is the author of several books. Vaneker also works as a consultant for the food industry, lectures in museums, and has curated exhibitions.

Paul van Reyk is a Sri Lankan caterer and cooking instructor, a food writer, and restaurant critic based in Australia, and also has traveled extensively in Papua New Guinea. Paul has a Master's degree in gastronomy from Adelaide University.

Susan Weingarten is an archaeologist and food historian at Tel Aviv University, Israel. She is a regular contributor of articles on food in the late antique Jewish Talmudic sources.

INDEX

Note: Page numbers in **boldface** reflect main entries in the book.